WELLINGTON

FIELD MARSHAL THE DUKE OF WELLINGTON BEARING THE
SWORD OF STATE

After the portrait by Sir Thomas Lawrence in Windsor Castle
[By gracious permission of His Majesty the King]

WELLINGTON

Being an account of the *LIFE & ACHIEVEMENTS* of
ARTHUR WELLESLEY, 1st Duke of Wellington

Marquess of Wellington, Earl of Wellington in Somerset,
Viscount Wellington of Talavera, Baron Douro of Wellesley,
IN THE UNITED KINGDOM;
Prince of Waterloo IN THE NETHERLANDS;
Duke of Ciudad Rodrigo IN SPAIN;
Duke of Vittoria, Marquess of Torres Vedras, and Count of Vimiero
IN PORTUGAL;
Duke of Brunoy IN FRANCE;
Field Marshal and Commander-in-Chief of the British Army,
Colonel of the Grenadier Guards;
A Marshal of the Armies of SPAIN, PORTUGAL, THE NETHERLANDS,
RUSSIA, AUSTRIA and PRUSSIA;
A Grandee of the First Class in SPAIN;
A Knight of the Garter, of the Holy Ghost, of the Golden Fleece,
Grand Cross of the Bath, of St. Andrew of Russia, of Maria Theresa,
of St. Hermenegilda of Spain, of the Red Eagle of Brandenburg, &c., &c.
A Privy Councillor; a Member of Parliament;
First Lord of the Treasury;
Lord High Constable of England; Constable of the Tower;
Constable of Dover Castle; Lord Warden of the Cinque Ports;
Lord-Lieutenant of Hampshire; &c., &c.
Chancellor of the University of Oxford.

---

by

RICHARD ALDINGTON

WILLIAM HEINEMANN LTD
LONDON   ::   TORONTO

FIRST PUBLISHED 1946

PRINTED IN GREAT BRITAIN AT THE WINDMILL PRESS
KINGSWOOD, SURREY

Contents

Illustrations

Maps

WELLINGTON

An intimate friend having remarked in familiar terms to Sir Arthur Wellesley, when at Hastings (1806), how he, having commanded armies of forty thousand men in the field; having received the thanks of Parliament for his victories; and having been made Knight of the Bath, could submit to be reduced to the command of a brigade of infantry? "For this plain reason," was the answer, "I am nimmukwallah, *as we say in the East; that is, I have ate of the King's salt, and, therefore, I conceive it to be my duty to serve with unhesitating zeal and cheerfulness, when and wherever the King or his government may think proper to employ me."*

WELLINGTON'S DISPATCHES, Vol. 2, p. 616.

THE BOY ARTHUR WESLEY, *About* 1780
ARTIST UNKNOWN
From the Duke of Wellington Collection

CHAPTER I

By Way of Introduction

"THE DUKE . . .
"The old Duke . . .
"In the old Duke's time . . ."
Elderly people used such phrases in my presence at the beginning of
this century; and though I heard them with the careless inattention of a
child, I knew perfectly well who was meant. In the England of 1900
"the Duke" could only mean one person. In my case there were
special reasons for knowing about "the Duke" since during the better
part of three years I lived near the old town of Walmer, and my school
overlooked the park of Walmer Castle, the official residence of that
quite useless dignitary, the Lord Warden of the Cinque Ports. New
boys were always informed: "You know, the Duke of Wellington
used to live there"; and with equal truth they might have been also told
that he died there. Skirting the castle and grounds on dismal crocodile
walks, we speculated enviously on the surmised luxury, idleness, and
splendour enjoyed by the invisible (and doubtless absent) Lord
Warden.

Out of such accidents do we form the indelible impressions of childhood, so that to this day "the Duke" still carries an impression of
grandeur which was fortified by a most unlikely arbiter of human
splendours, a housemaid.

It happened in this complicated way. The late Marquess Curzon of
Kedleston, visiting Calcutta as a young man, discovered a cousin of his
own ancestral home in the pompous Government House built by
Richard Wellesley, Governor-General of India and elder brother of
Wellington. Curzon instantly formed the ambition "to pass from a
Kedleston in England to a Kedleston in India"; and this in time he
actually did with uncommon pomp and ostentation. Having achieved
the historical ambition of living in Lord Wellesley's old boots,
nothing then remained for the noble Marquess on his return to
England but to sleep in the Duke of Wellington's old bed.

How was this to be done? Even Curzon's high opinion of himself
could not claim that he ought to be Commander-in-Chief of the army
or that there were any just grounds why Apsley House should be his

A*

residence; but he finally solved this tremendous problem by having himself appointed Lord Warden (which gave him the right to live at Walmer Castle) and celebrated the occasion by a gorgeous military procession through the streets of Dover. I very well remember watching that procession from the front windows of my father's office in Dover. It was a hot sunny day and the sun poured directly down into Castle Street, which was lined with soldiers from the garrison regiments in warm red coats, heavy spiked helmets and immaculate pipe-clayed belts and pouches, not to mention rifle and bayonet and other articles of equipment. They took up their position at an early hour and waited, and went on waiting, for, as befitted an ex-despot of the gorgeous East, Lord Curzon and his procession were extremely late. Every now and then I heard through the open window an ominous clatter from the street; and presently a stretcher would come by, bearing a white-faced limp soldier in a faint or a very red-faced soldier with sun-stroke, victims of Army regulations on clothing and Lord Curzon's ambition. Theirs not to reason why.

Eventually Lord Curzon himself passed through the decimated ranks towards the end of a long procession and immediately preceded by a gorgeously attired cavalry band mounted on splendid horses and raising a din with their kettle-drums and trumpets which made the windows rattle. Treacherous memory suggests that his lordship rode upon an elephant, but this can hardly have been the case. In the first place he would have had to borrow an elephant from the Zoo or a circus, and in the second place such a demonstration of despotism would have been violently resented by the large "radical and nonconformist element" in Dover. So memory must have mixed the procession actually beheld with accounts of Lord Curzon's fantastic durbar in Delhi.

Small boys are not apt to reflect on the social and moral implications of a foolish and costly pageant, and I must confess I was pleased and impressed by the noise and uniforms and flashing bayonets. Lord Curzon, I thought, must be a very great man.

The Curzons took up their residence at Walmer Castle and in a few days were quite forgotten, while his lordship doubtless revelled in the happiness of living in Wellington's rooms and perhaps sleeping in Wellington's bedroom—though probably he did not sleep in the Duke's austere and narrow camp-bed. But apparently the Curzons had difficulty in keeping their domestic servants, and one of these rejected young women came to us as housemaid.

With my natural propensity to low company I soon became friendly with this young woman and would sit with her in the kitchen, or hang about in the scullery helping to clean knives in a machine which, by the way, we fed with Wellington Emery Knife Powder. Her favourite topic was the hardships and insults she had endured in "the castle". It appeared that on her very first meal there she was sitting alone at the table when the upper butler entered the servants' hall. As she continued to eat unmoved, he walked over to her and hissed: "Stand hup when you see your betters!" And she had to stand hup. Passing then by a natural transition from the upper butler to Lord Curzon, she muttered angrily: " 'Im indeed! Oo's 'e, I'd like to know, putting on airs as if he was the great Duke 'isself, God bless 'im!"

I fell into a reverie. Here was I a humble and sometimes a scolded friend of a housemaid who had to stand hup to Lord Curzon's butler, who in turn no doubt had to stand hup to Lord Curzon, that impressive master of military processions and kettle-drums. Yet he, the Great Curzon, I deduced, would have been compelled to stand hup to the Duke of Wellington. What a tremendous swell the Duke must have been!

Thus, more than half a century after his death, vague memories of Wellington lived on in the hearts of the people in the place where he lived and died, and were unconsciously passed on by them to children.

A little later came Wellington as National Hero, a figure who can scarcely be missed by any English schoolboy or even the most casual visitor to London. In the misleading abbreviations of preparatory school history he appears for a moment in meaningless triumph at Assaye and Argaum, vanishes, reappears in a record half-page rush from Torres Vedras to Toulouse, defeats the Emperor (apparently in the same campaign) in a decisive paragraph at Waterloo, and then seems to make a final exit covered with patriotic wreaths. Several lessons later he pops up unexpectedly as Prime Minister in 1828 and temporary stop-gap for Peel in 1834, only to be buried with great pomp and adulation in 1852. In the English history of my boyhood the Duke was emphatically labelled "a good thing".

The trouble with National Heroes is that they are too much of a good thing. They are more simple-minded and far less amusing than the downright black and white figures of newspaper cartoonists, and equally incredible. These wax-work dummies of great men are accepted by children in mute if inattentive acquiescence (what else can they do?) but the adult mind, if it thinks of them at all, is apt to reject them with cynical amusement. When the debunking biographies of the long armistice found a wide and amused public, it was not (I suggest) because of any special depravity in that public, but simply because as children they had been bored and outraged by a long series of National Heroes—political, naval, military, literary, religious. This very natural reaction against making too much of a good thing out of the past was exploited by biographers who appeared to think that everybody was rather ridiculous except themselves.

Clearly it is again the National Hero Wellington who is commemorated in so many public monuments and street names. The stranger arriving in London from Southampton will almost certainly be put down at Waterloo Station, and very likely his taxi will take him along the Waterloo Road, over Waterloo Bridge and up Wellington Street to the Strand. If he should happen to walk down Piccadilly to Hyde Park Corner he will come on the now grimy Apsley House (the Duke's London residence), opposite which is an equestrian statue of Wellington, while behind the house and just inside the park is the bombastic metal Achilles made from some of the cannon captured at Waterloo.

So much ostentation of glory very naturally was apt to stir the transatlantic visitor to criticism, and I myself have heard murmurs to the effect that after all who cares about the Peninsular War and anyway the Prussians won the battle of Waterloo. I have to confess that there was a time when I added my own tribute of disrespect to these murmurs, for during a considerable period I looked upon Wellington (in so far as I knew anything about him, which certainly wasn't much) with a good deal of disfavour. He seemed to be just the type of man I most dislike: a fox-hunting aristocrat of the Protestant Ascendancy in Ireland, a Dublin Castle man, an Anglo-Indian, a professional soldier with a laugh like a horse with whooping-cough, a martinet who opposed the abolition of army flogging and unpardonably described his men as "the scum of the earth", a Tory who fought the Reform Bill of 1832 to the death and opposed many of the long overdue changes in England, a prodigious collector of titles, orders and monetary rewards.

The strongest influence in disparaging Wellington was one which affected a great many other people besides myself, and it was simply the incessant stream of Napoleonic propaganda which continued from the nineteenth into the twentieth century. Now, in history as in other human concerns it is all very well to give the devil his due, but there is something disquieting about the almost fanatical boosting of the archdictator throughout the period which was at least pretending to apply the principles of democracy. I have seen the statement printed several times that more books have been written about Napoleon than any other human being. There are at least two reasons for this, one being that a good many individuals and at least one nation could not reconcile themselves to the abnegation of personal power, the acceptance of equality, which are essential in a genuine democracy; and the other that in France the Bonapartists were an active political party. Thus there were at least two reasons for a Napoleon cult, quite apart from the tendency of biographers (except the debunkers) to idealize their victims.

When the Emperor said farewell to his troops at Fontainebleau in one of those melodramatic speeches which set one's teeth a little on edge, he gave what seems a curiously inadequate motive for not having died on the battlefield, which he admitted he ought to have done. He said: "It remains for me to tell in writing what we have done together." This may have been purely rhetorical, it may have been one more instance of that fraudulent claim to learning and literary genius which Napoleon found so useful in dazzling the French, or it may have been a hint of what he actually did after Waterloo—namely, create a Napoleonic legend with the sole purpose of creating a Napoleonic dynasty for his son. It is naïve to think that the books and records of conversations emanating from Saint Helena have any concern with historical truth. They are propaganda for the King of Rome; and this applies also to the writings of many of the Marshals and especially to the publication of the Emperor's Letters where everything is omitted which might show him in an unworthy or unsuccessful action.

This Bonapartist propaganda was in many cases spread deliberately and knowingly, especially between 1815 and 1870, but it was also passed on more or less unwittingly by later writers who did not take the trouble to make certain of even quite notorious facts. Thus, Mr. Emil Ludwig makes the Prussians beat off the final attack of the Old Guard (plus the divisions of Marcognet, Alix, Donzelot, and Bachelu) on Wellington's army; and Mr. Hilaire Belloc manages to write a chapter on the Peninsular War without mentioning either the name of Wellington, the presence of an English army during six years, or any of the operations in Portugal which were so unpleasant for the Emperor's Marshals and their reputations. There is plenty of evidence to show that before Waterloo, while Wellington was only engaged with the Marshals, the Emperor was far from unjust to him. There are a good many examples in Napoleon's official correspondence, but perhaps the most striking example occurred during the famous conversation with Metternich just before the renewal of the war in 1813. The Emperor with his usual energy and skill had been urging the reasons why Austria should not join the coalition against him, and a very important one was that the Allies had not a single good general; and then Napoleon suddenly interrupted and contradicted himself: "No, no, it is true they have Wellington." Even during the Elba period I have found at least one example of fair and even generous mention of the Duke by the Emperor; but after Waterloo this magnanimity wholly disappeared, for the reasons I have given.

Thus the Napoleonists as well as the Bonapartists, following obediently their master's voice, dropped easily enough into the habit of disparaging and then ignoring the Anglo-Irish general who did as much as any human being to cast the great man from his eminence; until finally we reach such enormous and possibly wilful blunders as those just recorded of Messrs. Belloc and Ludwig. And I have to admit that, like a great many other people, I was influenced against Wellington by this propaganda simply because I was too ignorant to know that it was propaganda, and had not the least idea even where to look to find the answers to it.

So far as I am concerned I have every reason to suspect that I should have remained an unconscious victim of all this brilliant Bonapartist propaganda until the end of my life but for a purely fortuitous event which started me off on a course of reading of Peninsular War and Wellington books. On my first visit to the Peninsula in the early 1930's I stayed at the Bussaco hotel, a pseudo-Manueline palace built for Dom Manoel II, but not finished when a revolution caused him to flee the country. The hotel stands in the beautiful park-garden full of magnificent trees which belonged to the monks of the old monastery; and this very monastery was Wellington's headquarters before the battle of Bussaco fought against Marshal Masséna, Prince d'Essling, "the spoiled child of Victory", in 1810. I learned from my guide-books that on this occasion at any rate Victory had frowned on her spoiled child, for he lost five thousand men in a series of futile attempts to thrust the Anglo-Portuguese from the lofty ridge which shelters the monastery lands from the east.

The next day I walked up to the stone obelisk, commemorating the deeds of the Portuguese in the battle, and then along the ridge. I am neither a military historian nor an arm-chair strategist, but, during the first or futile World War, I was given some instruction in military principles and spent a good deal of valuable time on battle-fields. Looking at that old battle-field of Bussaco, where every trace of conflict had long since disappeared, I was impressed by the notion that, while it was certainly foolhardy to attack such a position from the east, the man who decided to hold it and succeeded in maintaining it even after a French column reached the crest under cover of fog— that man was no fool as a general. In fact at Bussaco I had before me an exaggerated example of the "Wellingtonian position", that skilful choice of ground which, added to masterly knowledge and handling of the kind of troops at his disposal, enabled this Irish fox-hunter to defeat one by one all the best generals of his age, including the Great Master.

There is nothing like an object lesson for removing prejudice and pointing up ignorance. With no ulterior motive I began reading up Wellington's campaigns, and in time visited most of his battle-fields in Portugal, Spain, and southern France. I wish now that I had studied them much more carefully and that I had taken notes, but at any rate I managed to get a rough idea of what happened, which is about as much as anyone ever learns about a battle. And so the mysterious "old Duke" I heard about as a child gradually took shape in my adult mind as a human being, a man who influenced human destiny more than is usually granted outside more or less interested circles in his own country. There is of course a pro-Wellington legend of the English which has done him as much harm as the anti-Wellington legend of the Napoleonists.

The strong aristocratic bias of Wellington's nature and the indisputably reactionary line he took up as a politician have led people into very erroneous notions of Wellington's character. Few men have had so many brilliant enemies, contemporary and posthumous; and between their clever misrepresentation and the awkward hero-worshipping of his adherents it is none too easy to discover his true character, especially since more apocryphal anecdotes are told of Wellington than of any other Englishman. It sounds paradoxical to say so, but he was fundamentally more akin to blunt, straightforward men like Grant and Washington than to the flamboyant creatures with whom he was associated. He wore good-humouredly the tinsel and gold-lace forced on him so lavishly, but it is noticeable that on every opportunity he put them aside. The Duke of Wellington had to do many things and put up with many people Arthur Wellesley disliked; and probably there were few men he liked less than his fatuous admirer, the Prince Regent, for whom he won so many victories. Wellington was a master of the obvious and the immediate, and the most striking aspect of his intelligence is a shrewd horse sense which in the long run amounted to genius, or at any rate sufficed to defeat genius. Strong common sense, honesty, integrity, unceasing hard work, a resolution to make himself obeyed, and an unflagging belief in ultimate triumph—these were the main qualities which enabled him to persevere and at last triumph in his long unequal duel with the tremendous military power of the French Empire.

Wellington had no literary or artistic gifts or taste, and very sensibly laid claim to none. At any rate he avoided by Philistine modesty the pretentious errors which sometimes made Napoleon ridiculous, as when he made François I a Bourbon instead of a Valois and thought the battle of Pavia was won by Italians instead of Spaniards and Germans. Yet he was certainly as well-read as Napoleon, and probably had a more exact knowledge of the countries in which he waged war. At any rate I have nowhere come across any example of a mistake by Wellington so foolish as that which Tolstoy mocks at so bitterly in Napoleon, i.e. his expecting to meet *boyars* at Moscow long after the rank and title had been abolished. On the other hand, Napoleon understood France and Frenchmen as Wellington never understood England and the English. There is a very good reason for this; until he was nearly fifty he was little more than an occasional visitor to England, and he imbibed his political principles in the conquered territories of Ireland and India. The curious thing is not that he was a Tory, but that on the whole he was sensible enough to hold staunchly to the belief that even the Tory party must yield to the constitutionally expressed will of the people. The insinuation of French Bonapartists and some English Whigs that Wellington hoped to make himself a military dictator of his country is utterly absurd. It is an interesting fact that the one English general who did make himself the tyrant of his country was not the royalist Marlborough or the royalist Wellington, but the republican Cromwell.

I believe that the clue to Wellington's austere integrity as a public man is to be found in the words quoted at the beginning of this work:

"I am *nimmukwallah*, as we say in the East; that is, I have ate of the King's salt, and, therefore, I conceive it to be my duty to serve with unhesitating zeal and cheerfulness, when and wherever the King or his government may think proper to employ me."

Sentimental loyalism was common among Tories especially when their interests lay in the same plane as their chivalry, but it will be observed that Wellington speaks of "the King *or his government*"; and in that tangle of more or less subtle fictions and anomalies which the English call a constitution this would have enabled him to serve under any government carried on in the King's name even if it were hostile to the King. What he was trying to say is that as a soldier he considered himself a public servant independent of party politics and owing obedience to any lawful government. Much later in life Wellington expressed a similar idea by saying that he considered himself "the retained servant of the *monarchy*". The stress on monarchy may be explained partly by the uprush of loyal sentiments experienced by so many elderly gentlemen for the youthful Victoria, but chiefly by the fact that the Duke had been almost forced to become a Tory since only the Tories trusted and employed him. Certainly he had no reason to devote himself to any of the royal family before Victoria, since with the exception of George IV (whom Wellington thoroughly despised) they all hated him, particularly York, Cumberland, Clarence (William IV), and George III. I refuse to believe that the Duke of Wellington was animated by any romantic sentiments of loyalty when he could remark of his Sovereign: "Dammee! he looks and talks so like old Falstaff I'm ashamed to enter a room with him."

Wellington's more than sixty years of incessant labour were the sacrifice of an unusually conscientious and successful public servant, as soldier, administrator, diplomat, and (in later days) benevolent custodian of the realm. True, he was highly rewarded, but he often groaned at the abusing of his goodwill:

"Rest! Every other animal—even a donkey—a costermonger's donkey—is allowed some rest, but the Duke of Wellington never! There is no help for it. As long as I am able to go on, they will put the saddle upon my back and make me go."

Perhaps the reason for this perpetual drain on his energy lay in the fact that it was a unique experience both for the Crown and for Ministers to have at their disposal the Wellingtonian practical horse sense. Guessing that it would never be replaced, they felt they should make every use of it while it lasted. In 1851, when the Duke was a very old man of eighty-two, the first World Exhibition was held in the Crystal Palace at Hyde Park. Unluckily, the trees enclosed in the huge steel and glass structure harboured large numbers of sparrows, whose presence was most undesirable in view of the many precious exhibits lying unprotected beneath them. What was to be done? Clearly, it was impossible to shoot them without shooting the Crystal Palace to pieces, and bird-lime was too slow and uncertain. Under intense pressure from public opinion Her Majesty sent for the Duke of Wellington and blushingly explained the dilemma of the birds. "Try sparrow hawks, Ma'am!"

A life of such heroic public service, however highly rewarded, strikes a reader of the mid-twentieth century as feverish compensation for a frustrated intimate life. True, he was successful to an amazing extent, yet this success was only an inadequate substitute for more intimate satisfactions never attained. Underneath the cold exterior and matter-of-fact bluntness was a more emotional nature than has been supposed. Every now and then in the official correspondence one comes on a letter or batch of letters of unusual vehemence or pessimism; or there is a bitterly denunciatory General Order which amazes and offends his army; or there is a sudden severe punishment of an individual (e.g. Ramsay at Vittoria) quite unlike the Duke's usual calm if inflexible justice—and in each case it means that for a moment his nerves got the better of even his superhuman repression. Wellington was a man frustrated in his affections. His good-natured father died when Arthur was a boy, and he grew up entirely overshadowed by a superficially more brilliant elder brother who was adored by the mother. There is good evidence that at one time Lady Mornington despised Arthur and that he knew it; and the fact that she soon changed her mind could not remove the shock and its consequences. He never again trusted a woman, and his very numerous affairs brought him no satisfaction. Late in life he admitted that it had been pleasant to be run after by pretty and attractive women, but vehemently denied that any woman had ever loved him. He may have been wrong here. He seems to have forgotten his wife, but then he had fallen out of love with her before he married her, and only went through with it because of the strange protocol about engagements of his class and time. Such a man may find at last a real outlet for affection in his children, but Wellington's were mere babies when he left in 1808 to fight the Peninsular War, and young strangers when he returned permanently in 1818. At last these frustrated affections dwelt lightly and wistfully on a niece and daughter-in-law, an old flame and her husband (the Arbuthnots), and other people's children.

He was always greatly depressed by his victories, unable to forget the casualties; and they say he broke down completely when the Surgeon-General brought him the first casualty lists after Waterloo. Yet the Waterloo dispatch, written after that outburst of emotion, is such a dry formal document that the American minister in London was uncertain whether it really announced a victory or not. And this may stand as a warning of the difficulty, perhaps the impossibility, of deducing the true nature of a very reticent and repressed man from a vast mass of documents, mostly official, and a lot of printed gossip, mostly uncritical.

CHAPTER II

The Anglo-Irish Wesleys

OUR story begins in 1769, which was a year of comparative peace under what seemed the assured security of ancient hereditary monarchies. Contrary to common belief these states were not in the hands of incompetent foolish despots and servile ministers of their pleasures. It can scarcely be said with any show of truth that Catherine the Great and Frederick the Great were either foolish or incompetent. Carlos III in Spain, and the Marquess of Pombal in Portugal, are still remembered by their countrymen as clever and efficient rulers who have never been equalled since. Joseph II of Austria was to acquire the singular fame of provoking a rebellion of his subjects by democratic reforms which they were too conservative to understand. Sweden was about to see the energetic Gustavus III put an end to the ridiculous political factions of the Hats and Caps, in that even more ridiculous constitution of four legislative chambers which were required to act in harmony, and of course never did. Poland's curious system of elective monarchy was seen to be impractical, a recipe for anarchy and civil war; but her powerful neighbours had decided to deal with that by partition. The smaller states, even the powerful and republican Holland, were tranquil; and everywhere in Europe the educated wealthy strove to acquire that "universal spirit of politeness" which according to Mr. Gibbon had spread itself throughout the French nation.

At the head of this majestic if ossified combination, united by ties of mutual enmity, was the great and populous kingdom of France. And therein lay concealed the weakness of the whole system, for His Most Christian Majesty was undoubtedly bankrupt, had been since 1709, and was only kept going by a method which judiciously combined secrecy with muddle. There was no regular budget, so that even the finance minister did not know the fiscal position; and as it was forbidden to publish any figures relating to national receipts and expenditure nobody could tell him. Even though Louis XV did not say: "After us the deluge", he probably knew what was coming better than most people. There is a reasonably authentic story that he was driving in a new carriage with Choiseul, and asked the prime minister how much he thought it had cost. Knowing that the King was always swindled Choiseul guessed high, but far below the truth. Indignantly he said that positively it was high time this sort of thing was dealt with. The King laughed cynically, and gave him full powers to try. After a long and thoughtful silence Choiseul admitted his impotence, for to deal with the minor vested interests and venerable abuses involved in the carriage swindle would mean abolishing other abuses and interests *ad infinitum*; so that to buy the King a new carriage at a reasonable price required so many changes that they might cost the King his throne. The two decided to leave things as they were, and to leave the bill to posterity.

The fact is that France had so far outgrown its old organization that even as early as 1769 an efficient reform by orthodox means was probably impossible. Nobody made the attempt, and the most civilized nation in Europe continued to live under a complicated and wasteful set of internal arrangements which had long been obsolete. The perfection of their prose and the urbanity of their manners could not atone for the fact that their whole fiscal system and most of their laws and customs were absurd, unjust, and defective. But if the abuses and mistakes of the *ancien régime* were politically disastrous, it is important to remember that the system developed great social and cultural charm. Talleyrand's often quoted remark that those who had not known life before 1789 had never known "*la douceur de vivre*" is typical of innumerable testimonies. A unique civilization had been evolved, and contemporary memoirs (e.g. Marmontel's) show that it was by no means limited to the privileged few, though they sustained and diffused it. Even the austere and practical-minded William Pitt recognized this in his own fashion when he gravely told an inquiring abbé at Reims: "It is true you have no political liberty, but you have far more civil liberty than you imagine."

However peaceful this year 1769, little warriors and leaders of warriors were being born all over Europe. The greatest of them all was born in August in Corsica under disturbed conditions. For some time the Corsicans, led by Boswell's hero, General Paoli, had been rebelling against their suzerain, the decrepit republic of Genoa. In despair, the Genoese sold to the French the rights they were unable to enforce, and the French proceeded to ingratiate themselves with their new subjects by the time-honoured method of making war upon them. The secretary of the Coriscan general was a minor noble of Florentine descent, Carlo Buonaparte; and in the midst of these troubles his handsome wife, Letizia, bore her second son. They called him Napolione.

Three months earlier a similar happy event had befallen a family of the Anglo-Irish *noblesse*, for on the first of May 1769, at Merrion Square, Dublin, Anne, lady of Garett Wesley first earl and second baron Mornington in the kingdom of Ireland, lay in of her sixth child, Arthur. A curious fact about this recently ennobled family is that its real name was not Wesley or Wellesley, but Colley. The Colleys were an old and fairly wealthy English family, having been granted land in Ireland by Henry VIII; but the Wesleys were wealthier and claimed that their ancestor had come over as a standard-bearer to Henry II. Late in the seventeenth century a Garett Wesley had married an Elizabeth Colley, and as they had no children he looked round for some worthy young kinsman to inherit his large estates. It is said that this tempting offer was made to a distant English relative, then a schoolboy at Westminster, Charles Wesley, brother of the famous and saintly John. But this offer (if made) was unaccountably refused, and eventually Mr. Garett Wesley adopted his wife's youngest nephew, Richard Colley, on condition that he took the name and arms of Wesley.

The estates inherited by Richard Colley (now Wesley) were in Co. Meath, and his country-seat (long since burned down) was Dangan, not far from Dublin. Among other valuables he inherited the rotten borough of Trim, which gave him a seat in the Irish Parliament. This body of legislators was exactly modelled after the parent body at Westminster, from Lord Chancellor to Sergeant-at-Arms, with a Lord-Lieutenant to represent the king. But it was in fact merely a stately farce. Elections were infrequent, the Lord-Lieutenant was usually absent, a government majority was secured in both houses by distributing patronage, sinecures, and titles; and a still unrepealed act of Henry VII forbade the introduction of any bill that was not approved by the English Parliament. During much of the eighteenth century the affairs of Ireland were "managed" by the Primate with a mixture of repression and bribery.

Since the Archbishop was the real ruler of the country, the Protestant prelates of eighteenth-century Ireland formed a body of more consequence and dignity than those in England. They were usually high-spirited men, renowned for their patriotism and plain speaking. A pleasing example of the making of an Irish ecclesiastical patriot is afforded by the career of Dr. Theophilus Bolter, who was appointed to the see of Clonfert; whereupon Dean Swift immediately waited on the new Bishop and expressed the hope that his lordship would "serve his country" in the house of Peers. The Bishop demurred:

"It is a very small bishopric, and I shall never have a better unless I oblige the Court."

"When you have a better," said Swift, "I hope you will become an honest man. Until then—farewell."

The interview and dialogue were repeated when Dr. Bolter became Bishop of Elphin, but at last he reached the archbishopric of Cashel. Once more Swift called with his suggestion, and this time the new Archbishop replied with grave conviction:

"I well know that no Irishman will ever be made Primate, and as I can rise no higher in fortune or station, I will now zealously promote the good of my country."

This spirited combination of plain speaking with a proper attention to higher interests was diffused among the lower ranks of the Irish Protestant clergy, if we may believe the story of The Rev. Mr. Philips and the Bishop of Cloyne. This clergyman entertained his visiting superior with great hospitality, which included some excellent fish. As the Bishop was about to enter his carriage, he turned and said:

"My dear Philips, you have been extremely kind to me, and there is but one thing more which can add to my obligation, that is to drown yourself in the river which produces your excellent fish, that I may give your living to my son Joe."

"I thank your lordship," said the bowing parson, "but I would not even hurt the last joint of my most useless finger to save your lordship, your lordship's son Joe, and all your lordship's family, from the gallows."

Many have wondered where and how the Duke of Wellington acquired that habit of blunt plain speaking which offended squeamish souls; it seems probable that he derived it from his spiritual pastors and masters. The Duke always defended the Church of England. "It is that," he said, "which makes us what we are—a nation of honest men."

Some further glimpses of eighteenth-century Irish society in general and the Wesley family in particular may be found in the gossipy letters of Mrs. Pendarves (née Mary Granville) who later took as her second husband an Irish Dean, Dr. Delany. She arrived in Ireland from England on a long visit in 1731, three years after Mr. Wesley had inherited his "fortune". As was fitting she started off with a Bishop, Dr. Usher, who had a house in Dublin, "furnished with gold-coloured damask, virtues, and busts, and pictures that the Bishop brought with him from Italy". It is impossible to say what these decorative "virtues" may have been, but if like the busts and pictures they came from Italy they sound suspiciously popish.

Mrs. Delany (as it is convenient to call her) was greatly pleased with Ireland or at least with that small section of it who, like wealthy people in all times and places, live chiefly for pleasure and dwell like the gods of Olympus far above the common miseries of poverty and labour, hiding and hidden from them in a golden cloud of bank-notes. She remarked with surprise that most people she met were "much the same as in England—a mixture of good and bad", and it was even more surprising to find that they behaved themselves "very decently, according to their rank". But she also noticed in them a heartiness and "great sociableness" which reminded her of Cornwall, and led her to surmise that there must be "a good deal of tittle-tattle". Could this indeed be Dublin?

Before long, Mrs. Delany began a tour of country houses. Already at Bishop Usher's house she had noted the quantities of food, "six dishes of meat" at every meal and "universal cheerfulness". But that was nothing to the country, where families were "not solicitous of having good dwellings or more furniture than is absolutely necessary", but where she never saw a dinner with less than fourteen meat dishes or a supper with less than seven. Very soon she and her friends went "jaunting" with Mr. Wesley on a light picnic to Butlers Town, wherein frail nature was sustained on "cold fowl, lamb, pigeon pye, Dutch beef, tongue, cockells, sallad, much variety of liquors, and the finest syllabub that was ever tasted". Having "devoured as much as possible" they went to music, Mrs. Delany to the harpsichord, Mr. Wesley to his fiddle, while the children danced. "We danced two hours; the master of the house fiddled and danced the whole time; then we went to supper, and had a profusion of 'peck and booz' and extravagance of mirth". The party broke up reluctantly at one-thirty in the morning.

Inspired perhaps by Mr. Wesley's profuse "peck and booz", Mrs. Delany accepted an invitation to Dangan, which she did not regret. She found her host "improving" his property with trees, canals, and classical statues. There were three canals and a boat on each; "we carry our music on board, hoist our flag and row away most harmoniously". The family seemed to live mostly in the great hall, which had an organ and a harpsichord, and as "every one does just as they please" it must have been a lively place except, perhaps, during family prayers. Breakfast, for instance, which began at ten, consisted of chocolate, tea, coffee, toast and butter and "caudle"; and those who had finished eating at once sat down to the organ and harpsichord, while others played battledore and shuttlecock. As everybody ate so much, Mr. Wesley insisted they should walk four miles a day, and presented them with "walking-staffs". No wonder Mrs. Delany declared: "The more I am acquainted with Mr. Wesley, the higher my esteem rises for him. He has certainly more virtues and fewer faults than any man I know. He values his riches only as they are the means of making those about him happy."

Seventeen years later, in 1748, Mrs. Delany was at Dangan again. Mr. Wesley was now Lord Mornington, promoted for services which escaped the notice of history, but still the "same good-humoured, agreeable man", engaged in music, improvements, eating and making everybody happy. There was now an important addition to the family, "my godson, Master Wesley", who at thirteen was already a prodigy. Some interest attaches to this youth, who was to be father of the Duke of Wellington and three other successful sons. If Mrs. Delany can be credited he was a good scholar, and his hobbies included music, shipbuilding, and fortification. He was "not a little mortified" that his godmother would not let him salute her arrival by firing the cannon on his ship and fortified island. She adds that he was "a child among children" and "tractable and complying" to his elder sisters.

Provokingly enough, at this point Mrs. Delany's letters become reticent about the Wesleys and her interesting godson. From other but colourless sources we learn only that young Mr. Garett Wesley became M.P. for Trim in 1757, and, very soon after, Lord Mornington on the death of his father. Mrs. Delany notes that a musical academy had been opened in Dublin, "all ladies and gentlemen", with Lord Mornington as president and conductor. There can be no doubt of the young man's musical gifts. Trinity College, Dublin, made him Doctor of Music, and eventually Professor. If his serious music was above ordinary taste, he achieved great popularity with his songs and glees—"Gently Hear Me, Charming Maid", "Here in Cool Grot", "Come, Fairest Nymph"—some of which were rendered more than fifty years later amid applause and encores by the Prince Regent, known to the disrespectful Mr. Creevey and his friends as "Prinny".

Meanwhile the young lord had hoped to marry a duke's daughter, but at the last moment a rival turned up with "double his fortune and perhaps half his merit". He then turned to Miss Anne Hill, daughter of an ex-banker, but niece of a viscount. Perhaps to show his false first love that he at any rate was above sordid motives, Lord Mornington waived aside the father's hints that the young lady's fortune was inadequate to her suitor's rank. He did not desire any fortune, he would settle on her "£1,600 a year jointure and £500 a year pin money". If she had any fortune, "be desired it might be laid out in jewels for her". Mrs. Delany shook her worldly-wise head over this romantic transaction, and cynically hoped "she will prove deserving of this pretty behaviour, and make him happy", adding ominously, "he is a very good young man on the whole; but where is the perfect creature?" Meeting them just after the honeymoon she acknowledges reluctantly that they are "a pair of good-humoured young things", but "I think her education not finished enough, nor her judgment sufficient to get the better of some disadvantages he has had in his education".

Whatever those disadvantages may have been, it is clear that Lord Mornington was financially extravagant. He was renowned not only for his music, but for his "kindness and hospitality". He had a number of children, of whom eight survived. His barony was raised to an earldom (still Irish) but that must have cost him something, probably a great deal. And he continued his father's "improvements". The garden with canals and classic statues became a park of eight hundred acres with a large lake and a broad walk copied from that at Versailles. When Arthur Young visited Dangan in the 1770's he noted that "the plantations are extensive" and (*ominously*) that "his lordship is making many improvements". The lake had increased from twenty-six to one hundred acres and "his lordship has planned a considerable addition to it". Anyone who has tried to run a country estate with "ornamental improvements" as a hobby will ruefully acknowledge that there are few more effective means of getting rid of money. Add to this a dowerless wife, a large family, a hospitable nature, a rise in the peerage, and a mind more concentrated on glees and oratorios than on rent-rolls and husbandry. . . .

In 1774 there was a mortgage. It was only for £1,000, but the fact that a supposedly wealthy man had to raise so small a sum was ominous. By way of economy Lord Mornington moved his family to London, where he was haunted by a mysterious debt for the sum of £16,000, and grew fretful under the hardships of living on a mere £1,800 a year. When his lordship began buying lottery tickets, it was evident that the financial situation was serious. And then, rather suddenly and with a complete disregard for his responsibilities, he died in Knightsbridge in May 1781 at the age of forty-five, leaving his widow and children (the eldest, Richard, was just twenty-one) in "what may fairly be described, looking to their social position, as very straitened circumstances". In July of that year the new earl was compelled to raise a mortgage of £8,000, and four years later another for £10,000. Within half a century the "large fortune" over which Mrs. Delany had exclaimed so rapturously had been almost literally fiddled away.

CHAPTER III

The Fool of the Family

SUCH were the family and the kind of life into which the future Duke of Wellington was born, so far as may be known from these accidental and scattered references. Evidently these Irish Wesleys were amiable and gifted, but like all economically favoured classes they enjoyed a pleasant and luxurious life at other people's expense. The music and the feasting and the ornamental waters and the chivalrous gesture to Miss Hill and the children's education had to be paid for by Lord Mornington's tenants.

It can at least be said for the first two Morningtons that they were not absentee landlords and that the people on their land appear to have been better treated than most Irish tenants. The only first-hand evidence on this point is that of the agricultural expert, Arthur Young, who rode over Lord Mornington's manors in 1776, and jotted down some of his observations.

The "cabbins", as he calls them, were built of mud walls nearly two feet thick and well thatched, and warmer than the average English cottage, but some of the Irish cabins had no chimneys. All were well supplied with potatoes, "every cottage swarms with poultry", most had pigs and at least one cow. Young adds: "If the Irish cabbins continue like what I have hitherto seen, I shall not hesitate to pronounce their inhabitants as well off as most English cottagers."

This is all very well so far as it goes, but in summing up his impressions of Ireland at the end of his book Young expresses his indignation at the oppression of the Irish in words of considerable warmth. "The language of written law may be that of liberty," he says, "but the situation of the poor may speak no language but that of slavery." Religious and political subjection had been reinforced by economic measures which destroyed Irish trade, measures forced on the unreluctant English Parliament by the clamours of enlightened industrialists. Since these measures ruined Protestants and Catholics alike, the Anglo-Irish as well as the Irish, it is not surprising that the country seethed with anger, hatred, and rebellion.

Possibly this general economic distress had as much to do with the decline of the Wesley fortunes as the Earl's extravagance; but the retreat to England was certainly not for the purpose of economizing, since London was a much more expensive place than Dublin or Co. Meath. The plain fact is that, like other people in their position, they were afraid to stay in Ireland. George III and his friends, after getting rid of the elder Pitt, had contrived to involve themselves in a world war against the American colonies, France, Spain, Holland, and an angry league of hostile neutrals which included Russia, Prussia, and all Scandinavia. Command of the sea was temporarily lost, the British garrisons were withdrawn from Ireland, and there was grave danger of a French invasion. Under the pressure of these events, measures were passed to give some relief to Irish Catholics and Irish trade; but the Irish may be excused if they thought that this was due more to foreign dangers and the swords of the Irish volunteers (Protestant) than to justice and goodwill.

There was a period during this long and disastrous war when it looked as if the whole structure of the British Empire were about to collapse. But even George III and his Ministers could not entirely quell the energy and courage of the people they ruled. The American colonies were indeed lost, but Warren Hastings and Carleton saved India and Canada, while Eliott held out grimly through the three years' siege of Gibraltar until Rodney regained control of the seas and relieved him. Nevertheless, the peace treaties of 1783 were so bad from an English point of view that the world believed England could never recover, and that France was completely established as the dominant world power. The Gordon riots of June 1780, when for nearly a week the mob burned and pillaged London and more than four hundred people were killed and injured, gave the impression that the state of affairs at home was as bad as that abroad; and to some extent it was.

In these circumstances of public and private misfortunes, Arthur Wesley passed his boyhood and youth. He seems to have been a lonely, awkward boy, often in bad health, the ugly duckling and the problem child of his family. He was idle, dreamy, shy, and eclipsed by his two elder brothers—William, who took the name Pole on meritoriously inheriting an estate, and Richard, the second earl, who had a brilliant career at Eton and Oxford. Young Richard Mornington was an excellent classical scholar, and attracted the attention of statesmen by his Latin poetry and Greek scholarship. In those days such accomplishments were an almost certain passport to distinction. As a learned bishop wrote to a young man at Oxford: "I cannot too strongly impress upon you the importance of Greek, a thorough knowledge of which often leads to positions of dignity and emolument. Besides, it was the language of Our Lord."

Young Arthur Wesley had no such claims. From the little school at Trim, near his Irish home, he was moved to "Mr. Brown's academy at Chelsea", which seems to have had little merit beyond the fact that it was cheap. A fellow pupil remembered that Richard Mornington once came to see his young brother and, at his departure, gravely tipped him a miserable shilling—poignant evidence of the young earl's financial difficulties. Presently Arthur and his younger brother Gerald (who was only nine) were sent to Eton, where they kept unhappy company at the bottom of their form. As Gerald afterwards became a Doctor of Divinity he cannot have been so impervious to classical learning as Arthur, who in after-life made it a rule never to quote Latin. He made no friends at Eton, though he fought with "Bobus" Smith (afterwards Advocate-General of Bengal) and licked him in spite of, or because of, the fact that young Wesley was clearly and palpably in the wrong. He very seldom played cricket or rowed, but went swimming by himself or took long solitary walks. Hence the saying that the battle of Waterloo was won on the playing fields of Eton.

During the long vacations Arthur Wesley stayed with his mother's family in North Wales, where his dearest friend was the blacksmith's mate, named Hughes. The boys went off on long excursions in the mountains, but, as will happen, they quarrelled and got into a fist fight, which after a lot of slugging the blacksmith won. However, as Mr. Hughes boasted on many a winter's evening for many a year at the village pub, "Master Wesley bore no ill will", and they were better friends than ever.

It was evident to a discontented family that Arthur had learned absolutely nothing at Eton; and Eton is expensive. Head of the family Richard had passed from the obscurity of the Irish House of Lords to a seat on young Mr. Pitt's side of the House of Commons, and already "had a place". William had taken up the white man's burden of the borough of Trim, but what on earth was to be done with Arthur? He was now a great gangling boy of fifteen, shy and husky-voiced, and so uninterestingly awkward that girls were apt to mislay him at parties and go home with someone else. His chief occupation was scraping on the violin, a habit he had learned from his dear father, and the family now knew to its cost where that led.

The old rule was that the fool of the family went into the Church, but Arthur couldn't even learn enough Latin and Greek to do that. The only alternative was to buy him a commission in the army and to hope that he might slowly rise by the passage of time and the death of senior officers. Consulted *pro forma* on this subject, Arthur unexpectedly demurred. He didn't want to be a soldier. What did he want to do? Well, he rather thought he would like to be a financier. This was tactless as well as absurd. Neither the Dowager Countess nor the Earl liked to be reminded that the aristocratic family tree was smeared with banking or that they were in debt. Patiently they pointed out that the most Arthur could hope for was an allowance of £125 a year from Richard's encumbered estates, scarcely sufficient to compete on equal terms with Barings and Rothschilds.

Lady Mornington settled this difficulty with the decision we associate with dowagers and that extreme sense of the practical which elderly ladies often show in money matters. In those days the French had the military reputation the Germans have now; therefore Arthur must go to a French military academy; but before he could do this with the slightest profit, he would obviously have to learn French. So Lady Mornington removed herself and Arthur (and possibly some of the younger children) from expensive London to cheap Brussels, and arranged to share the expenses of lodgings and a tutor with one, Jack Armytage, the son of a wealthy baronet. In exchange for what was perhaps more than his fair share of the expenses, young Jack Armytage received an invaluable return—"the prestige of Lady Mornington's protection". Jack Armytage afterwards married an heiress and spent a long (he lived to be ninety-two) and useful life, driving a four-in-hand every day from Northampton to Barnet to meet the mail-coach, and then back again. All he remembered of the year in Brussels was that he and Arthur Wesley did very little work, went out into gay society a great deal, and that Arthur was always playing the violin. Forty years later at the Doncaster races he heard a voice say: "I'll be damned if that isn't Jack Armytage," and had the honour of shaking hands with the Duke of Wellington, who assured him that in 1815 care had been taken in Brussels that their old tutor should not be annoyed or molested.

In 1785 Arthur Wesley was dispatched to the military academy at Angers, which was directed by the engineer, Pignerol, but seems to have been intended for turning out cavalry officers since its chief feature was a riding school. There are no legends of Wellington at Angers such as are told of Napoleon at Brienne. Indeed, his life there is the same story of ill health and loneliness and such lack of interest in existence that he is reported by one contemporary to have spent his time "lying on a sofa playing with a white terrier".

There is exaggeration in this, a determination on the part of admirers to make the Duke of Wellington in youth an Admirable Crichton of laziness and ignorance. It makes a good story; but, if true, how is it that only a year or two later we hear of his "reading a great deal", of his intense curiosity about "any new invention or discovery", and his "power of rapid and correct calculation"?

Whether Arthur Wesley did or did not acquire formal and military knowledge at the Angers academy is not of much significance. The significant thing is that the first year or two of comparative freedom from restraint, the most impressionable time in a very young man's life, were spent in friendly intercourse with the French *noblesse* just before the Revolution. They formed his manners and taste, set his standards, gave a bias to his mind and his political and social thinking. Wellington did not hate the French as Nelson did, and as Blücher and the Prussians did. He fought his duel to the death with them, but fought it as far as possible in accordance with the unwritten laws of honour and courtesy of the old régime.

Angers lies in a part of France which remained Catholic and royalist at the Revolution, and from the districts round about came terrific counter-revolutionary uprisings which very nearly overthrew the Republic. The *noblesse* Arthur Wesley knew were very different from the wealthy courtiers of Versailles, who, like the contemporary Spanish grandees, were kept as pampered prisoners of the monarchy. Many of these provincial nobles were so poor that they had no more than fifty louis a year, but from them came most of the officers of the army and navy and colonial service, many of the lower clergy and provincial magistrates. Their daughters became nuns or married retired officers who preferred virtues to a dowry. They seldom rose beyond the rank of colonel or post captain, for the high lucrative posts went to the *grande noblesse* who had the favour of Versailles. The provincial *noblesse*, who were the cadres of the armed forces and did most of the fighting in war time, saw Versailles only twice in their lives: once when as hopeful young men they were permitted to bow to majesty on receiving their commissions, and once when the handful of grey-haired veterans who survived received a royal nod and the Croix de St. Louis as the reward for a lifetime of service. In spite of their poverty and ill-requited service they maintained their traditions of loyalty, religion, and frugal elegance, and it was of them Burke was thinking (not of the dissipated Parisians) when he praised "the unbought grace of life, the cheap defence of nations, the nurse of manly sentiment and heroic enterprise".

Dangan, Dublin, Kensington, Eton, Brussels, Angers—it is scarcely possible to think of any combination of influences more likely to confirm a youthful aristocrat in the prejudices of his caste. The new ideas which were to shatter the old régime and eventually to dominate Europe until the revival of ruthless military despotism in our own time had scarcely penetrated to any of these places, least of all Angers. If Arthur Wesley found any mitigation of the stern code of aristocratic honour and military service at Angers, it would only be in *galanterie*, for whose sins the Church had much compassion—Paolo and Francesca are in the highest, not the lowest, circle of hell. Wellington showed little or no Protestant bigotry in his treatment of Roman Catholics and in his attitude to them, at home, in Ireland, or abroad. On the other hand he never at any time showed the slightest trace of that gushing benevolence and tearful sentiment which was so common in the enlightened upper classes of France both before the Revolution and for a year or two after it started. The guillotine was set up by pedantic sentimentalists who wept over the "ravishing spectacle of a virtuous old man digesting in the sun".

If Arthur Wesley founded his manners and morals on those of the *noblesse* in and about Angers, he was quite right; they were by far the best human beings he had known, far superior to the overeating place-hunters who oppressed Ireland, and to the Great Whigs and Tories of London with their immense incomes, their endless political intrigues for office and sinecures, and the complicated adulteries which can hardly be said to have lost half their evil by losing all their grossness. With Burke's magnificent if wrong-headed tirades running in his mind, Arthur Wesley could scarcely see his former Angers friends as anything but innocent and heroic victims of revolutionary mob frenzy—whence perhaps his intense dislike of crowds and popular demonstrations. Some of these French friends died on the guillotine, some in the sacking of their houses, some in Carrier's *noyades* at Nantes. One of them, the Duc of Brissac, was murdered at Versailles in 1792, at the head of Louis XVI's constitutional guard.

It was lucky for Wellington that he did not also acquire the French *sensiblerie*, which had some passing influence even on so fine a nature as Wordsworth's. In later years a woman who was none too friendly to Wellington described him as "an original man, proud, simple, and great". That man was potentially existent in the thin, red-faced youth of seventeen who came back to England from Angers after an absence of two years. There had been no faintest chance for the originality and greatness to be displayed; the simplicity might be and was mistaken for stupidity, and the pride could easily show itself as mere awkwardness and reserve. Yet like all gifted people he must have had some inklings, however inarticulate and vague, of latent energy and power. The misfortune was that so far as we know he had not yet made a single intimate friend, nor had he found any older person who either understood or sympathized with him.

He certainly got neither from his own family, if he ever expected such a thing. Lady Mornington, the banker's daughter, liked material success or at least the promise of it, especially after life with a husband who was merely a gentleman and a musician. Her two elder sons were satisfactory, more than satisfactory—meritorious. Here was William who had shown his merit by having an estate left him, and was doing wonderfully well in the Irish Parliament, supporting the errors of Government as member for the hard-worked family borough of Trim. Far more imposing was Richard, the head of the family. Already in his twenties he had proudly proved that an excellent knowledge of the classics does "lead to positions of dignity and emolument", for he was close friends with Mr. Pitt and sat on the Treasury bench as a junior Lord of the Treasury. Lady Mornington had reason to be proud of her two elder sons. But she was not at all proud of Arthur—then. When he was sent to Angers she had announced contemptuously that he was "food for powder and nothing more".

Did Arthur know that this was his mother's opinion of him? Who can tell? But the mother who was capable of saying that, whether in a sudden flash of maternal exasperation or as a considered judgment, can hardly have appeared to her son as either sympathetic or very affectionate; and so once more Arthur was repelled and driven back into himself. Brother Richard appears to have shared his mother's views on the distasteful subject of his brother. He was too busy with Parliamentary duties to give Arthur much of his time, and he could hardly be expected to pierce that inarticulate reticence, absorbed as he was in the success of his Ciceronian eloquence in the House and in the dignity of sitting shoulder to shoulder with that elusive historical character, "Conversation Brown, a three-bottle man on the Treasury bench". But Richard did do something for his brother. He wrote on his behalf a begging letter to his friend, the Lord-Lieutenant of Ireland, in terms of dignified superiority and condescension:

"There is a younger brother of mine," he wrote, "whom you were so kind as to take into your consideration for a commission in the army.

B

He is here at this moment, and perfectly idle. It is a matter of indifference to me what commission he gets, provided he gets it soon."

On the strength of this enthusiastic testimonial Arthur Wesley was gazetted as Ensign in the Seventy-Third Foot, a Highland regiment which was under orders for India; and the date was March 7, 1787.

CHAPTER IV

Debts Public and Private

THE organization of the British army in the eighteenth century was weird and wonderful. The wonder is not that they were so often defeated but that they were ever victorious, and the super-wonder that even a Wellington with all his infinite patience, attention to detail, and knowledge of what ought to be done, was able at last to make so magnificent a fighting machine as the Army of the Peninsula.

The men of that army were recruited from the poorest classes, were miserably paid, fed and housed, and savagely flogged. It was very difficult to get recruits even in times of national danger, desertion was frequent, so that regiments were seldom up to strength and, as service was for life, the men were often too old and weak for fighting and marching. They were drunkards, they could "be trusted neither in victory nor defeat", for in either event they deserted or straggled after plunder and drink. In his moments of anger with their misbehaviour the Duke called them "the scum of the earth" and vowed they enlisted "for nothing but drink". Matters had been improved greatly between 1787, when the Duke entered the army, and 1809, yet here is what he says in one of his numerous representations to the Secretary for War— in this case Castlereagh:

"It is impossible to describe to you the irregularities and outrages committed by the troops. They are never out of the sight of their officers, I may almost say never out of the sight of their commanding officers of their regiments, and the general officers of the army, that outrages are not committed; and notwithstanding the pains that I take, of which there will be ample evidence in my orderly books, not a post or a courier comes in, not an officer arrives from the rear of the army, that does not bring me accounts of outrages committed by the soldiers who have been left behind on the march, having been left sick, or having straggled from their regiments, or who have been left in hospitals."

Behind these regulars was the home defence force of the militia. The men of the militia were more respectable characters, but their officers were amateurs who made all sorts of fantastic stipulations limiting the conditions of service. Proposals for raising one such volunteer regiment were laid before William Pitt, who read through a long list of things this regiment was not to be required to do "except in case of actual invasion". Finally he came to the condition: "The regiment is not to be sent out of the Kingdom"; whereupon, he added; "except in case of actual invasion".

In other words the English middle classes wanted victory, but were not prepared either to fight in person or to pay enough to the men who did fight for them.

All the honours and "emolument" of the regular army were reserved for the aristocracy. Commissions were obtained by purchase, by appointment through influence, and (very, very rarely) by promotion from the ranks. The promotion of officers was not by merit, but by seniority, purchase, and favour. Purchase and favour could nearly always triumph over merit and seniority. Time after time a subaltern or field-officer with no money but his pay would see his junior rise over his head by purchase. Officers, particularly general officers, were extremely jealous of their seniority, and would risk losing the whole army rather than endure to see another general with a month's less service put to command them. There was no staff college, and members of the staff were appointed by influence at home or to please a particular general. Until Sandhurst was founded in 1802, the only training college was for engineers and artillery officers at Woolwich; but cadets were appointed directly by the Ordnance department. There were usually only a handful and even some of these were found to be totally uneducated. The office of Commander-in-Chief was not revived until 1792, and then it was given to George III's son, the Duke of York, who was ignominiously defeated whenever he took the field and was later involved in money scandals connected with the sale of commissions. He functioned at the head of a mysterious administrative body known as "the Horse Guards", not that they were guards or rode horses but because they had offices at that address. Wellington suffered much from them, and invariably referred to them sarcastically as "those gentlemen". In 1826 he told Croker: "I can't say that I owe my success to any favour or confidence from the Horse Guards; they never showed me any, from the first day I had a command to this hour."

The army, then, was not altogether a brilliant prospect for a younger son of a large family with an allowance of £125 a year. It cannot have been with very high hopes that this raw young Ensign joined the depot of his regiment; but yet, as he afterwards remarked with his usual sober realism, "I wasn't so young as not to know that since I had undertaken a profession I had better try to understand it". That he was in earnest about this he proceeded to prove in a rather curious manner; he "had one of the privates weighed in his clothes only, and then with all his arms, accoutrements, and kit in full marching order". Obviously the reason for this was to find out how much a man had to carry on active service and what proportion it bore to his own weight. It must have been heavy, for the old musket alone was nearly twice as weighty as a modern rifle. From this little episode we may draw two deductions, not very favourable to the British army of that time. In the first place, the weight to be carried by a soldier should have been laid down in Field Service Regulations; in the second place, no officer should command men until he has drilled and marched as they have to do wearing their equipment. But the fact that an Ensign not yet eighteen, with only a few days' service, should have seen the necessity for this knowledge is significant. It showed a recognition of the importance of the private soldier very rare in those days.

This serious-minded young subaltern was not destined to spend his youth on the barrack-square or in unnoticed service as a junior officer in India. It is wonderful what a few months of military training and a becoming uniform will do for a young man in female eyes and hearts. Wonderful, too, what the word spoken in time or the carelessly scrawled signature of the great and powerful may do to lift that same young man quickly and easily over the first difficult steps of a career. Lady Mornington looked at her younger son in his new neat red tunic, and suddenly changed her mind about him. The lanky thin boy was seen to be an elegantly slender young man; what had appeared to be excessive reserve and shyness was now seen in its proper light as the modesty befitting an officer and a gentleman; what had been Frenchified manners were now seen to be Taste refining British Sobriety. Ensign Wesley looked well in the King's red uniform which, all later observers agreed, also suited the Duke of Wellington excellently; and the Ensign showed signs already of that extreme neatness and austere elegance which later brought the Duke the nickname of "the Beau". As was proper, the first person to notice it was his mother. Arthur was no longer "food for powder"; he was a "charming young man". Richard must be made to "do something" for him.

It was not so difficult after all. Mr. Pitt had shown his usual good sense in making friendly advances to the promising young classical scholar who might turn out to be a useful political ally; and young Mornington had shown his good sense by guessing that Pitt (only a year older than himself) was going to dominate English politics, and guessing right. Two generations of Pitts worked with two generations of Grenvilles. In 1787 a Grenville was created Marquess (later Duke) of Buckingham and in November of that year he was appointed Lord-Lieutenant of Ireland. Richard Wesley knew of the appointment before it was made public. He spoke a word in time, and among Buckingham's first acts as Lord-Lieutenant was the appointment of Ensign Arthur Wesley as one of his aides-de-camp. Nor did august patronage stop there. More words were spoken, and by way of a Horse Guards Christmas present, Ensign Wesley discovered he had been gazetted Lieutenant in the Seventy-Sixth Foot, with seniority, December 25, 1787.

Lady Mornington was delighted. With aristocratic disregard for punctuation and syntax, she wrote enthusiastically to her friends, the celebrated Ladies of Llangollen:

"There are so many little things to settle for *Arthur* who is just got into the Army and is to go to Ireland in the capacity of Aid De Camp to Lord Buckingham, and must be set out a little for that, in short *I must* do *every thing* for him and when you see him you will think him worthy of it as he really is a very charming young man, never did I see such a change for the better in any body he is wonderfully lucky, in six months he has got two steps in the army and appointed Aid de Camp to Lord Buckingham which is ten shillings a day."

There was just one shadow (there always is) in this otherwise bright picture. Like the Seventy-Third, the Seventy-Sixth was under orders for India, and the King insisted that it should sail with what Lady Mornington in her distress described as "its full compliment of officers". There would have to be another exchange and that, she feared, would "cost some money", as well as time. In this she was mistaken, for in January 1788 Lieutenant Wesley was transferred to the Forty-First, apparently without expense; and soon after started for Dublin. Unluckily, there was always the chance that these English line regiments might be transferred to distant and unhealthy stations in the East or West Indies, far from the founts of patronage. But the Lord-Lieutenant was powerful and his kindness inexhaustible: with a stroke of the pen he transformed this subaltern of the line into a cavalryman, by appointing Mr. Arthur Wesley to the Twelfth Light Dragoons, a regiment which had slumbered more or less peacefully in Ireland for seventy years.

That year, 1788, when the young Lieutenant took up his modest duties as a very junior aide-de-camp to Dublin Castle, was the last of the old regime in France. The help which France had sent (rather against the wishes of Louis XVI) to the American colonies in their struggle against the English turned into a dangerous boomerang. The Frenchmen who saw the birth of the new republic and watched it triumph over apparently hopeless difficulties were profoundly impressed. So in varying degrees were many Frenchmen who stayed at home. If these things could be done in America, why not in France? But the analogy was deceptive, and they were misled by the word "revolution". The American Revolution was a successful rebellion against a distant, unintelligent, and restrictive authority. It was a national uprising for independence, and when the English had been finally defeated the "revolution" was over. The new form of government was a natural evolution of the English Parliament, modified by the theories of French and English Utopians, but much more by real political needs; and it was conceived and administered by men acquainted with the methods and difficulties of representative government. Whatever internal dissensions there might be in the new republic they were not acute enough to be disastrous, and there was very little danger of attack from abroad.

Not only the British colonies in America, but all colonies of all European powers in the eighteenth century were bound to the mother country by jealously exclusive trade regulations, in exchange for which they received military protection against other predatory powers and any native inhabitants who happened to have survived. Under date 1667 John Evelyn reported of the New Englanders that they were "exceeding peevish and touchy" about their rights, and of doubtful loyalty, but in the middle of the eighteenth century the American colonists (as Fenimore Cooper proudly tells us) were conspicuous by their fervent loyalty. And well they might be. The French in Canada were building a line of forts along the Ohio to meet another line coming up the Mississippi from New Orleans. The English colonies were being encircled with evil intent; but this danger was swept away by the extraordinary series of triumphs of the Seven Years War. Cheered on by the active emissaries of the Duc de Choiseul, Americans then raised a cry for independence and freedom of the seas; and freedom of speech could easily be added as a war-cry, since it cost nothing.

Standing more or less unitedly on this solidly realistic platform, and perfectly familiar with the subtleties of Parliamentary language, Americans could indulge without danger in sublime and universally fraternal rhetoric. They had practical aims, and were determined to achieve them. On this basis they were able to build with confidence in the future.

The French also had a practical problem to solve, but they met it in a very different way. The public mind of France between 1788 and

1790 was in a strange state of emotional benevolence. Almost everyone who could read or write called himself a philosopher, and two "philosophers" could not walk down a country lane together without embracing and weeping over the enchanting pastoral sight of a cow suckling her calf. The French deputies to the National Assembly had little interest in a subject so prosaic, so devoid of sentiment, as the national debt. They wished to make France a new heaven on earth, and were confident they could do so by making speeches and abolishing by decree the most cherished weaknesses and abuses of human nature. Since they were idealists, who each knew he was right while all disagreed, they soon began to quarrel in the name of fraternity, and to achieve equality by cutting off each other's heads. Freedom was acquired by persecuting religion, confiscating property, the introduction of conscription (borrowed from that freedom-loving land, Prussia), by the institution of police spies known as concierges, and the printing of unlimited paper money.

Meanwhile the French national debt flourished exceedingly. It is impossible, owing to the imperfect method of accounting, to say what it was in 1789; but as the interest is given as 236 millions of francs annually, it could hardly have exceeded 5,000 millions. The revolutionaries confiscated property of the Church, the Crown, and the aristocracy amounting to about that sum; yet by 1796 the face value of the paper assignats was estimated at something between 45,000 and 48,000 millions of francs. The bonds issued by the Republic fell by 70 per cent, and "were soon completely worthless". The assignat of 100 *livres* paper was worth 96 *livres* cash in January 1790; by January 1795 it was worth 18; and in March 1796 a man with 24 *livres* in hard cash could buy 7,200 *livres* paper.

One example out of many must serve to illustrate the extraordinary corruption of the new republic. In 1797 the United States sent Commissioners, led by Charles C. Pinckney, to negotiate with the French Republic for compensation to American citizens for the loss of merchant vessels seized by French privateers. The American delegates left France indignantly when they discovered that the price of "compensation" was a bribe of £50,000 to the Minister of Foreign Affairs, and a "loan" of $13,000,000 to the heads of the Directory.

These men of the Directory had been welcomed by France as a release from Robespierre and the Terror; and it is not surprising that General Bonaparte in his turn was enthusiastically greeted as a release from the corruption of the Directory. They had pillaged France for themselves; he pillaged Europe for himself and France. By 1801—

1802, his Finance Minister, Gaudin, had consolidated the debt and at last balanced the budget. But this was only achieved by selling old Crown lands, by ruthless exactions from conquered countries, and by the windfall of 50,000,000 francs (in 1803) for the Louisiana purchase. Thus was settled the financial problem which had compelled Louis XVI to summon the General States in 1798.

The outer world saw and knew very little of this subterranean financial chaos, for it was naturally astonished and in most cases horrified by the surface drama of the National Assembly, the Convention, and the Communes, symbolized by the guillotine, the September massacres, the Vendée, and the *noyades*. The Dauphin was starved and ill-treated into a witless, cowering, scarcely human creature, fortunately soon released by death. The King and Queen followed and preceded many other victims of the guillotine, which soon became also the effective means for carrying out those frequent changes of government so popular in France.

Europe could not long maintain the attitude of a spectator, thrilling pleasantly or unpleasantly to the rapid series of tragical disorders which afflicted France, and complacently certain that at long last the threat of French military aggression was removed. "Poor France, that kingdom is now in a state of complete dissolution," wrote Mr. Gibbon; and such was the opinion of millions who knew far less about history than he did. But as early as 1792–1793, an ambitious war party gained control of the Revolution, began recklessly scattering declarations of war, and alarmingly announced that the Republic was about to "liberate the captive peoples of Europe" (if not of the world) by force of arms.

There were people who, wise after the event, claimed to have foreseen what would happen if the General States were called in France; but it may be justly suspected that most of these prophetic anecdotes have been antedated. In spite of the fruitful lessons of innumerable religious wars in which incalculable numbers of people were tortured, killed, imprisoned, or ruined owing to differences of opinion about the meaning of the Gospels, not many people could have foreseen what was to be inflicted on mankind between 1789 and 1815 in the name of Liberty. It seems improbable that even an artful fox like Talleyrand foresaw that large numbers of persons would be imprisoned in the cause of Liberty, others guillotined in the name of Fraternity, and that the sacred cause of Equality would call for dictators who wielded absolute power undreamed of by any monarch then living, including the Tsar. Nor can it have then appeared very

B*

likely that an immense popular movement, aiming especially at universal benevolence and perpetual peace, would result in a series of unprecedented imperialist wars, involving all Europe from Lisbon to Moscow, from Copenhagen to Sicily, and including Egypt, Palestine, and India.

On the other hand, at the beginning of this new experiment there was a tremendous amount of goodwill towards it in England. It was piously hoped that "France may now enjoy the inestimable benefits of a regular constitution". One of the purposes of Burke's *Reflections* was to give these thoughtless well-wishers a good fright. In any case the majority in England were soon redeemed from their benevolent attitude by the Republic's attack on the sacred rights of property (then a potent if unavowed form of religion), by the death of the King, by the official abolition of Christianity, and finally by the declaration of war. A minority defended France throughout, chiefly for reasons of political opposition to the Government, but a few because they could discern the generous ideas and ideals beneath all the violence and perversion. Another minority, with George III at its head, was against it from the beginning, for obvious reasons of unenlightened self-interest.

Although very little is known about Arthur Wesley's life and opinions during the period 1788–1794, there is some reason to think that he belonged to the last group—those who disapproved of the Revolution from the beginning. One of the few facts recorded about his life as aide-de-camp in Dublin is that he had begun to read, in that desultory way which Dr. Johnson thought the best way. Significantly, a list of his books drawn up at a rather later period contains a copy of Mackintosh's *Vindiciae Gallicae*, one of the ablest of the English books defending the aims of the French revolutionaries. The book was a reply to Burke's *Reflections*, and was published in 1791, so Wesley evidently made some slight effort to acquaint himself with the other side of the question.

The official duties of a Dublin aide-de-camp were not heavy, but social obligations were numerous and hard on a limited purse in a court which was conservatively described as "gay and extravagant". With an allowance of £125 a year and ten shillings a day from the army, it was not very easy to keep up with people who remarked thoughtfully that "a man can *jog along* on £40,000 a year". Consequently, the young man began to get into debt; and then, before he was of age, was sent electioneering. Richard, in his wisdom, had decided that the time had come for brother William to move to

Westminster, and that Arthur must now be the member for Trim. After being initiated as a Freemason, Arthur went off to interview the free, independent, and honest voters of his constituency. Even in a pocket borough, life was not all beer and bribery for the candidate. One old elector came up to Arthur Wesley and said his political conscience was troubled and his vote uncertain until he knew what was going to be done about a bond for £70 in his possession, drawn by Lord Mornington, but unpaid. The young candidate met this candidly; he would have nothing to do with it, for such a transaction (he held) would "vitiate my return". In that election he first showed his genius for obstinate defence. Although "plagued with requests of all kinds", he refused to make any promises whatsoever. Arthur Wesley was returned for Trim, and took his seat in spite of the notorious fact that he was not yet of age, and therefore illegally elected.

Life now became busier. In addition to Castle and Parliamentary duties (such as they were) he was gazetted Captain in the Fifty-Eighth Foot on June 30, 1791. Sixteen months later he transferred once more, to the Eighteenth Light Dragoons. Both these regiments were on the Irish establishment, and presumably both promotion and transfer came through the patronage of the Lord-Lieutenant. This switching from one branch of the service to another and back again now looks oddly irresponsible, but may have had its advantages for a future Commander-in-Chief who thus learned to handle units of infantry and cavalry. Long after his wars were over the Duke told Croker that he owed much of his success "to the attention I always paid to the inferior parts of tactics as a regimental officer". And he explained that before a man can "group divisions" and "move an army" he must understand "the mechanism and power of the individual soldier, then that of a company, a battalion, a brigade and so on". Since he first saw action as a battalion commander, he must have acquired his knowledge as a subordinate officer between the years 1791 and 1793.

It would seem that any young gentleman in his early twenties was sufficiently occupied by learning simultaneously the profession of a soldier and the art or craft of a politician, with the addition of considerable reading, violin-playing, and the flirtations of the Dublin Castle set. Such was not the view of brother Richard, who ruthlessly employed him in addition as land-agent for the Dangan estates. Hard work, but good training for a man who was to spend his life in a triple task of fighting, political negotiation, and administration. Someone who saw young Wesley in the Irish Parliament in those days—"a

young man, in a scarlet uniform, with very large epaulettes"—was told
that he spoke seldom but "always to the purpose". It was fortunate
for him that he had the gift of speaking and acting "to the purpose",
for he had a lifetime of needing them before him.

Suddenly there occurred a complication—he fell in love and wanted
to marry the lady. Her history, at any rate at that time, is a blank, for
she does not seem to have impressed anybody except Captain the Hon.
A. Wesley and another officer, Lowry Cole. Nobody seems to have
left any account of her, and even Mr. Guedalla can only suggest that
she was "bright-eyed", not an uncommon thing in young women.
She was the Hon. Catherine Pakenham, sister of an Irish landowner,
Lord Longford, and therefore entirely eligible, but without "fortune".
The suitor was also eligible except in one, indeed the same, respect;
and Lord Longford had to point out that the brother of one Irish peer
could not marry the sister of another with no more "fortune" than a
captain's pay, an aide-de-camp's allowances, and an increasing
number of debts to Dublin tradesmen. The refusal was polite but
definite, and nothing was left the young couple but to vow eternal
fidelity and to hope for better financial times. The humiliation went
deep, so deep that Wellington had a lifelong horror of debt, and in his
old age contrived to forget that he had ever been in its toils. "Never
get into debt," he said to the Army Chaplain, Gleig. "It makes a slave
of a man. I have often known what it was to be in want of money, but
I never got into debt." Was this wishful thinking or a mere lapse of
memory?

When this happened, Arthur Wesley was twenty-four, a Captain
of Dragoons with no active service to his credit, an obscure back-
bencher in the Irish Parliament. But younger men were commanding
regiments, and Pitt had been Prime Minister at twenty-three. If
Wesley had ambitions he had every reason to feel that he was dropping
behind in the race. Yet 1800 had come and gone when he told a friend
that the height of his ambition was "to be a Major-General"; and all
he was looking for in 1793–1796 was a "genteel competence" which
would allow him to marry Kitty Pakenham. It was precisely that
which was unattainable, for fate or the conspiracy of events or chance
had determined that Arthur Wesley should not settle down as a young
married man with an undistinguished if lucrative sinecure.

The conspiracy of events was complicated in the extreme, but
interesting to us here only in so far as it affected the career of a young
Captain of Dragoons in Ireland. In France the Revolution roared on
destructively, and to everybody's surprise (including their own) the

French managed to stave off the Prussian and Austrian invasion. For this they were more indebted to the imbecility and slackness of the enemy and to the remnants of the old royal army than to the revolutionary fervour of the volunteers. At the "great victory" of the Revolution at Valmy only two battalions of *sans-culottes* were engaged; the rest of the 36,000 French troops were old regulars. At the decisive moment the Prussians did not push their attack, probably because the ground was a little too muddy for precise and ponderous movements. And the battle was so feebly contested that out of 70,000 troops engaged on both sides the total casualties were less than 1,000, most of them French. But already the famous demi-brigades were being organized; conscription was gathering together the material for armies of undreamed-of size, and unintentionally forging incomparable weapons for the coming military dictator.

In Downing Street sat the haughty-nosed Mr. Pitt, a young man already weary with office, doomed to die at forty-seven with all the symptoms of old age brought on by worry, overwork, and disappointment. Pitt has been presented to posterity as a warmonger, but in 1792 he was not only unprepared for war, he did not even want it. He wanted another fifteen years of peace to heal the wounds of the disastrous American-French-Spanish-Dutch war. True, when the French King was imprisoned, Pitt had been forced to break off open diplomatic relations in deference to the feelings of George III, but he maintained secret but friendly relations through Talleyrand and Chauvelin. Both diplomats reported that England would remain at peace if Holland were not attacked, for England had a defensive treaty with Holland. To prove his sincerity, Pitt in 1792 made a conciliatory speech and reduced still further his already dangerously depleted navy and army. The British navy was reduced to 16,000 men; and there were only 151 ships of the line fit for sea. (By 1799 there were 120,000 men, and in 1814 no less than 1,168 effective ships of the Royal Navy.) What the army was we have already seen, and the only improvement was a slight increase in the pay of the private soldier. The reforms which were to make possible the Army of the Peninsula had not even begun.

Gestures of peace from weakness are always futile, as the English-speaking world never learns. They were futile in 1792. The revolutionary governments needed plunder and prestige, needed to employ the huge armies of starving ragged men they had called into existence and were afraid to disband. After a struggle, the war party in France had its way, and when the King's head had been cut off (to conciliate the other kings) war was declared on Holland and England in February 1793. To make everything snug and fraternal, the harmless Spaniards were included, and another Great European War had begun.

War is not so welcome to professional soldiers as is usually supposed by a wishful-thinking public, eager for safety and the thrills of victory. It disarranges the peaceful habits of barracks, and makes havoc with the sacred routine of soldiering. But it has its compensations, among them the fact that the right sort of casualties makes way for promotion among survivors; while an officer may go far if he is lucky enough to be successful and sufficiently friendly with his commander to be noticed for it and also possesses connections with influence in the Government. The dreary treadmill of promotion by seniority is accelerated. All this was quite as clear to Captain Wesley, A.D.C., as it was to every other officer; but he also knew that captains are very rarely mentioned in dispatches.

A higher rank was clearly desirable before proceeding on active service, but since patronage had exhausted its benevolence the only way to a step up was by purchase. Just how Richard Wesley was persuaded is not clear, but he agreed to sell the family home of Dangan with all its "improvements" for £36,000. An unspecified sum was loaned to Arthur, who in April 1793 was gazetted Major, and exactly five months later Lieutenant-Colonel of the Thirty-Third Foot, a Yorkshire regiment, otherwise known as the First West Riding. The Colonel of the regiment (who had little to do with it except to draw the pay and allowances) was no other than Cornwallis; for the Horse Guards were fraternally fond of officers who had been defeated in America.

Whether it was the influence of Kitty Pakenham or a sense of obligation to Richard or a belief that now or never was the opportunity to make a career, it is a fact that the young Major took his duties seriously. There were to be no more Dublin frivolities, no more debts and time-wasting. Card-playing had involved both, and, like many other young officers, Wesley took a vow to abandon it for ever; unlike them, he kept his vow. A more difficult and intimate sacrifice was called for. Music was the one art he cared for and understood, it was the link with childhood and his father, the consolation of his curiously lonely existence. The young Field-Officer gave up violin-playing; some say he burned his violin. In any event, he never played again; and music made way for ever to drill, tactics, organization, strategy, work.

Such virtues and good resolutions would never influence the Horse

Guards. Distinguished active service was the thing, and the new Major discovered to his chagrin that he had been gazetted to a regiment which was at the bottom of the roster for foreign service. He wrote urgently to Richard asking him to use his influence with Lord Westmorland to procure the command of a composite battalion of flank companies which was being formed. Fortunately the application failed, for though the Government had sent a weak expeditionary force to co-operate with the Austrians in the defence of the Low Countries, their main idea was to cut off French trade; to which end they were reinforcing the West Indian garrisons where the troops suffered heavy casualties from yellow fever and misguided notions of hygiene in tropical countries.

Perhaps these applications were not altogether abortive, and may explain why Arthur Wesley was appointed Lieutenant-Colonel of the Thirty-Third in September 1793, the very month in which Dangan was sold. But evidently neither Major nor Lieutenant-Colonel met the requirements of the guardians of Kitty Pakenham's virtue, especially while debts remained unpaid. Perhaps that confession of modest ambition made nearly ten years later in India meant that Kitty's relatives set as the goal the rank of Major-General or its financial equivalent in civil life. In 1793 that was a long way off, and however much Arthur Wesley might fret for the opportunities of active service, there was nothing for it but to obey orders and stay with his regiment.

And here, oddly enough, for the first time we come on evidence that this young man was a born soldier and that he had not wasted his time as a junior officer. He spent as much time as possible with his regiment, taking infinite pains with its organization and training. He drew up a set of standing orders which were admitted to be a model; and one inspecting general after another was forced to confess that the Thirty-Third was the best drilled and most efficient regiment in the Irish command. The routine of soldiering went placidly on, and then suddenly the barracks of the Thirty-Third at Cork was in a buzz of excitement and activity—orders had come for the battalion to join a small force whose modest objective was to invade northern France. And then, since the army would not be the army without orders and counter-orders, the bustle and excitement as suddenly vanished; the Thirty-Third was not to go after all!

The real orders came eventually, as they always do; and on June 25, 1794, the Thirty-Third Foot landed at Ostend, to join the expeditionary force under the Duke of York which was supposed to be defending the Netherlands in co-operation with the Austrians. The

10,000 reinforcements which included the Thirty-Third were a wretched crowd in the main, more resembling Falstaff's company of conscripts than a trained army. Many of the junior officers were untrained, and owed their commissions merely to the fact that they had collected a certain number of recruits. And what recruits! "They were the off-scourings of the nation, who could be purchased at a cheap rate by the crimps—criminals, decrepit old men, raw boys, the half-witted, the feeble-minded, and even down-right lunatics." The transport corps, known officially as the Royal Waggon Train, were nicknamed the "Newgate Blues" because of the colour of their uniform and because most of them were ex-convicts. Some of the infantry drafts were sent out lacking arms and accoutrements, and none of them had any overcoats. The hospital staff was made up of "drunken apothecaries, broken-down practitioners, and every description of rogue", and fully earned their nickname of "The Shambles". Finally, there were only four generals to an army of 40,000 (25,000 British); the Austrians soon went off and left their allies in the lurch; and they were expected to defend the Netherlands against 150,000 French! Such was a British expeditionary force when George III was King, when the Commander was one of his sons, and when Mr. William Pitt was Prime Minister.

The amazing fact is not that the campaign was one long retreat, but that this lamentable army managed to put up such a number of good fights. For this they were indebted to a few good regimental officers, to a sprinkling of old well-disciplined soldiers, and to the excellent musketry drill which made even a raw British battalion superior in fire-power to an equal number of the best continental troops. But they had nothing else to withstand the shock of Pichegru's demi-brigades, and hardly any skirmishers to meet his swarms of *tirailleurs*. The doomed little army had to fall back and fall back, continuously losing men, until in late November a rear-guard of three battalions under Lt.-Col. Wesley was trying to hold the line of the Waal. By this time the British contingent was reduced to 21,000, of whom only 10,000 were effectives.

The young Colonel who was given this responsible post had come under fire for the first time on September 25, 1794, and had handled his regiment well; but that hardly seems a reason for making him responsible for the safety of all that was left of the army. Head-quarters was thirty miles away and "a scene of jollification"; so much so that during the whole period from November to January the Commander-in-Chief never once visited the front line. While the staff ate and caroused, the shivering regiments on the Waal watched the French dancing the "Carmagnole" on the opposite bank. By night (Colonel Wesley wrote to a friend), "the French keep us in a perpetual state of alarm; we turn out once, sometimes twice, every night; the officers and men are harassed to death, and if we are not relieved, I believe there will be very few of the latter remaining shortly". The Colonel himself had not had time to change his clothes for weeks and spent "the greatest part of the night upon the bank of the river". So neglected was the commander of the rear-guard that letters from England told him "more of what was passing at headquarters than headquarters condescended to tell him".

His apprehensions about losing the men were soon enough realized. The Waal froze, the French crossed the ice, and the dismal retreat continued to the Yssel, and then back towards the Ems. March discipline vanished; the supply system broke down, and the starving soldiers fought each other for what little subsistence the poor country afforded; when they wakened at dawn from their icy bivouacs they found the earth was strewn with the frozen corpses of men and horses; and at last, of 25,000, a bare 6,000 staggered into their embarkation base. With polite irony the Hanoverian General, Walmoden, reported to the Duke of York: "Your officers, their carriages, and a large train are safe, but the men are destroyed." The whole campaign was a disaster and a disgrace, a monument to the incompetence, corruption, and cynical selfishness of Government, the Horse Guards, and the Staff. Nineteen thousand men were lost, but the Duke of York's travelling carriage and voluminous baggage were saved. Wellington never forgot that campaign, but he could very seldom be persuaded to speak of it. "The system was wretched," he said briefly, and again: "I learned more by seeing our faults and the defects of our system in the campaign of Holland than anywhere else." And finally, with a very grim expression on his face: "It has always been a marvel to me how any one of us escaped."

The British army had paid a high price for teaching its future General how not to wage war.

CHAPTER V

A Failure Leaves for India

IT was in March and April of 1795 that the dejected remnants of this expeditionary force were shipped home. Having seen what was left of his men safe on the Ems, the officer commanding the Thirty-Third did not wait for them but went on ahead. With his cocked hat pulled over his beaked nose, and the scarlet-lined military cloak wrapped closely round his spare body as protection against North Sea winds, the young Colonel had much to think over as he paced the deck or leaned against the bulwarks under the cloud of white sails. As far as was decently possible he would avoid the company of the ship's officers, for though the British navy in war-time is thoroughly familiar with the task of evacuating what is left of the army, there is often a touch of irony in the politeness and efficiency of its officers. Possibly, as military historians assert, Colonel Wesley meditated on problems of transport and supply, and on "the tactical value of missile-action against shock-action". Possibly, in spite of his allegedly cold heart, he remembered the dreadful scenes on the retreat and felt the soldier's regret for men's lives wasted in supreme efforts of useless courage, suffering, and death. But even the iron Duke was human, and it is possible that he thought chiefly of Kitty Pakenham, of his own career, and of the wretched state of politics in England and Ireland.

From the point of view of reputation and promotion Lt.-Col. Wesley had not advanced one inch after ten months of very trying active service. The fact that he personally had done his duty and more than his duty efficiently and well meant nothing. Napoleon voiced the sentiments of mankind when he said tersely: "Give me lucky generals." Whether Lt.-Col. Wesley knew it or not, as he sailed home his countrymen were singing a ribald song about:

> "The grand old Duke of York,
> He had ten thousand men;
> He marched 'em up to the top of the hill,
> And he marched them down again."

For it suited the purpose of the office-hungry Whigs rather to discredit the Duke of York and the Government than to use their influence in

Parliament for the reform and improvement of the army. One of the minor miracles of representative government, even when tempered by rotten boroughs, is that the Opposition usually knows even less about practical methods of waging war than the Government. As a matter of fact a certain reorganization and reform of the army were begun by the discredited Duke of York; but obviously, the Horse Guards and the Government would be too much occupied in trying to justify themselves in Parliament to worry about subordinate officers and their careers. Least of all would they call attention to their own inefficiency by promoting an efficient young Colonel. What they wanted was to have the whole disreputable campaign forgotten, and they succeeded so well that to this day it is hard to find information about it.

The result of Lt.-Col. Wesley's meditations was simple and decisive; he made up his mind to abandon active service in the army and to seek for political or administrative office. As he put it with his usual horse sense: "I see the manner in which the military offices are filled," i.e. by favour. Even though he was potentially the best officer in the army, the Horse Guards knew nothing about it and did not want to know. And then, whatever the Duke may have said afterwards, Colonel Wesley was certainly worried about his debts, euphemistically described as "the necessities under which I labour" in the numerous applications for posts he made in 1795. Unfortunately there was now a new Lord-Lieutenant, Lord Camden, who was less convinced of young Wesley's talents and merits than Buckingham or Westmorland; and though it is natural to suppose that Lord Camden would scarcely have been appointed to that post if he had been really qualified for it, he certainly possessed one valuable gift in a ruler—he knew how to say "No" to importunities.

The commander of the Thirty-Third called on the Lord-Lieutenant of Ireland at his London residence and stated his claims—probably bluntly and without suavity—to something genteel and confidential in the Irish Government; and was eluded. Being still aide-de-camp, he followed his chief to Dublin; and Richard wrote asking as a personal favour that Arthur might be grandly promoted—as Secretary at War for Ireland! It is not known what Lord Camden said in reply to Lord Mornington, a personal friend of Mr. Pitt and member of the board of control for affairs in India; but it is certain that he did not appoint Arthur Wesley as Secretary at War for Ireland.

What was to be done? Well, Arthur Wesley was also member for Trim, and perhaps some service to Government in debate might be noticed. Most unexpectedly he got a chance, and took it with courage;

for he had to answer no less an orator than Grattan. In the absurdly exaggerated Parliamentary language of the time, Grattan denounced Lord Westmorland for having denuded Ireland of troops for the unlucky war in Holland. He would not listen to the (for once sensible) government defence that new recruits had been raised to take their place; it was "a trick . . . a fraud", Lord Westmorland must be impeached. An opposition baronet had described the new recruits as "ragamuffins", in which Mr. Grattan fully concurred. And the thumping peroration ended with the statement that: "It is a striking circumstance, that in a debate where the conduct of Lord Westmorland towards the Irish army has been so publicly and so loudly arraigned, not one veteran of the army, nor any old officer, had ventured to defend him."

The member for Trim caught the Speaker's eye, and for the first time in two years Lt.-Col. Wesley spoke; and the House listened:

"What did the Act require? 12,000 men for the national defence. Were they or were they not in the country? It was admitted that the public service demanded troops to send abroad, and an addition was therefore made to the establishment by Parliament. Was it the new levies just recruited that were to be sent abroad to meet an enemy, or the disciplined soldiers? The question answered itself, and justified sending the old regiments out of the kingdom, and retaining new corps.

"He congratulated that hon. baronet on his military sagacity, who would send ragamuffins upon foreign service; but he assured the hon. baronet that however he might treat the new levies with contempt, they were not objects of contempt to the enemies of their country."

Even after the Duke of York's campaign an hon. baronet in Opposition could not go quite that far; and there are times, even in Parliament, even in an Irish Parliament, when plain horse sense wins the day. But if the hon. and gallant member for Trim expected the Government to reward this service to a former Lord-Lieutenant, he was mistaken. "A certain object of mine in this country" was no nearer achievement than it had been; and when Parliament rose, the hon. and gallant member retired to his constituency, and wrote a curious and interesting letter to his chief. Evidently brother Richard had been consulted, and evidently Lt.-Col. Wesley had remembered his old hankering for the realms of finance. This is what he wrote:

"I assure you nothing but the circumstances under which I labour would induce me to trouble Your Excellency's Government at any time and the Offices to which Lord Mornington has desired me to look are those at the Revenue and Treasury Boards and considering the persons who are at present at those

Boards, and those it is said are forthwith to be appointed to them, I hope I shall not be supposed to place myself too high in desiring to be taken into consideration upon the first vacancy at either of them. . . .

"You will perhaps be surprised at my desiring a civil instead of a military Office. It certainly is a departure from the line which I prefer; but I see the manner in which the military Offices are filled, and I don't wish to ask you for that which I know you can't give me. . . ."

There were more references to "the necessities under which I labour" and an admission that "Your Excellency and Mr. Pelham" might be "of opinion that the Offices at those Boards might be too high for me". It was a strange letter to be written by the future Duke of Wellington, and if we were not solemnly assured that it was his work we might almost suspect the hand of Wilkins Micawber. Thus the Colonel humbled himself for the sake of Kitty Pakenham, and humbled himself in vain. The Irish Revenue and Treasury Boards lost an almost unique opportunity of acquiring the services of an honest and capable servant.

Still Wesley did not abandon hope of a well-paid job and Kitty Pakenham, for in the early autumn he wrote again and suggested himself as Surveyor-General of the Ordnance for Ireland; but still Lord Camden said "No". Nothing then was left but to abandon all hope of office and of Kitty and to rejoin his regiment, now under orders to proceed overseas to the fever-stricken West Indies. In writing to commend him on this resolution, the Lord-Lieutenant thought it well to quench any lingering spark of hope, by adding: "I shall be very glad if I can make some arrangement satisfactory to you against you come back" (yellow fever casualties in the West Indies often ran up to 50 per cent) "but if a vacancy should happen in the Revenue Board I fear the Speaker's son must have the first."

That was final, and evidently there was nothing to be obtained in Ireland so long as Lord Camden was in control. Considering the modesty of the requests and what the applicant achieved in the next twenty years, this series of rebuffs surely ranks with those legendary rejections of great authors' manuscripts which afterwards turn out to be masterpieces. It would be interesting to know how Colonel Wesley received these refusals, and how he resigned himself to the penury and insignificance of colonial service as commander of a regiment of foot. It is impossible to know. He has left no record, and none of the people who in later days discussed his life with him dared to question him about this period. We may surmise that these wounds to his pride may have been one reason why he never afterwards solicited any employment, promotion, dignity, or honour. We may also surmise that he suffered in his affections as well as in his ambition. Going overseas on active service meant that at best he could not be home for several years, and therefore it was "farewell for ever" to Kitty Paken-ham. In view of what afterwards happened nobody can make much of a romance out of these two; but there seems no reason to doubt that they were in love in 1795, and that the seemingly final parting was not easy.

Getting away from England proved to be almost harder, and much more tedious and dangerous. The West Indian transports which sailed from Portsmouth in November 1795 were driven back by a violent gale. They set out again in December, only to run into a series of new gales. The fleet was dispersed, some of the transports eventually reaching their destination, while after seven weeks of hopeless beating about at sea the Thirty-Third and their Colonel were driven back to Poole in Dorset, where they hung about miserably for nearly four months. So persistently adverse and violent were these gales that religious persons considered them a divine judgment on whatever national sins they themselves were not inclined to, while the more frivolous pointed out that at any rate they saved an ill-defended and thoroughly seditious Ireland from French invasion. Harassed by this six months of useless buffeting and hanging about, Colonel Wesley fell sick of an unspecified fever—perhaps a touch of malaria picked up in Holland.

This must have been a wretched period for one of the most energetic men of action of an energetic epoch. And more months of inactivity were ahead, for while Lt.-Col. Wesley lay ill the Thirty-Third sailed for India—in April 1796. Soon he was in Dulbin on convalescent leave, clearing up the affairs of Trim and trying to make arrangements about his debts—he even "mentioned these embarrassments" to the Lord-Lieutenant, who was politely sympathetic but totally unhelpful. In May 1796 he was promoted full Colonel, perhaps as a kind of con-solation prize for exile from England and all hopes of political office. At any rate, it was the most which could be obtained by Lord Morn-ington's influence. In June the new Colonel was in London making last-minute purchases, and at the end of the month he was off at last, in a swift frigate, which enabled him to catch up with his regiment at the Cape of Good Hope. They reached Calcutta in February 1797. And so far as England knew or cared that was the end of Arthur Wesley and his politico-military career. Every convoy which sailed for the East in those days carried its complement of eager young men, full of high spirits and cupidity, in the service of the East India Company. And what happened to them? Some were killed and maimed in the wars; some were sent home in disgrace, either for flagrant incompetence or a too public breach of the languidly applied rules against bribery, corruption, and oppression; many more died, usually with appalling suddenness, of the diseases brought on in a tropical country by insane excesses in eating and drinking; some survived and a few succeeded. After twenty years or so the few survivors returned home, with their pockets full of more or less well-gotten gold, tradition- ally but not necessarily with shrivelled sallow complexions and sepoy moustaches, but inevitably with semi-oriental habits and manners, tedious old men of forty with odd eating habits who married faded young women unable to do any better for themselves, and settled down to soothe disordered livers at Bath or Cheltenham, cursing India and eternally regretting it. Lords of creation in the East, they were nobodies at home, except for what little consideration they could buy. "Nabobs" they were nicknamed contemptuously, and lived out their remaining days of opulence surrounded by the envy and derision of their fellow-countrymen for whom they had conquered or administered an Empire.

There were differences between Colonel Wesley and the average run of young men hopefully converging on Calcutta in search of fortune with or without reputation, differences which are worth noting. It was a great advantage, for instance, to go out as colonel and not as an ensign, for ensigns were so poorly paid in India up till 1800 that they could not possibly meet the ordinary expenses of a junior subaltern. And it was certainly a unique chance for the Colonel that within a year Lord Mornington came out as Governor-General. But the great difference is one which is unspectacular but so characteristic that it must not be passed over—namely, an intelligent and methodical preparation for the task ahead. Colonel Wesley took with him a well-chosen library of books on India, and spent the months of the long voyage in learning what they had to teach him. When he landed at Calcutta, he brought with him a considerable theoretical knowledge of military, political, and economic conditions in the country in which he was to serve. The books he read have long been obsolete, so that there is no point in listing them and they mean nothing to a modern reader; but the significant point is the strange spectacle of a British officer in the 1790's seriously preparing *before* undertaking a re-sponsibility.

While we have this indisputable evidence that Colonel Wesley was serious about his profession and career, we have other evidence that he was far indeed from being a dull military pedant. Thus, Captain Elers of the Twelfth Foot, who met the Colonel in September 1796 at the Cape, speaks of him as being "all life and spirits". His debts were a matter of common gossip at that time, and the same authentic voice hints that Kitty Pakenham was already forgotten in a flurry of flirtations and love affairs. At the Cape there was a Miss Henrietta Smith who attracted the Colonel's attentions. These may have been rewarded, for even to the masculine judgment of Elers the Colonel strongly resembled John Philip Kemble, whose "noble countenance" made him the matinee hero of the epoch. Elers was particularly struck by Wesley's clear blue eyes and "remarkably large aquiline nose". The lobes of his ears were joined to his cheeks, which was "also the case with Lord Byron". Elers is positive that Wesley talked "remarkably quickly", which would indicate an active mind and discredits the belief that even at this early date the future Duke was an inarticulate *militaire*. Clearly, however, he was no longer pining for Kitty Pakenham and had recovered from the long depression of spirits engendered by his sufferings from fever, the Duke of York, Lord Camden, and the Mornington family.

Such, so far as we know, was Colonel Wesley when he landed in India. But what sort of life, what kind of people had he come out to? What were the first impressions of persons like himself just arrived from England? Women usually have a sharper eye for such details than men, and we are fortunate in possessing just such a first impression from the pen of Mrs. Eliza Fay, the wife of a debauched barrister, who landed in Madras about a decade earlier. To her eyes it was a scene of "Asiatic splendour combined with European taste . . . flowing drapery, stately palanquins, elegant carriages, innumerable servants, and all the pomp and circumstance of luxurious ease and unbounded wealth". With surprise she observed that "the ladies here are very fashionable"; indeed "I found several novelties in dress since I quitted England". She also noted another side of the picture, "Europeans languishing under various complaints which they call incidental to the climate", but which Mrs. Fay is bluntly certain would have resulted from the same mode of living in any climate. She was quite right about the "complaints". Under the date 1790, we find that convivial diarist, Mr. William Hickey, making this entry: "The breaking up of the rains this season was attended with much fatal illness, and a number of the European inhabitants of Calcutta were carried off; in the month of September alone there were upwards of seventy funerals."

The plain facts are that they are too much, they drank far too much, and had too many servants. Sir Philip Francis, afterwards so venomously critical of Warren Hastings's "luxury", had 110 servants for a family of four. Rents were high (Francis paid £500 a year for "a large but mean house") but provisions were very cheap. A friend of the Francis family writes to a friend in America: "Even the recreations of this Country are little Riots. Thirty people at Breakfast, fifty at Dinner. Suppers at Midnight, Dances till Daylight. But we are reforming apace. To instance the Ceremonies of the Table. We now only toast Healths and Sentiments in Gills and half-pints of Claret." A Bombay dinner in 1784 consisted of "every joint of a calf . . . nearly half a Bengal sheep, several large dishes of fish, boiled and roast turkeys, a ham, a kid, tongue, fowls, and a long train of et ceteras". The numerous "bachelors' parties" were nothing but a series of terrific drunks, followed by excruciating hangovers which give one a headache even to read about. After one such party (at which I regret to say Colonel Wesley was present) Mr. Hickey was unable even to rise from his bed for forty-eight hours. No wonder the cemeteries filled rapidly.

This vulgar society cannot have been very congenial to a young Colonel with elegant French breeding and aristocratic prejudices. It is hardly possible to imagine Colonel Wesley at one of the dinners where "instead of drinking a glass of wine with a gentleman it was usual to throw a chicken at his head, while the Ladies pelted with sweetmeats and pastry". Most probably such scenes were already becoming a thing of the past when the Colonel arrived, for Lord Cornwallis had cleaned out much of the corruption and peculation which supported the vulgarians, and had set the good example of a simpler and more decorous manner of living. In any case, there is so much direct and indirect testimony to Wellington's abstemious habits that he can only very rarely have joined his contemporary Anglo-Indians in their table excesses. His favourite dish was roast saddle of mutton, but he was so indifferent to food that he often failed to notice what he was eating. It is said that he would eat rancid butter without perceiving anything disagreeable about it, and he certainly offended the gluttonous Cambacérés in later life by failing to take any notice of a specially prepared dish. After the Peninsular War his Spanish aide-de-camp, General Alava, complained bitterly that every night when he asked: "When do we move off?" the answer was: "At dawn"; while the invariable reply to the question: "What shall we have for dinner?" was: "Cold meat." "I came to hate the words *at dawn* and *cold meat*."

As to wine, Wesley's limit was "four or five glasses at dinner and a pint afterwards". This would be considered a very liberal allowance now, but was modest indeed in those days of unlimited bumperizing in half-pint glasses.

The tastes and habits of Mr. William Hickey of Calcutta had been formed on pre-Cornwallis lines, and he continued to live in a style of profuse extravagance and awe-inspiring excesses of the bottle. It is certain that on at least one or two occasions Colonel Wesley joined Hickey's parties. Mr. Hickey dined frequently with the regimental mess of the Thirty-Third, and reports that "they lived inimitably well, always sending their guests away with a liberal quantity of the best claret". But here the guiding and convivial spirit was not Colonel Wesley, but the second-in-command, Colonel Sherbrooke. At his country residence, Mr. Hickey encountered "eight as strong-headed fellows as could be found in Hindostan", with whom he drank "two-and-twenty bumpers in glasses of considerable magnitude"; after which the President "said everyone might fill according to his own discretion, and so discreet were all of the company that we continued to follow the Colonel's example of drinking nothing short of bumpers until two o'clock in the morning, at which hour each person staggered to his carriage or palankeen". If Colonel Wesley was not the discreet President, he was undoubtedly one of the indiscreet guests. But a week of glory for Mr. Hickey was when he entertained General St. Leger, Colonel Wesley, "the Dutch Governor", and other officers and gentlemen for the races. One afternoon alone they consumed turtle soup and fat deer, with champagne, claret, hock, and madeira, and, not unwarrantably, "the day went off with the utmost hilarity and good humour". Major Bradshaw and Captain Forrest offered "several choice songs", followed by the Messieurs Birch with "delightful catches and glees". Finally the hilarity reached such a pitch of classic elegance that the General sang "The British Grenadiers" with high spirit.

General St. Leger was not unknown to Colonel Wesley, for he too was "a survivor of the Duke of York's arduous and unfortunate campaign upon the Continent"; but, unlike Colonel Wesley, the General was "a professed judge of every circumstance connected with good living", and indeed had "damaged his health and fortune in the service of H.R.H. the Prince Regent", who appropriately succoured his faithful servant with a Staff job in India. It is scarcely necessary to add that India soon completed what Prinny had begun—the General died suddenly of apoplexy. He has a slight but sentimental interest for us, since the earliest in date of the majestic series of Wellington dispatches relating to India is a memorandum on horse artillery addressed (at his request) to General St. Leger who wanted flattery and support for a pet theory. He didn't get it. The dispatch is clear, comprehensive, definite, and somehow not untactful; but its judgment on the General's project might be summarized as "most desirable in theory, but too expensive and impractical except on a very small scale". Perhaps the General was too much absorbed in good living to observe the wholly unfamiliar note of competence and decision in this otherwise insignificant report. He would doubtless have died of apoplexy at once, could he have known that the subordinate officer he patronized so genially was a future Commander-in-Chief.

Command—that was what Colonel Wesley needed in order to act effectively, and command was almost impossible to obtain, owing to the large numbers of incompetent senior officers and their frantic jealousy of the privileges of their seniority. In April 1797 there was a ray of hope. The witches' dance of European politics had brought Holland and Spain into war on the side of France, and it was therefore legitimate though perhaps hazardous to form plans of attacking Batavia and Manila from India with a mighty expeditionary force of 1,400 men. Evidently Arthur Wesley (however little the public yet knew of him) had already acquired some reputation in Indian military and government circles. The Governor-General, Sir John Shore, "a good man, but cold as a greyhound's nose", unexpectedly consulted Colonel Wesley on this expedition and even proposed to make him commander. The omniscient Colonel was not in the least taken by surprise. He seemed to know all about the dispositions of the Dutch forces and the "slight brick wall" which defended Batavia, the citadel which "is not within shot of the artillery-ground" but "has no guns mounted on the land side". The troops (he said) ought to rendezvous at Tanjore in Malaya, advance on Batavia, and then proceed to Manila, "the principal object". But "ships cannot lie in Manila Bay in safety during the south-west monsoon. . . . This difficulty would be removed if they would determine to attack a fort, Cavite, which commands the entrance of a bay in Manila Bay, which is sheltered from the south-west monsoon". On the other hand, "if they begin by Manila itself, Cavite falls of course afterwards". The one objection from the Colonel's point of view was not the difficulty of the enterprise but his strong private opinion that the destruction of Batavia was morally unjustifiable—a strange scruple in an officer on the verge of his first independent command.

Unluckily there was (as always) a pestilential senior officer named Doyle on the horizon, and we find Colonel Wesley writing to Richard, Lord Mornington, under date April 17, 1797, as follows:

"It was proposed by Mr. Speke, the Deputy-Governor, to give me the chief command of the expedition; but I desired the person who communicated his wishes to me to decline it in my name, and to propose Doyle. If any thing should prevent Doyle from accepting it in case they offer it to him, and they should afterwards offer it to me, I intend to accept of it; taking the chance that the large force they intend to send, the known pusillanimity of the enemy, and my exertions will compensate in some degree for my want of experience."

This magnanimity was ill-rewarded, for nothing more was said of Colonel Wesley as commander, and the Madras Government appointed an officer "who knows his incapacity", for it was General St. Leger. The Colonel reported this to his brother in a letter of May 20, 1797 (the day before he joined Mr. Hickey's racing and drinking party) with the comment: "He is mistaken if he supposes that a good, high-spirited army can be kept in order by other means than by the abilities and firmness of the Commander-in-Chief." Naturally, the expedition was held up by innumerable delays, and the Colonel grew melancholy. Wistfully he reminds his brother that in a year of absence from England no letter had reached him from any of the family, and adds: "I wish you would let my mother &c, know that I am well." Astonishingly enough, the climate of India suited him, and he always maintained that it cured him of his youthful sickliness and weakness. In other respects he disliked India, "a miserable country to live in, and I now begin to think that a man well deserves some of the wealth which is sometimes brought home, for having spent his life here". And he continues pessimistically: "The natives, as far as I have observed, are much misrepresented. They are the most mischievous, deceitful race of people I have seen or read of. I have not yet met with a Hindoo who had one good quality, even for the state of society in his own country, and the Mussulmans are worse than they are. Their meekness and mildness do not exist."

That was written to Lord Mornington on July 12, 1797, but on July 27 we find Colonel Wesley writing again in rather better spirits, for he had just received official confirmation of an important piece of news which had been rumoured for some time—Richard had been appointed Governor-General of India, and raised to the English peerage as Baron Wellesley. Arthur Wesley knew his brother too well to expect to receive any extraordinary favours. He offers his service "to your Government", but adds soberly that "I can't expect to derive any advantage from it which I should not obtain if any other person were Governor-General". This is not quite true, for one of the characteristics of Richard Wellesley's rule in India was his almost unerring gift of choosing able subordinates, which cannot be said truthfully of his predecessor and immediate successors. Not until Lord Dalhousie came out in 1848 was there so brilliant a Governor-General of India as Lord Wellesley. But it was just as well for Colonel Wesley to form no high hopes of any unfair promotion from his brother, who (unknown to him) had determined to break entirely with the bad old traditions of nepotism and jobbing patronage which had lasted so long in Indian affairs. In rebuffing a possible attempt on those lines Lord Wellesley wrote sternly to his friend, Sir Chichester Fortescue, in these terms:

"Your nephew will be appointed a writer next season, I hope to Bengal; and when he arrives in India in a regular manner I will give him every encouragement and assistance; and if he deserves it (not otherwise), I will take care that he shall rise as quickly as the regulations of the Company's service, and the attention due to the merit of others, will permit: *more I will not do for my own brother.*"

That was decisive.

Meanwhile the expeditionary force for the Eastern islands set sail, with Colonel Wesley in no more important position than commanding officer of the Thirty-Third Foot. He distinguished himself, however, by a sharp brush with the authorities, in which he claimed and eventually received for himself and his regimental surgeon full charge of the health of his own men, as against the claims of the naval surgeons. Whereupon he drew up a code of thirty-six "Regimental Orders for on Board Ship" which left nothing in the matter of health, cleanliness, exercise, and discipline to the unaided imagination of the troops. Behind this there was neither the jealous desire to keep every little bit of authority nor any wish to coddle the men, but the purely practical aim of arriving at the destination after a long voyage with as few sick as possible. It is worth noting that this was not the last occasion on which Wesley came sharply into conflict with naval officers in the matter of their authority over his men while on board ship. A certain naval captain ordered one of Wesley's soldiers to be flogged, and then heard these rather disturbing words: "Certainly the man must be flogged, but I shall *make my report* and you will abide the consequences." The man, we are told, was not flogged after all.

The expedition never reached either Batavia or Manila. They landed at Penang in September 1797, and were immediately recalled by Lord Hobart (the Governor of Madras), who was worried by "the intrigues of the French" and the "threatening attitude of Tippoo Sultan". With some wisdom he decided it was safer to have the troops back in India. Colonel Wesley alone did not waste his time, but made a thorough survey of Penang and presented Government with a ten-page report on the advantages of holding that port and just how to make it moderately secure from "insults and plunder". He thought it had "great economic possibilities".

CHAPTER VI

India and its Problems

"ON the 26th April, 1798, Lord Mornington first beheld the 'coral strand' of the coast of Coromandel. On that day he anchored in the roads of Madras; and after the excitement of a passage through the surf which perpetually rages on these romantic shores, placed his foot upon the soil of India, and was saluted by the guns of Fort St. George."

The new Governor-General paused long enough at Madras to add his name to the lengthening list of those who had failed to solve the ancient problem and hoary scandal of the Nawab of Arcot's debts. In May he proceeded to Calcutta, "the city of the sun, glittering with palaces, gardens, and groves, branching banian-trees, palm-trees of every variety, bright green peepuls, tall bamboos and flowers of every hue", which he reached on May 17. Two days later Arthur Wesley changed his name to "Wellesley", obviously at his noble brother's request. The inflated language of the contemporary historian just quoted seems appropriate to Lord Mornington, whose most conspicuous foible was his love of display, "bursting forth", as a sardonic Anglo-Indian noted, "like a constellation in all his pomp and splendour among us". "Marquis Wellesley," says the same critic, "was in no way sparing of the Company's cash. His Lordship's own establishment of servants, equipages &c, were extravagant in the superlative degree, not only in point of number, but splendour of dress. . . . His Lordship also determined upon building a palace suitable to his magnificent ideas . . . and at the same time commenced a second palace at Barrackpore. The grounds were laid out with extraordinary taste and elegance, upon different parts of which he erected a theatre, a riding-house, with probably the finest aviary and menagerie in the world."

As the Governor-General stepped ashore, revolving these and other magnificent projects, his matter-of-fact brother Arthur was drawing up a memorandum to "The Agents on Clothing for the 33rd Regiment" which winds up "and I shall have the satisfaction of knowing that I have already saved one year's clothing for the Colonel". It is hardly possible to imagine a clearer example of the contrast between the two brothers. In the language of his own time, Lord Wellesley was "a gentleman of enlarged views" (some added "enlarged head") but apt to overlook details of expense and execution. Such details might be usefully left to his brothers, Arthur and Henry, for Lord Wellesley had brought the latter with him as secretary. To Arthur Wellesley the immediate result of his brother's arrival as Governor-General was a great increase in hard unremunerative work of a secret nature. Between June and August 1798, for instance, he supplied the Governor-General with no less than eight confidential and detailed memoranda on military and political problems.

The presence of the English in India is due to a set of historical accidents which justify the statement that "the British Empire was founded in a fit of absent-mindedness". The Cape passage to India was discovered by the Portuguese in 1497–1498, and for a century they disputed the trade with the Dutch. In 1600 Queen Elizabeth authorized the founding of the East India Company, for the purpose of trade only, not of acquiring territory. Twelve years later a Portuguese fleet tried to destroy the Company's ships off the coast of India, and were defeated. Thereafter the East India Company was engaged in constant warfare successively and sometimes simultaneously with the Portuguese, Dutch, and French companies, all striving for the monopoly of the Eastern trade. Missionaries were added by all as an afterthought.

Grants of land were made by Indian princes for the settlement of the European trades—Portuguese Goa and French Pondichéry still remain in India as relics of their former influence. Madras was founded by the English in 1639, Calcutta in 1686. These were Company settlements, but Bombay was a possession of the Crown, having been ceded in 1661 as part of the dowry of Charles II's Portuguese wife—odd as it seems that he should have a wife.

These settlements prospered, but throughout the eighteenth century the British East India Company was involved in a life and death struggle with the French, in which Clive finally defeated Dupleix. The fight between the Europeans was complicated by a typically oriental caprice on the part of the Nawab of Bengal, who without provocation suddenly descended upon Calcutta in 1756, and imprisoned 146 of the English inhabitants in a small jail only eighteen feet by fifteen. By morning all but twenty-three of the whites had died of heat and thirst. Clive promptly avenged this horror by the battle of Plassey, and astonished the world by defeating a Mohammedan army of 50,000 men and 50 guns, with less than 3,000 men and 8 guns. In the subsequent treaty about 900 square miles of Bengal were ceded to the Company. Thus began armed conflict with Indian princes and the acquisition of territory larger than small city sites. Bengal was acquired by Warren Hastings. Hyder Ali of Mysore, father of Tippoo Sultan, attacked and nearly captured Madras which was saved at the last moment by Eyre Coote. In 1790 there was another war with Tippoo Sultan, which resulted in his paying an indemnity and ceding part of his dominions, with the full intention of regaining both at the first opportunity.

India in 1798 undoubtedly provided plenty of opportunity for the exercise of Lord Wellesley's abilities, and he needed all the help he could get from his two gifted brothers. The problem at that time was not, How can India govern herself? for the collapse of the Great Mogul's power had split the country among warring princes and usurpers who oppressed their own subjects and plundered those of their rivals. Apart from the great province of Bengal, the areas directly under British or French rule were small. Inevitably one of these powers would have to enforce peace and order, or they would have to abandon their trading establishments altogether. Naturally two European powers could not be expected to co-operate for this desirable end, so they continued to fight it out as they had been doing indecisively for at least half a century previously.

It has sometimes been doubted whether in 1799 there was any danger from the French, but the fact that such doubt could be expressed merely shows how successful Lord Wellesley was. General Bonaparte's expedition to Egypt was decided in March 1798 and he remarked significantly: "The master of Egypt must eventually be master of India." His instructions from the Directory contain these words: "The army of the East shall take possession of Egypt; the Commander-in-chief shall *chase the English from all their possessions in the East which he can reach* . . ." The attack from this side failed, because Nelson destroyed the French fleet at Aboukir, and Sir Sidney Smith defeated the French army at Acre. Whereupon Napoleon left his army to die or be captured, and returned home to announce his victories. How deeply he yearned to invade India may be seen from the fact that he twice attempted to arrange for a land invasion from the Caucasus in co-operation with the Russians; and on the second occasion an advance-guard of Cossacks had actually started when luckily for the English Napoleon quarrelled with the Tsar Alexander and decided to advance on Moscow instead.

In 1798 Lord Wellesley could not possibly know how events would turn out in Egypt and Syria, and indeed the last body of French troops in Egypt did not surrender until late in August 1801. Meanwhile, there was danger to British rule from India itself. The passive

c

policy of Sir John Shore and general inertia had weakened the armed forces of the Company, while French officers had raised and trained large native armies for the Nizam of Hyderabad. Tippoo Sultan of Mysore, and the chiefs of the Mahratta Confederacy—Scindia, Holkar, and Berar. The most hostile of these princes was Tippoo. Lord Wellesley was alarmed by receiving a copy of a proclamation issued by Malartic, Governor of the French island of Mauritius, in which he called for volunteers to go to the aid of Tippoo who (said the Frenchman) "only awaits the moment when the French shall come to his assistance to declare war against the English". The Governor-General was also informed that some of these French officers had already landed and had joined Tippoo at Seringapatam.

The effect of this news on the Governor-General's "enlarged views" was an impulse to declare war on Tippoo immediately. Luckily for him and his cause he first consulted his military brother, and received a masterpiece of cool common sense in reply. Certainly, Colonel Wellesley wrote, this offensive alliance with France is a perfectly good *casus belli*, but "the consequence of that alliance has been an addition to the forces of Tippoo of 150 men at most" and he is "never likely to get more than 3,000 French troops". Moreover, "we are not in the fortunate circumstances which are desirable before we enter into a war", and "if we are to have a war at all, it must be one of our own creating; a justifiable one, I acknowledge; one which we shall think necessary". And so "is there any danger in deferring the war to that period when your resources will have revived, when you will have the benefit of the assistance of all your allies?"

In other words: "Don't go to war unless it is unavoidable and if possible, just; but, above all, don't get into a war until you are *prepared*."

When he read that document Lord Wellesley paused, for he was no fool. Perhaps he held a conference with his brothers, but in any event emissaries were dispatched to the Mahrattas and to the Nizam. The influence of Scindia and a not unnatural desire to wait and see which side looked like winning induced the Peshwah to elude these overtures; but the Nizam, an old ally, agreed to dismiss his French officers and to join with the Company. Meanwhile Colonel Wellesley with the Thirty-Third was sent to Madras as an unofficial chief of staff, to organize the army there and "to keep Lord Clive on the right road". The voyage began unpropitiously, for the ship ran on a reef, and "she was got off, I may almost say, by the bodily strength of the soldiers". Moreover, the Calcutta contractor had supplied inferior rum and infected water—

"nearly every man has had the flux; I have had it; fifteen men have died of it. It is unpardonable, as I warned him of it, and I am afraid I must make a public complaint of him."

The difficulties of keeping Lord Clive "on the right road" were considerable. He had only just been appointed Governor of Madras, and apparently for no better reason than that he was son of the great Clive. Colonel Wellesley found him "a mild, moderate man, remarkably reserved, having a bad delivery, and apparently a heavy understanding". The Colonel surmised that Lord Clive had been misled and frightened by his advisers, and indeed one of them had reported: "I can anticipate nothing but shocking disasters from a premature attack upon Tippoo in our present disabled condition, and the impeachment of Lord Mornington for his temerity." Were there not Acts of Parliament specifically forbidding the East India Company to increase its territory or to make war upon the Indian princes except in case of Indian aggression? There were. But like all attempts to legislate neutrality, these Acts were doomed to be eluded; for what is an act of aggression? If Lord Clive wanted to wait until Tippoo and the French invaded his territories (in which event he would most probably be defeated) the Governor-General held that alliance with a power which hoped "to chase the English from all their possessions in the East" was distinctly aggressive. Besides, Lord Wellesley intended to have the better army, which would clearly put right on his side. Evidently Lord Clive could be made to see reason, for Colonel Wellesley was able to report that "I doubt whether he is so dull as he appears, or as people here imagine he is"; besides, "he is convinced of the necessity of the measures in which you are embarked".

Having accomplished this diplomatic errand, the Colonel of the Thirty-Third was free to put in an immense amount of extra hard work in the thankless task of reorganizing the Indian army; for, as the autumn of 1798 passed, the protracted correspondence between Tippoo and the Governor-General showed no signs of the peaceful solution Colonel Wellesley had advised. An army therefore was to concentrate at Vellore, about a hundred miles from Madras, and a hundred and eighty from the final objective, Seringapatam, Tippoo's capital; and it had a formidable task ahead. Tippoo possessed a French-trained field army of 47,000 regulars and 30,000 garrison troops, well equipped, and with artillery. Their most dangerous contingent was a body of about 13,000 light cavalry, adepts at eluding a general engagement, at cutting off stragglers and small detachments, and destroying supplies ahead of an invading force. The only method of meeting this was for the invading army to carry its own supplies. With unwearied patience the unofficial chief of staff turned himself into the unofficial quartermaster-general, interviewed strings of *brinjarries* (native grain dealers) for rice supplies, collected transport bullocks by the thousand, heaped up "beef, biscuit and arrack" for the European troops, and for the sepoys provided a strange assortment of commodities, including "rice, doll, sweetmeats, ghee, oil, betel-nuts, tobacco, bhangarah, massaulah and greens".

Unfortunately, it was one thing to know what ought to be done and to know how to do it, and quite another thing to secure obedience without the necessary rank and authority to enforce it. The bullocks ordered were not supplied; the battering train ordered to Vellore was not sent; the commanding General turned up, neglected to continue Colonel Wellesley's methods of collecting food, and was faced with famine; a Colonel bringing up a detachment forgot about feeding his men and sent panic-stricken letters demanding supplies. The General called on Colonel Wellesley to meet the emergency ("during two nights . . . I was in bed only two hours; and had black grain merchants teasing me almost the whole time that I was employed upon other business"), and when the emergency was met, the General appropriated the credit to himself. No wonder Colonel Wellesley wrote to his brother Henry that his "situation is an awkward one and without remedy". No wonder he looked forward wistfully to the day when the slow wheel of promotion by seniority would bring his name among the Major-Generals. However austere his sense of duty, it must have been irritating for Wellesley to drudge day and night doing the Commander-in-Chief's work for him and then to be told coolly that no public acknowledgment would be made of his work "for fear of creating jealousy in other officers"! There was every prospect that the campaign, every detail of which he had planned and organized, would be credited to others, while he was limited to the functions and reward of a mere Colonel of Foot.

Then happened a curious, unexpected accident. A certain Colonel Aston (another of the Prince Regent's numerous ex-friends in India) was in command of the regiments concentrating at a place called Arnee, preparatory to joining the main body at Vellore. In December, this Colonel Aston was mortally wounded in a duel, and his command went to the nearest senior Colonel, who happened to be Colonel Wellesley. He was thus placed unexpectedly in a position to super-intend the final preparations with his predecessor's full authority of an acting Major-General. Yet such was the negligence of the Madras

Government in providing money that the Colonel had to sell his own horses and borrow money from other officers to carry on the public service. Luckily, the Governor-General yielded to his brother's urgent calls and came down from Calcutta to Madras; whereupon affairs at the base were conducted with some reason and efficiency. But now the Governor-General himself introduced a new and awkward complication—by proposing to join the army in person. Since Lord Wellesley was an autocratic civilian with no knowledge of fighting he would have been an intolerable nuisance at the front; and since he was the supreme head of the British Government in India his presence would merely serve to undermine the authority of the actual military commander, General Harris. It would be as much of a nuisance and general paralysis of military efficiency as having the Prince Regent at headquarters. The misplaced desire of brother Richard for military glory aroused Arthur's wrath; and Colonel Wellesley wrote one of those letters for which the Duke of Wellington was afterwards famous and feared:

"I am entirely ignorant of the objects which you may have in view in coming, which may certainly counterbalance the objections I have to the measure; but it appears to me that your presence in camp, instead of giving confidence to the General, would in fact deprive him of the command of the army. . . . All I can say upon the subject is, that if I were in General Harris's situation, and you joined the army, I should quit it."

The Governor-General stayed where he was.

Slowly the patient work of drilling, equipping, and organizing went on, and at length, under date February 4, 1799, the Colonel was able to write his brother: "The ponderous machine is now nearly prepared, and all we have to do is to put and keep it in motion." True, Colonel Wellesley might march only as Colonel of the Thirty-Third, but the chance of Aston's death had enabled him to make "the ponderous machine" efficient, and that was what mattered. Then, just as the army was about to march, he had another piece of luck. As an ally, the Nizam of Hyderabad sent a contingent of about 16,000 troops under the direction of his vizier, Meer Allum, and the intention had been to brigade them with Colonel Aston's European regiment. Meer Allum asked for Colonel Wellesley and the Thirty-Third, so that he went after all as commander of the army's left wing.

Early in March the "ponderous machine" got under way, and must indeed have been an extraordinary sight. The army of about 36,000 moved in a vast hollow square about three miles by seven, protected by cavalry, and itself protecting an enormous and bizarre convoy of about 200,000 camp-followers, 120,000 bullocks, vast numbers of camels, donkeys, horses and elephants, carrying the supplies with ponderous and noisy slowness, amid ceaseless trumpeting, braying, bellowing, and whinnying. Would it reach its destination and achieve its purpose? Before the army started, Colonel Wellesley was none too optimistic. He pointed out to the Governor-General that they were late in starting and that affairs "have been already in some degree mismanaged"; and so "I am glad you are prepared for a failure. . . . It is better to see and to communicate the difficulties and dangers of the enterprise, and to endeavour to overcome them, than to be blind to everything but success till the moment of difficulty comes, and then to despond".

That was in February. On March 9, 1799, the Colonel writes still cautiously but with an evident lift of spirits: "We are going on well; have got Oodeadroog, Batingerry. Anchittydroog, and Neilgherry." But when they reached Bangalore the transport bullocks were failing in "the most alarming manner". The Colonel investigated and discovered "a parcel of absurd, impracticable, shop-keeping regulations . . . under which no great undertaking could ever prosper". He persuaded the General to abolish them immediately and also to destroy "many stores . . . absolutely useless excepting as lumber, and which I had pressed the General to leave behind him at Vellore". Clearly, but for Colonel Wellesley's energetic interference the "ponderous machine" would have stuck at Bangalore, facing a disastrous retreat of discouraged sepoys harried by light horse. His will and energy forced the half-competent Generals to do the right thing, and: "*Camp near Allagoor, 25th March, 1799*. . . . I write to inform you that we are going on now as well as you could wish. There is not *now* a doubt but that we shall bring that monstrous equipment to Seringapatam, and, in that case, we shall certainly take the place."

There was a battle on March 27, and Tippoo's troops fought well. "His infantry advanced, and almost stood the charge of bayonets of the Thirty-Third, and his cavalry rode at General Baird's European brigade." At the critical moment, Tippoo mishandled his artillery, his troops engaged were totally destroyed "without loss to us", and the rest withdrew in panic. In other words, Colonel Wellesley's staff work had solved the military problem—he had brought enough of the right kind of troops with enough supplies to the right place at the right time. The ponderous machine stopped, fought its action, won, and slowly moved on. It was the reward of months of intense, patient work, prodding subordinates to action, silently correcting the mistakes of

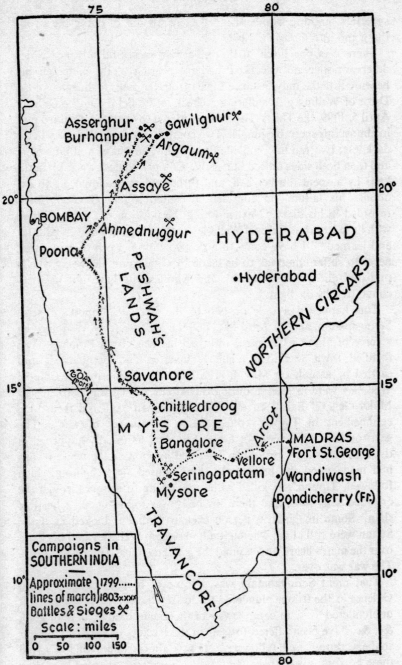

Asserghur   Gawilghur
Burhanpur   Argaum

Assaye

BOMBAY

Ahmednuggur   HYDERABAD

Poona

PESHWAH'S LANDS

                Hyderabad

NORTHERN CIRCARS

GOA (Port.)

Savanore

Chittledroog

MYSORE

Bangalore   Arcot   MADRAS
                      Fort St.George
          Vellore
Seringapatam   Wandiwash
Mysore
                  Pondicherry (Fr.)

TRAVANCORE

Campaigns in
SOUTHERN INDIA

Approximate) 1799......
lines of march) 1803 xxxx
Battles & Sieges ✗
Scale : miles

0   50   100   150

superiors, arguing wooden-headed Generals out of doing the wrong thing and into doing the right. . . .

There was one hitch in this otherwise successful advance which deserves notice, not because it had any bearing on the campaign, but because it is the only instance (apart from the siege of Burgos) of the Duke of Wellington's suffering a check in the field. On the night of April 5, 1799, the Thirty-Third were ordered to capture a fortified post in almost impenetrable jungle. Two companies missed their way in the darkness; two ran into enfilade fire and lost an officer and nine men; and then both sides retired hurriedly. Colonel Wellesley was hit in the knee by a spent musket ball, and turned up at headquarters to announce his failure "in considerable agitation", as General Harris recorded in his diary. Next morning the position was easily carried with little loss, but Colonel Wellesley made a note of a lesson paid for and learned: "I have come to a determination, when in my power, never to suffer an attack to be made by night upon an enemy who is prepared and strongly posted, and whose posts have not been reconnoitred by daylight."

This happened a mile or two to the west of Tippoo's capital, Seringapatam, and on April 14 (1799) the Madras army was joined by a force of about 6,000 men, who had marched from Bombay. The fortified town was then regularly invested and bombarded, and carried by assault on May 4. The Nizam's contingent and Colonel Wellesley were in reserve during this attack, which was entrusted to Major-General Baird, an old soldier who had "suffered from long confinement in Tippoo's dungeons as a prisoner of war". The garrison kept up a very hot fire at first, but, as usually happened in these Indian sieges, resistance collapsed as soon as the white troops had made good the breach. In the confused street fighting which followed, Tippoo was killed as he was trying to escape through the crowded sally-port, and there his body was found under a heap of slain. Some imaginative person exclaimed that it looked as if the Sultan were still alive; whereupon horse-sense Wellesley laid his hand over the man's heart, and assured the gentlemen that Tippoo was dead. The war was over.

That night Seringapatam was a scene of hideous confusion and violence as the troops plundered the town. "Scarcely a house was left unplundered . . . in camp jewels of the greatest value, bars of gold, &c, &c, have been offered for sale in the bazaars of the army by our soldiers, sepoys and followers." It was almost impossible to avoid these horrors, for at that time armies everywhere regarded it as their

THE STORMING OF SERINGAPATAM

A line engraving after the painting by Peter Krafft

right to pillage captured towns, and officers who were injudicious enough to interfere were frequently shot by their own men. Wellington never accepted this view, since he believed that war should not be waged with civilians, that it was both good policy and common decency to treat conquered peoples humanely. By the rules of the service, prize money was allotted for material captured, and the troops should be content with that. They never were; and the Duke never succeeded in enforcing his orders against pillage until the very end of his active military career, and not completely even then.

Seringapatam gave him his first lesson in dealing with situations of this kind. Early on the morning of May 5, General Baird was sitting at breakfast with his Staff when Colonel Wellesley came in and showed a written order from the General in command appointing him (Wellesley) military commander of Seringapatam. Baird flushed with anger. He was a hot-tempered man, and since he had led the assault, considered he was entitled to the command of the town. As he put it dramatically: "Before the sweat was dry on my brow, I was super-seded by an inferior officer." Baird rose in a fury, saying to his officers: "Come, gentlemen, we have nothing more to do here." "Oh, don't do that," said Colonel Wellesley politely, "stay and have breakfast."

There were indeed excellent reasons why General Baird should not have been allowed to hold the military command of the captured city of Seringapatam. Long years afterwards the Duke explained them. "Baird," he said, "was a gallant, hard-headed, lion-hearted officer; but he had no talent, no tact. He had strong prejudices against the natives; and he was peculiarly disqualified from his manners, habits &c, &c, and, it was supposed, his temper, for the management of them. He had been Tippoo's prisoner for years. He had a strong feeling of the bad usage which he had received during his captivity . . ." All very good reasons, it would seem, for not giving him power over the native population.

The new commander had his hands full. At ten that morning he wrote advising the General to stay away because "we are in such confusion still". Among other troubles the keepers of Tippoo's tigers had fled, and the starving animals were violent. At 12.30 p.m. he wrote asking for the Provost-Marshal to be sent immediately—"until some of the plunderers are hanged, it is vain to expect to stop the plunder". A third report says "things are better", but urges that troops be confined to camp with hourly roll-calls. And then with characteristic irony: " . . . it would be very advisable that the officers of the army should suspend the gratification of their curiosity, and that

c*

none but those on duty should come into the town. It only increases the confusion and the terror of the inhabitants." On the morning of April 6, the Colonel was able to report: "Plunder is stopped, the fires are all extinguished, and the inhabitants are returning to their houses fast. I am now employed in burying the dead, which I hope will be completed this day, particularly if you send me all the pioneers." In each of the principal streets dangled from gallows the lifeless body of a British soldier or a sepoy as a grim warning to the rest of the army.

The harsh measures were successful. All Tippoo's family (including his sons and numerous harem) and the chief inhabitants had been saved, as well as the granaries, powder factories, the huge stores of ammunition, the palace and the treasury—which contained more than a million sterling in coin and jewels. The strength of the place may be judged from the fact that over 1,200 brass and iron cannon were found mounted on the walls or in the arsenal. Large numbers of muskets (most of them, significantly, captured from the Company) were also found. All these had to be checked and inventoried, barracks built for the troops, ruined houses rebuilt, and repairs to the fortifications begun. One by one Tippoo's surviving generals and ministers came in "under cowle" as it was called, i.e. a guarantee of peace and safety of person. The family of the former Hindu Rajah (whose throne had been usurped by Tippoo's father, Hyder Ali) were found miserably huddled in one room of the palace, where the women could not live in *purdah*—the gravest of insults. To their surprise they found themselves released, treated with respect, and the late Rajah's nearest descendant, a small boy, had the bewildering experience of being saluted ruler of Mysore. True, the Company annexed some of Tippoo's territories, and others were ceded to the Nizam; but even this reduced Mysore was larger than it had been before the days of Hyder Ali—Wellington was always in favour of moderation.

Plenty of work in these and many other directions, but nothing to show for it in the way of promotion or credit. True, the Colonel received his share of the prize money, but it was inadequate to his expenses. "Since I went in to the field in December," he wrote privately to the Governor-General under date June 14, 1799, "I have commanded an army with a large staff attached to me, which has not been unattended by a very great expense, particularly latterly. About six weeks ago I was sent in here with a garrison, consisting of about half the army and a large staff, and I have not received one shilling more than I did in Fort St. George. The consequence is that I am ruined." This was unpleasant enough, and at the same time we find the Governor-General complaining that the services of Colonel Wellesley had not only gone unnoticed, "but his promotion is protracted so studiously, that every intriguer here believes it to be delayed for the express purpose of thwarting me".

Although the campaign ended on this note of frustration and irritation, the victory was immensely popular with an army which had not forgotten Tippoo's past and the old scores to be paid off. When Hyder Ali made his attack on Madras in 1770, he had defeated a small English army and would have tortured and massacred the prisoners but for the protests of his French officers. As it was, the commander, Colonel Baillie, died in a Seringapatam dungeon; and the fate of the others was very disagreeable. As soon as Tippoo succeeded his father he ordered that "the handsomest and youngest of the European soldiers should undergo the repulsive ceremonies of Mohammedanism. They were drugged with a delirious stuff called *Majum*, which rendered them insensible, and in this state they received the initiatory rite. These wretched men were then compelled to act as drill-serjeants to Tippoo's slave battalion of boys, who had been kidnapped from the Carnatic". General Mathews and his officers, captured in 1782, fared no better. The General and seventeen of his officers were poisoned, and others died or went insane in the dungeons. (Baird was one of those tough enough to survive until rescued by Cornwallis.) It was natural, then, that Colonel Wellesley should be popular with the officers in the Indian army who knew how largely the success was due to him. Significantly, the Governor-General began to receive letters from junior officers petitioning that they might be "allowed to serve in any future operations under Colonel Wellesley".

CHAPTER VII

The Freebooters

THE military commander of Seringapatam was not appointed to a sinecure. He had to keep his own ruffians in order and employed on useful but inexpensive work; there were disorders and petty rebellions to suppress; the engineer officer in charge turned out to be both incompetent and recalcitrant, and had to be removed; there was dishonesty in the disposal of the captured stores which had to be pursued through many tedious sittings of a court martial; there was endless administrative correspondence. He drew up for the Madras Government "A Regulation for the Due Administration of Justice within the Fort and Island of Seringapatam", twelve pages long, divided into twenty-nine sections.

The Governor-General, eager for the prosperity of his new ally, the Rajah of Mysore, required a report on "the different kinds of esculent vegetables, the modes of cultivation, and machinery adopted for watering the grounds; the different breeds of cattle, the extent and tenures of the farms, and the usual price of labour; the cultivation and the preparation of cotton, pepper, sandal-wood, cardamums, and the means by which these may be extended, the state of manufactures and manufacturers, the climate and seasons of Mysore; the general condition of the inhabitants with respect to food, clothing and habitations, as well as the subdivisions of castes and tribes prevalent among them". Fortunately he was thoughtful enough to send a Fellow of the Royal Society to help with this prodigious inquiry, which was not completed until long after the Governor-General and Colonel Wellesley had returned to England, and was then probably pigeon-holed as "another of Lord Wellesley's extravagancies".

These are the inevitable trials of those who are willing to accept the thankless task of ruling others, but in this case they might have been easier to bear if the Governor-General had not been so subject to "enlarged views" and infrequent but peremptory and contradictory orders from the King's Government. Colonel Wellesley was hardly settled in Seringapatam (the first satisfactory job he had ever had) when brother Richard in Calcutta proposed that he should drop everything, and proceed to England for the purpose of overwhelming the enemies of the Governor-General of India. The Colonel responded gloomily but loyally (June 23, 1799): "I am very willing to go if it is thought that I can be of any use." Having injected this note of uncertainty, the Governor-General reflected, and changed his mind. Arthur was not to go, but the project of a descent on Batavia was always held in reserve to be brought up whenever other business was urgent. The Colonel must have felt considerable relief when he could announce that he was going to visit the posts and forts along his frontier—it was harder to reach him there. He was off on August 19, 1799, and was at once busy with reliefs and detachments, with *vakeels* (native envoys), and the misdeeds of *killadars* (governors of forts) and *polygars*, who are defined as "natives who consider themselves independent; they inhabit forts, hills and woods, armed with pikes and matchlocks". Perhaps the polygars were not very different from the numerous bands of freebooters who had to be patiently but grimly suppressed: "There is a place called Ey Goor, four or five coss from Munserabad. You will be pleased to destroy it, and hang all persons either in it or Munserabad that you find in arms." The most dangerous of these freebooter leaders was one Dhoondiah Waugh (or Dundia Wao) who was hotly pursued by a couple of armed columns but fled over the Mahratta frontier, where it was forbidden to follow him.

Late in November, Colonel Wellesley was back with his garrison at Seringapatam, and there he might be seen every morning on parade dressed in "a long coat, the uniform of the 33rd Regiment, a cocked hat, white pantaloons, Hessian boots and spurs, and a large sabre, the handle solid silver, and the mounting of the scabbard of the same metal, but all gilt". He defied regulations to the extent of never wearing powder, and wore his hair cropped close, being "convinced the wearing of hair powder was very prejudicial to health as impeding perspiration". Off parade he still had plenty to do in addition to his perennial problems of bullocks, rations, pay rolls, polygars, and injuries to the feelings of other officers. For instance, was it necessary for the surgeon of the Thirty-Third to keep a record of all case histories and forward it monthly to the Surgeon-General in Ceylon? The Colonel thought not, but then he had to take up the problems of obtaining a chaplain, arranging more and still more pensions for Tippoo's innumerable family, arranging for the upkeep of the royal tombs (which "cost a pretty penny") and the delicate subject of new wardrobes for the ladies of the zenana. These ladies were a great embarrassment, as may be partially gathered from the following confidence to a sympathetic brother colonel:

"Within these few days I have received an application from a very respectable man (Père Dubois) to have returned to their husbands the wives of about 200 Christians, and other unmarried Christian women, whom Tippoo had carried off from their husbands and friends upon different occasions when he visited the Malabar coast and Canara, and who were placed, and are now supposed to be, in his Zenana. I have refused to comply with this request, although the refusal is unjust, because, the Company having taken this family under its protection, it is not proper that anything should be done which can disgrace it in the eyes of the Indian world, or which can in the most remote degree cast a shade upon the dead, or violate the feelings of those who are alive." [Letter to Lt.-Col. Doveton, Seringapatam, Dec. 24, 1799.]

He did however supply a list of names of such women and when someone suggested the list was incorrect, the Colonel coolly responded:

"If the name of any woman still alive should have been omitted, and her husband should be married again, the breach of the law will not be very criminal either in the priest who marries them or the man who is married; and as it is not intended that these women should ever quit the Zenana, it will never be known whether the lists are correct or otherwise."

Horse sense, but it was perhaps fortunate for Colonel Wellesley that there were as yet no missionaries in Seringapatam to make a hullabaloo about this cynical handling of sacred rites and obligations. Thus the winter of 1799 passed more or less peacefully into the spring of 1800, enlivened by a couple of riots between dissident castes and by preparations against the province of Wynaad where, it was said, "the annihilation of the Pyche Rajah will have a great effect on the minds of the disaffected, with which this province abounds". Meanwhile rumours and reports increased of the return in force of Dhoondiah Waugh and his robber bands. This native hero, who modestly called himself King of the Two Worlds, had been an enemy of Tippoo, but later entered his service, and, having offended that capricious ruler, was discovered by the British in one of the Seringapatam dungeons, "destined to a painful death" (probably by impalement) which the gentle Tippoo had not time to carry out. All Tippoo's captives were inconsiderately released without any inquiry, and Dhoondiah repaid his benefactors by gathering together the disbanded remnants of Tippoo's army and other local Robin Hoods for purposes of plunder. After being chased out of Mysore in 1799 he retired to the country of the Peshwah, but:

"*Seringapatam, 20th April,* 1800. The progress Dhoondiah has made in Savanore, and the large force he has collected, have induced me to order three regiments of cavalry into the field, and to the northward. I have besides at Chittledroog the 77th Regiment and three battalions of sepoys. . . ."

"*Seringapatam, 1st May*, 1800. Dhoondiah is getting on in Savanore; he has been joined by Rajahs, Polygars, and disaffected and discontented of all descriptions, and he is now employed at the siege of Dummul. . . ."

"*Seringapatam, 5th May*, 1800. . . . Dhoondiah has beat a detachment which Appah Saheb sent to impede his progress in Savanore, consisting of 5000 cavalry and a large body of infantry. He is . . . very close to our borders."

"*Camp, 20th May*, 1800. General Orders. The troops to march to-morrow. . . ."

It was not a campaign in which the gentlemen of the army could take much pleasure, and the commander himself referred to the King of the Two Worlds in a fit of exasperation as "a despicable enemy". Despicable or not, he was as elusive as the Pimpernel of fiction, and if Colonel Wellesley had not received permission to pursue him into Mahratta territory, the chase would have been vain. (It was nearly called off at the outset by a letter from the Governor-General offering once more an "expedition to Batavia".) In addition to the usual troubles, jungles had to be negotiated and rivers crossed by basket boats, while the military problems involved co-operation with more or less friendly Mahratta allies and keeping the King of the Two Worlds on the run by constant marches and countermarches.

Bad news came through early in July. Goklah, the Mahratta ally, was reported "beat". Dhoondiah had cut his rear-guard to pieces, killed Goklah, then destroyed all his main body but the horse, capturing cannon and supplies. This was awkward, but the Colonel pushed on, sending out a separate column under his second, Colonel Stevenson. On July 14, 1800, a fort with a garrison of 600 was captured, but Dhoondiah escaped. Goklah's surviving cavalry joined on July 20; Dummel with 1,000 men was taken on July 25; and at three in the afternoon of July 30 they at last caught up with the main enemy body. "I surprised his camp . . . with the cavalry; and we drove into the river or destroyed everybody that was in it, took an elephant, several camels, bullocks, horses innumerable, families, women, children." Two lieutenants and some white troops swam the river and captured six guns, but the King of the Two Worlds escaped.

This disaster cost Dhoondiah 5,000 men, but still he baffled pursuit, crossing the Malpoorba River with Colonel Stevenson hot after him. All August was spent in a military hide-and-seek, and it was not until the night of September 9, 1800, that the robber's camp was reported only nine miles off. After "passing a most anxious night", Colonel Wellesley set off at dawn with his four cavalry regiments, with which small force in single line he immediately charged and overthrew the enemy. The King of the Two Worlds was slain and his body brought into camp by the Nineteenth Dragoons. It was a daring feat, for the attackers were outnumbered at least by four to one, and the slightest hesitation or wavering would have meant being cut to pieces; and it is the only occasion on which Wellington personally led a cavalry charge. A four-year-old son of Dhoondiah was found in the camp; and Colonel Wellesley rescued him, paid for his upbringing, and on leaving India handed over to trustees a sum of money for his education. What was left of Dhoondiah's forces was dispersed or captured by Colonel Stevenson the next day.

Thus ended the King of the Two Worlds and the campaign, but so much remained to be done that Colonel Wellesley was not back in Seringapatam until late in November. While the troops may have found some compensation in their unauthorized plunder of the camp, the Colonel had gained nothing for himself but military experience. For three months a force of less than 40,000 indisciplined guerrillas had occupied the attention of five cavalry and eight infantry regiments (four of them European), all highly disciplined troops under experienced officers. It was a useful if tedious object lesson in what could be done by guerrillas when they had plenty of room to operate and knew the country. We may be certain that there was a nook in the Colonel's brain where that object lesson was pigeon-holed for future reference, though we may be equally certain that he did not then foresee a time would come when he would operate in conjunction with guerrillas instead of against them.

Colonel Wellesley had not even reached Seringapatam on his return march when a special messenger brought him from Calcutta a portentous document with many numbered clauses. Briefly, His Excellency the G.-G. had abandoned Batavia (the Admiral had refused to co-operate without the King's orders), and now proposed to collect a force at Trincomalee, Ceylon, with the purpose of (a) repelling a now improbable French attack on India; (b) capturing by surprise the French island of Mauritius; (c) proceeding to the Red Sea to join the forces fighting the French in Egypt. Colonel Wellesley was appointed to command the army, and ordered to proceed to Trincomalee without delay.

Here was the opportunity for pursuing bigger military game than tiresomely elusive bandits, and the Colonel obeyed his orders with high hopes. For his successor he left long and precisely worded memoranda on the steps to be taken to complete the "pacification" of

Mysore. Several of the brighter young officers were glad to throw up safe and lucrative posts under the Madras Government to follow his fortunes as members of his staff. He was already at Trincomalee on Christmas Day, 1800, and at once plunged with zest into passionate correspondence of this kind: "Sir, I have to request that you will supply . . . 150 casks of beef, of 360 lbs. each, and 2,000 gallons of Bengal rum . . ." and "What is the distance from the Pavillon to the place at which it is proposed that the troops should land on Cooper's Island?" The Governor of Ceylon received a brief epitaph from Colonel Wellesley which posterity has remembered but not always applied: "I don't recommend that he should be informed of the object of the expedition until the disclosure of it to all India is not likely to be prejudicial to the operations."

These high spirits and bright prospects were not destined to endure. Dispatches came in from England ordering the transfer of a large expeditionary force to Egypt; and without waiting for orders from Calcutta, Colonel Wellesley at once shipped his men to Bombay to be nearer the point of rendezvous and to gather supplies unobtainable in Ceylon. This anticipation of orders was intelligent, but a dangerous precedent, as the Governor-General angrily pointed out. And before this misunderstanding was cleared up a worse blow fell. Infuriated generals had descended upon the Governor when they heard that a command had been given to his brother; and as a result the Colonel received an official letter informing him that he was superseded by Major-General Baird; the Batavia and Mauritius expeditions were cancelled in accordance with the instructions from London, and as large a force as possible was to go to Egypt.

Colonel Wellesley was very angry. For once in his life he forgot he was *nimmukwallah*, and complained—not officially to the Governor-General, but in a private letter to his brother Henry, the Governor's secretary:

"... I shall always consider these expeditions as the most unfortunate circumstances for me, in every point of view, that could have occurred; and, as such, I shall always lament them.

"I was at the top of the tree in this country; the governments of Forts St. George and Bombay, which I had served, placed unlimited confidence in me, and I had received from them both strong and repeated marks of their approbation. Before I quitted the Mysore country, I arranged the plan for taking possession of the ceded districts, which was done without striking a blow; and another plan for conquering Wynaad and re-conquering Malabar, which I am informed has succeeded without loss on our side. But this supercession has ruined all my prospects, founded upon any service that I may have rendered.

. . . has there been any change whatever of circumstances that was not expected when I was appointed to the command? If there has not, (and no one can say there has, without doing injustice to the Governor General's foresight,) my supercession must have been occasioned, either by my own misconduct, or by an alteration in the sentiments of the Governor General. I have not been guilty of robbery or murder, and he has certainly changed his mind; but the world, which is always good-natured towards those whose affairs do not exactly prosper, will not, or rather does not, fail to suspect that both, or worse, have been the occasion of my being banished, like General Kray, to my estate in Hungary. I did not look, and I did not wish, for the appointment which was given to me; and I say that it would probably have been more proper to give it to somebody else; but when it was given to me, and a circular written to the governments upon the subject, it would have been fair to allow me to hold it until I did something to deserve to lose it." [Letter of March 23, 1801, Bombay.]

It was undoubtedly a situation to infuriate any man. Brother Richard had put the Colonel in a false position which might have wrecked his career, and had also grievously injured at least half a dozen officers who had thrown up their jobs to follow Colonel Wellesley's fortunes only because they believed in him. There was (as he said) no need to offer him the command, but having given it, the Governor-General should not have withdrawn it without explanation. But then, how could he explain to the world that he had sacrificed his brother to the row raised by the Major-Generals in Bengal? It is not surprising that Arthur Wellesley was angry, and that the private letters to "My dear Mornington" ceased abruptly, and were not resumed for a long time. Apparently he did not even trouble to acknowledge a very gracious epistle from Richard giving him the Hobson's choice of going to the Egypt expedition as second-in-command or returning to Mysore. Perhaps the Colonel was a little weary of his task of restraining and directing the Governor-General's "enlarged views" of military policy, which had some of the fantasy inseparable from civilian strategy; and he was certainly heartily sick of doing the donkey work of organizing campaigns in the background while other officers took the curtain and the bows.

Fortunately for his honour as a soldier, the Colonel had time to think; he remembered he was *nimmukwallah*, that his duty was to the service, and he determined to support General Baird loyally and to let him take the credit for all Wellesley's careful work of organization. Indeed, rather to their mutual surprise, he and Baird got on well together, at least well enough for the Colonel to decide definitely that he would see the thing through. But just as he was about to sail, the warmth of his feelings or more probably a Ceylon mosquito brought on an intermittent fever. A letter written on March 31, 1801, to Henry

Wellesley, announces a fever attack on March 25, and also shows that the resentment had not cooled down:

"I am quite distressed about my officers who followed me through the Mysore country. However, I have seen enough already to be certain, and if I do not go, matters will be uncomfortable; and if I well can, I will go. I have the satisfaction of finding that there is not a man here who would have come, had he known what was likely to happen to me, if he had the power of refusal. Indeed, in this respect, the feelings of the greater part of the army agree with mine."

After all, he did not follow the expedition. He had scarcely recovered from the fever when he developed an unpleasant skin complaint, known as Bombay itch, probably from infected bedding at the hospital. The doctors treated this with nitrous baths, which the Colonel humorously complained were so strong that they scorched his towels. An equally nitrous final letter was dispatched to "My dear Mornington" on April 16, 1801; and early in May he was back in Seringapatam, heartily wishing he had never left it. On the way up from Cannanore he was accompanied by Elers, who noticed that the last attack of fever had turned the Colonel's hair grey at the temples, although he was only thirty-two. Elers noted also that he kept "a plain but good table" and that he was "very abstemious with wine". He was very even in his temper, "laughing and joking with those he liked, speaking in his quick way", and fighting his few battles over again with a devoted staff. His greatest concern was the fear that he would be superseded by some Major-General newly arrived from England, for as he said: "We want no Major-Generals in Mysore, they're so damned inefficient." Before the party reached Seringapatam an overland dispatch from England came in, with the information that the Governor-General had been awarded a pension of £5,000 a year for the conquest of Mysore and that all senior colonels had been made Major-Generals. At once Colonel Wellesley was all animation:

"Do you happen to have an Army List, Elers?"
"Yes."
Elers went off for the List, and came back, saying:
"I'm sorry to tell you, Sir, it doesn't include you as Major-General. You are within about five or six of it."
The Colonel was silent, and then said sorrowfully:
"My highest ambition is to be a Major-General in His Majesty's service."

CHAPTER VIII

The Fighting Mahrattas

COLONEL WELLESLEY celebrated his return to Seringapatam by another attack of fever, and then settled down to the humdrum life and multiple duties of his garrison command. Even as he lay on his sick bed he was informed that a robber chief, the Rajah of Bilghy, had escaped; and that the ladies of Tippoo's ex-zenana again needed new clothes. After a weary chase the Rajah was recaptured, but the superannuated ladies of Seringapatam were as much trouble as the starving tigers found after the assault. It was a great relief when orders came to transfer them elsewhere about a year later (May 1802), and the Colonel wrote with sardonic satisfaction to the unfortunate officer who was now to be responsible for them: "I have the pleasure to inform you that the first detachment of ladies, being those devoted to the amusement of old Hyder, march to-morrow morning for Vellore." Apart from an expedition against the Bullum Polygar, who was easily captured in a forest which had hitherto defied all the Company's forces, there was little to do but to drill and discipline the troops, build new roads and bridges and a hospital, settle complicated matters of exchange, and encourage the rice, pepper, and teak trade. "I have some thoughts of going home next winter," he wrote, "if I don't see some prospect of being actively employed in India." Gone were the days of hectic parties with Mr. Hickey and his like, and wisdom had come hand in hand with sobriety:

"I know but one receipt for good health in this country, and that is to live moderately, to drink little or no wine, to use exercise, to keep the mind employed, and, if possible, to keep in good humour with the world. The last is the most difficult, for, as you have often observed, there is hardly a good-tempered man in India."

Here and there in the vast mass of correspondence about details of Indian military and civil administration, there are curious, though too rare, glimpses of the Colonel's own points of view. It is startling, and certainly pleasant, to find a soldier and a Tory who is not wedded to the policy of the "strong hand". Writing of conditions in Malabar, he says:

"I acknowledge, however, that I long for the return of civil government. Although a soldier myself, I am not an advocate for placing extensive civil powers in the hands of soldiers merely because they are of the military profession, and I have always opposed the idea excepting in cases of necessity."

In his own province he practised what he preached, and left civil government as far as possible to the Rajah's vizier, Purneah, whose abilities, the Colonel asserted, "astonished" him. And apparently their joint efforts were successful, for the Colonel was able to report:

"The Rajah's government is in a most prosperous state: the country is become a garden where it is inhabited, and the inhabitants are returning fast to those parts which the last savage had forced them to quit. . . . The Rajah's treasury is rich . . . Purneah has repaired numberless tanks . . . and there is every prospect that this prosperity will be permanent."

Inspired by these results, the Colonel sent to Bombay for a large cargo of seed potatoes which he presented to Purneah in the hope that "we shall make potatoes as flourishing in Mysore as they are in Ireland"—which might have been put more tactfully but was meant well. Gardening and agriculture seem to have been very much in the Colonel's mind at this time, for the ladies of two brother officers were much surprised when instead of sending them flowers he presented them with bunches of celery and cabbage plants. Scandal went further and said that the Colonel did not limit his attentions towards officers' ladies to presents of vegetables. There were rumours that the Colonel's "very susceptible heart" had been laid at the feet of a Mrs. Captain F——, and not without success. Objections were voiced, not by the lady's husband, but by the Colonel's own aide-de-camp, West, and by a certain Lady Tuite, both of whom considered the situation "highly immoral and indecorous". The result was that Colonel Wellesley refused to shake hands with Lady Tuite and was not on speaking terms with his own aide-de-camp. "The Colonel, in after-life, proved most grateful to the lady, and provided by his interest for some of her children."

So life in the garrison town droned on, with only occasional whispers from the outer world. Mr. Pitt had resigned and was succeeded by Mr. Addington, known to his many enemies as "the Doctor" (his father had been a prosperous physician) which prompted Sheridan to greet the new Government with an old rhyme, to the delight of the House:

"I do not love thee, Dr. Fell;
The reason why I cannot tell;
But this I know, and know full well,
I do not love thee, Dr. Fell."

As a good Tory, the Colonel shook his head at these tidings, and at the rumours of peace with France, which he surmised (and rightly) would prove to be only a truce. Belatedly "the gentlemen in Leadenhall St." (as he called the East India Company's Directors) recognized his services in the affair of the King of the Two Worlds by a grant of 10,000 *pagodas*, though the honour of the thing was greatly reduced by similar awards to four subordinates. Even the news, received in the late autumn, that he was at last gazetted Major-General (seniority, April 29, 1802) failed to move him to any expression of excitement or gratitude. Perhaps the promotion had come too late, perhaps ambition had taken a higher flight, for over in Paris was another general officer, three months his junior, and not only Commander-in-Chief of the greatest army in the world but First Consul and Consul for life— dictator of France. Ten thousand sepoys and Mysore were small beer in comparison; and campaigns against Tippoo, Dhoondiah, and minor Rajahs and Polygars trifling compared with Lodi, Rivoli, the Pyramids, and Marengo. The whole world was ringing with the name of Napoleon Bonaparte, but, outside the services and a circle of friends, who had heard of Major-General the Honble. A Wellesley? Was he destined to return home with a modest competence, and to end his days as a General on half-pay, entertaining the ladies with oft-told stories of Seringapatam and the Bullum Polygar?

Such thoughts may sometimes have intruded on his sleepless hours during suffocating nights before the monsoon rains, but if they did he never mentioned them; and the only trace of disappointment is the negative one that there were still no letters to "My dear Mornington". Secret information and confidential reports, still loyally supplied, were sent to the Governor-General by way of his private secretary. And then, late in the autumn of 1802, the drowsy torpor of Seringapatam was shattered by momentous local news:

"Fort St. George, 9th Nov., 1802

"My dear General,

The Peshwah's and Scindiah's troops have again been defeated by Holkar, with great slaughter . . . the Peshwah has fled . . . we shall be required immediately to send a force. . . . The Commander-in-Chief will accordingly send the orders necessary . . . the necessity of this case supersedes all other considerations . . . measures must be conducted with as much concealment as possible. . . ."

The Mahratta Confederacy (nine-tenths Hindu and one-tenth Mohammedan), was a formidable power, occupying an area of 970 miles by 900, with a united force of about 200,000 cavalry and 100,000 infantry. The Mahratta power dated back to 1680, when the Rajah of Sattara defeated the Great Mogul, Aurungzebe, and his Portuguese allies; and seized much of his territory while admitting his nominal suzerainty. By 1800 a most singular supersession of real authority had occurred. Allum Shah, the descendant of the Great Mogul, was a captive in Delhi, but so too was the descendant of the Rajah of Sattara in his own dominions; the authority of that prince had been usurped and made hereditary by his chief minister the Peshwah. But, so rapid were these feudal changes, that already the Peshwah had been reduced to a not very secure hold on the Sattara territories, while the remainder of the empire was ruled by his nominal subordinates, Gaikwar of Baroda, Scindia of Gwalior, Bhonsla of Berar (or Naghpur), and Holkar of Indore, with a multitude of minor chieftains, engaged in the perpetual civil war of feudal lords. Though cavalry made up the greater part of the various Mahratta armies, their powerful artillery and infantry were French-trained, and many of the officers were European adventurers, mostly French, but a few English. In the early 1790's Cornwallis had made a treaty of alliance with the Peshwah (possibly exaggerating his real importance) but it had never been ratified, because the Peshwah's nominal subordinates, but real masters, would not allow it. Defeated and driven from his capital in 1802, the Peshwah rather belatedly remembered this treaty, and within twenty-four hours applied to the British Resident for military aid to recover his dominions. Lord Wellesley decided to support the Peshwah against his rebellious chieftains, but shrewdly insisted on a new and more stringent treaty, which was ratified by both sides in December 1802.

Outwardly the quiet of Seringapatam was unbroken by these events; Major-General Wellesley could keep a secret and had a good poker face. Confiding in nobody, he set secretly and rapidly to work, and we heard no more of gardening and ladies. Orders were sent out to form supply and transport depots, the arsenal was set to work turning out 30,000 cartridges a day, the troops were unostentatiously trained in the type of warfare to be expected, and emissaries were dispatched to discover which of the minor chieftains were friendly and which hostile to the Peshwah. Supply, transport, tactical training, intelligence were organized for whoever should take command; which in time proved to be a Lieutenant-General Stuart, otherwise unrecorded in history.

The preparations took time, and it was not until February 8, 1803, that the busy military commander of Seringapatam was able to leave for advanced headquarters, still apparently ignorant of what part he was to play. At length, about a month later, his orders arrived. The main body of the army under General Stuart was to remain on the frontier of Mysore; Major-General Wellesley was to advance with about 10,000 men, join Colonel Stevenson with another 8,000 of the Nizam's troops, coming from Hyderabad, and then make a long march on Poona, the Peshwah's capital. Once more the "ponderous machine" of an Indian army moved forward (March 8, 1803), and once more, thanks to careful preparation, with complete success. Major-General Wellesley's emissaries had done their work well, and by April 4 (1803) six minor chieftains loyal to the Peshwah had joined, bringing more than 9,000 native troops with them. Colonel Stevenson's contingent met them on April 15, and the slow procession moved on, now some hundreds of miles from its base. The otherwise uneventful military promenade had a dramatic ending. News came in that the Mahratta chief in Poona intended to burn the town as soon as the relieving force appeared. Major-General Wellesley at once made up his mind. Leaving his infantry and artillery to come on as quickly as possible, he started off with his cavalry at nightfall on April 19, made a forced march of forty miles over a mountain range, and at three o'clock next day clattered into the streets of Poona, as the surprised Mahratta "marched off with some precipitation" in the opposite direction, in too much of a hurry to burn the town.

Followed a period of tedious *pourparlers* with the Peshwah, who was uncertain in his loyalties and intentions. Moreover, as the exasperated Resident reported, "his mind is religious, and given to the observance of superstitious customs, which occupy much of his time". He could not make up his mind, for instance, which day would be really auspicious for re-entering his capital. In fact, he could not bring himself to take this important step until May 13, 1803; and, so far as carrying out his side of the treaty now that he was safely restored, he did nothing at all with majestic indolence. The other Mahratta chiefs were less religious or more enterprising, for they were reported across the frontier of Hyderabad on a plundering invasion, much to the alarm of the Nizam and his officers. With a complete understanding of the nature of allies, the Major-General at once sent off Stevenson and the Nizam's troops to make feints in front of the enemy, and prepared to follow as soon as he could replace his huge casualties in transport bullocks. Since the Bombay Government had omitted to send even one of the thousands he had required of them in anticipation of precisely this event, he was reduced to helplessness until he could collect them himself. It was not the first time and far indeed from being the last when he was impelled to remark innocently "if I'm not at hand everything seems to go wrong".

When he was able to move again, there followed weeks of tedious negotiations. It was a matter of "face", for though both sides wanted peace and were anxious to retire, the side that retreated first would be as much defeated as by a lost battle in the field. All through July they negotiated, and the Major-General met the interminable crafty or childish excuses for delay and more delay with smiling patience. He was waiting for the weather, and even on August 1, 1803, he still seemed hopeful of peace. It became evident, as soon as the weather suited, that the Mahrattas were trying to trick him into retiring; and once convinced of that, he acted with a speed which staggered them. On August 6 he broke off relations; on the seventh he marched and issued his proclamation to the inhabitants; on the eighth he attacked and took the town of Ahmednuggur; on the ninth he placed his batteries against the reputedly impregnable fortress; and on the tenth the garrison of 1,400 surrendered. The Mahratta troops, particularly the Arabs, lost heavily in the fight for the town. The quantities of stores captured were "astonishing", for the Mahrattas had never dreamed that the place could be captured, and had made it a chief depot.

He was off again on August 17 (1803) moving steadily north-westward into Mahratta territory, and on August 21–22 sent his army over the river Godavery in wicker boats. There were provoking delays owing to the slowness of convoys in bringing up supplies, and the advance was necessarily cautious since somewhere ahead lay the combined armies of Scindia and Berar. At this distance from the base the sepoys could not be used as spies—they were nearly as conspicuously different from the inhabitants as Europeans; and the army had to grope its way on with no better intelligence than that of the local *hircarrahs* or messengers. Stringent checks and counterchecks were devised, and the bringers of important news were interviewed by the General himself. Yet, in spite of all this care, a slight misunderstanding produced a most dangerous situation, which was only saved by the General's quick decision and unbreakable will and by the devoted courage of his troops.

On September 21, 1803, all the *hircarrahs* reported the enemy in force at a place called Bokerdun. It was decided to march in two detachments (the other under Colonel Stevenson) by converging roads, and to attack together on September 24. The Mahrattas were at Bokerdun all right, but that happened to be the name of a district as well as of a place. Thus, about 1 p.m. on September 23, after a march of twenty-four miles, Major-General Wellesley with about 5,000 men and 17 guns suddenly came on the whole Mahratta army of at least 50,000 men with more than 100 guns, drawn up with one river to their front and another on their left near the village of Assaye (or Assye). Many of the enemy's officers were European (mostly French and a few English or Irish adventurers) and, according to the *hircarrahs*, there was only one ford and that most obviously controlled by the enemy's artillery.

What was to be done in this scrape? Wellesley had made it a rule never to fight the Mahrattas on a position of their choosing, but he had an even stronger rule—never to retreat before Orientals, no matter what the odds. Far to the right his quick eye noticed two villages facing each other exactly on opposite sides of the river, and he immediately deduced a ford. Sending word at once to Colonel Stevenson, he made a flank march across the enemy's front, and crossed the ford, hoping that the enemy troops would not be able to manœuvre in time to meet this sudden move. Here he was mistaken, and he found them with their right on the river Kaitna, their left on the village of Assaye, and their 100 guns all concentrated on a front of about a mile. Wellesley immediately attacked the guns with the bayonet, and though the gunners stood until they were bayoneted, the supporting Mahratta infantry fled. Unluckily, in spite of precise orders to the contrary, the Seventy-Fourth Regiment was led straight into Assaye and cut to pieces, and the cavalry had to be used prematurely to save the remnants. Moreover, there were many of the first line of Mahratta gunners who feigned death, and turned their guns on the rear of the attacking troops as they swept by. The commander of the British cavalry, Lt.-Col. Maxwell, was killed, leading a charge against a huge mass of enemy infantry. The Seventy-Fourth Regiment lost every officer killed or wounded and four men out of every five. Wellesley himself had two horses shot under him; and most of his staff officers were wounded. There were five hours of this desperate fighting before the Mahrattas finally fled, leaving behind 1,200 dead and 98 guns. But the casualties to the small attacking force of 5,000 were comparatively enormous; Europeans, killed 164, wounded 411; Natives, killed, 245, wounded, 1,211; total 2,031. Several of Wellesley's guns were put out of action and 300 cavalry horses killed; the enemy fled only from the bayonets of the Seventy-Eighth and the remaining sepoys.

Critics of the battle lament that the victory was not immediately followed up; but after the long march and the battle, the surviving troops were utterly exhausted. The surgeons were too few to attend to the wounded, and the exhausted commander himself sat miserably with his head between his knees, with a dead officer on one side and a wounded one on the other. But his victory was decisive, for in addition to losing nearly all their guns and ammunition, the Mahrattas retreated in the greatest haste and confusion. While the main army rested, Colonel Stevenson's detachment took the fortresses of Burhampoor (October 16, 1803) and Asserghur (October 21, 1803). These actions were a repetition of the capture of Ahmednuggur, thus described by a Mahratta leader:

"These Englishmen are strange people, and their general is a wonderful man. They came here in the morning, looked at the wall, walked over it, killed all the garrison, and returned for breakfast."

Scindia asked for an armistice, which was granted on November 23, but almost at once he broke its terms, and with the remnants of his army joined the Rajah of Berar at Argaum (or Argaon), where Wellesley came up with them on November 29, in the afternoon. The attack was delayed by a panic in three of Wellesley's sepoy regiments, but, "luckily, I happened to be at no great distance from them, and I was able to rally them and re-establish the battle". This time nothing else went wrong. The enemy's crack troops (supposed to be Persians) were destroyed, his cavalry repulsed, and "their whole line retired in disorder . . . leaving 38 pieces of cannon and all their ammunition". The cavalry pursued for miles, dispersing fugitives, and capturing camels, elephants, and baggage. About 3,000 of the 30,000 Mahrattas were killed, while Wellesley's casualties were only 344.

The Mahrattas now fled north about fifty miles to the great mountain fortress of Gawilghur, followed rapidly by the Company's army. This was another of these supposedly impregnable fortresses, but "the heavy ordnance and stores were dragged by hand over mountains and through ravines" nearly thirty miles, on roads built by the troops themselves; and it was stormed on December 15, 1803. What was left of the large garrison surrendered, and the war was over. Berar accepted the peace terms offered, on December 17, and Scindia on December 30; the treaties were signed, and dispatched to the Governor-General for ratification. Peace indeed was general on all Eastern fronts, for after Assaye the Major-General received an enthusiastic private letter from his august brother in Calcutta; resentment melted in the sun of triumph, and after nearly three years of sullen silence, "My dear Mornington" was tacitly forgiven by a letter from "ever yours most affectionately, Arthur Wellesley".

CHAPTER IX

A Minor Hero Returns Home

WHEN, in December 1803, Major-General Wellesley signed the two treaties which successfully ended his share in the Second Mahratta War, he still had before him another fifteen months of Indian service; yet at thirty-three he had made his reputation in India as a soldier and administrator, and, which is more important, had learned virtually all the lessons India had to teach him in either activity. His only fighting in 1804 was one of his swift and devastating attacks on freebooters, involving a forced march of sixty miles with infantry in twenty hours; and the only significance of the action lies in the fact that he had so completely gained the confidence of the troops both European and Native that they could and would do for him things which other commanders found impossible.

Measured ·gainst the numbers and ferocity of modern warfare, these armies and their achievements are insignificant; and even in their own time they were inconspicuous when seen against the perspective of the Revolutionary and Napoleonic wars. But they had their importance. Lord Wellesley's treaty of Bassein with the Peshwah was one of the most important in the whole history of the British in India; yet it would scarcely have been worth the paper it was written on but for Arthur Wellesley's six-hundred-mile march from Mysore to Poona. And that in turn would have been useless if it had not been backed by the long campaign decided at last in the brief and bloody crises of Assaye and Argaum. True, this campaign was linked with and was subsidiary to General Lake's campaign in the north, but unlike that campaign it had to excuse no failures, such as the defeat of Colonel Monson's force.

Little of Arthur Wellesley's life in India was spent within reach of the Governor-General's refined and ostentatious luxury, or the indulgence and extravagance so much valued by Mr. Hickey and his kind. Very nearly half of it was spent in the anxieties of campaigning and in the discomforts of a moving camp. By chance a young political officer of those days, Mountstuart Elphinstone, has left a realistic record of "a camp day" on one of Major-General Wellesley's marches:

"General [i.e. reveille] at half-past four. Tent-pins rattle, and I rise and dress while they are striking my tent. Go to the front, and to the Quartermaster-General's tent, and drink a cup of tea. Talk with the staff, who collect there until it grows light. The assembly beats and the General [Wellesley] comes out. We go to his breakfast-table in front of his tent and breakfast; talk all the time. It is bitter cold [November 15] and we have our great-coats on. At half after six, or earlier or later, we mount and ride. The General generally rides on the dusty flank, so nobody stays with him. Now we always have coursing a mile or so out on the flank; and when we get to our ground from ten to twelve we all sit, if our chairs have come up, or lie on the ground. When the tent is pitched, we move in, and the General lies on the carpet, and we all talk, until breakfast is ready. Then we breakfast off fried mutton, mutton chops, curries, &c. and from eleven to two get to our tents, and I arrange my hircarrahs, write my journals, read Puffendorf . . . and sometimes talk politics and other privities with the General. At two or three I eat a loaf and drink two glasses of port-and-water. And when it grows dark . . . I get shaved, and walk about head-quarters lines until it is pitch dark, and then dress, go to dinner; and we all talk about the march, and they about their former wars and this war, and Indian courts and politics. At nine we break up; and the Quartermaster-General and Major of Brigade and I hold a committee, and settle whither we march next day; and then I go to palanquin. All this is extremely pleasant. . . ."

. . . But monotonous, and the reverse of that Oriental splendour and luxury which the heated imaginations of Opposition speakers in Parliament attributed to commanding and other officers in the Indian service. So monotonous indeed was this camp life that the smallest episode was eagerly taken up, repeated, and discussed, particul␣␣␣y if it gave any chance for a laugh. There is something pathetic in the General of a victorious army writing privately to the Governor-General of India to share with him such a schoolboy joke as this:

"Malcolm writes from Scindia's camp, that at the first meeting Scindia received him with great gravity, which he had intended to preserve throughout the visit. It rained violently; and an officer of the escort, Mr. Pepper, an Irishman, (a nephew of old Bective's by the by,) sat under a flat part of the tent which received a great part of the rain that fell. At length, it burst through the tent upon the head of Mr. Pepper, who was concealed by the torrent that fell, and was discovered after some time by an 'Oh Jasus!' and an hideous yell. Scindia laughed violently, as did all the others present; and the gravity and dignity of the durbar degenerated into a Malcolm riot—after which they all parted upon the best terms."

It is not surprising that the Major-General suffered from lumbago, and that he began to think of going home to England. Lord Wellesley had been resigning office but retaining it ever since his arrival in India; but the Major-General did not send in his resignation until he discovered by accident that his appointment to the Madras Staff had never been sanctioned by the Horse Guards. The shrinking sensitive-ness of the true military man was hurt by what he maintained was a "lack of approval from His Majesty and His Royal Highness", though it was more probably due to a clerk's oversight. However, at the request of the Governor-General, this resignation was withdrawn, but only for a few months. It became effective as soon as there could be no doubt that the Governor-General was about to be superseded at the insistence of the East India Company Directors, who wanted dividends, not the glories and responsibilities of an empire. Possibly, even probably, Lord Wellesley's offence was not so much his alleged extravagance, still less any real or supposed infringement of laws against expansion, but the unpardonable crime of believing in free trade. The enormous profits of the East India Company were due to its almost complete monopoly of the Eastern trade, so that the Governor-General's leanings towards a liberal trade policy naturally excited the deadliest passions in these respectable merchants. Even the King's Ministers wavered in their support of Lord Wellesley; and Arthur Wellesley indignantly urged him to go home.

Meanwhile, the Major-General's last year in India was marked by some tardy recognition of his military successes, some of it official, but the rest spontaneous and therefore all the more pleasant. Early in March 1804 the remnants of the army of Assaye and Argaum were back at Poona, and their General was about to proceed to Bombay after a year in the field and a brilliant campaign. Just before he left, he received a letter from "the officers who served with the division of the army under your immediate command" asking his acceptance of a gold vase (afterwards changed to a "set of gold plate of 2,000 guineas") "to express the high idea they possess of the gallantry and enterprise that so eminently distinguish you". To the soldiers of that age the journalism which is so important to their successors was at best a matter of indifference, more frequently a cause of annoyance and contempt. But competent praise such as this was highly valued. The field officers and senior subalterns who signed the letter were at once professional critics and executants—it was the orchestra respectfully greeting the composer-conductor. Government honours might be influenced, popular applause was ignorant and fickle, journalists could be bought to write anything; but this was the unpurchasable judgment of his peers, and Wellesley's earnest reply shows gratitude as well as a genuine surprise.

In Bombay he was given a public reception which included a salute of fifteen guns, a procession through streets lined by troops, an address in extremely pompous language, and a dinner at the theatre which was decorated with "an elegant transparency of General Wellesley's arms, fixed so as to face the company. The utmost conviviality prevailed . . ." A few days later came a letter from the Governor-General at Calcutta, enclosing an address and resolution of the inhabitants: "that a sword of the value of £1,000 be presented to Major-General the Hon. A. Wellesley . . ." in recognition of his services. General Wellesley's answer to this has unfortunately been lost, but his brother's Ciceronian acknowledgment more than atones for it:

"Gentlemen, This honour is peculiarly acceptable to the warmest sentiment of my heart. The zeal of fraternal affection and of private friendship cannot furnish expressions of approbation equal to those which the services of Major-General Wellesley demand from my public duty. . . . ."

It is impossible to find gush of this kind in all the thousands of Wellington letters and dispatches, although he did write foolishly to young women; and his chief preoccupation in Bombay at that time had nothing to do with graceful or effusive acknowledgments of public honours. He was devising means for clothing troops who would have had to pass the monsoon in rags if their commander had relied upon the official channels of supply.

Mid-May 1804 saw the Major-General back in camp near Poona, still anxious to resign and return to England. But all such plans were suddenly interrupted by news which sent him hurrying to Madras and thence to Calcutta—brother Richard was in military trouble and needed comfort and aid, for Colonel Monson had contrived to lose five good battalions in the war with Holkar. Heroically Arthur Wellesley refrained from saying "I told you so", for he had opposed the war on moral and military grounds, and had not been consulted on methods and strategy. By the middle of August 1804 Arthur Wellesley was in Calcutta and remained there until November, turning out detailed memoranda on a dozen different subjects, political and military, for the Bombay Government as well as for the Governor-General. On November 17, 1804, General Lake defeated Holkar at Farruckhabad, and Wellesley was on board a frigate bound for Madras and Seringapatam; the Governor-General had persuaded him to stay on "a little longer".

The consent was reluctant, for he was more and more anxious to be done with India and to take a place, however modest, in the tremendous military drama unfolding in Europe. His hesitations turned to resolve in February 1805: "Five ships arrived this morning, which left England on the 4th September. General Lake was made Lord Lake of Delhi and Laswarree, and I a Knight of the Bath, on the 1st September. Henry is gone as plenipotentiary to Madrid. I determined last night upon going to England." The insignia of the Order did not reach him until several days later "in a box" which "was kicking about the *Lord Keith*, which arrived here ten days ago, and was brought to shore by a passenger who went to the ship by accident to look for his own luggage, and he informed me yesterday that he had got it". The notification was officially recognized on February 25; and thenceforth he was Sir Arthur Wellesley.

Many were the valedictory messages and letters to and from Sir Arthur on his departure, but there are three which are especially interesting. The first is dated Fort St. George, February 28, 1805, and is addressed to The Magistrate at Seringapatam, and reads:

"I herewith enclose a bond, No. 2713, of 1804–5, for the amount of one thousand star pagodas.

"I wish to place this sum of money in the charge of the Court of Seringapatam, for the benefit of Salabut Khan, the son, or the adopted son, of the late Dhoondiah Waugh.

"I am desirous that the Court should be his guardian, and should superintend his education, the expense of which will be defrayed out of the interest of this sum, and a sum of two hundred pagodas already in the hands of Lt.-Col. Symons. . . ."

This chivalrous but wholly practical gesture towards the child of a fallen foe may be linked with the farewell letter to Purneah, the Dewan of Mysore. Ever since the death of Tippoo, Wellesley and Purneah had been the rulers of Mysore; and a strong friendship had grown up between them. Long before this, Wellesley had written to another English officer deploring the fact that "Purneah does not realise how highly we think of him"; and later, after he had sailed for England, a letter to the Resident (March 20, 1805) has the rather wistful line: "In case Purneah should write to me, I wish you would send me a translation of his letter." The farewell letter to Purneah is dated from Madras, March 2, 1805, and contains these lines:

". . . I have obtained permission to go to England, and I shall commence my voyage in a few days. I part with you with the greatest regret; and I shall ever continue to feel the most lively interest for the honour and prosperity of the government of the Rajah of Mysore over which you preside.

"For six years I have been concerned in the affairs of the Mysore government, and I have contemplated with the greatest satisfaction its increasing prosperity under your administration. . . . Upon the occasion of taking my leave of you,

D

I must take the liberty to recommend to you to persevere in the laudable path
which you have hitherto followed. Let the prosperity of the country be your
great object; protect the ryots and traders, and allow no man, whether vested
with authority or otherwise, to oppress them with impunity; do justice to every
man. . . . As a testimony . . . of my sincere regard and of my gratitude for many
acts of personal kindness and attention . . . I request your acceptance of my
picture, which will be sent to you from Bengal."

Many were the expressions of public regard conveyed to the
departing soldier in addresses from various bodies, but the most
gratifying was that from the native inhabitants of Seringapatam,
though perhaps in the privacy of the mess the famous whooping
laugh rang out over the flowery paragraphs:

"Gratitude for the tranquillity, security and happiness we have enjoyed under
your auspicious protection, since this country was thrown by Divine Providence
under the just and pacific waving banners of the Honourable Company; respect
for the brilliant exploits you have achieved, which strengthened the foundation
of that tranquillity; and reverence for your benevolence and affability, glow all
at once in our hearts with such force, that we are unable to find language
sufficient to express our feelings and regret on the occasion of your departure."
[The signatures include Mohammedan as well as Hindu names.]

Thus ended a service of almost exactly eight years during a period
which Sir Arthur thought was "probably the most eventful of the
history of the British nation in India". For at least three years of that
time he had lived under no roof more luxurious than a canvas tent; he
had learned the benefits of frugality at table and of great personal
cleanliness (rare enough even among the aristocracy of the time); so
that he reversed the experience of most Europeans and, in spite of his
fever attacks, left India in better health than when he arrived. Or
rather, his general health had become so good that a few weeks at sea
saw him recovered from the fatigues and "wasting away" he had
suffered latterly in Madras.

The change from a life of incessant activity and responsibilities to
the six months' rest cure of a voyage round the Cape to England must
have been startling by its contrast, but the best remedy in the world for
overworked servants of Government. To be sure, there was the
inevitable discomfort and even danger of storms (we have Sir Arthur's
own word for it that he was "very sea sick" on this voyage) and the
still greater danger of French privateers—for in this very year of
Trafalgar no less than 507 British merchant ships were captured or
sunk on the high seas. For the long days of lazy tropical weather Sir
Arthur had provided himself with plenty of the newest English fiction

available in India, but as H.M.S. *Trident* dipped and splashed her way towards Saint Helena the ex-governor of Mysore could not refrain from penning a letter on the lumber resources of that country and a memorandum on the causes and possible cure of Indian famines and another on the employment of Negro troops in India (he was against it). On June 20, 1805, the convoy reached Saint Helena, and there Sir Arthur heard the disagreeable news that brother Richard had been superseded by Lord Cornwallis—a snub from the Company and the Government.

Both the island of Saint Helena and its Governor delighted the returning General. The Governor, he wrote, "is a good man, but a quiz, of a description that must have been extinct for nearly two centuries. I never saw anything like his wig or his coat." In view of later complaints about the island, it is interesting to note that exactly ten years before Waterloo, Sir Arthur writes of Saint Helena with enthusiasm: "The interior of the island is beautiful, and the climate apparently the most healthy I have ever lived in." True the horses and roads were "very bad"; but "my health has been much mended by the voyage, and particularly by a short residence upon this island. . . I do not recollect for many years to have been so well as I have felt latterly, and particularly since I have been here".

On July 10, 1805, the convoy left Saint Helena for the last lap of the voyage, and inevitably the thoughts of the returning General dwelt less on the India he had left for ever and more on himself and what the future might hold for him in England. As a younger brother of an impoverished Irish peer he had not done too badly. At thirty-six he was Major-General, a Knight of the Bath, and "victor of Assaye and Argaum", for which he had received the thanks of King and Parliament. The world had heard about that, but what it did not know about was this soldier's gift of organization added to his unerring good sense as a commander in the field. Some of the officers in the Indian army may have known it, but most certainly not the disposers of fate at the Horse Guards, by whom an Indian victory was looked on as a liability rather than an asset. At that moment a vast French army under one of the great military leaders of history was encamped with hostile intent on the Straits of Dover, and Nelson was still feverishly hunting the French battle fleet. Seldom in its history had England so much need of a great soldier, and not a person in England knew that the sepoy General on the *Trident* was the man all England was clamouring or praying for.

He could afford to wait. "I am not rich in comparison with other people," he wrote a general who pressed him not to leave India, "but very much so in comparison with my former situation, and quite sufficiently so for my own wants." And he could end with the assertion that his savings "have rendered me independent of all office or employment". As Indian fortunes went it was a modest one, something over £30,000, every shilling of which had been honestly earned. Many a lawyer and writer to the Company went home with more money than the man who for six years had been virtually dictator of the wealthy state of Mysore, with unlimited opportunities for graft. If he had chosen to abuse that power while remaining within the law and custom of the time, he could have brought home a quarter of a million. His eight years' service had earned Sir Arthur Wellesley a capital sum equal to about six months' income of Lord Castlereagh, the Minister to whom he would report on arrival.

It was a certainty that one of Sir Arthur's first and chief occupations would be the defence of his brother's actions and policy, for few public careers were more dangerous than that of a successful and energetic Governor-General of India. Impeachment, with its attendant anxieties and expenses, was reserved for those Governors who added to the British dominions and influence in India, while those who did nothing or lost ground were commended; yet nobody, including the impeachers, ever contemplated restoring what had been annexed. The reasons why Lord Wellesley did not drink the same bitter cup as Clive and Warren Hastings are three: The private enemy in Parliament lost his seat and committed suicide; the public was engaged in a great war and was weary of Indian affairs; there was no evidence against him. But this was for the future to reveal.

Meanwhile the aged Cornwallis had arrived in Calcutta to serve a second term as Governor-General, his very presence a rebuke to the gorgeous Richard Wellesley. Cornwallis was a favourite of George III, and imitated his master in his manner of speech and in a real or affected love of simplicity and dislike for show. When he came ashore, Lord Wellesley, as a mark of respect, sent off a tremendous collection of staff officers, servants, and carriages to wait on the new Governor-General. Seeing this pompous display Cornwallis turned to his secretary and asked:

"What? What? What? What's all this, Robinson, hey, hey, hey?"

"My Lord, the Marquis Wellesley has sent his equipages and attendants as a mark of respect, and to accompany your lordship to Government House."

"Too civil, too civil, too civil by half. Too many people. Don't want 'em, don't want one of 'em, haven't lost the use of my legs, Robinson, hey, hey, hey? Thank God, I can walk, walk very well, hey, Robinson, hey? Don't want a score of carriages to convey me half a mile. Certainly shan't use 'em."

So the new Governor-General—or old Governor-General restored —walked to Government House, where the Marquess Wellesley received him with much respect and state, and led him to breakfast in a magnificent apartment where a fine band of music played martial airs. As they passed through one splendid room after another, Cornwallis showed his appreciation:

"Upon my word, Wellesley, you have shown much taste here, much taste indeed, Wellesley. It is very handsome, very handsome indeed, Wellesley."

Later he was conducted to a set of apartments which had been specially prepared for him, but Cornwallis thought them much too large and expensive and therefore jumped to the conclusion that they must be Lord Wellesley's own rooms:

"I shall not take your rooms, Wellesley. They're too large, much too large for me, I should be lost in them, I should prefer a smaller place on the ground floor. I therefore request, nay, I insist, Wellesley, you continue in the rooms you are used to, which will gratify me exceedingly."

A day or so later his physician, Dr. Fleming, had occasion to call on his lordship, and ventured to ask how he liked the new palace.

"Like it, Fleming! Like it! Not at all, not at all! It's as much too large as the other was too small. I shall never be able to find my way about it without a guide, nor can I divest myself of the idea of being in a prison, for if I show my head outside a door, a fellow with a musket and a fixed bayonet presents himself before me. I won't have this continued, I won't indeed, Fleming. Wellesley may do as he likes, but I won't be thus pestered, and I must have quiet and retirement. I shall order every sepoy downstairs and let them remain in their guard-room —proper place for them."

Such was the gossip of Calcutta even before Lord Wellesley had left for England, as recorded by the bibulous Mr. Hickey who was animated by no special malice; and it is not hard to see how such talk, exaggerated and inflamed by malice and envy, could in Parliament quickly reach the point of charges of oppression, ambition, and disordered luxury. The Directors of the East India Company were enraged with Lord Wellesley because they had been told (untruly) that he intended "to overthrow their authority". They extended this suspicion and dislike to his brother, whom they avoided receiving at first on various pretexts, but really because "they were apprehensive lest by any mark of personal attention to me they should afford ground for a belief that they approved of any of the measures in the transaction of which I had been concerned". History is full of stories of ingratitude, but there is something particularly piquant in the spectacle of these wealthy and plethoric tradesmen refusing even to see the lean soldier who had held and extended their dominions, and who had brought their army to a state of efficiency it never knew before or since. And he actually regarded it as a triumph worthy of record that they eventually invited him to "one of their Wednesday dinners"!

Mr. Pitt was out of town when Sir Arthur Wellesley reached London (September, 1805); but, as in duty bound, he immediately called officially on Lord Castlereagh at the Colonial Office. He was informed that his lordship was engaged, and was shown to a waiting-room, where "I found a gentleman, who, from his likeness to his pictures and the loss of an arm, I immediately recognised as Lord Nelson. He could not know who I was but he at once entered into conversation with me, if I can call it conversation, for it was almost all on his side and all about himself, and in, really, a style so vain and so silly as to surprise and almost to disgust me". Something intelligent was said by the unknown military gentleman, to whom Nelson was talking on topics, and in a manner he supposed likely to interest the friends of George III and the Duke of York who held most of the lucrative army posts; and suddenly the Admiral made an excuse to leave the room and consult the office-keeper.

"Who is that gentleman in the room with me?" he asked.

"Major-General Sir Arthur Wellesley, my lord."

The Admiral was sobered by this news, "for when he came back he was an altogether different man, both in manner and matter . . . in fact, he talked like an officer and a statesman. The Secretary of State kept us long waiting, and certainly for the last half or three quarters of an hour I don't know that I ever had a conversation that interested me more."

Not the least remarkable aspect of this curious little story is the fact that Castlereagh kept Nelson and Wellington hanging about in his ante-room for more than an hour.

On top of the Admiralty building in Whitehall in those days was a semaphore telegraph station by which orders and important news were relayed to and from Plymouth. Less than two months after this conversation the look-out men in London were electrified by the news

SIR ARTHUR WELLESLEY, 1804

After the painting by Robert Home
[*The National Portrait Gallery*]

VISCOUNT CASTLEREAGH

After the portrait by Sir Thomas Lawrence
[*The National Portrait Gallery*]

which began coming in from the waving arms of the next signal station: "Combined French Spanish fleet defeated Trafalgar 18 enemy ships surrendered remainder fled lord Nelson killed in action . . ." England was saved. The long threat of invasion was at last blown into vapour by the guns of Trafalgar; yet there was little public rejoicing. The destruction of the last grand fleet Napoleon put into commission seemed to Nelson's countrymen scarcely a compensation for his death. And later somewhere in that intensely silent crowd which watched the great Admiral's coffin on its way to St. Paul's stood an obscure sepoy General recently returned from Calcutta.

CHAPTER X

"So Bright an Example of Constancy"

"INSTEAD of calling upon Pitt, I rode with him from Wimbledon Common to London." A conversation between Pitt and Wellington would be even more interesting to overhear than one between Nelson and Wellington, but all we learn is that the two "rode very slowly" and had "plenty of time for discussion". Apparently what they discussed was "our late system in India"; at least on this particular ride, when Sir Arthur did most of the talking and Pitt listened. What did Pitt think of this still youngish General, defending his brother's Indian policy in his blunt horse-sensical way? Seemingly Pitt was impressed in his favour; for though, as befitted a returned East Indian soldier, the General went off to Cheltenham immediately after this September ride, he reported in December: "I have seen Pitt several times" and "he has always been very civil to me."

They met again in November at the country-house of Lord Camden, the former unfriendly Lord-Lieutenant of Ireland. It was a large house party, which included the whole Cabinet, and every day Pitt "used to ride 18 or 20 miles, and great pains were taken to send forward his luncheon, bottled porter, I think, and getting him a beefsteak or mutton-chop ready at some place fixed beforehand. The place was always mentioned to the party, so that those kept at home in the morning might join the ride there if they pleased. On coming home from these rides, they used to put on dry clothes and to hold a cabinet". The one member of the party who could not sit in on these discussions was Sir Arthur Wellesley, who held no office; and there is a touch of irony about this since he was the man destined to make Pitt's policy effective. It was a strange coincidence that he should have met both Nelson and Pitt in the last few weeks of their lives, as if they unconsciously handed on to him their great task, their uncompromising struggle against France and the Napoleonic dictatorship. For many a future session of war-weary Parliaments, the anti-Bonaparte government was only kept in power by the growing reputation and victories of the sepoy General who had waited patiently outside the door when Mr. Pitt held his informal Cabinets.

History was kind to him again, for Sir Arthur was one of the guests at that most memorable of Guildhall banquets—one of the occasions which lifted that function above its low level of a business men's feast—when Pitt was saluted as the saviour of England and the future saviour of Europe and made his brief but unforgettable reply: "Europe is not to be saved by any single man. England has saved herself by her exertions, and will, as I trust, save Europe by her example." "He was scarcely up two minutes," the Duke would say of the speech, "yet nothing could be more perfect." But great speeches are powerless against fate, and England's example at Trafalgar had no effect on the decision at Austerlitz—the blow that broke Pitt's heart. In January he lay dying, and the world was told that his last words were: "My country, how I leave my country!" though what he actually said to Canning were the more modest if less poetic words: "I am sorry to leave the country in its present situation." That was prosaic enough for Wellington to have said and to approve. Did he ever learn what Pitt thought and said of him in those last days? It is high praise Addington has recorded:

"Sir Arthur Wellesley is unlike all other military men with whom I have conversed. He never makes a difficulty or hides his ignorance in vague generalities. If I put a question to him, he answers it distinctly; if I want an explanation, he gives it clearly; if I desire an opinion, I get from him one supported by reasons that are always sound. He is a very remarkable man."

Mr. Addington's memory of what Pitt said about General Wellesley may have been unconsciously influenced by later events, for as a soldier Wellesley had no opportunity of serving Pitt. In December 1805 he did sail for Bremen as a mere General of Brigade in a force which was to operate against Napoleon from Hanover, in the hopes of influencing Prussia against France. Austerlitz put an end to that as to many another scheme, and after only a six weeks' promenade in Germany, Sir Arthur was back in England, with his Pittite friends out of office and the Fox-Grenville alliance in control. "*We* are not actually in opposition," Sir Arthur wrote a friend, "but we have no power." "We" of course meant the Wellesleys for Richard was back in England, having arrived just in time to take a last farewell of his friend and leader, William Pitt. There certainly can have been little hostility from one side of the Government, for Lord Grenville was an old and staunch friend of the family. And though Sir Arthur went off to Hastings with the humble assignment of a mere brigade to drill, he had little to complain of—in October 1805 he was gazetted to the staff, and in January 1806 to the colonelcy of the Thirty-Third, vice Lord

D*

Cornwallis, deceased in Calcutta. As he wrote a friend, "these appointments have made me rich".

Perhaps the brigade at Hastings was not intended as a snub by Government. After all that was the very place which had been chosen for successful invasion seven hundred and forty years earlier, and it might be still considered by Government the post of honour in the defence of England. It is worth recording that Sir Arthur Wellesley was one of the few people in England who thought that if the French did succeed in landing in force they would have little difficulty in occupying the country. "Our military system," he said afterwards, "was very faulty; orders were sent from four or five different departments—everybody pretended to give orders." When somebody objected that the French army could not have subsisted in England: "I have seen them in Spain, with every communication cut off, live on their own horses. I knew what they would do in this country—eat everything, burn the towns, and carry off the women."

French invasion and its highly probable success if attempted were not the only worries Sir Arthur had to deal with in the spring of 1806. In the first place he had to return to Parliament, for the enmity to Richard Wellesley (now back in England, insulted rather than consoled by his new title of an *Irish* Marquess) had come to a point in one Paull, an Anglo-Indian who had got himself elected to Parliament with no other purpose than that of making himself unpleasant to the former Governor-General. Lord Grenville offered the pocket borough of Rye, so that Sir Arthur might defend his brother in the lower House, but this brought up some rather delicate points of political etiquette. However much Sir Arthur might be in earnest when he said he was *nimmukwallah*, he could hardly fail to realize that as he grew older he inclined more and more to agree with the Tories, whereas Lord Wellesley, though no great democrat, inclined more to the Whigs. How would Sir Arthur's Tory friends feel if he sat for a Whig borough? Apparently they saw the situation in a favourable light; Sir Arthur received from Castlereagh so generous a letter ("your first and only consideration must be the protection of" Lord Wellesley's "character and services from unjust aspersion") that he hesitated no longer. His election as a nominal supporter of the Ministry of All the Talents cost him £367—a year's income of the former Dublin Castle aide-de-camp.

Almost certainly this link with Captain Wesley escaped the attention of Sir Arthur, who in the spring of 1806 was very intimately concerned with a more interesting if more embarrassing echo of his past. Nearly ten years elapsed since he had abandoned his violin and sought a modestly lucrative Irish post—for the sake of Kitty Pakenham. Had he wholly forgotten her in India, where whispered gossip linked his name with married ladies; where his accounts showed numerous purchases of elegant shawls and jewellery, though not for Kitty Pakenham; and whence he wrote many letters, but none to Kitty Pakenham? As she never wrote to him, might he not have reasonably concluded that after nine years she had forgotten him? A wilful silence of nine years on both sides seems sufficient quietus for any love-affair.

Walking in Cheltenham not long after his return, Sir Arthur met an Anglo-Indian lady, sister-in-law of the Governor of Madras and wife of a general not otherwise eminent in history. From this lady, General Wellesley learned, perhaps with more surprise than delight, that Catherine Pakenham had not forgotten him, that she had formed no other attachment (not even with the fascinating and eligible Lowry Cole) and that, in short, their romance was in exactly the same state it had been in 1797, except that he was thirty-seven instead of twenty-eight, and she was thirty-three instead of twenty-four. The revelation cannot have been anything but embarrassing, and it was distinctly unromantic that the hint should have to come from one of the lady's friends. In the ethics of sentiment as understood in Sir Arthur's age and social class, release from an engagement, however obviously unsuitable the couple might be for marriage, could only come from the lady. Many a novel of the epoch hinged on this very situation, and the ingenuity of novelists was strained to the utmost to find new pretexts for releasing the honourable hero from a prior engagement so that he could marry the real heroine.

Needless to say, Sir Arthur Wellesley did the right thing—he renewed his suit and was instantly accepted. Whether the conventionally right and honourable thing was also the best thing from the point of view of human happiness is a question. The gossips of the United Kingdom, from Miss Maria Edgeworth in Dublin to Queen Charlotte in London, did their best to make a romance out of a situation which the Queen hopefully referred to as "so bright an example of constancy"; but a more accurate epitaph on the marriage is supplied by a military historian who gloomily refers to Kitty Pakenham as "not the right woman for him". Just where and how she was "wrong for him" is impossible to say at this distance in time with a contemporary conspiracy of silence. It is clear that he soon learned to endure other long separations from her with great courage; indeed, within a week of marriage he went off to woo his constituency, and left to his clergyman brother the task of bringing the bride to her new home in London; and before long his attentions to other ladies became notorious. Whatever Lady Wellesley's hidden defects, she possessed one which was public, and above all others likely to annoy her husband—she gushed, and (horror of horrors!) she gushed over him. After a lifetime of enduring that sort of thing from "My dear Morning-ton", it must have been intolerable to find it recurring in an aggravated form in his own home. How far she carried these public demon-strations may be illustrated by one sinister anecdote. After the battle of Salamanca, some officious person brought her the captured French eagles; whereupon she struggled free from her restraining attendants and embraced the eagles, screaming: "They are mine, they are mine!" and then fainted away.

On the other hand it must be admitted that specifications for the perfect wife of a great military commander do not seem ever to have been drawn up, and probably would not be filled if they were. Did not Fyodor Karamazov marry the one woman who had no sexual at-traction for him? Yet the Duke certainly avoided the matrimonial misfortune of his great hero, Julius Cæsar, and his great opponent, Napoleon Bonaparte; for Kitty Pakenham was every inch a lady, in the chastest sense of the word.

Parliamentary duties claimed the attention of Lady Wellesley's husband that session. In May 1806 an indictment was presented to the House of Commons, beginning with these portentous words:

"Article of Charge of High Crimes and Misdemeanours committed by Richard Colley Marquess Wellesley, in his transactions with respect to the Nabob Vizier of Oude."

Sir Arthur defended his brother against these and other obscure charges, and on the whole very successfully, though he worked under the heavy disadvantage of a full knowledge of the facts and a loyal determination to stick honestly to them. Such considerations weighed little with Lord Wellesley's persecutors, who, needless to say, cared rather less than nothing for the inhabitants of India, but a great deal for their own political careers. For instance, in a pathetic speech Lord Folkestone pointed out how Lord Wellesley had supposedly under-taken military measures against the aggression of Zemaun Shah, "a mere pretext—they were continued there after the death of the Shah and the dismemberment of his dominions"—in spite of the fact that the Shah survived Lord Folkestone's speech forty-seven years. For

CATHERINE, FIRST DUCHESS OF WELLINGTON

After the drawing by Sir Thomas Lawrence made in 1814

[*Reproduced from the monograph on Sir Thomas Lawrence by
Lord Ronald Sutherland Gower. The Duke of Wellington's Collection*]

two years these desultory proceedings dragged on, involving the unlucky Richard Wellesley in legal expenses amounting to £30,000, and only terminating when Mr. Paull followed a strange fashion of British legislators of the day and cut his own throat. All Sir Arthur gained from it was a closer acquaintance with the "radical" Mr. Creevey, with his inordinate appetite for office and turtle soup and his bitter enmity for "the Wellesleys".

"You will have seen that I am in Parliament," Sir Arthur wrote to a friend in India from Hastings on July 31, 1806, "and a most difficult and unpleasant game I have had to play in the present extraordinary state of parties". And some months later from Deal: "You will have heard with astonishment of Paull's attack upon Lord Wellesley. The impudence of this gent in setting himself up for Westminster has afforded an opportunity of unveiling him to the public, and his character is now well known. Only think of that fellow standing for Westminster, and having been not far from carrying his election!!!" And again, in February 1807: "I was the first person who discovered that the characteristics of Paull were perseverance, effrontery, and impudence; and when you conceive such a character, you will not be astonished at all at what he has done, notwithstanding the kicks, cuffs, and buffeting which we gave him last year in Parliament, and all that he still threatens."

It is not easy to discover Mr. Paull's motives, unless he was the mere tool of a faction at East India House, since Richard Wellesley appears to have treated him very kindly in India. But whatever Paull's personal motive, his supporters in the House of Commons were playing the lowest kind of party politics. Naturally Richard Wellesley was no more above criticism than any other minister or emissary of Government, and there was certainly criticism of his policy in the Cabinet itself. But in this period (1806–1808), when Wellesley was involved in continual worry and expense to justify himself, England had only two gains to show for more than ten years of costly and bloody war with France. Nelson had won them control of the sea (which incidentally included the power to occupy Malta and Sicily at will); and Wellesley had won them control of India, and hence of the vast Eastern trade which enabled them to defy Bonaparte and his continental blockade indefinitely. Supposing Lord Wellesley had contrived to lose India to the French? There would have been no Parliament left to impeach him.

That most of his brother's critics knew little about India neither surprised nor annoyed Sir Arthur Wellesley, who was well acquainted with the fact that exact knowledge and candour do not have, and very seldom have had, much to do with criticism of Indian affairs. What did influence him (and it could scarcely have been otherwise) was the realization that the people who talked unscrupulous nonsense about India for their own political advancement were the very same people who talked most sanctimoniously of "democracy" and "reform". It was as if fate had determined to make him a Tory; and then went on to clinch the matter by making him Chief Secretary for Ireland.

This was a strange reversal of affairs when the humble suitor for a minor post in the Irish Revenue returned ten years later to rule that country on a salary of nearly £7,000 a year. (The Lord-Lieutenant now was the Duke of Richmond, who relied on "my dear Arthur" for everything, and was quite incapable of running the machine of government without "Arthur's" assistance.) And this appointment itself came about through a curious political whirligig. The Grenville-Fox government, who came into power at Pitt's death and distinguished themselves by turning out all his friends, found they too could not come to terms with Napoleon, as they and their supporters had been urging their predecessors to do. Nor were they any more successful with the war than Pitt's government, for if that had the dismal record of Ulm and Austerlitz and the fall of Austria to its discredit, the Ministry of All the Talents had to plead guilty to Jena (October 1806) and the collapse of Prussia. Fox died in September 1806, and the Government had been "strengthened" by the addition of the henpecked Lord Holland, only to find itself at loggerheads with George III on the now hoary topic of Catholic Emancipation.

George III made it a matter of conscience not to permit seats in Parliament to his Catholic subjects. He said it was contrary to his coronation oath. Some thought he really believed this; some thought he only did it to annoy; and some thought he was merely mad as usual. At all events when Catholic Emancipation was mentioned to him by his Ministers he first reproachfully threatened to go officially mad, and then accepted the Government's resignation. This occurred somewhat unexpectedly in March 1807 (barely a month after Napoleon's reverse at Eylau) and thus the Tories were once more in power, nominally under the senile Duke of Portland, actually under a dual leadership of Castlereagh and Canning.

There had been two rebellions in Ireland in less than a decade, so there was every reason why Canning and Castlereagh should want to hand over the responsibility for that exasperating country to a soldier, well acquainted with Ireland and holding an excellent administrative record. What does seem curious is that a Government, which only came into power because it promised the King not to press Catholic Emancipation, should choose as its Secretary for Ireland the very man who as Prime Minister carried the measure in the next reign and who actually had stated in a letter written on November 19, 1807:

"Our policy in Ireland should be to endeavour to obliterate, as far as the law will allow us, the distinction between Protestants and Catholics; and that we ought to avoid anything which could induce either sect to recollect or believe that its interests are separate or distinct from those of others."

Another principle he enunciated about Ireland, which sounds surprising in a Tory Chief Secretary, was that "government ought to do what is just towards the governed, let the consequences be what they may". On the other hand, he had no illusions whatsoever about Ireland or the relations between Ireland and England. As he saw it, Ireland had originally been occupied for purely military reasons—to prevent a flank invasion of England—so that the English were there as conquerors and were most naturally hated as such. "I lay it down as decided that Ireland, in a view to military operations, must be considered as an enemy's country," Sir Arthur wrote in May 1807, and later in the same memorandum he put down these weighty words:

"I shall conclude this part of the subject by telling you that I am positively convinced that no political measure which you could adopt would alter the temper of the people of this country. They are disaffected to the British government; they don't feel the benefits of their situation; attempts to render it better either do not reach their minds, or they are represented to them as additional injuries; and in fact we have no strength here but our army."

A Chief Secretary for Ireland who held such views was not likely to be disappointed, and perhaps had a better chance of carrying out his cold policy of "doing what is just" than those who set out with warmer but less realistic views. But it is quite evident that Sir Arthur had no intention of linking his destiny too closely either to Ireland or to politics. His acceptance of the Irish post was conditional. " . . . Ministers have told me that they consider me at liberty to give up the office in Ireland whenever an opportunity of employing me professionally will offer, and that my acceptance of this office, instead of being a prejudice to me in my profession, will be considered as giving me an additional claim to such employment."

There is no need to imagine any powers of second sight in the making of these arrangements. Sir Arthur's experience in India had given him the military knowledge and confidence in himself he lacked in 1796, and by this time he knew enough of the other generals to know that they deserved his contemptuous "damned inefficient". (Sir John Moore was proving to be the exception to the rule.) Sooner or later, Ministers would have to use Wellesley on an expeditionary force, and indeed they had already sought his advice on such fantastic projects as the invasion of Mexico and Venezuela; meanwhile, he would look after Ireland for them, and hope that this service would induce them to support him when the time came against the inveterate mistrust and even hatred inspired in the Horse Guards by that unspeakable monstrosity, an efficient British General.

Employment with an expeditionary force came in August 1807, but not in the circumstances a patriotic officer would have wished and not on an errand which could arouse much enthusiasm. Although the Danish campaign of 1807 was successful and perhaps a first turning-point for England in the fortunes of this long hard war, the morality of the affair was doubtful, and hence it long remained in the same obscurity which so rightly concealed the Duke of York's earlier campaigns. Yet, but for Canning's prompt if illegal action, England might well have been crushed and all hope of resistance to the Emperor's military dictatorship of Europe would have disappeared.

What happened was this. After the battle of Friedland (June 14, 1807), Alexander of Russia gave up all hope of further resistance, and England's last remaining ally of any real power was gone. Napoleon and Alexander met at Tilsit "to divide the world between them". It was believed that there were secret clauses to this treaty, directed against England, and that Napoleon hoped to bring against its hitherto unconquered fleet the united navies of France, Russia, Sweden, Denmark, Spain, Portugal, and North Italy. The first step (so Canning was led to believe) was to be the taking over of the important Danish navy by a land invasion. In a private letter to Lady Bessborough, the British envoy extraordinary to Russia, Lord Granville Leveson Gower, certainly hints at some such dire threatenings:

"Whilst in England Politicians are occupying themselves in squabbles in Parliament, and the People in following Sir F. Burdett's Chair, the most deadly blows are aiming at the very existence of the country; for be assured that the dangers which threaten England at the moment infinitely exceed what we ever before apprehended." [Memel, July 15, 1807.]

Now Leveson Gower had hitherto been very optimistic ("you who were always so sanguine", Lady Bessborough says anxiously in replying) and therefore must have received very serious news, probably the same which on July 19 determined the British Cabinet to take the serious step of seizing the Danish fleet—for Denmark was a neutral. The action was loudly condemned, not only by Denmark but all over Europe; and, after all, it was but reasonable to feel a tender hesitation in criticizing the violences of an almost omnipotent aggressor, while applying the severest moral standards to a small island people fighting for their existence. What made the expedition all the more wicked was its complete success; indeed, an eye-witness noted that he never saw Napoleon in such a rage as when he heard the news that the entire Danish navy had been captured by the English. Eighteen ships of the line, 10 frigates, and 42 smaller ships would have been a useful, perhaps decisive, addition for his invasion of England.

The expedition succeeded partly because of the element of surprise, but chiefly because it had a precise and possible objective, and there was a proper co-ordination of the naval and military forces, which in turn was due to the appointment of intelligent commanders. Yet in spite of the conditions on which Sir Arthur had accepted political office, he had considerable difficulty in going on this expedition. Ministers of course were fully aware of the negotiations between Napoleon and the United Irishmen and of the Emperor's guarantee that Ireland should be treated "like America in the late war"; and they naturally wanted to keep their competent soldier in Dublin. Even when he had insisted on going, the elderly generals at the Horse Guards did their best to thwart him, appointed him to command the Reserve, and gave him a "second-in-command" as a "dry nurse". They were quite sure an Indian officer and a "politician" could not possibly command an army.

The "dry nurse" in this case was Brigadier-General Stewart, a competent officer, and "during the embarkation, the voyage out and the disembarkation", Sir Arthur allowed him to "do everything", for "I saw no kind of objection to anything he suggested". The troops landed on August 16, 1807, and Copenhagen was invested on the eighteenth. On August 26 a small Danish army attempted to raise the siege, and Wellesley's force was detached to meet it. "Stewart, as usual, was beginning his suggestions and arrangements, but I stopped him short with 'Come, come, 'tis my turn now'. I immediately made my own dispositions, assigned him the command of one of the wings, gave him his orders, attacked the enemy and beat them. Stewart, like a man of sense, saw in a moment that I understood my business, and subsided with (as far as I saw) good humour into his proper place."

The battle at Kioge on August 29, 1807, was pretty well a foregone conclusion, since the raw Danish levies could not have been expected to stand up to Wellesley's trained infantry. Fifteen hundred prisoners were taken and considerable casualties inflicted, while not a single British officer was lost "and but few men of the 92nd and 95th; some of the officers of hussars have been wounded, and a few of the men". Sir Arthur was less concerned with his victory than with the fact that owing to the mistake of a Hanoverian general, the plan was not completely carried out and some of the Danish army escaped. The episode is worth noting only since it was to be repeated again and again on greater battle-fields against a far more formidable foe. The Danish general seems to have been well satisfied with the treatment of his conqueror: "Penetrated with gratitude for your human and generous conduct towards me and all the officers prisoners . . ." he wrote. An invading army can never expect much warmth and friendliness from the invaded, but Sir Arthur's care in protecting civilians received some response. A certain Tönnejen wrote to him on September 4:

"It is an obligation to me to thank you most sincerely and of my heart for the protection you have given me in these days your troops have laid in my neighbourhood. I can never forget it; I shall still remember it; and I beg you most humbly that you will never withdraw me this protection so long your troops are staying here; it will still be a comfort to me and family in letting us live in rest and security."

The Countess of Holstein wrote (in French) to thank Sir Arthur for his protection of her peasants; and the good example even influenced the ranks, for a private soldier (Rifleman Harris of the Ninety-Fifth) boasts that he protected a family with "five very handsome daughters" from "a set of rough and ready Riflemen, unscrupulous and bold". So at any rate the neutrality of Denmark was violated with every conceivable politeness by all ranks, while a steady bombardment of Copenhagen was maintained until half the town was on fire and compelled to surrender. The terms were drawn up and signed on behalf of the British army by Sir Arthur. And though Ministers dallied with the idea of occupying the country, Sir Arthur was against it and anxious to leave now that the fighting was over and the real object of the expedition achieved. He reached England by October (ahead of the captured fleet) and in December was once more in Dublin Castle, ruling the country in the name of the Duke of Richmond and dispensing patronage with that "mixture of aristocratic

hauteur and cold contempt" which made him so unpopular with the
gentlemanly beggars who then infested Government.

A friend in India wrote suggesting that Sir Arthur might return
there; for, since the departure of the Wellesleys, matters had not gone
too well in that distant part of the Empire. In replying he said:

"I don't think it probable that I shall be called upon to go to India. The fact
is that men in power in England think very little of that country, and those
who do think of it feel very little inclination that I should go there. Besides
that, I have got pretty high upon the tree since I came home, and those in power
think that I cannot well be spared from objects nearer home. At the same time
the Indians in London are crying out for my return. . . . You will see the
accounts of our Zealand expedition, which has had great effect in London, and
has added to the popularity and strength of the ministry." [Dublin, Oct. 15,
1807.]

"I have got pretty high upon the tree since I came home" is a
curious echo of his phrase about his position in India seven or eight
years earlier, when Seringapatam seemed to him "the top of the tree".
There is no reason to doubt his sincerity; and those who speak of
"Wellesley's ambitions" as so strong a motive in his career seem to
forget how comparatively modest those ambitions were. His "pretty
high upon the tree" went a little higher in the first half of 1808. In
February he received the formal thanks of Parliament (it had been
Assaye before, and now it was Kioge); and in April he just scraped
into the Lieutenant-Generals, his name being last on the list of
promotions. A few days later he entered his fortieth year, twenty-one
years of which had been spent in the army. If he had died then, or if
his career had carried him no further up the tree, he would have been
little more remembered than scores upon scores of other successful
soldiers, sailors, and administrators. He might have had his chapter
in the history of British India and his paragraph in English history.
Students of British military history might have been struck by his
extraordinary promise (or they might have ignored him), and if his
Indian dispatches had ever been printed they would have had their
few admirers. But General Wellesley would have been no more
known to the world at large than such of his Indian friends and
superiors as Generals Lake and Baird. How he celebrated his birthday on May 1, 1808, we do not know, or indeed if he celebrated it at
all. He was in London that day for certain, and seems to have written
no official letters; so perhaps he took a brief vacation and spent part of
the day with Lady Wellesley and their two little boys. In any case,
though he did not know it, this was the last time he would ever have the

chance to spend a peacefully obscure birthday. He was about to move into history, and his climb "pretty high upon the tree", with which he was so contented, was no more than a preparation for what was ahead. It is true that he went off with what might be called a brilliant false start, but it was so brilliant that the interruption could only be temporary.

A few weeks after this birthday he received an official document which began:

"*His Royal Highness the Commander in Chief to Lieut.-General the Hon. Sir A. Wellesley, K.B.*

"Horse Guards, 14th June, 1808

"Sir,

"His Majesty having been graciously pleased to appoint you to the command of a detachment of his army, to be employed upon a particular service, I have to desire that you will be pleased to take the earliest opportunity to assume the command of this force, and carry into effect such instructions as you may receive from his Majesty's ministers.

"The force, which his Majesty has been pleased to place under your command, consists of the following corps:—

Royal Artillery	9th Foot
Royal Staff Corps. Detachment	38th „
29th Foot	40th „
32nd „	60th „
50th „	71st „
82nd „	91st „
5th „	95th, Four companies

4th Royal Veteran Battalion. . . . [&c., &c.]"

CHAPTER XI

Boney's Invincibles

THE expeditionary force entrusted to Sir Arthur Wellesley had originally been collected with the idea of operating against Spain in her great colonies of South America. It was now ordered to co-operate with Spanish armies in the defence of Spain against France; and what it actually accomplished was the liberation of Portugal. What had happened to make this sudden reversal? The change was not in England, which alone of the powers, great and small, never wavered in its opposition to Bonaparte and never changed sides; though it must be confessed that the task of resistance seemed to grow more and more thankless and hopeless, as ally after ally was crushed and went over to the enemy. After Austerlitz and the humiliation of Austria had come Jena and the savage crushing of Prussia, followed in turn by Friedland and the abandonment by the Tsar Alexander of his alliance with England. The "Continental System" of excluding English shipping and English goods from all ports was now to be extended from the Baltic to the Mediterranean, from Russia to Portugal. Sweden, Denmark, and Portugal were to be coerced into joining the great land blockade, and . . . "the British Carthage" would be wiped out. There had never been any doubt of the earnest wish of successive French governments to destroy England through the destruction of her trade. As early as January 1793 a report to the French Revolutionary Committee of Defence had used these words:

"The credit of England rests upon fictitious wealth; the real riches of that people are scattered everywhere. Asia, Portugal and Spain are the most advantageous markets for the productions of English industry; we should shut those markets to the English by opening them to all the world. We must attack Lisbon and the Brazils, and carry an auxiliary army to Tippoo Sultan. The Republics of Italy offer you maritime prizes, the loss of which will fall on English commerce."

Bonaparte merely carried on the same policy but with more success. It is a mistake to suppose that his combination of the Continental System and privateering was without serious results. Privateers accounted, on an average, for a loss of $2\frac{1}{2}$ per cent of *all tonnage clearing British ports,* trade was dislocated, and in 1810–1811 England was near to famine.

We have seen what happened to Tippoo Sahib (who never got his French "auxiliary army") and to the Danish fleet, since Sir Arthur Wellesley was concerned in the successful liquidation of both these problems. Sweden, in spite of Sir John Moore, was lost; but events in the Iberian Peninsula at last gave England the opportunity for a permanent front on which to wage serious war against Napoleon, instead of wasting men, money, and supplies on futile expeditions which at best resulted in what Sheridan called "filching sugar islands".

Since 1795 Spain had been a more or less servile ally of France, and under the energetic handling of Napoleon had paid him an annual tribute of 72,000,000 gold francs—one of the ingenious devices by which the government of the Empire showed a supposedly balanced budget. The government of Spain was in the hands of a lamentable quartet: Carlos IV, a semi-imbecile sportsman who wished to be excused the labours of kingship while enjoying its privileges; his Queen, Maria Luisa, intriguing and domineering; the royal *cicisbeo,* Manuel Godoy, Prince of the Peace, who ran the country as he robbed it; Ferdinand, Prince of Asturias, who would have liked to overthrow Godoy, but was too much of a coward to attempt it.

On his return to France in July 1807, Napoleon started to weave an extraordinary and Machiavellian plot against these feeble and sub-servient allies. He began by massing troops at Bayonne, and then after the usual bullying threats and propaganda lies, sent Junot with an expeditionary force against Portugal—of course with the connivance and knowledge of the Spanish government. His army had only just crossed the frontier when a curious treaty was signed at Fontainebleau, partitioning Portugal between the King of Etruria, Godoy (who was to be called Prince of the Algarves), and France. The purpose of this elaborate farce is still not clear, except that it was evidently a trap; but at this moment (autumn 1807) the Spanish royal family played further into Napoleon's hands by a quarrel as extraordinary as Godoy's secret treaty. The Prince of Asturias was arrested and accused of plotting to dethrone and even to murder his parents, though all Ferdinand had actually been doing was to intrigue secretly with Napoleon to marry any available female of the Bonaparte family in exchange for the Emperor's support against Godoy.

Meanwhile Junot had reached Lisbon with a very exhausted but totally unopposed army on November 30, 1807; only to find that at the last minute the British ambassador had persuaded the feeble Prince

Regent of Portugal (the Queen of Portugal was as mad as the King of England) to escape to Brazil, with the fleet, the treasury, and most of the wealthy families. Eight days earlier, Napoleon had sent another 25,000 soldiers into Spain; in January 1808 they were followed by 30,000 more; and towards the end of that month the French-controlled press suddenly attacked the Prince of the Peace in the ominous familiar style. In February the great fortresses of Pamplona, Barcelona, San Sebastian, and Figueras were occupied through acts of treachery. By March there were nearly 100,000 French troops in Spain, and the terrified Godoy was on the point of flying to South America with the King and Queen; but the mob rose to prevent the escape, and to save Godoy's life, Charles abdicated in favour of Ferdinand. To make confusion worse confounded, Charles then withdrew his abdication, and the various members of the family were lured over the French frontier by the Emperor on various pretexts and kidnapped into "honourable captivity" after being forced to renounce their rights to the Spanish throne. After these delicate but elaborately unnecessary preliminaries, the way was at last opened to appoint Joseph Bonaparte to be "His Most Catholic Majesty, King of Spain and the Indies". Even Napoleon admitted, in cooler days, that it would have been both more honourable and more sensible to declare open war.

Clearly it is not possible to set any definite historical date as the moment when Napoleon's vast empire and vaster dreams of ambition began to decline, unless it is put very late and obviously in the retreat from Moscow. French royalists were naturally inclined to see at least an ideal moral date of condemnation in the murder of the Duc d'Enghien; but there is another date, equally moral and ideal, and at the same time marking a moment after which the Grand Army never had a day of complete peace until its great leader abdicated at Fontainebleau. The date is May 2, 1808, when the populace of Madrid rose in savage fury against Murat and his occupying regiments, and were in turn massacred with even greater savagery and fury. Probably not more than 1,000 Spaniards and French perished in the four hours of street fighting, and most of these were Spaniards, but it was a dreadful and dramatic moment in history, the opening of the long and bloody Peninsular War. For the first time Napoleon had a truly national war on his hands, and that war never ceased until it had spread to all Europe.

It might be said with truth that Ferdinand was a worthless person undeserving of the devotion of the meanest peasant who died in his cause; that the old Spanish government was quite rotten; that Joseph Bonaparte was a far better man and that he wished to govern Spain intelligently and well; and that eventually the restored government of Ferdinand pushed Spain back towards the Middle Ages rather than forward to better times. All this and more might be said and would be true, but would not change the fact that Napoleon's cynical behaviour was so outrageous, so insulting to a great and proud nation that they had either to fight him to the death or to feel degraded for ever. So far as Spain was concerned it was truly a war of the people, for the Juntas and generals were incompetent and the regular armies almost invariably unsuccessful. But it is precisely because the Spanish people resisted Napoleon for nearly seven years in spite of all these handicaps that their fight was so heroic.

From Madrid the revolt against the French and their treacherous infiltration spread to Asturias, Galicia, and eventually to every other province of Spain. It seems certain that Murat in Madrid misjudged the situation after the suppression of the rising on May 2; but, what is more important and startling, the Emperor himself misjudged it, and had indeed miscalculated from the beginning. He imagined that he had only a series of local riots to deal with, and most of the troops he had sent into Spain were not the veterans of the Grand Army but second-line battalions, raw conscripts, the mere overflow of the depots. Hence the series of French reverses which shook the legend of French invincibility. Hurrying ahead a little in time, we find that in late June 1808 Marshal Moncey was repelled from Valencia with the loss of 1,200 men; Saragossa under the leadership of Palafox defied Lefebvre and Verdier throughout the summer, and eventually drove them off with the loss of 3,500 men and 54 guns; finally, the most astonishing of all, Dupont and nearly 18,000 men surrendered to the Spaniards at Baylen on July 23–24. Baylen caused a sensation in Europe, for it was the first time an Imperial French army had surrendered, and the Spaniards talked long and loud of their triumph over "the victors of Jena and Austerlitz". This was a slight exaggeration since nearly all the surrendered troops were second-line conscripts, while General Dupont himself had never before held an independent command. Moreover, Baylen itself proved a mixed blessing, for until they had destroyed most of their own armies, the Spanish generals were always trying to repeat it and suffering most dreadful defeats—unwise victims of "the spirit of the offensive". But in the summer of 1808 the situation of the various French detachments in Spain was undoubtedly unpleasant and even perilous, while a complementary rising in

Portugal embittered the life of Junot and his men who had hitherto enjoyed months of uninterrupted and lucrative plunder. The wrath, dismay, and astonishment of the French at this resistance were inexpressible except in the words of one of their own great poets, La Fontaine:

> "Cet animal est très méchant;
> Quand on l'attaque, il se défend."

One of the first and most sensible actions of the Asturian Junta was to send accredited representatives to ask for aid in London, where they arrived on June 4, 1808. As we have seen, Sir Arthur Wellesley's commission as General of an expeditionary force was dated June 14, so that for once the British Cabinet acted promptly—at least on paper. Indeed the question must have been settled even earlier, for it was on the evening of June 14 that Sir Arthur discussed Irish affairs with a young M.P. to whom he was temporarily handing over their management in the House. This young man was J. W. Croker, afterwards Secretary of the Navy, an arrogant and omniscient person much disliked by his friends and now chiefly remembered for his infamous attack on John Keats. He was, however, an able executive, and left valuable notes on Wellington. On this particular evening, Croker relates that while he was making some memoranda, Sir Arthur "seemed to lapse into a kind of reverie, and remained silent so long that I asked him what he was thinking of". The reply was so memorable that it must be recorded in full:

"Why, to say the truth, I am thinking of the French that I am going to fight. I have not seen them since the campaign in Flanders, when they were capital soldiers, and a dozen years of victory under Bonaparte must have made them better still. They have besides, it seems, a new system of strategy, which has out-manœuvred and overwhelmed all the armies of Europe. 'Tis enough to make one thoughtful; but no matter: my die is cast, they may overwhelm me but I don't think they will out-manœuvre me. First, because I am not afraid of them, as everybody else seems to be; and secondly, because if what I hear of their system of manœuvres be true, I think it a false one as against steady troops. I suspect all the continental armies were more than half beaten before the battle was won. I, at least, will not be frightened beforehand."

Croker was a good party man and a clever journalist, but it does not appear that he knew anything much about military affairs and phraseology, although he did once try to prove to the Duke of Wellington that he did not know the difference between a scarp and a counterscarp. It therefore seems probable that he has misreported the subject of Sir Arthur's reverie and that the British General was not musing over grandiose Napoleonic plans of strategy (a waste of energy in the commander of about 10,000 men) but over the new French tactics which had so far baffled every army in Europe. Sir Arthur believed he had found the answer to those hitherto triumphant French tactics. Light infantry would deal with the cloud of *tirailleurs*; the excellent French cavalry must be held off the flanks of a position and otherwise met in square; the charge of the Napoleonic column could be crushed by the fire-power of the British line; and the *trouée* (break-through) of the Napoleonic artillery could be avoided by keeping the main line of troops on a reverse slope. The essence of the whole situation was the fact that, whatever their other faults, the British infantry of the time were better drilled in musketry and steadier under attack than any other troops in the world. Not only could they load and fire more rapidly and accurately than their opponents, not only was their fire discipline so good that their musketry could be halted in a second, but their formation in line enabled every musket to be in action, while the French formation in column kept over two-thirds of the muskets out of action. When an English battalion of 600 muskets met a French battalion of similar numbers, the English had 600 muskets firing, the French only 132. And the same disposition held whether the English were attacking or defending. When the pre-cautions named were properly taken, the "thin red line" was irresistible not because the British were supermen but because "600 well-aimed bullets are four times as powerful as 132".

Yet so stupid are soldiers, even the greatest, that Napoleon's Marshals (Junot, Masséna, Soult, Victor, Ney, Marmont) and Napoleon himself were all defeated by these simple means to which they could find no answer and which they seem scarcely to have observed. Napoleon's columns at Waterloo were defeated in exactly the same way that Junot's were defeated at Vimiero seven years before. What the French Marshals did about it was to belittle their opponent and his men, to conceal their losses and to find innumerable excuses; but they failed to explain why the small though gradually increasing army of the Peninsula moved eventually from Lisbon to Toulouse and Bordeaux, or why the French army under Napoleon himself fled from Waterloo. There was one French officer of the Peninsular War more candid than the rest. This was Lieutenant-Colonel Bugeaud who later became a Marshal of France, and who forms an interesting contrast with the gifted General Foy who after the war deliberately misrepresented the conduct of his victorious enemies because "it is necessary that the soldier in the ranks should not only hate his enemy, but also despise him"! In a private letter, as well as in his secret journal, General Foy admitted that what he wrote in his formal history was false. Here in contrast is the very interesting admission of the future Maréchal Bugeaud, which explains the tactical success of the British Peninsular Army better than any other short statement and has the advantage of being an admission of a brave enemy and of giving a vivid account of the feelings and experience of French soldiers in a Peninsular battle:

"I served seven years in the Peninsula, and during that time we sometimes beat the English in isolated encounters and raids which as a field officer detached I was able to prepare and to direct. But during that long period of war, it was my sorrow to see that only in a very small number of general actions did the British army fail to get the better of us. We almost invariably attacked our adversaries, without either taking into account our own past experience, or bearing in mind that the tactics which answered well enough when we had only Spaniards to deal with, almost invariably failed when an English force was in our front.

"The English generally held good defensive positions, carefully selected and usually on rising ground, *behind the crest of which they found cover for a good part of their men*. The *usual obligatory cannonade* would commence the operation, then, in haste, without duly reconnoitring the position, without ascertaining whether the ground afforded any facilities for lateral or turning movements, we marched straight forward, 'taking the bull by the horns'.

"When we got to about a thousand yards from the English line the men would begin to grow restless and excited: they exchanged ideas with one another, their march began to be somewhat precipitate, and was already growing a little disorderly. Meanwhile the English, silent and impassive, with ordered arms, loomed like a long red wall; their aspect was imposing—it impressed novices not a little. Soon the distance began to grow shorter: cries of 'Vive l'Empereur! En avant à la baïonnette!' broke from our mass. Some men hoisted their shakos on their muskets, the quick-step became a run: the ranks began to be mixed up: the men's agitation became tumultuous; *many soldiers began to fire as they ran*. And all the while the red English line, *still silent and motionless*, even when we were only 300 yards away, seemed to take no notice of the storm which was about to beat upon it.

"The contrast was striking. More than one among us began to reflect that the enemy's fire, so long reserved, would be very unpleasant when it did break forth. Our ardour began to cool: the moral influence (irresistible in action) of a calm which seems undisturbed as opposed to disorder which strives to make up by noise what it lacks in firmness, weighed heavily on our hearts.

"At this moment of painful expectation the English line would make a quarter-turn—the muskets were going up to the 'ready'. An indefinable sensation nailed to the spot many of our men, *who halted and opened a wavering fire*. The enemy's return, *a volley of simultaneous precision and deadly effect, crashed in upon us like a thunderbolt*. Decimated by it we reeled together, staggering under the blow and trying to recover our equilibrium. Then three formidable

Hurrahs terminated the long silence of our adversaries. With the third they were down upon us, pressing us into a disorderly retreat. But to our great surprise, they did not pursue the advantage for more than some hundred yards, and went back with calm to their former lines, to await another attack. We rarely failed to deliver it when our reinforcements came up—with the same want of success and heavier losses." [L'Armée française en 1867, Général Trochu; quoted by Sir Charles Oman in his *Wellington's Army*, 1912. The italics are the author's.]

The obvious question is why, if they were as good as that, did they not drive the French straight out of the Peninsula and over the Pyrenees, instead of taking six years? There is a complex of answers, but the most obvious and important one is that these highly trained infantry were rare animals and during a large part of the war there were at least ten French soldiers in the Peninsula to each one of them. They were only able to remain there because of a peculiar set of circumstances, such as existed in no other European theatre or possible theatre of war, and because they had a General who alone grasped the whole situation and was competent to deal with it. There were certain advantages in being a mere "sepoy General" in Spain which the great French Emperor overlooked.

It seems unlikely that General Wellesley had yet come to a complete understanding of the major strategical and tactical problems of war in the Iberian Peninsula that June night in London as he talked quietly with Croker. After all he had to go there and see for himself before that could happen. Nor was his confidence in himself and his men based in the least upon a new weapon he was to try out, Major Shrapnel's "explosive shell loaded with lead shot". He was thinking of what he had seen done by his troops in India and possibly of an engagement between French and English troops which had occurred at Maida in Calabria in 1806, and is now forgotten, being embalmed rather than commemorated by the "Maida Vale" of modern London. An English force of about 5,000 men under General Stuart had met a French force of about the same or larger numbers under General Régnier with startling results—they knocked out and captured 2,000 of the French with a loss of only 320. As the French scholar and pamphleteer Courier, who happened to be serving in Régnier's army, put it: "With our good troops, and with equal numbers, to be defeated and broken up in a few minutes—such a thing has not been seen since the Revolution." General Stuart did nothing with the victory his troops had won for him, and its significance was overlooked except by Wellesley and a handful of the British officers who were at Maida and afterwards became famous in the Peninsula—among them

Kempt, Colborne, Oswald, and Cole. One of Wellington's greatest
assets was that the enemy began by under-estimating him and his
troops, that each Marshal in turn learned his lesson by bitter experience and then became so over-cautious that he could be bluffed,
as Marmont was on the Coa, Soult in the Pyrenees, and Ney at
Quatre Bras.

Although it still had appalling defects of organization on the home
front, even the first nucleus of the Peninsular Army was a very
different body from the army over whose rear-guard Colonel Wesley of
the Thirty-third had watched so gloomily and anxiously in 1795. The
evils of political influence and purchase among the officers still
existed, but had been mitigated by the establishment of a Military
Training College in 1801 and by the valuable experience of active
service. Moreover, there was now more promotion from the ranks
(though Wellington himself disapproved of it), and it seems to have
been the practice to send out a certain number of blank commissions
over each big action. The career and achievements of Sir John Moore
can only be touched on incidentally here, but once and for all it must
be clearly stated that one of the important factors in Wellington's
success was the system of army training introduced and applied by
Moore.

The greatest improvement in the quality of the rank and file was due
to a measure of Lord Castlereagh, whereby militiamen of one year's
service and upwards were encouraged to volunteer for the regular
army and the resultant gaps were filled at once by ballot or draft.
Large bounties were paid—and nearly always spent immediately on
drink. But, as a number of Peninsular War diaries by men in the ranks
show, there were many men who had joined up for patriotic motives,
though there was still too high a proportion of blackguards and even
of criminals. Towards the end of the war when Wellington needed to
issue his own silver and gold coinage in France, he had no difficulty in
finding a score of expert coiners in the ranks of his own army. These
were the type of men responsible for the marauding which annoyed
their commander so intensely, and also those responsible for the
excesses at Badajoz, Ciudad Rodrigo, and San Sebastian. But this was
a necessary evil due to the fact that rogues and vagabonds would fight
for their country when the trading classes on the whole refused;
though it is true that there were a few Methodists in the ranks, even
among the officers. Military punishment was still harsh and bar-
barous, and was itself a fatally effective means of turning good soldiers
into bad ones.

Probably the greatest handicap to Wellesley if not to the army itself was the clique of old generals headed by the Duke of York at the Horse Guards. They exercised a despotic and unintelligent control of the army, dating their foolish ukases from "Stable Yard", whence the saying "Straight from the Horses' mouth". Having been conspicuous failures on active service, they exercised their old age in a diligent and pedantic insistence on obsolete methods and traditions which ought to have been abolished; while they and their defenders blamed all their errors on the civil powers whom they bullied and threatened into adopting their policies and then turned round and abused as "politicians". They particularly disliked younger and distinguished generals who had achieved unmistakable success in the field, especially Sir John Moore and Sir Arthur Wellesley. It seems incredible, but it is a fact that Sir Arthur had barely started on his expedition to Portugal when the Horse Guards insisted on superseding him by Sir John Moore, and putting over that excellent general two elderly Guardsmen, cronies of the Duke of York, Sir Harry Burrard and Sir Hew Dalrymple, both as senior as they were stupid. Sir Harry had been beaten in America (always a sure method of military favour from George III), while Sir Hew had apparently seen active service only with the Duke of York and happened at that moment to be buried from human ken as Governor of Gibraltar. The disastrous results of this intrigue will become apparent a little later. Meanwhile, the brilliant gentlemen of the Horse Guards gave Sir Arthur an army of 18,000 foot with only 390 cavalry (they had to fight a Napoleonic army of all arms!) while they forgot the transport entirely, and there would have been none if Sir Arthur had not managed to get Castlereagh's permission to take horses and drivers from Ireland!

On July 12, 1808, Sir Arthur Wellesley sailed from Cork for Corunna on a fast frigate, H.M.S. *Crocodile*, while the main body of his troops (about 10,000 strong) followed in slow convoy. He arrived at Corunna on July 20, 1808, a crucial date in his life and indeed in world history, for from that time on there were always British soldiers in the Peninsula, who in spite of infinite difficulties, disappointments, and opposition remained there until they at length transferred the war to the soil of France. He arrived three days before the battle of Baylen when the Galician Junta was feeling gloomy over a terrific defeat of Cuesta's army, which however they dishonestly represented to Sir Arthur as a great victory. Cheered by English supplies of arms, ammunition, and money, they gave the English General a good deal of optimistic and misleading information, including the really dangerous statement that Junot had only 15,000 men in Portugal, when in fact he had 26,000. And this was by far the best French army in the Peninsula, for 17 out of Junot's 22 battalions were veterans of the Grand Army.

After a visit to Oporto, where he found a belligerent bishop who promised to supply horses and mules, Sir Arthur landed his troops at the mouth of the Mondego River, just opposite Coimbra. (The reason he could do this at all was that a plucky student of Coimbra University had assembled some armed peasants, turned out the French garrison from Figueira da Foz, and then handed over the fort to British marines.) The landing occupied the time from August 1 to August 5, and on the last day General Spencer intelligently turned up from Andalusia with about 5,000 extra men, having sailed to join his colleague the moment he heard of Baylen. Meanwhile before even his army had begun to land, Sir Arthur heard of his triple supersession by the kindly gentlemen at the Horse Guards. He took it well, writing to Castlereagh (H.M.S. *Donegal*, August 1, 1808):

"All that I can say upon that subject is, that whether I am to command the army or not, or to quit it, I shall do my best to insure its success; and you may depend upon it that I shall not hurry the operations, or commence them one moment sooner than they ought to be commenced, in order that I may acquire the credit of the success."

It would be interesting to know what was Castlereagh's response to this austere magnanimity, which was an indirect rebuke to his shuffling capitulation before the forces of Stable Yard, but his reply (if written) does not seem to have been preserved. If we may judge from the former experience of the kind in India, Sir Arthur must have been very angry, however well he concealed the fact in writing, and certainly, even one who had eaten the King's salt might well be exasperated by a second supersession from command before he had even had a chance to make one mistake. But this time there was a chance to achieve a success, since some days must elapse before these other generals could arrive.

At any rate, he took no risks. The series of General Orders Wellesley issued to the troops are admirable in their prudence and foresight. George III's Protestant conscience would have been hurt if he had learned that in this Catholic country his troops were to present arms when the Host passed them, and "officers and soldiers not on duty are to halt and front it; the officers to pull off their hats, and the soldiers to put their hands to their caps". A greater difficulty was the scarcity of mules and horses ("let nobody ever prevail upon you to send a corps to any part of Europe, without horses to draw their guns," he warned Castlereagh) and even Portuguese bullock carts with their squealing axles were so hard to collect that the army could not march until August 9, 1808. But then it went off in the highest spirits, even though, as Rifleman Harris notes, the infantry carried "a weight sufficient to impede the free motions of a donkey" and the first day's march was hampered in addition by "a burning sun above our heads, and our feet sinking every step in hot sand". But soon the army was passing through the beautiful rich country of central Portugal, and everyone was still in high spirits except perhaps the Commander of the Forces, who had most of the worrying to do. On top of all other troubles, Wellesley was painfully learning about the generals of allied powers, who had evolved a scheme of behaviour peculiar to themselves. The Portuguese General Freire astonished and exasperated his British colleague by a luxuriant display of temperament—one day he and his army were entirely at Sir Arthur's orders, the very next he coolly appropriated for himself all the stores his government had collected for the English; then he demanded that England should supply his army with bread; and finally proposed an insane march inland directly away from the field of operations on which he had previously agreed. Eventually Sir Arthur had to move on Lisbon with no help from the Portuguese army except for a contingent of about two thousand—all he could be certain of feeding. Allied generals were to be a source of much discomfort and danger in the next few years, so it was perhaps as well to begin early.

Early in the evening of August 15 (1808) the advance-guard ran into French outposts in and near the pleasant little town of Obidos; and next day the action of Roliça was fought with a small French army of about 5,000 men under General Delaborde. Wellesley's chief difficulty with his army was to restrain their "indisciplined valour". At Obidos the riflemen outposts pressed on too far and would have been wiped out to a man if not rescued by a brigadier with some experience, and Sir Arthur's careful flanking movements at Roliça were wrecked by the lack of discipline of Colonel Lake who rushed the Twenty-Ninth Foot prematurely into action and cost the army his own life and 478 other casualties before the French were driven back with the loss of guns and prisoners. In spite of the small number of men involved, the Duke in later days would never allow that Roliça was only a skirmish. It was "one of our most important affairs" and "terrible hard work to drive off the French". In fact both sides could claim some advantage, for while the English had driven their enemies from two strong positions,

S

Corunna

Lugo

Santiago

Astorga

Sahagun

Vigo

Mejorga

Medina de
Rio Seco

Valladolid

Zamora

Oporto

Amarante

R. Douro

Medina
del Campo

Avintas

Salamanca

Coimbra

R. Mondego

Ciudad
Rodrigo

Figueira
da Foz

Guarda

40°

R. Tagus

40°

Leiria

Obidos

Rolica

Vimiero

Cintra

Torres Vedras

LISBON

Badajoz

1808-09 Campaigns in
**PORTUGAL &
WESTERN SPAIN**
Approximate line of march
Wellesley 1808 xxxxx
Moore 1808 ....
Battles & Combats ✗
Scale: miles

0   50   100

E

the French had fought a delaying action and had eluded an attempt to cut them off. But Wellesley's army was delighted by its success, and many a letter home enthusiastically described the clash of the fight, the glittering arms and bright uniforms of the troops manœuvring over the rolling mountainous country under the brilliant blue sky of Portugal. In that first action Sir Arthur did more than "give the French a beating"; he captured the heart and imagination of his own army.

Pushing on rapidly after the enemy, the army found food and bad luck awaiting them at Vimiero; they were reinforced by two fresh brigades, and their victorious General found Sir Harry Burrard anchored in the bay. It had been Sir Arthur's intention to push on immediately in the direction of Lisbon to meet Marshal Junot who had set out at once with about 13,000 men; but the leisurely successor absolutely forbade any movement whatsoever, in the grand tradition of Horse Guards Generals. So leisurely was this gentleman that he decided to stay on board ship for another day "to finish some letters", while Sir Arthur returned disconsolately to camp, and at six o'clock the next morning (August 21, 1808) he was writing to Castlereagh:

"You will readily believe, however, that this determination is not in conformity with my own opinion, and I only wish that Sir Harry had landed and seen things for himself with his own eyes before he had made it."

What a change in tone in a letter written next day!

"As I am the most fortunate of men, Junot attacked us yesterday with his whole force, and we completely defeated him!"

Not three hours after the gloomy letter to Lord Castlereagh was sealed a "cloud of dust was seen on the road from Torres Vedras", and this turned out to be not Sir Harry Burrard but Junot and the French army. When Sir Harry did arrive the battle was already successfully under way, and luckily he had sense enough not to interfere with the orders of his immediate inferior in military rank and infinite superior in military ability.

Unlike Roliça where the redcoats had to charge uphill and then beat off the counter-attack of greater numbers, Vimiero was a typical Wellingtonian position of the defensive kind. Junot recklessly sent his men to the attack in column formation, and the long red lines waited for them in that ominous silence which afterwards played such havoc with French nerves. On came the French in their clean white uniforms victory seemed in their grasp, when suddenly round after round of grape smashed into them from a hidden battery, a shattering volley of musketry rolled from the steady infantry, and with a startling cheer the red lines charged them with the bayonet in front and in the flank. The two French brigades reeled back in astonishment and dismay, leaving behind them the Colonel of the 82*ième* dead and Generals Charlot and Delaborde wounded. Junot galloped up to rally them and sent them back to the charge, led and protected this time by their grenadiers, "all fine-looking young men, wearing red shoulder-knots and tremendous-looking moustaches". This imposing appearance utterly failed to impress their enemies, for as the exulting British riflemen rapidly picked them off they shouted to each other: "There goes another of Boney's invincibles!" And as the survivors of Junot's brigades fell back a second time in even worse confusion, a legend died—with their "long-nosed bugger" to direct them the British infantry would never again believe, like the rest of Europe, that "Boney's armies are invincible".

The battle was not yet over. Junot sent Kellermann with the last of his reserves to reinforce the brigades of Brennier and Solignac, and to launch a desperate attack on Wellesley's extreme left, where there was terrific hand-to-hand fighting in and about the cemetery. Just as the French infantry were wavering, Sir Arthur galloped up to his handful of cavalry shouting, as he raised his hat to them: "Now, Twentieth, now's the time!" and the little group of horsemen charged with such dash that Junot and his staff only just eluded capture. It was the very crisis of the battle, and as the French hesitated or retired in confusion, smoke-blackened staff officers galloped to Sir Arthur's side for the expected permission to launch the final counter-attack and pursuit. Generals Fane and Anstruther could hardly hold back their stamping, shouting, swearing infantry, who saw the victory for which they had fought for three hours slipping from them. "Charge!" they shouted, "Damn it! Tell us to charge!"

A sudden change came over the battle, the leaden hand and brain of Sir Harry and the Horse Guards descended heavily on the army. Sir Arthur Wellesley was at the side of his new chief pleading eagerly for action: "Now's your time to advance, Sir Harry. The enemy are completely beaten, and we shall be in Lisbon in three days!" The man who had just won a decisive battle was brushed aside, and to its anger and bewilderment the victorious army was ordered to stand where it was instead of pursuing the beaten enemy. Staff officers crowded round the two disputing Generals, and as Sir Arthur at last turned away in disgust and annoyance they begged him for the orders he could no longer give.

"What do we do now, sir?" they asked eagerly.

"Shoot partridges."

"Shoot Sir Harry Burrard" might have been the most sensible order, though perhaps a little prejudicial to discipline and not much good, for next day he was superseded by the arrival of Sir Hew Dalrymple. It is hardly surprising that these two old gentlemen were bewildered and even frightened by the success which fate and Sir Arthur Wellesley had placed in their hands; they had never before known anything but defeat and the only successful generals they had ever met were those of the enemy and Sir Arthur. Nodding hoary heads they agreed that it would be dangerous to advance. Sir Arthur had been too rash, there must be no more of it, further advance would be dangerous, far too dangerous. . . .

They were interrupted by Sir Arthur, who came in with what even their leaden eyes noticed as something rather like a grin on his face. He came to tell them that General Kellermann had just ridden into the lines with a trumpeter and a white flag to ask for an armistice and terms for the evacuation of Portugal.

CHAPTER XII

Losing a Peace

ACCORDING to Charles Greville, who was an intimate friend of the Duke of York and for many years quite the reverse to the Duke of Wellington, there was a simple reason for the Royal Commander-in-Chief's hatred of the General who was sneeringly referred to at the Horse Guards as "the politician" or "the Beau" and by Napoleon's propagandists as "the sepoy"—the Duke of York wanted to command the Peninsular Army, in spite of the notorious fact that he had already lost two expeditionary forces. York's wounded vanity easily won the support of the other senior Horse Guards Generals, who had every reason for disliking a successful junior; and so there was complete success for the intrigue by which Wellesley was superseded in the midst of a brilliant campaign, at the very moment of victory. It was an achievement to chuckle over in military clubs for a generation.

Such intrigues succeed partly because the ordinary men and women fighting, suffering, and paying for a war cannot believe them possible, partly because the victim never has positive proof and could not use it in the midst of war if he did have it. They are apt to be boomerangs to those who plot them, though in the England of 1808 George III's favourite son could ignore both the anger of public opinion and the displeasure of the government. Yet it is curious that eight months after Vimiero, York was forced to resign his high office, not for this intrigue but through public revelations of his scandalous life and the sale of commissions and promotions by his mistress, Mrs. Clarke. The victims of the intrigue were Burrard and Dalrymple, who most probably knew nothing about it, and in their futile vanity imagined they had been appointed to supersede Arthur Wellesley because they were his superiors in military skill.

There was one hitch in the success of the intrigue, for the gentlemen at the Horse Guards had overlooked the speed of Wellesley's mental movements and the promptitude with which he generally got them carried out. In any case, they doubtless imagined that he would be hamstrung by being given only 300 cavalry and no transport whatever. They gave him five or six weeks to flounder helplessly and to send in protests (which of course would be suppressed) and then they would be able to tell the world that "Wellesley is no good" and "had to be superseded". If the superseding generals failed in Portugal, so much the better; the Horse Guards did not approve of a Peninsular War unless, of course, the Duke of York was in command. And the hitch in the intrigue was simply that they were, as usual, too slow, and that before their stuffed shirts arrived on the scene Wellesley had already won two battles and ensured the deliverance of Portugal.

That was the position when Kellermann glumly turned up with his flag of truce to ask for an armistice. Junot, Duke of Abrantes, was so rattled that he would have been glad to get out on almost any terms. But instead of meeting an army advancing rapidly in triumph, Kellermann came on an angry and gloomy army doing nothing; and instead of meeting the clear-eyed, swift-thinking leader who had smashed two French armies within a week, he came upon two old bumbles so dull and so foolish that they could not even conceal from him their secret fears and groundless apprehensions. Kellermann knew English and heard Sir Harry and Sir Hew mumbling to each other about "our perilous position" and "Sir John Moore will not arrive for several days" and the like; and with quick-witted French impudence he demanded and (over Sir Arthur's protests) obtained terms for the armistice he had never dreamed of when he left Lisbon. This was an unhappy hour for Sir Arthur, for now the two old gentlemen who had wrecked his war proceeded to give away the hard-won benefits of his peace. Why did Sir Arthur put his name to this armistice? In a private letter to Castlereagh, dated August 23, 1808, only two days after the battle, he says:

"Although my name is affixed to this instrument I beg that you will not believe that I negotiated it, that I approve of it, or that I had any hand in wording it. It was negotiated by the General himself in my presence and that of Sir Harry Burrard; and after it had been drawn out by Kellerman himself, Sir Hew Dalrymple desired me to sign it."

It must be emphasized that this armistice was quite distinct from the famous or infamous Convention of Cintra, which was so nicknamed in accordance with good journalistic ethics because it had nothing whatever to do with Cintra, and because Cintra happened to be one of the few Portuguese place names known in England. Sir Arthur Wellesley did *not* sign the Convention, which was a second treaty laying down the terms on which Junot was allowed to evacuate Portugal; Sir Arthur *did* sign the armistice which was a treaty arranging for a suspension of arms after the battle of Vimiero. It was the

Convention which caused such an explosion of rage in England, and for signing which Sir Arthur was bitterly blamed, although he never even saw it until after it was made public. Among the few people who took the trouble to find out what really happened were some who severely blamed Sir Arthur for signing the armistice—they held he should have refused and have appealed to the Government and public opinion. But the Government, in the shape of his personal friend the Minister of War, Castlereagh, had already let him down badly by allowing him to be so insultingly superseded; and what responsible man in his senses would dream of entrusting his honour and his career to the vagaries of a public opinion which was swayed in any direction by hired writers—above all Sir Arthur Wellesley, who would neither hire journalists nor see them? If he had refused point-blank to sign the armistice the gentlemen at the Horse Guards would gladly have used an act of disobedience as an excuse to wreck his career. The military reasons for agreeing to an armistice are set out in the letter to Castlereagh already quoted. The same letter contains an interesting paragraph about Wellesley's relations with Sir Hew and the difficulties of his situation:

"I will not conceal from you, however, my dear Lord, that my situation in this army is a very delicate one. I never saw Sir Hew Dalrymple till yesterday; and it is not a very easy task to advise any man on the first day one meets with him. He must at least be prepared to receive advice. Then I have been successful with the army, and they don't appear to me to like to go to anybody else for orders or instructions on any subject. This is another awkward circumstance which cannot end well; and to tell you the truth, I should prefer going home to staying here. However, if you wish me to stay, I will: I only beg that you will not blame me if things do not go on as you and my friends in London wish they should . . ."

There were clearly moments and days when it was hard to remember he was *nimmukwallah*, especially when Sir Hew, to get rid of him, suggested missions which would have been humiliating to a very junior officer and were of course refused. Sir Hew wanted to get Wellesley home and to take the credit for his army's past and problematic future achievements; but that army showed an obstinate attachment to its first commander. The generals who had served under Wellesley at Roliça and Vimiero sent him a present of plate and a rhetorical address of congratulation, and similar addresses were signed by every staff and field officer in the army.

This cannot have been pleasant for Sir Hew, who speedily contrived to get himself and his colleagues recalled to England in disgrace.

Among the terms of his Convention were some which touched on Portuguese interests, which Sir Hew had signed away without even consulting the Portuguese authorities. The Bishop of Porto, who had done so much to help the British army, wrote an angry letter of protest to London where nobody from the Prime Minister down knew the terms of the Convention, for Sir Hew during two whole weeks forgot to send a copy home. Impatience and curiosity seethed to boiling point and then, when at last the terms were known, exploded in an absurd hysteria of rage, for the Convention of Cintra, though not good, was by no means so unfavourable as was asserted. The height of absurdity was reached when Sir Arthur Wellesley arrived in London to find that he above all was blamed by newspapers and public for a Convention he had not even signed, and was refused credit for the victories which had made possible any convention at all! There were caricatures of all three Generals "showing the white feather" and hanging from gallows, and evidence on all sides that an enlightened public demanded another Admiral Byng episode—Sir Arthur Wellesley was to be shot as an encouragement to other English generals not to imitate him.

Sir Arthur ignored all insults, refused to make any statement to journalists, or to allow his friends to make one on his behalf. It was sufficient for him that he "felt always conscious of the confidence of the army". But when Castlereagh and King George tried to wriggle away from him in his unpopularity, the reaction was swift. Castlereagh hemmed and hawed about taking Sir Arthur to the King's levee in his carriage, it might be better postponed, His Majesty might be embarrassed, the King's Minister. . . . Looking the Minister straight in the eye Wellesley said: "I will either go to Court to-morrow, or never go to Court again."

He went.

Enlightened public opinion continued its blithe utterances. When the news came of Roliça, Lady Holland remarked that at any other time she would have positively welcomed it, but now feared it might give a temporary popularity to Canning. Lady Bessborough twittered that Sir Arthur Wellesley should have *thrown up* his commission and *cut* off his *right* hand before signing the Convention of Cintra—which of course he did not sign. And a bright but unnamed gentleman who had never heard a shot fired in war made a great reputation as a wit by repeating: "All *I* can say about the Convention is that *I* spell humiliation, 'Hewmiliation.' " . . .

Of course there was a court of inquiry, which met in November, 1808 and consisted of seven of the most mature generals obtainable, who after long deliberation brought in such cautious and colourless findings that Castlereagh was obliged to write them a sharp letter asking them to state what they did mean. What they meant was to commit themselves as little and as ambiguously as possible, and above all to shield the two senior officers. Long after, the Duke of Wellington used to relate with glee a little story about this inquiry, referring to Sir Brent Spencer who had been supplied in the first instance by the Horse Guards as "dry nurse" and "second-in-command", but had almost instantly been converted into a warm admirer and loyal supporter of the man he had been sent to thwart. But at the inquiry Spencer suddenly remembered his old associates and swore that during the battle of Vimiero he had seen "a reserve of French strongly posted on the heights of Torres Vedras"; which, if conceivably true, would excuse Burrard for not following Wellesley's urgings to advance. Wellesley said nothing when the statement was made, but when the session ended went up to Spencer:

"Why, Spencer, I never heard of this reserve before. How is it that you only mention it now?"

"Oh," said Spencer cheerfully, "poor Burrard has such a large family!"

The most sensible comment on the eager desire of the Whigs, the journalists, and the public to have Sir Arthur Wellesley shot naturally came from him. It was, he said, "rather hard, as I was the winner of the two battles which had raised the public hopes so high, and had nothing to do with the subsequent proceedings but as a subordinate negotiator under orders of my superior officers."

Imperfectly whitewashed by this aged if friendly tribunal, Sir Harry and Sir Hew retired for ever to the obscurity from which the Duke of York had withdrawn them to the discomfiture of everybody but the enemy. The Emperor remarked crisply that he had intended to court-martial Junot, but the English had spared him the pain of punishing an old friend by their imbecile conduct in prosecuting the victor; and so Junot retired, though temporarily. Temporarily, too, Sir Arthur retired—to Dublin Castle once more, where he took up the routine of coercing an irreconcilably hostile people and of "appeasing what gentlemen call their feelings" and other people (including Sir Arthur) bluntly called "appetite for pensions and places".

CHAPTER XIII

Douro and Talavera

DURING that autumn of 1808, while Sir Arthur scandalized aged generals by his contempt for their military opinions, or dealt with official correspondence in Dublin, great events were happening in Spain. The Emperor, as was his custom, had announced them beforehand to his obsequious Legislative Assembly:

"Great Britain, it is true, has landed some troops in the Peninsula and stirred up an insurrection; but this is a blessing in disguise. That Providence which has always watched over the armies of France has blinded the English government and caused them to send an army to the Continent where it is doomed inevitably to destruction. In a few days the Emperor will place himself at the head of his troops, and with the aid of God, will crown the true king of Spain in Madrid, and plant his eagles on the ramparts of Lisbon."

Much of this grandiose programme of aggression was carried out. Blinded by conceit the Spanish Junta and generals disregarded the military advice of the English Cabinet (which was the advice of Sir Arthur Wellesley) and did what the Emperor had scarcely dared to hope they might do—they threw their brave but untrained and unsteady armies against the Emperor and his veterans in a foolhardy offensive in which they were utterly defeated. The Emperor restored his brother Joseph to the palace in Madrid, but he certainly failed to plant his eagles on the ramparts of Lisbon, and could not even occupy Andalusia and the south. Carrying out a plan suggested to Castlereagh by Sir Arthur Wellesley, an English army under Sir John Moore struck north of Madrid in the direction of Burgos, the nerve centre of French communications. Stung by the danger and the insult, the Emperor suddenly developed the tigerish energy of earlier days, marched at the head of his army as he urged them on forced marches through the snow over the Guadarrama pass, and sent Moore scurrying back to safety and his transports at Corunna. But the Emperor's access of energy soon flagged; he frittered away a fortnight at Valladolid doing nothing, then hurried back to France to crush one of the endless conspiracies against him, then grew involved with the divorce of Josephine and the Austrian marriage—and, in short, never again returned to Spain where his presence was so indispensable to his cause and where, for lack of his leadership, legions of his veterans lost their lives.

On the surface, affairs in Spain seemed prosperous enough for the Emperor, if not for Joseph. Sir John Moore's army shed stragglers by the hundred as it grumbled and tramped its miserable way over the rocks and snow of Galicia. Soult was given charge of the pursuit with hints of plunder and rule in Portugal from his Imperial master, but he could not catch Moore until that General turned on the French and broke them at Corunna, falling himself in the hour of triumph. So exhausted were Soult's men by the long chase and this battle that, far from being able to overrun Portugal, they were only too thankful at being able to stumble into Oporto for rest and refreshment. Meanwhile Sir John Cradock lay in Lisbon with the nucleus of the army with which Wellesley had taken the city, the Spaniards were trying to reorganize their armies in the South, and guerrilla fighting broke out in any part of Spain as soon as the French grip relaxed; General Beresford, an old friend of Sir Arthur's from East Indian days, was busy drilling and organizing the Portuguese; and Sir Arthur himself had ideas and a plan. Besides, it was now certain that the Austrians would once again try their luck at fighting "Boney" in the spring of 1809.

The death of Sir John Moore at once made him a national hero; and those who had given him little enough support in his lifetime discovered him to be infallible when he was dead. Moore had said he did not believe a British army could be maintained permanently on the Continent and had coined the unfortunate phrase "littoral warfare", which was a more technical expression for "hit and run". He had also reported that the "frontiers of Portugal are indefensible". Since Moore had been a Whig and Wellesley was a Tory, it was clear that the Opposition would bitterly oppose the latter in his plan of defending Portugal and maintaining a British army in the Peninsula. Even Government was uncertain, particularly since Canning favoured a campaign in Andalusia based on Cadiz, the holding of which port would have been a great help to British trade. Only Castlereagh supported Arthur Wellesley and his plan. With 20,000 well-trained and well-equipped British troops (4,000 of them cavalry) with 30,000 newly trained and newly equipped Portuguese regulars and 40,000 militia, Sir Arthur believed he could hold Lisbon against any force the French could maintain in the field at that distance, and that "so long as the contest should continue in Spain" this army "would be highly useful to the Spaniards" and might "eventually decide the contest".

The Cabinet was convinced; an almost abject memorandum from them to the King secured his reluctant consent; and Sir Arthur prepared to return to Lisbon. Lady Wellesley gave a farewell party in Dublin and was sent off to Malvern with the children, while her husband very nearly disappeared prematurely from his command in a shipwreck. An agitated aide, who rushed into Sir Arthur's cabin and announced hysterically that all was over, received from Sir Arthur the stolid assurance: "In that case I shan't take off my boots"; and H.M.S. *Surveillante*, after all, landed them safely in Lisbon on April 22, 1809. But alas for hopes of Austrian success and a diversion of Napoleon's forces to the East! On that very day the Austrians were defeated at Eckmühl; exactly three weeks later Napoleon entered Vienna, and towards the end of May came Aspern and Essling, which cost the Emperor 20,000 casualties, but shook the Austrian army badly. On July 6 Napoleon put an end to the war by the brilliant if expensive battle of Wagram. To keep the scale of operations clear, it should be said that Napoleon took 165,000 men into the battle of Wagram; while at the same date his armies in the Peninsula numbered 280,000, soon to be raised to 350,000.

Luckily the slow communications of that age prevented these dismal tidings from reaching Wellesley in the first and energetic weeks of his second campaign in Portugal. The future being hidden (as a rule, mercifully) from men, Sir Arthur did not realize as he landed in Lisbon that he had five years of fighting ahead; and who would have guessed that "so young a Lieutenant-General" would return home as Field-Marshal and a Duke? It is not the habit of prosaic men of action to dwell on such fantasies. What weighed on Sir Arthur was the problem whether he should first attack Soult in north Portugal or Victor in Spain. Scruples about superseding Sir John Cradock were fortunately removed by learning that Sir Arthur had arrived in the nick of time to prevent that thunderbolt of war from evacuating his army in a panic, although the nearest French outposts were more than two hundred miles away.

A sudden gust of briskness and expectation pervaded the hitherto languid British troops in Lisbon as they felt once more the energetic impact of the will which had directed them at Roliça and Vimiero. Within ten days Wellesley had accomplished more than had been done in Portugal since he handed over the command to Sir Harry and Sir Hew. Cradock was ceremoniously consigned to Gibraltar; the decision was made to attack Soult; and the army was concentrated on Coimbra where he reviewed them on May 7 (1809). Wellesley found he had 16,000 British, 11,000 Portuguese, half of whom had never been in action. He had not enough light infantry, he was deficient in artillery, particularly in horse-artillery and he still had no engineers and no siege-guns. With this force he proposed to attack Soult's 23,000 veterans, who held a strong position on the far side of the deep, swift, and wide Douro. But in warfare each side has its special troubles. Soult's were that guerrillas had virtually cut him off from his base and the other French armies, while he had just discovered an alarming political conspiracy in his own camp.

Once more, as its diarists testify, a British army set off in high spirits, and after some skirmishing with rear-guards which netted about a hundred prisoners, found itself halted on the south bank of the Douro with the bridge blown up, no fords, and all boats apparently destroyed or removed. So confident was Marshal Soult that he had confronted Wellesley with an impassable obstacle that he even neglected to post guards on the river, and instead sent patrols towards the sea while he himself occupied a large house with a splendid view of the Atlantic. The English always had come by sea, and no doubt they would be obliging enough to do so this time.

Military operations now came to resemble an adventure story with a smug moral—the Idle and the Industrious Generals. Next morning while the Marshal was still fast asleep and his staff were dallying over a leisurely breakfast, Wellesley had already reconnoitred from the Serra Convent, had sent off Major-General Murray with a detachment to cross the river at Avintas, and ordered officers to find at least one boat. His immediate staff could see for themselves on the opposite bank of the river a large building (the Seminary) surrounded by a wall with only one gate, a position which could be held with only a few troops if they could somehow be got across, while all the approaches were commanded by British artillery skilfully hidden on the Serra heights. While staff officers, bred in the best Horse Guards tradition, were gloomily proving to each other that no boats could be found to cross and that even if they were found the "operation was too risky" they heard the profane voice of Wellesley exclaim calmly:

"By God! Waters has done it!"

And, by God! Waters had. Waters was a staff captain, one of Wellesley's young men, and he had intelligently discovered a Portuguese barber with a skiff hidden in the rushes. Promptly requisitioning skiff, barber, peasants, and a prior, Waters crossed the Douro and began slowly bringing back four large empty barges. As the staff watched breathlessly, Sir Arthur sent word to the Third Foot (the

Campaigns in
PORTUGAL &
WESTERN SPAIN
Approximate lines
of march, 1809
Against Soult ×××××
   ,,   Victor ......
Battles & Combats ✗
Scale: miles

0   50   100

Buffs) to advance to the water's edge under cover in readiness to cross at once. For nearly an hour the barges plied to and fro, the Buffs were over and fortifying the walls, General Paget had crossed, more troops were crossing, when suddenly a galloping horse clattered into the court-yard of Soult's house, the Marshal abruptly awoke and his staff were electrified into action by the most unpleasant news that the English were crossing the Douro.

The first French attack was made over the open, and vanished under the shrapnel of the 18 guns hidden in the convent grounds; and the English forces in the Seminary steadily increased. After three hours of fighting the French had achieved nothing, and the Marshal (forgetting the Portuguese civilians and their hatred of the French) called up the regiments from the quays. Instantly every available boat was manned by patriotic citizens, and in a surprisingly short time they had ferried over the British Twenty-Ninth and the Portuguese Sixteenth regiments. Soult saw the game was up, and his army saved him the trouble of a decision by frankly running away, "throwing down their knapsacks and arms, so that we had only the trouble of making many prisoners every instant, all begging for quarter and surrendering with great good humour". Charles Stewart (Castlereagh's brother) charged the fugitives with a handful of cavalry, but Murray hung back in a half panic, and as usual with a British army the men and officers were slack in following up; and so. far too many of the French escaped. There was a certain satisfaction apparent nevertheless when General Wellesley and his staff sat down to the excellent dinner and vintage wines which had been prepared for Marshal Soult and his epicures.

Late that night (May 12, 1809) Soult was staggered to learn that Beresford and his Portuguese had driven Loison out of his position at the bridge of Amarante and were thus across this main line of the French retreat. Up to this moment Soult's conduct had been feeble, unworthy of a Marshal of the Empire; but he met this apparently final disaster with magnificent spirit and energy. Brushing aside all hints of surrender, he ordered the immediate destruction of all his artillery, ammunition, transport wagons, plunder, and every kind of impedimenta, and made a dash for Galicia by almost unknown mountain tracks. The Marshal shed prisoners and horses as Moore's army had lost them, and before he brought the bulk of his ragged starving army to safety from the pursuit he had lost upwards of 6,000 men, while he left behind 58 guns in Oporto in addition to a large unknown number destroyed. Thus, within four weeks of Wellesley's landing in Lisbon, not a Frenchman remained in Portugal except as a prisoner or a fugitive; and this had been achieved at the expense of no more than 500 casualties.

The dark spot in this otherwise cheerful picture was that the bulk of Soult's army had been allowed to escape, an error or unavoidable failure which caused plenty of trouble later. Yet Wellesley had held out no hopes of any spectacular capture and indeed had warned Hookham Frere (letter of May 9, 1809): "I am afraid it is not in my power, with the force which I have at my disposal, to prevent him (i.e. Soult) retreating into Spain." Perhaps the most cheerful omen was the confidence engendered in the army, particularly the hitherto untried Portuguese, who gave Wellesley the nickname of "Douro" from this the first victory he gave them. He on his part was or professed to be equally pleased with them, and snubbed General Mackenzie for disparaging them:

"You are in error in supposing that the Portuguese corps will not fight. One battalion has behaved remarkably well with me; and I know of no troops that could have behaved better than the Lusitanian Legion did at Alcantara the other day. . . ." [Letter of May 21, 1809.]

It was just as well that commander and army had the encouragement of these early successes, for they needed all their mutual confidence to carry them through the trials and disappointments of the next eighteen months, which the Duke always admitted was "the most trying part" of the war. Yet when Sir Arthur called off the now hopeless pursuit of Soult and began concentrating on Abrantes for an advance into Spain even his cautious and realistic temperament seemed to have every reason for hope. He had not then learned the horrors of co-operating or trying to co-operate with Spanish generals, not yet perceived the full extent of the delays, disappointments, and discomfiture which awaited the commander who expected punctual and effective support from Spanish and Portuguese Juntas. Not until August (1809) did Wellesley learn that his Austrian allies had failed and that the grand British diversion to Walcheren (which had starved his own army of supplies and reinforcements) had achieved little but the infection of many fine regiments with malaria. In May and June 1809 the situation looked very hopeful. The Emperor, it could reasonably be assumed, would be pinned down in Austria and unable to send any help to Spain; the Walcheren expedition might succeed in spite of its leaders; thanks to Moore, Andalusia was still in Spanish hands with the intact but raw armies of Cuesta and Vanegas; Soult and his men seemed out of the picture for months to come; Ney's corps was involved with Romana and his Galicians, Suchet was in a mess in Aragon, and Victor while theoretically threatening central Spain was actually in a panic about a possible joint attack from Wellesley and Cuesta.

This was exactly what was planned, and not badly planned, in spite of the exasperating amount of discussion demanded by Spanish pride and Spanish lethargy. Vanegas was to threaten Madrid with 25,000 Spaniards, and if possible retake it, in any event hold up any reinforcements to Victor. Wellesley with his 20,000 British, but no Portuguese, was to join Cuesta's 35,000 and march on Madrid from the west. Trant and Wilson with their guerrillas would supposedly look after the left flank, and simultaneous guerrilla disturbances would be evoked in all the provinces.

Such were the hopes; but annoyances began before ever Sir Arthur left Portugal. The Government in London failed to send him cash to purchase supplies and transport animals. The troops, particularly the Irish, started plundering and molesting the inhabitants. No reinforcements came as promised. The Spanish Junta promised everything, but it was always for *mañana*, for nothing ever turned up to-day. And then when at last the army managed to move into Spain, Sir Arthur made the acquaintance of that perplexing, and anachronistic phenomenon, El Capitan-General Don Gregorio de la Cuesta, and was forced to the exasperated comment:

"I can only say, that the obstinacy of this old gentleman is throwing out of our hands the finest game that armies ever had."

Nor did a closer acquaintance with the septuagenarian and his army kindle Sir Arthur's military enthusiasm. The guides who were to bring him to inspect the Spaniards at Almaraz ominously lost their way, and the inspection had to be made by torch-light. Even by this deceptive and romantic illumination the spectacle was more picturesque than reassuring. Wellesley noted at once that the men were mostly too young and the generals far too old. Cuesta himself was so decrepit that he had to be held on his horse by pages, and in a council of war he patriotically but fatuously refused to discuss plans in the common language of French, and through interpreters contributed nothing to the discussion but the simple though inoperative word, "No".

Riding back next day with his Quartermaster-General, Sir Arthur shook his head doubtfully over their experiences and delivered himself of this prophetic utterance on Cuesta's army:

"I'm sure I don't know what we are to do with these people. Put them behind stone walls, and I dare say they would defend them, but to manœuvre with such a rabble under fire, is impossible. I am afraid we shall find them an encumbrance rather than otherwise."

Sir Arthur was greatly worried about his left flank (but not, as events proved, sufficiently worried) and asked Cuesta to send out a flank guard of 10,000. Cuesta refused, hesitated, eventually sent 600. No supplies came from the Junta, and the British were already half starved. With maddening persistence the Spanish generals utterly refused to move when action was possible, and then threw their half-trained levies into grandiose actions when the favourable moment had passed and crushing defeat was inevitable. On July 22 (1809) they came suddenly on Victor with only 22,000 men near Talavera, and Wellesley at once entreated Cuesta to seize this golden opportunity for a combined attack next morning. Until midnight the hidalgo could not make up his mind and then at last consented. Wellesley had his men in position at 3 a.m., but not a Spaniard could be found and when at last General Cuesta was discovered (reclining on cushions beside his couch) he had changed his mind—he would not fight that day! Next day, when it was too late and Victor had escaped to join King Joseph and Sebastiani, Cuesta came up burning for the fray and insisted on pursuit when pursuit was becoming dangerous. "I am afraid he will get himself into a scrape," Sir Arthur commented after refusing to go with him. "If the enemy should discover we are not with him, he will be beaten or must retire. In either case he may lose all the advantages which might have been derived from our joint operations and much valuable time. . . ."

Exact but helpless prescience! Cuesta rushed towards Madrid only to learn on July 25 (1809) that he had run into a concentration of 55,000 enemies, Vanegas having totally failed to carry out his part of the manœuvres. By a strange but lucky mischance, Cuesta did not launch his hopeless attack but retreated on his ally who was grimly starving at Talavera. Even then he left most of his army in a situation of extreme peril during the whole night of July 26, merely because Wellesley had suggested to him the only way to extricate it; and the reason the Spaniards escaped was because the French never dreamed that any general would make such a blunder. But Talavera was the place to stand if the allied armies were to do anything, and after infinite arguing (Cuesta afterwards made the absurd boast that "he made the Englishman get down on his knees and beg") the Spanish General agreed to fight and agreed to dispose his army in a strong position so steep and broken up by olive gardens and stone walls that the Spaniards could come to little harm if they kept their posts and might even intimidate the French if they refrained from running away.

This, unfortunately, was exactly what they could not do. In the late afternoon of July 27 (1809) Sir Arthur had been forced to gallop out himself and rescue one of his retiring advance brigades which had got into a mess, and then thought he had better see what was happening to the Spaniards. He reached their positions just as some of Victor's light cavalry and horse-artillery made a demonstration; whereupon the Spanish infantry fired a tremendous volley which did no harm to the enemy whatsoever and then, in the words of Sir Arthur himself:

"Nearly 2,000 ran off . . . (not 100 yards from the place where I was standing) who were neither attacked, nor threatened with an attack, and who were frightened only by the noise of their own fire; they left their arms and accoutrements on the ground, their officers went with them. . . . They are really children in the art of war, and I cannot say that they do anything as it ought to be done, with the exception of running away and assembling in a state of nature." [Letter to Castlereagh, August 25, 1809.]

This must have been cold comfort for the unfed British troops who fought such odds at Talavera for so many hours. After dark on July 27, Victor made a night attack on Hill's corps, which was beaten back with loss after nearly capturing that efficient and popular English General. Against the advice of King Joseph and Marshal Jourdan, Victor attacked again next morning. Sir Arthur was there and ordered the regiments to retire behind the slope and to lie down, a manœuvre fatally misinterpreted by the French Marshal as a retreat. His over-confident men were smashed by volleys and thrust back by the bayonet, and a single division lost 1,300 of its men in forty minutes. It was after this that the famous episode occurred when thirsty men on both sides drank from the dark pools of the little Portina River which flowed between their opposing lines, and both sides fraternized and carried off their wounded.

The main French assault came at 2.30 p.m., on July 28 then 30,000 Frenchmen attacked along the whole British line. Sherbrooke with the Guards carried their triumphant counter-attack too far, suffered heavily, and would have lost the battle if Wellesley had not been on the spot and instantly remedied the mistake. About this time he was hit by a spent bullet, but did not even dismount, and listened with an unmoved face when they told him how Anson's brigade of cavalry on the extreme left had destroyed itself by charging into a deep ravine where men and horses lay heaped in death and agony. As if that were not horror enough, towards evening the long dry grass on the Cerro de Medellin caught fire, and the British wounded, their heads thrust in their haversacks, were burned or suffocated to death. But every French attack was beaten off, and, two hours before dawn on July 29, a weary, very hungry, but not disheartened little army stood to arms waiting for fresh attacks which never came. Joseph and Jourdan and Victor had had enough, and under cover of darkness had slipped away. The redcoats were down to third rations that day, but they found strength for a round of cheers as Craufurd and his Light Brigade joined them, after a forced march of forty-three miles in twenty-two hours. Indeed they had every reason for cheering. Talavera had no strategical results, but, in the actual fighting 16,000 British troops with 36 guns had met and defeated 26,000 French veterans with 80 guns, losing 5,000 men to 7,000 of Victor's.

The victory though "imperfect" was popular in England. De Quincey has left us a vivid description of how the news of Talavera was carried all over the island by the mail-coaches. We can imagine the great crowds in London cheering each of the bright red coaches as it left with "horses, men and carriages dressed in laurels and flowers, oak-leaves and ribbons", and feel something of the excitement which ran with the coaches along the open roads—"young and old understand the language of our victorious symbols, and rolling volleys of sympathising cheers ran along with us, behind us, before us". Vimiero, Oporto, Talavera—the British had waited long and wearily for a general who would lead their armies as successfully as Nelson had led their navies. They were sick of muddle and defeat, and Talavera (though no Waterloo) was a triumphant set-off to Walcheren. The Government was quick to seize the opportunity of sharing in the popularity won by its General. Lord Liverpool, the Minister of War, wrote him almost obsequiously (August 20, 1809):

"I congratulate you most sincerely on your most brilliant and decisive victory. The feelings of your friends on the occasion you will easily conceive, and I can assure you that ample justice is done you by all descriptions of persons in this country. It is universally felt that you have raised the British military character in the eyes of all Europe to a height which it has certainly not attained since the war of the Duke of Marlborough; and even those who look with most despondency to the result of the struggle in Spain are ready to admit that your victory has added strength and security to the country at home. . . ."

After more praise to the same effect and an assurance of "large discretionary powers" to "Lord Wellesley and yourself" (for Richard was now at last second fiddler to Arthur as ambassador to Spain) the

letter winds up with the information: "I have just had the satisfaction of receiving directions to prepare the warrant for your creation
as a Viscount and Baron."

And so Baron Douro of Wellesley and Viscount Wellington of
Talavera take the place of Sir Arthur Wellesley in history. It does not
appear that elevation to the peerage made the slightest difference to
him; and it is an amusing fact that the first time he signed the "Wellington" of his new dignity was in a letter which asked: "Would the
Regency give me leave to have a *chasse* at Villa Viçosa?" For by late
autumn they were back in Portugal once more, with Wellington grimly
determined never again to trust the promises of a Spanish Junta, never
again to co-operate with a Spanish army unless he could command it.
After Talavera everything seemed to go wrong all at once. Intelligence
service failed, so that a French field force of 185,000 was represented to
Wellington as only 125,000, while a combined force under Ney,
Mortier, and Soult were on his flank and rear almost before he heard
of them. Cuesta abandoned Talavera along with the 2,000 British
wounded, and soon after lost nearly all the French guns which his
allies had captured in the battle and had presented to him. Above all,
the Spanish Junta either would not or could not carry out their
promises of supplies, and Wellington's army was starving.

"For bread we took the corn of the fields," says a Rifle Brigade diarist, "and,
having no proper means of winnowing and grinding it, were obliged . . . to
rub out the ears between our hands and pound them between stones to make
dough . . . from which wretched practice we christened the place Dough Boy
Hill. . . ."

So much for the men. An officer of the same unit has left his record:

"After our stay at Talavera, during which we nearly starved, the army commenced its retreat, passing the bridge of Arzobispo in the most correct and
soldier-like manner, our Brigade forming the rear-guard. The army retired on
Deleytosa, the Light Brigade remaining in a position so as to watch the bridge
of Almaraz. Here for three weeks we nearly starved and our position received
the name of Dough Boy Hill. . . . We had a few dollars and as I could speak
Spanish I rode into the lines of the Spanish troops where I could always purchase some loaves of bread at a most exorbitant price."

No wonder the Commander of the Forces thundered at the Junta:
"I positively will not move, nay, more, I will disperse my army, till I am
supplied with provisions and means of transport as I ought to be."
But in spite of its sufferings and oft-repeated threats of dispersal, the
British army still remained in Spain, in and about Badajoz where they
could draw some supplies from the more friendly ally, Portugal. The

men suffered from dysentery and from "Guadiana fever" (malaria), which nobody at that time connected with the swarms of "mosquittos". As the news of Walcheren and the Austrian disasters came in, the dreary picture was not lightened by the dissolution of the British Government and a pistol duel between Canning and Castlereagh. The new Prime Minister was a lawyer, Spencer Perceval, who later on achieved the strange distinction of being murdered in the House of Commons in mistake for somebody else; Lord Liverpool took Castlereagh's place, and Canning gave way to Richard Wellesley. Perturbed by these mutations (for hitherto Castlereagh alone had been intelligent enough to support him unswervingly) Wellington posted down to Cadiz to see his brother before that dignified gentleman left for London. What they said to each other is not known, but it is known that the Spanish Junta, accustomed to generals covered with gold lace, feathers, and gorgeous escorts, were shocked by the sight of a Commander of the Forces travelling post alone with his military secretary, dressed in a plain grey frock-coat and a cocked hat covered with waterproof silk. It is also known that closer acquaintance with this Junta, who had already caused him much trouble, so gravely disturbed the English General that he immediately ordered his army to retire into Portugal.

Alas! remembering nothing and learning nothing, the Junta had determined on another general offensive, just at the exquisitely inappropriate moment when the Emperor had concluded a peace with Austria. Thoroughly alarmed by the rumours which reached him (for the Junta did not confide in him) Wellington refused to allow either his own or the Portuguese army to co-operate in wild offensive schemes doomed to failure:

"The consequence of undertaking such a plan," Wellington wrote, "would be that after a battle or two, and some brilliant actions by some, and the defeat of others, and the loss of many valuable officers and soldiers, the allies would be obliged to resume again the defensive positions they ought never to have quitted."

That was written on September 25, 1809. On October 18, the Duque del Parque attacked and beat the French at Tamames, the first Spanish victory in the field since Baylen. A month later (November 19, 1809) General Areizaga (Cuesta's successor in rank and incompetence) fought the disastrous battle of Ocaña, losing 4,000 men as casualties, 14,000 as prisoners, 50 guns, and 30 colours. Ten days later the victorious Del Parque was surprised and defeated at Alba de

Tormes, losing 3,000 men, 9 guns, and 5 colours, while his French opponent lost only 300 men! Thus, as Wellington had predicted, the ill-judged, ill-timed, and ill-prepared Spanish offensive began with a delusive success, and ended with crushing defeats which left all southern Spain open to the enemy.

The Junta had believed Wellington's withdrawal was due to personal pique and a fit of the sulks, such as they were accustomed to in their own generals, and to placate him they had offered Spanish chargers, the rank of Captain-General, and a force of 12,000 inefficient recruits. He accepted the first, referred the second to the pleasure of His Royal Highness, and refused the third. They never confided to him the plans of their offensive—his condemnation of any offensive at that particular time quenched that—but this did not prevent them from informing their own generals that Wellington was co-operating fully in the offensive or from blaming him afterwards for the failure he had so accurately predicted! Seeing a chance to sow mistrust between allies, the French propagandists took up the motive eagerly, sneered at Wellington for "doing nothing" while the gallant Spaniards died, and, hoping above all to get rid of the one competent general on the other side, the *Moniteur* propagandists professed to ask nothing better than the continuation of the "sepoy General" in command. It would, they said, greatly facilitate the French task of "driving the frightened Leopard into the sea." The pro-French party in Parliament obediently took up these points, and under date November 12, 1809, we find the Creevey diary noting: "The Wellesleys will now be beat if they are attacked properly; upon which I fire into our leaders for their meanness in not having attacked them long ago."

CHAPTER XIV

Bussaco and Torres Vedras

WERE the sepoy General and his army "doing nothing" in Portugal in 1809–1810? Well, as we have seen, he asked for and obtained permission to hunt foxes; and the fatigue parties who fed broken biscuits to his hounds were glad to steal some of the pieces to make up for the hungry Talavera days—an episode of which Lord Byron has made a most dishonest use. The officers, as we learn from one of them, were encouraged to go shooting; and there was a sudden double fashion for horse-racing and extravagant jockey clothes. Nor can it be said that Lord Wellington was in any sense a spit and polish martinet of the Horse Guards breed:

> "We had no unnecessary drilling," writes Lieutenant Grattan of the Connaught Rangers, "nor were we tormented by that greatest of all *bores* to an officer at any time, but particularly on service, uniformity of dress. The consequence was that every duty was performed with cheerfulness; the army was in the highest state of discipline; and those gentlemen who had, or fancied they had, a taste for leading the fashion, had now a fine opportunity for bringing their talents into play. . . . Lord Wellington was a most indulgent commander; he never harassed us with reviews, or petty annoyances, which so far from promoting discipline, or doing good in any way, has a contrary effect. A corporal's guard frequently did the duty at headquarters; and every officer who chose to purchase a horse might ride on a march. Provided we brought our men into the field well appointed, and with sixty rounds of good ammunition each, he never looked to see whether their trousers were black, blue or grey. . . ."

It should be added that this easy standard was applied only to veteran battalions which had shown their mettle in bloody fights. The rookies and the Portuguese had plenty of drill, exercise, and inspection; and their officers were liable to sudden eagle swoops of inspection, followed by memoranda of a sarcasm so withering it left the recipients feeling like old dried-up applies.

But if "the Beau" was not even soldiering in Portugal, what was he doing? First of all, and unlike almost everyone else on his side of the struggle, he had been doing some hard military thinking. He had maintained that Portugal was defensible, and now at forty, for the first time in his military career, he had to concentrate on the problem of fighting defensive campaigns. In October 1809 he went down to

Lisbon, spent some days riding round with Colonel Fletcher, the commander of his engineers, and on October 20 issued twenty-one specific orders, the results of which are known as the Lines of Torres Vedras.

A description of the famous Lines, with the redoubts, inundations, abattis, walls, escarpments, signal system, the many hundred guns, belongs to the military historian; and here, as in everything else relating to the Peninsular War, Oman is the man. But, granting that the Torres Vedras defences, on which thousands of Portuguese laboured during a year or more, made Lisbon more or less impregnable, what were the other factors on which Wellington counted? So exact was his foresight that the order for the Lines went out exactly one year before Masséna arrived in front of them with his army of 60,000 men. But what Wellington counted on was a complex of factors in which the surprise fortification of the Lisbon area was only one. It is worth summarizing them briefly to understand the success of a defence which everyone else, from the Emperor and the British Cabinet downwards, thought was impossible:

(1) Command of the sea—which enabled Lisbon to be fed indefinitely; while, if the worst came to worst, the English and Portuguese armies could be embarked on transports, to fight somewhere else.

(2) The training of at least 25,000 Portuguese regulars to a state of discipline and efficiency when a Portuguese brigade could be effectively linked with each British division.

(3) The delaying of the French advance by every possible means short of a battle, and by a battle only under most favourable circumstances or at a breaking point of government and civilian morale "clamouring for action".

(4) Starvation as a weapon of war. The ancient Portuguese law of the *Ordenanza* was to be revived, under which on the approach of an enemy all the men became militia, all the inhabitants left their houses and retired on Lisbon, destroying all food stocks on the way.

(5) The Portuguese militia were to hang on the flanks and rear of the invading army, cutting its communications, picking off stragglers and foraging parties, harassing in every way possible.

(6) The continued resistance of the Spanish people. Since the dispersal of most of the regular armies, there had been a great increase in guerrilla activity.

(7) Time.

Time, that was the most uncertain and most dangerous of all the complex of factors, and Wellington could not know that the Emperor had made the decision, fatal to himself, that in the Spanish War time was on his side. Wellington did know that Napoleon was not the Duke of York, and was apt to move with lightning speed and efficiency. More than once he doubted if he would have time enough to prepare his bag of surprise tricks; and hence the variations in mood traceable in his letters. Before the battle of Ocaña (November 1809) he had been cheerful, informing Liverpool that the enemy cannot "make an attack upon Portugal" unless "the Spanish armies should meet with some great misfortune". Even after that disaster he still thought prospects "by no means hopeless, notwithstanding the defeat of Areyzaga". In December he moved his headquarters to Coimbra, and on January 19, 1810, moved them north to Viseu. On that very same day Joseph and Soult made the strategic error of invading Andalusia instead of Portugal. Albuquerque with 10,000 men raced into "impregnable but ungarrisoned" Cadiz just ahead of the French, and "saved the cause of Spain in the south".

This event which should have cheered Wellington depressed him— he had counted on a more successful resistance in Andalusia. On January 31, 1810, we find him asking Lord Liverpool for instructions —was he "to defend this country to the last" or "turn my mind seriously to the evacuation"? (Evidently somebody was betraying Wellington's secret correspondence to the Whigs, for Creevey reports that Lord Hutchinson saw "his *last* despatch . . . written under the greatest possible fright, and [he] has pressed the Government for positive instructions. . . ." Lord Hutchinson, according to Creevey, said orders had gone to evacuate Portugal.) But all this was premature, for "the fright" happened in January, and it was not until April 17, 1810, that Masséna, *alias* Duc de Rivoli, Prince d'Essling, and *enfant gâté de la victoire*, was appointed to command the army of Portugal, with a nominal strength of 140,000 (86,000 effectives)— surely sufficient to "annihilate" 20,000 redcoats.

The Whigs made the most of the situation in the debates in Parliament. Mr. Ward thought that:

"Lord Wellington's exploits at Talavera left the cause of Spain as desperate as they found it, and in their consequences resembled not victories, but defeats."

Mr. Whitbread opined that:

"We held our ground in [Portugal] just at the will of the French Emperor, and at his option he would drive us out of it. But what could we expect from our present ministry?"

Day by day, week by week, month by month, work went on at the Lines; and Wellington gradually recovered his optimism. In February he had asked for the Fleet and an increase of transport tonnage, but on the last day of March he was positively drolling to the Secretary of the Horse Guards:

" . . . if I am in a scrape, as appears to be the general belief in England, although certainly not my own, I'll get out of it."

A few days later he was writing Lord Liverpool even more confidently: "I shall fight a battle to save the country," in spite of the "very bad" news of the Austrian marriage. Late in April Ney's men moved lethargically on the fortress of Ciudad Rodrigo, but obeying the Emperor's orders "to proceed methodically" they did not begin the siege until June 2. Masséna himself turned up next day, but so "methodically" was the siege carried out that Rodrigo did not fall until July 9—nearly a year since Talavera, and the great "Army of Portugal" had not even crossed the Portuguese frontier! Without knowing it, Masséna and the Emperor were playing Wellington's game, and as early as April 20 he wrote home cheerfully: "I do not know whether the state of tranquillity in which affairs have been for some time is advantageous to the French, but I know that it is highly so to us. The British army is increasing in strength daily . . ." On June 15, 1810, Colonel Fletcher reported the Lines "nearly completed", reinforcements arrived from England, and the regular Portuguese troops were brigaded with the British—"un tas de coquins" the Emperor had called them contemptuously, but Wellington liked the look of them. The day would come when he would call them "the fighting cocks of the army".

On July 20 (1810) Masséna "methodically" crossed the frontier and sat down to besiege Almeida. This fortress was meant by Wellington to hold out, and consequently had been well garrisoned and supplied. There was a scuffle on the Coa between Robert Craufurd's Light Division and Ney's advance-guard, both sides making mistakes and suffering losses; and then the French lines closed round Almeida late in August. A broken powder barrel carried at night from the magazine to the rampart laid a train which by the one chance in ten million was exploded by a bursting shell before it was noticed, killing five hundred of the garrison and wrecking every house in the town, "like the bursting of a volcano". Almeida had to surrender (August 28), and this disaster, added to the fact that Wellington had refused to risk his army and the whole Allied cause in a probably futile effort to save Rodrigo, exploded a volcano of criticism against him. Spaniards protested hotly; Portuguese looked glum, and a few even went over to the enemy; the French sneered at the sepoy General's "incompetence and timidity"; Whig members of Parliament croaked that "the Beau" would risk anything for the sake of self-glory in a battle; and patriotic newspapers published "accounts, not only of the numbers, but of the positions occupied by this army". Harassed by all these troubles, the Allied Commander stood aghast at the names of the generals and colonels suddenly forced on him at this crisis by the Horse Guards. Like Lord Chesterfield he tried to see the bright side: "I only hope that when the enemy reads the list of their names he trembles as I do"; adding, "I pray God and the Horse Guards to deliver me from General Lighthume and Colonel Sanders".

"Methodically," as the Emperor had ordered, Masséna's men advanced from Almeida; and as they slowly moved forward his troops discovered with surprise at first, then with anger, and finally with something like dismay, that they were entering a devastated country whose inhabitants had vanished. Towns and villages and hamlets were empty and ominously silent; no obsequious mayors came forward to placate the victors; crops had been reaped and removed; valuables and furniture had disappeared; even the grain mills were dismantled. It was a dress rehearsal of the "scorched earth", which met the Grand Army two years later in Russia.

Masséna floundered forward with an optimism born of unawareness, and advanced with majestic delays along the worst possible road (as his enemy gleefully noted), shedding horses and transport wagons at every mile. Trant and his merry militiamen swept down on the great artillery train, taking eight hundred prisoners. Swarms of *Ordenanza* hung on the French flanks, pillaging French supplies and cutting French throats. Yet when Masséna's feet were already in the cunning trap, pessimism in England was universal, Wellington himself noted "the croaking which prevails in the army", and the Portuguese Government worked itself into a panic, plagued him with feverish communications accusing innocent persons of espionage and recommending fifth columnists as men worthy of every trust, wrote him an angry letter about Almeida, and insisted that a battle must be fought "to save Portugal".

If "the Peer" (as subalterns now nicknamed him behind his back) sighed with impatience and damned the eyes of nearly everybody in private, who will blame him? especially since he gave no public sign of the almost intolerable burden of necessary and unnecessary worry put

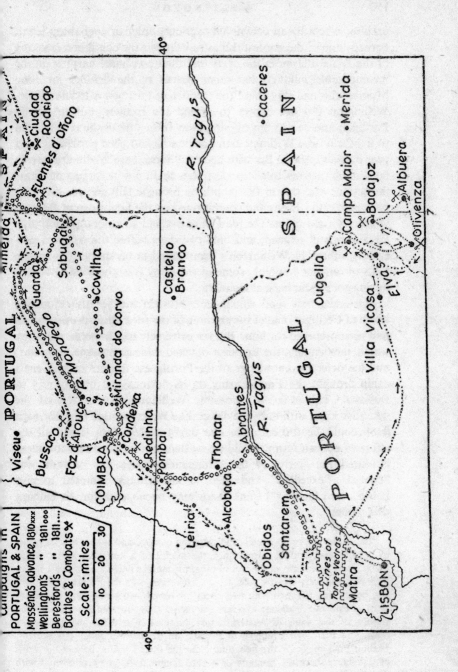

Campaigns in
PORTUGAL & SPAIN
Masséna's advance, 1810 xxx
Wellington's   " 1811 ooo
Beresford's   " 1811 ......
Battles & Combats x

Scale : miles
0   10   20   30

PORTUGAL
Viseu
Almeida
Ciudad Rodrigo
Fuentes d'Oñoro
Bussaco
Guarda
Sabugal
Covilha
Foz d'Arouce
R. Mondego
Miranda do Corvo
COIMBRA
Condeixa
Redinha
Pombal
Castello Branco
Thomar
Alcobaça
Abrantes
Leiria
Obidos
Santarem
R. Tagus
R. Tagus
Lines of Torres Vedras
Matra
LISBON

SPAIN
Caceres
Merida
Campo Maior
Badajoz
Olivenza
Albuera
Ougella
Villa Vicosa
Elvos

PORTUGAL

40°
40°

on him, except by an occasional over-curt order or over-sharp letter. Perhaps one of the hardest things to bear was the continued croaking of the Whig officers in the army and their continued harping on the incomparable military and other virtues of the defunct Sir John Moore, who had said that "the frontier of Portugal is indefensible". Wellington did not expect to defend the frontier, but to defend Portugal; and he was not running away from a battle, he only wanted to fight it on the Wellingtonian position he had been perfecting for a year outside Lisbon. But with his usual horse sense Wellington saw in September that his almost perfect plan could not be carried out in its perfection; and late in the month he brought Hill and his divisions back across the Tagus and concentrated on the high ridge of Bussaco which lay right across the road Masséna had so ignorantly adopted. Pessimism still reigned, and only two days before the battle, a pert cavalry officer in Wellington's army noted in his diary: "Everyone talks of our not standing, some of the army (viz. the First Division) having gone as far back as Coimbra."

Masséna's best road would have brought him on the Mondego north of Coimbra, and at the crossing of the river all sorts of surprises had been prepared for him. But the extremely bad Imperial maps (by which, incidentally, the Emperor directed these campaigns from afar) and the defective knowledge of the Portuguese traitors in Masséna's camp brought the French army on its devious and bumpy way to Bussaco. This was an admirable Wellingtonian position of the defensive kind, with only one defect (like Waterloo itself) the northern flank could be turned. Masséna might merely turn it and all the effort of concentrating would be wasted, but as no such movement appeared the spirits of the Commander rose; the position was "capital", "excellent", and then, "I am strongly tempted to give battle", and finally, "I think there may be no occasion to embark this winter".

"Far as the eye could stretch, the glittering of steel, and clouds of dust raised by cavalry and artillery, proclaimed the march of a countless army; while, immediately below me, at the feet of those precipitous heights on which I stood, their picquets were already posted. . . . This, then, was the French army: here lay, before me, the men who had once, for nearly two years, kept the whole coast of England in alarm; who had conquered Italy, overrun Austria, shouted victory on the plains of Austerlitz, and humbled in one day the power, the pride, and the martial renown of Prussia, on the field of Jena. To-morrow, methought, I may, for the first time, hear the din of battle, behold the work of slaughter, share the honours of a hard-fought field, or be numbered with the slain."

Such were the eve-of-battle reflections of one green young subaltern, who cannot be accused of under-estimating his enemy, as that enemy's General was about to do. And here is another subaltern's glimpse of the battle line forming at dawn, a hint of the prestige Wellington had already won in his army except with the inevitably intriguing generals and the irreducible Whigs:

"Lord Wellington lay amongst his soldiers, under no other covering than his cloak, and as he passed through the ranks of the different battalions, already formed, *his presence and manner gave that confidence to his companions which had a magical effect*."

It must be confessed that the battle of Bussaco does not add to the great military achievements and glory of the Prince of Essling. His reconnaissance was so incomplete that he fought without knowing there was a road by which his opponent could be turned; he under-estimated both the General and the troops opposed to him; and his recently discovered orders for the battle show that he thought he was turning Wellington's right when he was attacking his right centre. Hill and his two divisions had never even been seen by the French scouts or the Marshal's telescope! Masséna attacked as recklessly as if he indeed had only sepoys in front of him, but unhappily for the Allies he did this only at Bussaco—he was far too sharp-witted to ask for a second lesson of the kind.

On the morning of September 26, Wellington had his divisions either concentrated on the high road or strung out along the ridge. There was a heavy mist which entirely concealed the whereabouts of the French who could be heard crashing and clattering up the slope, and this fog alone saved them from a worse defeat and gave them what little temporary success they had. General Reynier (or Régnier), the man who had been defeated at Maida in 1806, commanded the columns of Masséna's left, and did not regain his lost reputation. (Reading the account of the battle the Emperor took a couple of quick pinches of snuff, and remarked: "Reynier at least might have learned something from Maida!") The three separate masses of Reynier's men were so ill co-ordinated that they attacked, not simultaneously, but at three different times. Heudelet's division blundered straight into some of Picton's men and never even reached the crest. Merle's division had better luck and struck a part of the ridge which was unoccupied. But, as always happened at the danger spot in any battle, the Peer was miraculously on the spot and sent Colonel Wallace with his Eighty-Eighth against the head of the French column just as part of the Forty-Fifth charged from the other side. "By God, Wallace, I never witnessed a more gallant charge!" Then Foy's brigade scared a regiment of Portuguese militia from the field, but were thrown back by Leith's men. A few minutes later Wellington had galloped to the right of his line, and Moyle Sherer heard him say to the General there:

"If they attempt this point again, Hill, you will give them a volley, and charge bayonets; but don't let your people follow them too far down the hill."

Wellington's orders on the field, Colonel Sherer noted, were "short, quick, clear, and to the purpose"; moreover, they "confirmed confidence" by their "mixture of simplicity and decision". In a moment Wellington was off at a gallop to his extreme left, where Robert Craufurd and his Light Division were knocking the heart out of Ney and his two divisions. The attack was such a costly failure that Ney on his own responsibility called it off. And well he might. Without achieving any object whatsoever, Masséna in a short time had lost nearly 5,000 men to his opponent's 1,200. Four of the attacking generals were killed or wounded, and a fifth was left prisoner; seven full colonels lay dead or wounded; while in Wellington's army no officer over the rank of major was killed. The *Moniteur* of course had no difficulty in arranging a propaganda victory for Masséna; but in private the Emperor snorted violent epigrams at the expense of his old friend.

Masséna was no fool and needed no second lesson. He made no further attack on the Bussaco ridge, as everyone in the Anglo-Portuguese army fervently hoped he would, but turned the position as he might have done unscathed at first. The victorious army immediately fell back on Lisbon, passing through the tumult of the evacuation of Coimbra, and groping their way to their positions in the line through the tropical rains of a Portuguese autumn. Masséna left all his sick and wounded at Coimbra under the guard of details and the sailors who were to man the British ships to be captured in Lisbon harbour; and then pushed on in pursuit, confident (in spite of Bussaco) that Wellington would either fly by sea or surrender. Before the French army's rear-guard had got many miles from the town, a startling rumour reached them—Trant and his militia were said to have surprised Coimbra, capturing 5,000 men and 80 officers. Masséna was annoyed, and his whole army shocked and angered, when this rumour proved to be entirely true. And yet another and more unpleasant shock awaited them as they pressed nearer to Lisbon:

"Passes, naturally strong, bristled here and there with the most powerful artillery," wrote a French officer, describing his army's first contact with the

Lines. "Art had vied with Nature in erecting defences where death could be dispensed, without sustaining any harm in return. Throughout the whole breadth of the peninsula in which Lisbon is situated, as if it had been all one fortified city, there reigned in all the posts of the English and Portuguese, the greatest silence, calmness and good order. Sloops of war in the Tagus flanked the right of their position; and a ball from one of their cannon killed General Sainte-Croix the first day of our arrival."

It is said that Masséna examined the Lines through his telescope with growing consternation, and finally turned to the Portuguese renegades on his staff, demanding angrily to know why they had not informed him of these terrific obstacles. They stammered that they had not known of Wellington's fortifications. "*Diable!* Wellington didn't build these mountains." But after all, it wasn't the mountains that mattered, and Masséna was merely evading. The mountains between Torres Vedras and Lisbon, and between the Tagus and the ocean, are mole-hills compared with the ranges Masséna had already passed. What worried him was the fortifications, and the men and guns behind them.

"Masséna is an old fox," Wellington admitted regretfully, "and as cautious as I am. He risks nothing." It was on October 14 (1810) that Masséna made his survey of the Lines of Torres Vedras; and the Anglo-Portuguese army gleefully awaited his attack, which never came. But for the lesson of Bussaco, he might have plunged; but the great battle so long planned for his destruction never took place. Instead of attacking he threw up some hasty and flimsy lines of his own and pretended he was blockading Wellington, a poor device which could not deceive his own troops, who could see the daily movement of ships in and out of Lisbon harbour, but did deceive the Opposition newspapers in London who gravely attributed to Wellington's army all the misfortunes of Masséna's. The greatest trouble of the French was hunger. True, they nearly had to meet a fierce attack as well, for as Wellington brooded over the situation from his eyrie on the great Agraça redoubt, he was heard to mutter: "Damned tempting, damned tempting." Then he added: "I could lick those fellows any day, but it would cost me 10,000 men, and as this is the last army England has, we must take care of it." Better to manœuvre the French out of Portugal, without casualties to his army, by the slow but certain weapon of hunger. So he rode back to headquarters and his endless correspondence, ironically acknowledging the lukewarm letter of Government thanks for Bussaco with its pompous announcement of a ribbon of the Bath for Beresford which, Lord Liverpool thought, might "produce a most favourable impression in Portugal". Wellington wrote back asking for 100,000 pairs of shoes for the army—"it may be obliged to make marches". As it could now only march forward, the hint should have been obvious.

But Masséna was bravely obstinate, and held on to his pretended blockade for a month. Then, finding the position impossible for more bluff, he slipped away under cover of a heavy fog on the night of November 14-15, 1810—a memorable date, for in spite of many disappointments and delays it meant that the third invasion of Portugal had failed, that the initiative had at last passed to Wellington. But Masséna did not leave Portugal; he fell back to fortified positions in and about Santarem (fifty miles from Lisbon) and stayed there in starvation and isolation until March 1811. The morale of his men was becoming poor—on November 17, for instance, a single squadron of the Sixteenth Dragoons picked up 112 prisoners from French foraging and marauding parties. And small wonder. While Wellington's men lived in comparative comfort and ease, Masséna between Bussaco and January 1, 1811, lost no fewer than 18,457 men in dead, sick, prisoners, and deserters.

Moreover, the *Ordenanza* cut off the French army so effectively that none of Masséna's couriers got through the blockade. Every messenger was captured, and his dispatches promptly forwarded to Wellington. To get news of his plight through to the Emperor, Masséna was forced to allow his final emissary, General Foy, an escort of 600 men. And when at last the Emperor's advice and succour arrived, what did they amount to? Foy brought back 1,850 men; Conroux got through with 7,500; and meanwhile over 12,000 of Masséna's sick had died—a net loss of over 3,000! The one really damaging effect of the Emperor's orders was a pure accident—a Spanish traitor surrendered the great fortress of Badajoz to Soult who was making a spirited but ineffective demonstration south of the Tagus.

What were they saying and thinking in England? Lord Liverpool, brushing aside the news of Masséna's retreat to Santarem, complained of "most disagreeable scenes in the two Houses"—for there was a political crisis, and one reason Masséna hung on in spite of his losses was the hope that at any moment the Tories would be out and the enlightened Whigs be in, with the consequent evacuation of Portugal. And while Parliament quarrelled, a distracted public could not make out what was happening and whether it should prepare for mourning or rejoicing:

"My Mother," writes Lady Bessborough, "has just been here. . . . She amus'd me with her puzzle at the different readings of the news from Portugal.

At Mrs. Howe's it was explain'd to her as very good, and a proof of Ld. Wellington's good Generalship making Masséna retreat, and Mr. Long had *betted* (for
the pleasure of betting with an Arch Bishop) that Masséna without a battle
would be forc'd to retreat into Spain before February. On her return home she
met with Ld. Carlisle, who assured her Masséna had not retreated, but taken
a better position, and plac'd us in a worse; that Ld. W. was no general at all,
and fell from one blunder to another, and the most we had to hope was his
being able to embark quietly and bring his troops in safety back to England,
which he thought very doubtful. My Mother tried to *console* him with her
account of it, but found he knew everything she could tell him, and thought it
all proof of ruin."

Loyal, sensible, but slightly too optimistic Mr. Long! You were
absolutely right, and the "Arch Bishop" of York was absolutely
wrong, but you lost your bet by thirty-two days. It was on February
19 that Masséna held a council of war to contemplate grim news:
Reinforcements from central Spain had turned back for lack of food;
Don Julian Sanchez had cut off a food convoy coming from Rodrigo;
the Tory Government had not fallen; and after exhausting every
conceivable excuse for delay the Horse Guards had at last sent
Wellington the reinforcements he needed to take the offensive. "On
the 4th March (1811) a large convent in Santarem was seen to be on
fire"; and at 5 a.m. on March 6 an urgent message came into
headquarters from Lumley's dragoons—the enemy had decamped!

Then, as Masséna's army sullenly fell back into Spain, there
developed a thrilling duel of war between Ney and Wellington—Ney's
rear-guard facing Wellington's advance-guard. On March 9, Wellington's cavalry was skirmishing with Ney's at Pombal, and on the
eleventh, Ney only just managed to extricate himself from a trap. On
the twelfth, Wellington cautiously but very skilfully manœuvred Ney
out of Redinha; he fell back on Condeixa, while Masséna abandoned
all hope of holding Coimbra. The thirteenth was a good day for
Wellington—Ney escaped from Condeixa only by the skin of his
teeth, the Hanoverian hussars had Masséna flying for his life; and the
two Marshals had a bitter quarrel. The fourteenth was not so good,
for though Wellington advanced fourteen miles, a newly arrived Horse
Guards General vexed him to fury by throwing away 90 good men out
of sheer stupidity. That night the French burned vehicles and baggage
at Miranda do Corvo to lighten the retreat, and on the fifteenth, Ney
was hustled over the river at Foz d'Arouce, losing 250 men and an
eagle. On the eighteenth, after a short rest, he was again overtaken and
hustled out of a new strong position at Ponte de Murcella; and next
morning he lost 600 prisoners, including an aide-de-camp. As the

British advance-guard pressed eagerly on, they found the road strewn more and more thickly with the bodies of dead men, with dead horses and mules, broken wagons and caissons. It was not indeed the retreat from Moscow, but it was a small-scale rehearsal for that disaster. On March 22 (1811) Masséna and Ney quarrelled violently again; and Ney went off to Valladolid, nominally under an arrest he refused to recognize. And finally Masséna himself had to abandon all hopes of further resistance, and retired on Rodrigo, losing 200 prisoners at Guarda, and over 700 casualties at Sabugal.

By the first week in April (1811) the only French left in Portugal were prisoners and the beleaguered garrison of Almeida. Napoleon's third invasion of Portugal had cost him 25,000 men, of whom 20,000 had died; and it cost Masséna his last command. On April 20, 1811, the Emperor sent orders to the Prince of Essling to hand over the command of the Army of Portugal to yet another Marshal of the Empire—this time Marmont, Duke of Ragusa. On that same day Wellington's Anglo-Portuguese were back in the very positions they had evacuated in August 1810, but back with increased numbers, with intact equipment, exuberant in spirits, and with a confidence in their leader which now could not be destroyed even by the united efforts of his hostile and mistrustful countrymen and the Emperor Napoleon.

The sepoy General, cried an enraged *Moniteur*, is waging war with all the ferocity he has learned in India, and shoots every poor Portuguese peasant who refuses to abandon his home.

"Mr. Speaker," cried an orator in the House, "If this be termed the defence of a country, the Portuguese or any other people may well exclaim, God defend us from such defenders!"

In February 1811, just at the time when Masséna was burying men by hundreds a week and quarrelling with his subordinate generals about possible methods of escape, a bright brave Whig exclaimed:

"Who is there mad enough to expect that we shall be able to drive the French out of the Peninsula, either by arms, or by negotiation? Where is the man, in his senses, who believes or will say that he believes, that we shall be able to accomplish this?"

And at the very moment when a despairing Masséna was being hustled out of Portugal but just before the news of his retreat reached London, the well-informed Mr. Freemantle thus warned the Government:

"It rests with the enemy to choose his day, to make his own dispositions, to wait for his reinforcements, to choose whether he will continue to blockade you, or whether he will give you a fair opportunity of contending with him in the field."

Best, bravest, and brightest of all perhaps were the remarks of Lord Liverpool who, after congratulations as polysyllabic as they were hollow on the defeat of Masséna, went on to complain that the Peninsular campaign was very costly, adding the suggestion, that, "now that the French have been driven out of Portugal", some of the British infantry battalions might be sent home as an economy! A French "morning state" of the army at this period shows a gross total of 354,461 French troops in Spain!

Such are some of the differences between fighting a war at home or at the front, for politics or from a sense of duty, as a soldier or as a civilian strategist.

CHAPTER XV

From Fuentes to Badajoz

JUNOT, Soult, Victor, Masséna, Ney. . . . Something had happened in Europe, there was an uneasy stirring of occupied peoples, a faint breath of hope after the bitter disillusion of imperial rule. One Marshal of France after another had failed against the same army and the same General; and whatever the Whigs might say, Europe was watching events in Portugal eagerly and hopefully. The Prussians were somewhat unintelligently putting up Lines of Torres Vedras round Potsdam; the Russians silently noting the effect of a devastated country in winter on a French army.

Wellington paid for his triumph. During the whole of this war his personal life was swallowed up entirely by his life as General. For three years he never slept out of his clothes, and throughout the war never left his army for a day except on public business. For days on end, he was on horseback from sunrise to sunset; many a time he had not a moment to eat during the whole twenty-four hours of a day; he learned to sleep by snatches at any odd time, anywhere. He had to train every one of his generals, create his own supply and transport organizations, fight battles without cavalry and sieges without artillery, suffer Horse Guards officers gladly, see his plans made vain by the vanity or incompetence or teachery of a Spaniard, the indolence of the Juntas, the parsimony and stupidity of his own government. His junior officers were too often careless, his men always drunkards, sometimes thieves. Small wonder that when Larpent joined the army in 1812 he was horrified to see how dangerously thin and worn Wellington looked, for "*everything* depends on this one man". He himself often described the two and half years between Talavera and the end of 1811 as "the trying period of the war".

The French army were out of Portugal, but they held or threatened all the frontier fortresses, and (incredible as it sounds) Wellington still had not been provided with a siege train, although the Peninsular War was three years old. All he could do was to blockade Rodrigo and Almeida, when to his intense annoyance a French supply train was allowed to slip into Rodrigo by the incompetence of the cavalry commander, Erskine, a personal friend of the Duke of York. To the

south of the Tagus, Beresford had taken the place of Hill (sick with
Gaudiana fever) and had managed to recover Campo Maior and
Olivenza. But it was Badajoz that mattered, and Wellington galloped
135 miles in three days to reconnoitre it, giving Beresford detailed
instructions for the blockade and orders to meet any relieving force
at Albuera. As he galloped north again, news reached him (April 29,
1811) that Masséna had somehow scraped together 48,000 men, and
horses for 38 guns, and was trying his luck once more—this time to
raise the blockade of Almeida.

Wellington determined to meet him at Fuentes d'Oñoro, just on the
Spanish-Portuguese frontier, with 10,000 fewer men and 10 more
guns. From soon after noon until dark on May 3 (1811) the French
infantry stormed again and again up the sloping street of the once
pleasant little village, only to be thrown back by fierce counter-attack.
A Highlander of the Seventy-First Foot says he fired 107 rounds,
adding "my shoulder was as black as a coal from the recoil of my
musket". The next day (May 4) Masséna suspended his attacks and
reconnoitred; and on the morning of May 5 he attacked the village of
Pozo Bello, held by Wellington's newest and weakest division, the
Seventh. During the withdrawal of this division, covered by the
cavalry and a demonstration by the Light Division, there occurred the
famous episode when Ramsay of the Horse Artillery charged the
French cavalry which surrounded him and successfully brought off
his two guns. It was an awkward moment of the battle described
in the official dispatch as "very critical circumstances" and judged in
homelier language by the honest admission: "If Bony had been there
we should have been beat."

But Boney wasn't there, and once more the fight raged in the
streets of Fuentes, where the "Highlanders lay dead in heaps" and
"the French grenadiers, with their immense caps and gaudy plumes, in
piles of twenty and thirty". At one moment the situation was critical
indeed. The Highlanders had been driven to the churchyard at the
very top of the village and were fighting among the tombs and grave-
stones when Sir Edward Pakenham (the Adjutant-General) galloped
up, exchanged a few sentences with the commander of the reserve,
Colonel Wallace of the Eighty-Eighth, and then rode off to meet
Wellington. In a moment or two Pakenham galloped back, shouting:
"He says you may go, come along!" And a desperate charge of the
Connaught Rangers cleared the French from the village for good and
all. Indeed it ended the serious fighting of the battle; on May 8,
Masséna was in full retreat, and on May 10, he ceased to command,

having lost 2,100 men to Wellington's 1,450. Yet Masséna had one last crumb of comfort—most of his garrison succeeded in escaping from Almeida owing to the stupidity of General Erskine, who dishonourably put the blame on two colonels, one of whom (Bevan) committed suicide in protest. "They were all sleeping in their spurs even," said Wellington contemptuously, and he described the failure to guard Almeida as "the most disgraceful military event that has yet occurred to us". But what was the use of protesting against generals like Erskine, when the Horse Guards persisted in sending out any friend of the Duke of York's who thought he would like a slice of Wellington's reputation?

Scarcely had Masséna's, or rather Marmont's, rear-guard vanished in the direction of Rodrigo when Wellington's thoughts went south of the Tagus. What had happened to Beresford? "My only anxiety now is on your side," Wellington wrote, "and I propose immediately to put in motion some troops towards the Alemtejo. . . ." On May 16, he was off at his usual high speed, following up these troops, when he received the news that Soult and Beresford had fought the bloodiest battle of the war at Albuera. Myers and Houghton were killed, Cole seriously wounded . . . and Beresford had lost more than 4,000 of his 10,000 troops, the Spaniards 1,300 and Soult 6,000. Napier's magnificent rhetoric—"Then was it seen with what a strength and majesty the British soldier fights . . ."—hides the fact that Albuera was an error,* not because it was a doubtful victory, but because at that moment the Allies simply could not afford to lose the men. Wellington's own private judgment ran thus:

"Albuera was a strange concern. They were never determined to fight it; they did not occupy the ground as they ought; they were ready to run away at every moment from the time it commenced till the French retired; and if it had not been for me, who am now suffering from the loss and disorganisation occasioned by that battle, they would have written a whining report upon it, which would have driven the people in England mad."

With twenty-five trained sappers, some inexperienced engineer officers, and a scratch artillery train which contained guns over two hundred years old, Wellington laid siege to Badajoz—an enterprise doomed to certain failure with such inadequate equipment. Then, in June, Marmont joined Soult as he marched to the relief, and Wellington fell back on Elvas and hopefully offered battle. But the Marshals

* Because that passage about the Fusileers is so often quoted out of context, Napier's dislike for Beresford and absurd cult of Soult makes his analysis of the battle unfair and untrue.

GENERAL SIR WILLIAM BERESFORD

After the drawing by Thomas Heaphy
[*The National Portrait Gallery*]

GENERAL SIR THOMAS PICTON

After the painting by Sir Martin Archer Shee
[*The National Portrait Gallery*]

were grown wary; Soult went off to rescue Seville from the guerrillas, and Marmont spread himself out in cantonments to feed. Leaving Hill south of the Tagus with 13,000 men, Wellington went north with the remaining 46,000 to blockade Rodrigo; but in September the town was revictualled by Marmont, and as Wellington reluctantly fell back before larger numbers, there were sharp local actions at El Bodon and Aldea da Ponte. On September 25, Grattan of the Eighty-Eighth actually saw Wellington and his staff with swords out fighting their way through a cloud of Montbrun's troopers. But the Marshal was afraid to risk a battle, retired, and from the Tagus to the Bay of Biscay the deadlock lasted out 1811. But another year had passed; a British army was still in the Peninsula; and war between Russia and France was now inevitable. Everywhere, whether wearied of war or not, men wondered what 1812 would bring.

The slim man in the grey frock-coat "upon whose life everything depends" was not without honour. Grudgingly the Horse Guards consented that he should be a full General, but with "local rank" only. Parliament had offered thanks "for the deliverance of Portugal"; and, more handsomely, Portugal itself offered the Grand Cross of the Tower and Sword, the title of Conde de Vimiero and a pension—the last of course refused. Mr. Whitbread, M.P. wrote a gracious letter confessing nobly that he had ceased to believe that Wellington was a liar. Yet in Parliament Mr. Whitbread was still a pessimist:

"Lord Wellington after pursuing Masséna to the frontiers had been obliged to fall back, his attempt on Ciudad Rodrigo had proved abortive; everything we could do for Spain had already been done. . . ."

So why not oblige Mr. Whitbread and his friend the Emperor Napoleon by withdrawing this ineffective army from the Peninsula? Yet there were hopeful signs too, or so Wellington thought. He reported with glee the daring feats of his friends, the Spanish guerrillas, who the Emperor angrily insisted were "bandits". Temprano, for instance, had rescued a British officer "at the very gates of Talavera"; "both the Empecinado and Mina" had been "very successful" and Longa likewise. Moreover, Julian Sanchez had succeeded in capturing the Governor of Rodrigo, General Renaud, along with most of the garrison's live cattle. Raiding was evidently the vogue, for hard on top of this came news that Hill had made a dash at Arroyo dos Molinos, surprising two brigades of Girard's division, and capturing 1,300 prisoners, 3 guns, and $5,000 of stolen money. Among the prisoners were the Prince d'Aremberg, a relative by marriage of the

F*

Emperor; General Bron; and more than thirty other officers. And from Andalusia came word of the incredible—a tiny Anglo-Spanish force had managed to hold Taiifa against almost overwhelming odds. Straws in the wind! And the man in the grey frock-coat was brooding over hopes and plans in the bleak upland village of Frenada, writing words which Mr. Whitbread and Lord Grey and Mr. Creevey and Mr. Freemantle would have called criminal folly:

" . . . the task would not be an easy one. But the difficulties are not insurmountable; and I think it is possible, with our maritime resources, to form and maintain an army in the Pyrenees. . . ."

As was proper, the deadlock was resolved by the orders of the Emperor.

It sounds a paradox, but one of Wellington's most valuable assets was that the Emperor would *not* give King Joseph full authority over the Marshals, and *would* interfere from a distance in military plans and operations. Even in those slow-moving days the greatest military genius could not hope to conduct campaigns at a distance of four to six weeks. The intelligence on which the Emperor based his orders was stale, and when the orders arrived the situation had changed. Moreover, he had never seen the country in which the war was being fought against the Anglo-Portuguese, and in those later years had fallen into a strange habit of building grandiose plans and issuing peremptory orders in defiance of bitter facts. That incomparable brain and energy were overreaching themselves. He could not be made to see that along the Spanish-Portuguese frontiers the roads were almost impassable, that communications were everywhere cut by guerrillas, and that his system of feeding on the country (instead of by supply system, such as Wellington's 5,000 pack mules) was an intolerable strain. He persistently over-estimated his own numbers, he obstinately undervalued the enemy.

In the autumn of 1811 the Emperor was fertile in Peninsular plans. First, Marmont was to borrow troops from Dorsenne and Soult (who would not have let them go), lay siege to Elvas, and then take Lisbon. Excellent plan—if Wellington had no siege train to capture Rodrigo; and just at that moment Marmont heard rumours that at long last a British siege train had arrived. But long before Marmont's respectful objections reached the Emperor, he had forgotten all about this scheme of capturing Portugal and had turned to something else. It was Valencia now. Affable Whig supporters in London had assured the Emperor that Wellington had so many sick that his English

troops were down to 20,000. It was not true, and as usual the Portuguese were ignored, but what matter? Marmont must detach 12,000
men to support Suchet's operations in Valencia (which incidentally
succeeded), with another 3,000 to keep communications open. But in
December the Anglo-Portuguese army was not 20,000, as the Emperor
believed, but 60,000; and just as Marmont was weakened by these
orders Wellington struck like a thunderbolt at Rodrigo.

Orders to engineers and artillery went out on New Year's Day, 1812;
to generals of division on January 8, on which day the fortress was
invested and an important redoubt stormed with the bayonet after
dark. On the thirteenth, the fortified convent of Santa Cruz was
stormed. On the fourteenth, a dismayed Marmont got the first news
(the guerrillas had managed to hold it up five days) and ordered a
concentration he hoped to complete by February 1. On January 19,
Wellington ordered the assault, which succeeded after fearful slaughter
and was followed by scenes of violence and brutal drunkenness.
General Mackinnon of the Third Division was killed; Craufurd of the
Light mortally wounded; Vandeleur, Colborne, and Napier were
wounded. The columns got mixed up at the breaches, and Harry
Smith of the Rifle Brigade found himself seized and throttled by a
gigantic Irish grenadier who called him a "French bastard", and only
desisted when Smith managed to gurgle an authentic "damn your
eyes". The tumult and the disorder spread as the French garrison
surrendered, and all the sots and bad hats of the attackers scattered for
drink and plunder. Officers had to stand guard over the Spanish
women, and as the disorder spread the "voice of Sir Thomas Picton,
with the power of twenty trumpets, proclaimed damnation to everybody".

Early next morning as Wellington rode into the town he met a
strange crew marching out, "some of them dressed in Frenchmen's
coats, some in white breeches and huge jack-boots, some with cocked
hats and queues; most of their swords were fixed in their rifles, and
stuck full of hams, tongues, and loaves of bread, and not a few were
carrying bird-cages."

"Who the devil are these fellows?" the Peer asked, and was considerably dashed at learning they were one of his best regiments, the
Ninety-Fifth.

Wellington's losses in the siege and assault were 1,121; the French
nearly 2,000, including the Governor, 60 officers, and 1,300 men
prisoners. But Craufurd was dead, and that was a loss Wellington
could never hope to make good. As for Marmont, the news that he

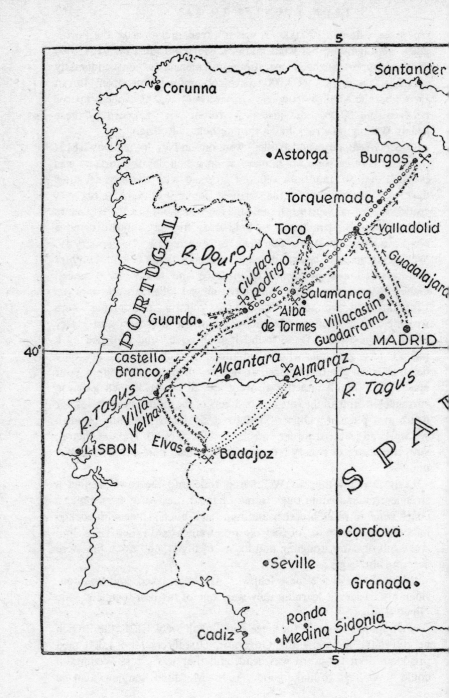

Campaigns in
PORTUGAL & SPAIN
1812
Approximate lines of march
Wellington's advance xxxxx
"   retreat o o o o o
Hill's raid on Almaraz.....
Battles, Combats & Sieges ✗
Scale : miles
0   50   100

had lost Rodrigo reached him on January 21, and he reported it to the Emperor as if it had been a supernatural event: "There is something so incomprehensible in this occurrence that I can make no observation." But while the Marshal was fruitlessly pondering the incomprehensible, Wellington had already begun to send his siege guns secretly south to Badajoz, sending the troops down in February, but remaining himself in the north until the last possible moment—for the Marshals had now formed the flattering belief that, where Wellington was, there trouble was to be expected. On March 16, 1812, Badajoz was invested.

Meanwhile news came from the outer world, bad and good. At this crucial moment Richard Wellesley chose to quarrel with the other members of the Cabinet, and resigned, bringing on himself from Arthur the crushing sarcasm: "In truth the republic of a cabinet is but little suited to any man of taste or of large views." The other news was that the Allied world had chosen to make a tremendous fuss about the capture of Rodrigo, and to make it the occasion for honouring the defender of Portugal. England made him Earl of Wellington, with Parliament voting him thanks and an annuity of £2,000, with K.B.s for Graham and Hill; Portugal made him Marquess of Torres Vedras; while Spain, ever grandiose, titled him Duque de Ciudad Rodrigo, Grandee of Spain of the First Class.

Wellington dreaded two things at the siege of Badajoz—bad weather and a joint relief army under Soult and Marmont. The weather indeed turned out to be vile, but the Emperor dispersed the greater danger by writing Marmont that Badajoz was no business of his, that Wellington would probably not dare to attack it, but that if he did Marmont was to march into north Portugal—in fact do what Wellington hoped but hardly dared to expect. In spite of this gift from the Emperor, the siege of Badajoz was costly and bloody, for the place was very strong, was defended by 5,000 men and a most determined Governor (Philipon), and time was short. The garrison made determined sorties, drenching rains flooded the trenches, the casualties in the attacking batteries were exceptionally high, the storming of Fort Picurina on the night of March 24 cost 319 out of the 500 attackers; and on April 4 news came that Soult (without Marmont) was only five marches distant. The general assault was ordered for the night of April 6, 1812.

That night was almost certainly the most terrible for Wellington and his army of any in the whole war. For more than two hours Wellington stood on a knoll overlooking the town in a little nook lighted by a small torch held by an aide-de-camp, and watched the storm which was a prolonged fury of artillery and musketry, "blue lights, rockets, combustibles of every kind hurled over the parapets and down the slopes into the ditch". Time after time the survivors of the Light and Fourth divisions rallied and attacked the breaches in utterly futile heroism, for the entrances were closed by immovable "*chevaux de frise* formed of cavalry sword-blades set in foot-square beams, and chained at the ends", while grape and musketry blasted into an- nihilation every column which tried to remove them. All through those hours staff and regimental officers came in with gloomy reports of nothing but failure and hideous casualties. Some time after mid- night an officer reported to Wellington that so many officers had fallen there were scarcely any left to lead the few remaining men. The Surgeon-General, who was standing near, saw Wellington's face as he received this news:

"I shall never forget it to the last moment of my existence . . . the jaw had fallen, the face was of unusual length, while the torchlight gave his countenance a lurid aspect; but still the expression of his face was firm."

Mistaking the doctor for a staff officer Wellington ordered him to go at once to Sir Thomas Picton and tell him he must convert his false attack on the castle to a real attack. He was apologizing for his error, when an officer rode up calling loudly: "Where is Lord Wellington?" and catching sight of him: "General Picton has captured the castle, my lord!" At once Wellington mounted and rode towards the castle, hearing on the way that the two other false assaults had succeeded, and that Philipon had fled to Fort San Cristobal. Badajoz and its five thousand men were taken, but at a cost of nearly that number of casualties, including very many officers.

A rumour had passed through the rank and file before the attack that "if we succeeded in taking the place there was to be three hours' plunder". Nothing could be falser, for Wellington in fact ordered his Provost-Marshal "to execute any men he may find in the act of plunder"; but the sack of Badajoz was truly appalling—"in less than an hour after it fell into our possession it looked as if centuries had completed its destruction". If Wellington in his anger described his army as "the scum of the earth", we must remember the unspeakable scenes at Badajoz, thus described by Captain Blakeney of the Twenty- Eighth Foot:

"What scenes of horror did I witness there! They can never be effaced from my memory. There was no safety for women even in the churches; and any who interfered or resisted were sure to get shot. Every house presented a scene of plunder, debauchery and bloodshed, committed with wanton cruelty on the persons of the defenceless inhabitants by our soldiery; and in many instances I beheld the savages tear the rings from the ears of beautiful women who were their victims, and when the rings could not be immediately removed from their fingers with the hand, they tore them off with their teeth. Firing through the streets and at the windows was incessant, which made it excessively dangerous to move out. . . . Men, women and children were shot in the streets for no other apparent reason than pastime; every species of outrage was publicly committed in the houses, churches and streets, and in a manner so brutal that a faithful recital would be too indecent and too shocking for humanity. Not the slightest shadow of order or discipline was maintained; the officers durst not interfere. The infuriated soldiery resembled rather a pack of hell-hounds vomited up from the infernal regions for the extirpation of mankind than what they were but twelve short hours previously—a well-organised, brave, disciplined and obedient British army, and burning only with impatience for what is called glory. . . ."

CHAPTER XVI

Salamanca and Vittoria

THERE was a pause while divisions reorganized, and the Peer rode north to straighten out the mistakes made in his absence. But with Rodrigo and Badajoz in their hands, the door was wide open to the Allies for the invasion of Spain; and the prompt handing over of the two great fortresses to Spanish garrisons soothed Spanish pride and Spanish suspicions. Then the worried Joseph and the Marshals were positively dismayed by Imperial orders withdrawing 27,000 veterans from Spain for the Russian campaign; and were still brooding over this when Hill made one of his swift and efficient raids. On May 19 (1812) he suddenly appeared before Almaraz, a vital little place on the French lateral line of communication, captured and destroyed Forts Napoleon and Ragusa, with 400 prisoners, 18 guns, a pontoon bridge, and large quantities of stores. Immediately on hearing the news Wellington ordered the repair of the great Roman bridge at Alcantara. These were ominous and obvious signs of a coming offensive, and the Marshals wrangled with each other as to where it would fall, each acrimoniously demanding the help he refused the other. And then, nine days before the Emperor started for Moscow, Wellington suddenly crossed the Agueda and moved swiftly towards Salamanca. The blow had fallen on Marmont.

The odds were still impossibly against Wellington, if his opponents had not been pinned down in garrisons, distracted by the guerrillas, and weakened by personal quarrels. Marmont still had 50,000 men; Soult, nearly 60,000; the Army of the North, 40,000; and behind them was Joseph's Army of the Centre. Against these armies Wellington could bring only 54 guns and 48,000 men, plus Hill's 18,000—a total of 66,000 when concentrated against a possible enemy concentration of at least 150,000. But Marmont was taken by surprise with his men scattered widely for subsistence, and was compelled to abandon the city of Salamanca, into which Wellington rode with his cavalry and the Sixth Division amid "the shouts and vivas" of the inhibitants who were "out of their senses at having got rid of the French, and nearly pulled Lord Wellington off his horse. . . . The women were the most violent, many coming up to Lord Wellington and embracing him. He was writing orders on his sabretash, and was interrupted three or four times".

Escaping the perils of the Spanish ladies, Wellington galloped to the comparative safety of the front line, where he contemplated the double problem of reducing the Salamanca forts and dealing with Marmont's field army. It was not until June 27 that the last of the forts capitulated, and meanwhile Wellington had suffered the disappointment of having Marmont refuse battle at the ridge of San Cristoval, a site described by military writers as "the ideal Wellingtonian position". The war passed into manœuvre, Marmont retreating until July 15, when he received reinforcements, and suddenly took the offensive. On July 18 the Peer and his staff got mixed up in the cavalry fighting, thus described by a delighted subaltern who witnessed their difficulties:

"Lord Wellington, with his staff, and a cloud of English and French dragoons and horse artillery intermixed came over the hill at full cry, all hammering at one another's heads in a confused mass, over the very ground I had that instant quitted. . . . I was highly interested in observing the distinguished characters . . . Marshal Beresford and the greater part of the staff remained with their swords drawn, and the Duke himself did not look more than half pleased. . . .'

On the night of July 21 there was a terrific thunderstorm, such as superstitious Peninsular veterans afterwards declared always preceded "the Duke's victories". Nevertheless on July 22 he continued his retreat and even sent off his baggage on the road to Ciudad Rodrigo, indifferent to the mutters and murmurs of an army who were fretting angrily for action with the French. Seeing the dust from this baggage train, Marmont concluded that for some reason his opponent was afraid to fight, and gave orders to cut off his retreat. In doing so he committed the two military sins of "marching across the enemy's front" and "over-extending his left".

It is said both commanders were eating a late and hasty lunch about two o'clock, Marmont on the hill known as the Greater Arapiles, Wellington on the ground beside a farm nearer to Salamanca. Wellington had tasted nothing since dawn, and as he ate a piece of bread and cold chicken, he remained on horseback intently watching the movements of the French. Suddenly he threw the food away, called to his staff, and was off like the wind on his thoroughbred "Copenhagen". Far out on his right he came on the Third Division, commanded that day by Kitty's brother, Sir Edward Pakenham. There were no waste words:

"Ned, move on with the Third Division, take those heights in front, and drive everything before you."

"I will, my lord."

GENERAL LORD HILL
From a drawing by George Richmond
[*The National Portrait Gallery*]

BATTLE OF SALAMANCA

Drawn and etched by W. Heath

A brief handshake, and Wellington was off again like a flash, to direct the great main attack of his Fourth and Fifth divisions and the cavalry. Marmont, realizing his danger and his error too late, started to mount his horse and was severely wounded. As the rapidly advancing roar and rattle showed that Pakenham was easily driving into the over-extended French left, the Fourth and Fifth divisions drove the French centre into confusion and there fell upon the French the staggering blow of Le Marchant's heavy cavalry brigade, "a whirling cloud of dust which moved swiftly forward carrying within the trampling sound of a charging multitude". The fine regiments of the divisions of Thomières, Maucune, and Brennier broke and fled, mere rabble "black with dust, worn down with fatigue, covered with sabre-cuts and blood". General Bonnet fell, and Clausel took his place, attempting a desperate effort to retrieve the day. Wellington threw in his large reserves, and two more French divisions broke and fled in disorder. No such rout had befallen a French army for many years. The Allies lost over 5,000 men, with 6 generals wounded and 2 killed; but the French lost 14,000, with 3 generals killed and 4 wounded (including Marshal Marmont), 136 officers and nearly 7,000 men prisoners (another 1,000 came in next day), 20 guns, 2 eagles, 6 colours. Perhaps the crowning triumph, though Wellington never saw it, was the note on the battle entered in his diary by General Foy who commanded one of Marmont's divisions: "It raises Lord Wellington almost to the level of Marlborough. . . . At Salamanca he has shown himself a great and able master of manœuvres. . . . It was a battle in the style of Frederick the Great. . . ."

Among the many apocryphal stories of Salamanca one of the most curious and unbelievable is that Wellington returned to the town that night and sat to Goya for his portrait. How could any commander possibly have done such thing with all the manifold confusions following a great battle to deal with? Wellington was certainly on the battle-field during the pursuit after dark on July 22; at dawn he was far ahead at Alba de Tormes, and seems to have been the only general present with the advance-guard when Bock's dragoons broke the retreating French squares and took one thousand prisoners.

The news of Salamanca reached the Emperor in a Russian bivouac and roused him to fury—had he not predicted, had he not warned them months before, that any reverse to Marmont's Army of Portugal "would be felt all over Spain"? England had the official dispatch on August 16 and went mad with delight, as unanimously as if the Tower guns booming the victory salute had quenched the Whig croakings for ever. Bathurst, the new Secretary for War, was obsequious, writing (as he said) "amid the acclamations of all London", sending "congratulations on this most eventful victory", and adding a string of "yeses" to military requests Wellington had been vainly making for months. Liverpool, now Prime Minister in the place of the murdered Perceval, was equally fulsome: "Most decided as well as brilliant victory which has for centuries crowned British arms . . . incalculable importance . . . never in my life saw anything equal to the enthusiasm excited . . ." Spain sent the Order of the Golden Fleece, and a rich florid voice in London ordered that "Arthur" "be advanced to the dignity of a Marquess . . ."

"What the devil is the use of making me a Marquess?" said the Peer to one of his staff. He was a little worried, for he was not absolutely certain that he had followed up his victory in the most effective way. Too many of the French had escaped, and he blamed a Spanish general for evacuating Alba de Tormes without permission and without reporting the fact. Following a grim trail of dead, sick, and straggling Frenchmen, the Allied army entered Valladolid on July 30 (1812), and Clausel fell back on Burgos with the remnants of Marmont's Army of Portugal. The British main body turned southward to Madrid, and as they came over the Guadarrama "the soldiers ran forward to catch a glimpse of the countless steeples . . . ten thousand voices vociferated 'Madrid! Madrid!'" On August 12 Wellington in his usual neat plain dress rode into Madrid at the head of the Fifty-First Foot, accompanied by only one staff officer. Already, five miles outside the city they had been met by a great crowd bearing laurel boughs, wine, flowers, bread, sweetmeats, strewing the road before them with palm leaves, and breaking into the ranks to march arm in arm with the men. As they entered the city, excited mobs, surged along shouting, "Viva Wellington!" while the church bells rang continuously and the women swirled round Lord Wellington, kissing his hands, his sword, even his horse and the ground he rode on, and cast down their silk shawls to make a path before him. The illumination after dark was so brilliant that "night seemed to be converted into day" and "the whole population of Madrid seemed to fill the streets". Wellington hastened to his headquarters at the Royal Palace and at once sat down to report this triumph to London:

"My Lord,

The army moved forward yesterday morning, and its left took possession of the city of Madrid, the King having retired with the army of the Centre by the roads of Toledo and Aranjuez, leaving a garrison in the Retiro. . . ."

The Retiro and its garrison were easily taken, and the operations provided a military entertainment for at least 100,000 Madrileños, who set up such shouts of triumph when the signal gun for the assault was fired that the British troops could not hear their officers' commands. The French Governor surrendered with 2,000 men, 189 guns, 20,000 muskets and huge quantities of food and clothing which proved most useful to the Spanish guerrillas. Other news, good and bad, came in as Wellington gave his army a few days' well-earned rest and plotted future moves. El Empecinado had captured the garrison of Guadalajara, 900 strong; Soult had evacuated Niebla, Ronda, and Medina Sidonia in the south; the siege of Cadiz was raised at last; Colonel Skerett had retaken Seville; Soult was abandoning all Andalusia and joining Suchet in Valencia. Against this, the Emperor had taken Smolensk and America had declared war—"We may depend upon it," Wellington commented, "that the mouth of the Channel and the coasts of Portugal will swarm with privateers."

In spite of Salamanca and withdrawals for Russia, the seemingly inexhaustible French reserves maintained the Imperial armies in Spain still at well over 200,000 effectives. Wellington had but 56,000, far too few for any of the great possibilities opened up by his victory. The best he could do was to gamble, and he chose to try and capture Burgos—at the moment when the Junta at last appointed him Commander-in-Chief of their armies, too late to be of any use for the campaign of 1812, just as all the reinforcements he had asked from England were sent out too late. The siege of Burgos lasted from September 19 to October 20, and ended in failure and a retreat.

Burgos was the nearest to defeat Wellington ever came upon in the Peninsular War. Perhaps he was tired, perhaps with the dreadful slaughter of Badajoz fresh in his mind he shrank from the ruthless throwing forward of men to certain death. At the funeral of Somers Cocks, the most brilliant of his younger officers, who was killed at Burgos, Wellington looked so gloomy and forbidding that no one dared speak to him. When at last Sir Benjamin D'Urban ventured a word, Wellington turned on him vehemently:

"If Cocks had lived, which was a moral impossibility since he exposed himself too much to risks, he would have been one of the greatest Generals we ever had."

And then relapsed into his glum silence. The uncalled-for and vehement defensive (a "moral impossibility" for Cocks to live) is interesting, since all critics agree the assaults on Burgos were made by insufficient numbers of inferior troops; Wellington was trying to spare the remnants of the old divisions who broke themselves in taking Rodrigo and Badajoz. Yet this does not explain why he had only three (!) siege-guns or why he neglected to bring up more from Madrid and Santander.

Soon it was useless to repine or argue about these errors and short-comings. The French reorganized their vastly superior numbers, and Wellington with his total of 80,000 (of whom 25,000 were uncertain Spaniards) faced a concentration of 110,000 excellent French troops. On October 21, 1812, he gave the order to retreat—just three days after the Emperor had left Moscow. It was a long retreat, and Wellington frankly admitted that it was "the worst scrape I ever was in". On the whole he came out of the ordeal pretty well—with 100,000 men after him he brought off his army with the loss of only 6,000, of whom 2,000 were lost in the last four days through no fault of their Commander. Compared with the retreat from Moscow, the losses were negligible. Oddly enough, and contrary to popular belief, it was not in the *retreat* from Moscow but in the *advance* on Moscow that the Emperor lost the bulk of his men, very largely through their infamous march discipline and inefficient commissariat. Napoleon crossed the frontier with 600,000 men, and had already lost 100,000 (sick, stragglers, deserters, chiefly) before he reached Smolensk. The number of men who started from Moscow on the retreat were only 108,000, while another 60,000 were operating on distant wings.* Compared with gigantic proportional losses like these, Wellington's loss of one man in fourteen seems small indeed.

The loss of two thousand men between Salamanca and Rodrigo during the four days, November 16–19, had this excuse—they received no rations during the whole period, owing to a mistake of Colonel James Gordon, the Quartermaster-General, who sent the army along one road and the supplies along another. It was not surprising that the starving men dropped from the ranks and robbed cottages, shot up the herds of pigs, and stole beehives. No wonder Wellington was furiously angry with them, for it is quite possible that he never knew the men had not received their rations. At any rate the curious story of Colonel James Gordon makes it not improbable. Gordon was a close personal friend of the Duke of York, and despite Wellington's protests was sent out by the Horse Guards to supersede the efficient and loyal Sir George Murray who was "promoted" to an unnecessary and

---

* Croker has recorded a long talk with the Duke on this subject, too long unfortunately to quote here. For the Duke's pondered thoughts on the Emperor's Russian Campaign, see Appendix.

unwanted post in Ireland. Gordon used his privileged position to send disparaging reports on Wellington to the Horse Guards (to please his patron, the Duke of York) and to supply secret and confidential military information to Opposition newspapers and M.P.s! Wellington had been very much worried about these leakages, and only discovered the channel when the pro-French London press published information from a confidential dispatch before even it had reached the Prime Minister, and when its contents were known only to Wellington, his military secretary (Lord Fitzroy Somerset), and Colonel Gordon. So dangerous was this Horse Guards intrigue of the King's son that Wellington and the Prime Minister were forced to correspond about it by private cipher; and so powerful were the Duke of York and his clique that the Cabinet did not dare to court-martial Gordon—it was not until four months after his act of treachery that he was removed, and then only on a polite pretext!

It is not necessary to think that Gordon deliberately sent the army's food on the wrong road from Salamanca; his natural incompetence would take care of that; but it does seem probable that he omitted to tell Wellington of his mistake and that his subordinates dared not do so, knowing full well that Gordon had far greater power with the dispensers of promotion and pay at the Horse Guards than the Commander of the Peninsular Army. If it could ever be shown for certain that Wellington was kept in ignorance of this essential fact it would go a long way towards excusing him for the Memorandum to Commanders of Divisions and Brigades (November 28, 1812) which offended his army so deeply. This memorandum was confidential to general officers only, but the confidence was at once violated (by whom? by Gordon?) with real damage to Wellington's popularity with his men. The wording of the document is sharp and shrill, an evidence of great fatigue and overstrained nerves:

" . . . the discipline . . . of the army under my command . . . has fallen off . . . to a greater degree than any army with which I have ever served, or of which I have ever read.

"Yet this army . . . has suffered no privations which but trifling attention on the part of the officers could not have prevented. . . .

" . . . nor has it suffered any hardships excepting those resulting from the necessity of being exposed to the inclemencies of the weather at a moment when they were most severe. . . .

" . . . Irregularities and outrages of all descriptions were committed with impunity, and losses have been sustained which ought never to have occurred. Yet the necessity for retreat existing, none was ever made on which the troops made such short marches; none on which they made such long and repeated halts; and none on which the retreating armies were so little pressed on their rear by the enemy. . ."

This is almost ridiculously severe, but it is only fair to say that in addition to the excusable outrages during the hungry days (November 16–19) Wellington had to complain of the following fairly damning list: (1) On October 24, all the troops at Torquemada were drunk and lost many stragglers incapable of marching. (2) In the last days of October, orders to burn a boat bridge and to blow up two land bridges were not carried out. (3) On October 30, the Fourth Division was so drunk at Valdemoro that several hundred men could not even stand and were easily taken prisoners. (4) The food in the Madrid arsenal was wasted and destroyed, instead of being given to necessitous Spaniards as ordered. (5) November 9, many drunks had to be left at Villacastin. (6) November 17, so many stragglers were out shooting pigs that troops coming up behind thought there was an action in progress. (7) November 17, Lieut.-General Paget captured by enemy. (8) Three divisional generals disobeyed their route march orders and nearly lost their divisions in consequence.

Yet if the army had behaved badly on the retreat, it had escaped the dreadful fate of the *Grande Armée* in Russia; and as the regiments settled down to winter quarters in Portugal their General could enumerate the successes of their last campaign with justifiable pride:

"We have taken by siege Ciudad Rodrigo, Badajoz, and Salamanca; and the Retiro surrendered. In the mean time the allies have taken Astorga, Guadalaxara and Consuegra, besides other places taken by Duran and Sir H. Popham. In the months elapsed since January this army has sent to England a little short of 20,000 prisoners, and they have taken or destroyed or have themselves the use of the enemy's arsenals in Ciudad Rodrigo, Badajoz, Salamanca, Valladolid, Madrid, Astorga, Seville, the lines before Cadiz &c.; and upon the whole we have taken or destroyed, or we now possess, little short of 3,000 pieces of cannon. The siege of Cadiz has been raised, and all the countries south of the Tagus have been cleared of the enemy."

In spite of the retreat, there was optimism in the Peninsula that winter, and everywhere the "Salamanca Song" was heard from the guitarists with its derisive refrain: "*Ah Marmont! Onde vai, Marmont?*" Everywhere there seemed to be a springing of hope, except oddly enough in Parliament, where Mr. Freemantle was "decidedly of the opinion that by the battle of Salamanca we have gained nothing but glory", and Mr. Ponsonby warned the House:

"It is useless to carry further an unprofitable contest; it is useless to waste the blood and the treasure of England for an unattainable object; it has been proved that the power of England was not competent to drive the French out of the Peninsula."

News travelled slowly in those days, and Mr. Ponsonby delivered his pessimistic oration just before the arrival of the famous Twenty-Ninth Bulletin of the Grand Army (which admitted its destruction) on December 3, 1812, from the village of Molodetchno. "The person of the Emperor is safe," it added. Meanwhile Lord Wellington (prophetically named Duque da Victoria by his Portuguese allies) had carried a lumbago-wracked frame from Frenada to Cadiz and from Cadiz to Lisbon, bolstering the morale of Juntas and arranging suosidies and troop levies; and it was not until January 19, 1813, that he read the momentous bulletin. He was in Lisbon at the time, and from a long contemplation of Napoleon's confession of failure in Russia, Wellington turned to the private letter from the Prime Minister accompanying it:

"There has been no example within the last twenty years of such a change of fortune. .... The most formidable army ever collected by Buonaparte has been substantially destroyed; and it remains only to be ascertained whether he will be able to escape, and with what remnant of that army with which he entered Russia in June last."

Yet there was one man who had always maintained that *Jonathan Wild the Great* could not continue to rule so great a part of the civilized world by "force and fraud", and had stuck to this view throughout the long years of apparently hopeless resistance. Wellington's reaction to the bulletin was interesting—he immediately dispatched Count Nugent to the Emperor of Austria with a brief message: "Lord Wellington expects at least to give employment to between 150,000 and 200,000 French troops in the next campaign." Austria had not joined the new coalition against France; she was France's ally and an Austrian princess was Empress of the French. Yet most Austrians, even the Austrian Emperor himself, disliked the French alliance, and might be very willing to break it if they saw a real chance of success.

Having dispatched this laconic temptation to change sides, Wellington rode rapidly back to headquarters, arriving at Frenada on January 23, after a last stretch of fifty miles in the saddle. Something seemed to have cured his lumbago; indeed he struck Mr. Larpent as "looking well" and being "in high spirits and great good humour with everyone". He impressed the new Deputy Judge-Advocate as being "very ready, and decisive and civil", but the pert little barrister admits that "going up with my charges and papers for instruction, I feel something like a boy going to school". Whatever it was that made Lord Wellington feel so cheerful and whatever the plans for "giving employment" to 200,000 French troops, he kept entirely to himself. Mr. Larpent observed him very closely and noted:

> "Lord Wellington reads and looks into everything. He hunts every other day almost, and then makes up for it by great diligence and instant decision on the intermediate days. He works until about four o'clock; and then, for an hour or two, parades, with anyone whom he wants to talk to, up and down the little square of Frenada (amidst all the chattering Portuguese) in his grey great-coat."

What he discussed with "any one he wants to talk to" we do not know, but it is absolutely certain the subject was not the next campaign. The Commander of the Forces seemed to have given himself the order, "Mum's the word", and to have made up his mind not to trust anyone after the Gordon betrayals. By way of confidential military information General Graham was let into a valuable secret: "Hounds are in good trim, and the foxes very plentiful." Consumed with curiosity, the Prince Regent tried to open a private correspondence, to which he received a chillingly dutiful answer, dispatched with the private remark to the Military Secretary: "What the devil have we to say to each other?" On February 10, 1813, a letter went confidentially to the War Minister, asking for a siege train to be sent to Corunna at once, though no reason was given for the choice of Corunna when the army's base was Lisbon. On February 24, Wellington reported home on Army Children's Schools in Lisbon, on a French failure to beat up Hill's quarters, and complained to Larpent: "My table is covered with details of robbery and mutiny and complaints from all quarters in all languages." But nothing was said to throw any light on plans (if any existed) for the next campaign.

The climate of Frenada is bleak and windy, and a puzzled staff could think of no reason for its being chosen as headquarters, except its proximity to foxes. They forgot its distance from Lisbon, the Portuguese Regency, and distinguished English visitors. At all events, Wellington continued in excellent humour and in March gave a feast and dance in Rodrigo under the pretext of investing his ancient rival for Kitty, now Major-General Sir Lowry Cole, with the Order of the Bath. True, there was a shell hole in the roof and another in the floor of the dance hall, but they hid the one with more or less stolen tapestries and put a sentry to warn dancers of the hole in the floor. There were fifty ladies and 150 men, and Wellington "rode full seventeen miles to Rodrigo in two hours to dinner, dressed in all his orders, was in high glee, danced himself, staid supper, and at half-past three in the morning went back to Frenada by moonlight, and arrived before daybreak at six, so that by twelve he was ready again for business".

Still there remained this obstinate silence about plans of campaign. In April, General Cotton, commanding the cavalry, learned that "I propose to take the field as soon as the appearance of green forage will secure food for the horses". Later in the month the British War Minister was told that "I propose to put the allied British and Portuguese army in motion in the first days of next month", and then a real hint of the line of surprise attack was dropped to General Graham:

"I rather think, between ourselves, I shall direct my march across the Lower Duero within the kingdom of Portugal."

Actually, the offensive did not get under way until May 22, but its plan and even its line of advance had been kept secret so carefully that by the time the junior strategists had begun to grasp the plan it was too late to write it in full to the newspapers. Briefly, the plan of the great offensive movement of 1813 was to surprise the enemy by starting off the main body of the allied army north of the Douro and then throwing the whole body (after Hill's men joined from the south) across the river Esla by pontoon. The whole army would then march direct on Burgos, constantly outflanking the French right wing; the continental vase was to be transferred eventually from Lisbon to Santander, where a siege train would be waiting in ships hovering off the coast.

Late spring rains and the slow movements of the clumsy pontoons delayed the start until May 22, but the army was "all cheerfulness, joy and anticipation", and even its austere Commander waved his hand as he crossed the frontier and called: "Farewell, Portugal!" He never saw Portugal again. Wellington began his march with Hill's detachment in order to divert French attention from the far larger allied movements under Graham in the north—for it was now a fixed idea with the Marshals that Wellington always moved with his main body. In four days Hill's men had regained Salamanca and were moving on Toro; and then Wellington with a few staff officers galloped furiously north from Salamanca at dawn on May 29 (1813), crossed the Douro next morning in a basket hauled by a cable, and by noon had joined Graham's main body. On June 3, Wellington made his junction with Hill at Toro; so that within twelve days of starting he had 80,000 men in striking distance of Valladolid. King Joseph and Marshal Jourdan, who had hoped to intercept the invading army at Salamanca, held long and unhappy council; and as a result of their deliberations a huge convoy of refugees and plunder from Madrid set

S. Sebastian
St. Jean de Luz
Irun
Maya
Lesaca
Roncesvalles
Ostiz
Sorauren
Pamplona

FRANCE

R. Ebro

● Barcelona

40°

Valencia ●

Murcia ●

Campaign in
PORTUGAL & SPAIN
1813
Approximate lines of march
Hill's advance □ □ □ □
Graham's advance ○○○○
Wellington's ride . . . . . .
Allied Armies' advance ✕✕✕✕
Battles, Combats & Sieges ✕
scale : miles
0   50   100

off again wearily, this time with the French army retreating from Valladolid to Burgos.

The Allies were in hot pursuit, a triumphant procession where they marched "singing even the last mile" each day. At Zamora, at Palencia, the seemingly endless lines of the Allied troops passed cheering and singing through streets vivid with bright tapestries and hangings; girls and even nuns showered them with rose petals; the church bells clashed and pealed jubilantly. "The sun shone brilliantly, the sky was heavenly blue, and clouds of dust marked the line of march of the glittering columns," wrote a romantic young officer. "The joyous peasantry hailed our approach and came dancing to meet us, singing, and beating time on their small tambourines. . . ."

"This singing psalms to me wastes time," wrote his matter-of-fact and impatient Commander, who wanted "certain ships loaded with biscuit and flour and certain others loaded with a heavy train of artillery and ammunition" sent off "*at once*" from Corunna to Santander. Even as he wrote, the outflanked French army had abandoned the line of the river Pisuerga, had fallen back on Burgos, and then had decided to abandon that also. On the morning of June 13, the castle of Burgos (the fortress which had turned the Allied army back in 1812) was blown up, and so hurriedly and unskilfully that more than one hundred French soldiers were killed. It was a dramatic moment. Embroidering a little, many years after the event, the Duke told Croker that "when I heard and saw this explosion I made a sudden resolution forthwith—instanter to cross the Ebro and endeavour to push the French to the Pyrenees. . . . Some of my officers remonstrated with me about the imprudence of crossing the Ebro. . . . I would not listen to advice, and that very evening I crossed the river. . . ."

But at that moment the French rear-guard suddenly lost touch with the Allied army, and found they were followed only by Julian Sanchez's guerrilla cavalry. What had become of Lord Wellington? they asked each other; and decided rather dangerously that he had halted "with his usual timidity". In fact he was taking his army over the mountains by roads which the French thought impassable, as indeed they were except in summer and to troops in high spirits:

"One while, the columns moved through luxurious valleys inter-sprinkled with hamlets, vineyards and flower-gardens," wrote a romantic officer, "at another, they struggled up mountain ridges, or pressed through alpine passes overhung with toppling cliffs. . . ."

Another enthusiast imagined himself "transported to the happy retreat described by Rasselas"; yet another talks more prosaically of buying a pat of butter "to nibble on the way" after having tasted none for two years; and a fourth describes the enjoyment of an "olio" of beef, fowls, rice, and a hare, with wine, rum, and brandy. Those who had to trudge every step of the way on foot and help to haul the guns over precipices were less romantic and festive. A private soldier's diary reads:

"We were so harassed by fatigue in our long marches that we never left the camp, and were too weary to pay much attention to anything that did not relieve our wants."

Such was the famous five days' march across the Cantabrian Mountains towards Vittoria, which the French only discovered too late, when Reille's division bumped into Wellington's First and Maucune's into the Light, as they debouched rapidly from the passes, and picked up a few hundred prisoners from the astonished and retreating enemy.

The complicated and decisive battle of Vittoria was fought on June 21, 1813, as the culmination of the manœuvres by which Wellington had hustled the French right across northern Spain in thirty days. The French army, 57,000 strong, with 153 guns, was drawn up behind the river Zadorra, and by an extraordinary piece of neglect none of the thirteen bridges was destroyed and only three covered by artillery. Wellington's attack started on his extreme right with Hill's corps and thence spread all along the line as the other columns (some belatedly) came into action. He himself started off with the Light Division, which was opposite the French centre. A peasant informed him of an unguarded bridge, and instantly he changed his plan to meet this unexpected piece of good fortune, sent Kempt's brigade over and a staff officer to order Lord Dalhousie immediately to attack with the Third and Seventh divisions. The staff officer could not find Dalhousie but ran into Sir Thomas Picton who was riding up and down in a civilian top hat and a rage, exclaiming: "Damn it! Lord Wellington has forgotten us." Taking the orders to Dalhousie on himself Picton sent his Fighting Third into action with the unforgettable operation order:

"Come on, ye rascals! Come on, ye fighting villains!"

They went into action, says an interested spectator, "like a meteor"; and indeed this somewhat unorthodox charge of General Picton's men really decided the battle, for they drove the French out of two positions, and by the time they were slowing down, Wellington had brought up his artillery and reserves for another attack, while on the far side of Vittoria, Graham's divisions and Longa's Spaniards decisively threatened the French flank and rear and main line of communication with France.

By four o'clock in the afternoon, Joseph had been compelled to throw in all his reserves, there was another furious artillery duel, and then the whole Allied army charged in a triple line of brigades.

"The sun was setting, and his last rays fell upon a magnificent spectacle—the red masses of infantry were seen advancing steadily across the plain—the horse artillery at a gallop to the front, to open its fire on the fugitives—the hussar brigade were charging by the Camino Real—while the second division . . . was extending over the heights upon the right. From a hillock Wellington viewed the retreating enemy and urged forward his own troops in pursuit. What a sight to meet a conqueror's eye! Beneath him the valley was covered for a mile with straggling fugitives—for the French army had totally lost its formation, and neither attempted to rally even or check the pursuit."

Joseph was forced to abandon his own carriage (which was found loaded with Italian pictures cut from their frames) and to flee across country to avoid imminent capture. The whole of the enormous French baggage train fell into the hands of the victorious army, and between them the Allied soldiers secured plunder worth over a million pounds sterling. Among the innumerable trophies was Marshal Jourdan's gold-mounted *bâton* of a *Maréchal de France*, which Wellington sent to the Prince Regent as a trophy. As Wellington galloped towards Vittoria with the Life Guards, to post them as sentries to prevent the sack and burning of the town, he passed through an amazing pandemonium and confusion:

"Cannon and caissons, carriages and tumbrels, waggons of every description were overturned or deserted. . . . Here was the personal baggage of a king— there the scenery and decorations of a theatre. Munitions of war were mixed with articles of virtu; and with scattered arms and packs, silks, embroidery, plate and jewels. . . . One waggon was loaded with money, the next with cartridges; and wounded soldiers, deserted women and children of every age everywhere implored assistance or protection. Here a lady was overtaken in her carriage—in the next calash was an actress or fille-de-chambre, while droves of oxen were roaming over the plain, intermingled with an endless quantity of sheep and goats, mules and horses, asses and milch cows."

Joseph lost all his artillery (151 guns), 415 caissons, 100 military waggons, huge quantities of ammunition, 2,000 prisoners; and he himself was flying at top speed with a disorderly multitude, which a few hours earlier had been an army, in the direction of Pamplona and the road to France. The power of Napoleon in the Peninsula was at an end. The unbelievable had happened. An event which a whole generation of politicians had spent years in proving to be impossible had dramatically occurred—a British army was in sight of the Pyrenees and in pursuit of a dismayed and routed Imperial army. Three days after the battle, Wellington summed up the situation, as he wrote to Richard Wellesley in his matter-of-fact style:

"King Joseph and his army must quit Spain; indeed, they have already this night retired from Pamplona."

By the beginning of July, Graham's detachment of the Peninsular Army had driven the French out of Irun and across the Bidassoa; Saragossa was recaptured; Pamplona and San Sebastian besieged; Clausel was retiring into France with the last remnants of "King" Joseph's army. Wellington's army now occupied the line of the Pyrenees from Roncesvalles to the Atlantic—a curious eyrie for a "frightened Leopard" which was to have been driven into the sea at Lisbon long ago.

The news reached London on July 3 amid tremendous rejoicings and a new shower of congratulations and rewards for the victor. "You have sent me," wrote Prinny, "among the trophies of your unrivalled fame, the staff of a French Marshal, and I send you in return that of England." The only difficulty here was that a baton for Field-Marshals was an armament unknown in the British army, so that the Horse Guards were compelled hastily to invent one with many mutterings about *the Fountain of taste*. Almost as important as the Regent's gracious notice was a letter from the Prime Minister:

"The information of your success, which will be transmitted to the north of Europe this night, will arrive there most opportunely, and cannot fail to produce the most important effects. If Austria would now declare, we might really hope to put an end to the tyranny which has been so long oppressing the world. . . ."

For the Emperor had recovered or seemed to recover from the Russian disaster with miraculous speed and efficiency. He had beaten the eastern powers at Lützen and Bautzen, and an armistice was arranged to discuss peace terms. Austria still hesitated, desperately anxious to join the winning side, but desperately uncertain which would win. Hence Napoleon's efforts to keep the news of Vittoria from the other powers at the conference, and the unwontedly strenuous efforts of the British Government to circulate it. They ordered a

G

reprint of the *Gazette* with Wellington's dispatch in German, Dutch, and French, and distributed copies at every continental port they could reach. The story is that Count Bubna got the news in Dresden and sent it on to Count Stadion (the Austrian envoy) by a special messenger, who arrived in the middle of the night. Stadion read the news of Vittoria by the light of a candle, and then with a whoop of joy rushed along the corridors knocking at the bedroom doors of emperors, kings, and ministers, shouting:

"King Joseph is dished in Spain!"

A few days later, Austria joined the Coalition against Napoleon.

CHAPTER XVII

Victory

WHY did not Wellington capture more than two thousand of the demoralized French army at Vittoria? Because, as every battle of the war proved, that obstinate creature the British private soldier had definite ideas about what was required of him and what he was prepared to do, and nothing could induce him to follow up any victory to the last ounce of energy.

Why did not Wellington invade France at once, seeing there was nothing but a beaten and disorganized army between him and Paris? Because the fortresses of Pamplona and San Sebastian still held out to his rear; and because for all he knew the Eastern powers might make a peace, which would bring down on him the Emperor and what was left of the Grand Army. At the time of Vittoria, Wellington had just heard of the armistice of Plaswitz. Moreover, he was convinced that if he once took his army into France, the Spanish government would never allow him to retreat back into Spain. On top of this he had very little ready money to pay for supplies in France; and he had no intention whatever of provoking a national uprising in France by robbing the peasants for his supplies.

So Wellington decided on caution, to blockade Pamplona (which was too strong to take by assault, but was luckily short of food) and to besiege San Sebastian, while waiting for some decisive move by Russia, Prussia, and Austria. Meanwhile, it was interesting to learn that Vittoria had thrown the Emperor into one of the wild fits of rage of his decline; that he had sent the unfortunate Jourdan into poverty and exile; that he had deposed Joseph and cruelly put him in the hands of his greatest enemy, Marshal Soult, who had been ordered "to recapture Spain and Portugal", but with fewer and worse men than had sufficed to lose them.

While Wellington watched the Pyrenees, Hill's men and the Spaniards kept guard over Pamplona, while Graham was ordered to capture San Sebastian by assault. He made sad work of it; and by July 25 had thrown away over 1,200 men against a loss of only 67 to the besieged. Wellington was in something of a quandary that morning, for news was coming in which seemed to indicate that a reorganized army directed by Soult was about to storm the passes, while the failure at San Sebastian was so serious it could not be neglected. In the end, Wellington rode over to Graham to make plans for a renewal of the assault, and as he made his way back to his headquarters at Lesaca after dark that night he met belated messengers bringing startling news which should have reached him much earlier. The nine days' battle of the Pyrenees had begun, and the first day's fighting was over before Wellington had even been informed. Soult had sent Reille and Clausel against the pass of Roncesvalles, where a mere six thousand of Lowry Cole's men held them up all day. Nearer the sea D'Erlon had attacked William Stewart at Maya, and had been held in a costly but heroic manner. Unfortunately, Cole was dilatory in reporting, and made a quite unnecessary withdrawal that evening.

"Our generals," Wellington once said, "are really heroes when I am on the spot to direct them, but when I am obliged to quit them they are children."

At four o'clock in the morning of July 26, Wellington was on his thoroughbred "Copenhagen" galloping inland as fast as he could pelt. He found the ever reliable Hill on the Bidassoa, ordered him to stand firm, and then galloped on towards Pamplona—the absence of news from that direction was most disquieting. At about eight that evening he heard with annoyance that Cole was still retiring, and promptly sent counter-orders. Oddly enough, the real damage had been done by the usually bellicose Picton, who had come walloping up to Cole's headquarters in hot haste that afternoon, dressed in a blue coat and top hat, and beating his charger with a furled umbrella he had hastily picked up in mistake for a switch. Although Picton had precise and urgent orders from Wellington *not* to fall back in his pocket at that moment, he ordered a retreat. Luckily, at the last moment Cole had an inspiration, and Picton agreed to let him continue to hold the hills which are in fact the key to the whole Sorauren position.

That night (July 26–27) Wellington slept at Almandoz, and was off again at dawn at full speed with a few of his staff, including the Quartermaster-General (Murray) and Lord Fitzroy Somerset, his secretary. Bad news kept meeting them on the way, and at Ostiz they heard Picton was actually falling back on Pamplona! Leaving Murray behind to control the movements of the reserve divisions coming up, Wellington galloped off on his thoroughbred at such a speed that only Somerset kept up with him. With a flying clatter of hoofs they galloped up to the bridge at Sorauren, and saw the whole impending battle laid out before them. Wellington made his decision instantly

GENERAL SIR GEORGE MURRAY

From a drawing by John Linnell
[*The National Portrait Gallery*]

WELLINGTON

After the drawing by Thomas Heaphy
made at the British Headquarters, 1813
[*The National Portrait Gallery*]

dismounted and wrote Murray a thirteen-line dispatch altering the divisions' line of march, with friendly but foolish peasants clamouring round him that the French were at hand—quite needlessly since anyone could see the French cavalry coming through the village street towards them. The dispatch was finished. Somerset dashed away with it in one direction, and Wellington, just eluding the French dragoons, cantered off to join his own troops. The orders so dramatically dispatched brought the relieving divisions up several hours earlier, and thus ensured victory. Otherwise, such romantic and irregular happenings were contrary to the Peer's severe tastes.

It was a day of dramatic moments and demonstrations for one who detested drama. Portuguese veterans who had been with Wellington at the recapture of Oporto suddenly caught sight of the slim horseman in his grey frock-coat and oilskin-covered cocked hat, and instantly set up their war shout: "Douro! Douro!" The long lines of redcoats heard the cry, knew what it meant, and their rattling cheers ran along the slopes. For once in his life, Wellington did not shrink in distaste from a demonstration. Indeed, he rode to a knoll so that all could see he was there. A well-bred officer remarked that he should "never forget the joy which beamed in every countenance when his lordship's presence became known"; and private soldiers grinned at each other: " 'Ere's Atty, 'ere's that long-nosed bugger that licks the French!" Everybody on the redcoat side of the line felt immeasurably relieved and heartened. Marshal Soult, hearing the prolonged cheers, guessed that heavy reinforcements had arrived; and decided to delay his attack until he had made an armed reconnaissance. And then came the usual Wellingtonian "victory thunder-storm", roaring more encouragement to the redcoats.

Wellington said of Soult that he was an excellent general until he got his troops on to the battle-field, because he then did not know what to do with them. Someone else epigrammatically remarked that after July 28 the battle of the Pyrenees turned out to be a repetition of Bussaco followed by an encore to Salamanca. It was not until noon that Soult launched his columns to the attack, and was easily beaten off "in the old style". On that day 18,000 British, Portuguese, and Spanish infantry in line defeated 33,000 French in column. Most remarkable was the feat of the surviving 400 men of the Fortieth Foot who had been badly mauled in the fighting on July 26, and with two Spanish battalions beat off three attacks of five French battalions. At the second assault, the Spaniards fled, and the position was only saved by the 400 of the Fortieth Foot charging 2,000 Frenchmen with the bayonet. Wellington's entire staff waved their hats and cheered this handsome feat of arms, for which they received a severe rebuke from the Peer, who held that it is no part of a staff officer's duties to shout encouragement or approval to regimental officers and men in action.

There exists a letter of the Emperor about this battle, not published in the official correspondence, which throws an interesting sidelight on his methods of composing bulletins:

"You had better circulate the news that in consequence of Marshal Soult's victory the siege of San Sebastian has been raised, and 30 siege-guns and 200 waggons taken. The blockade of Pamplona was raised on the 27th. General Hill could not carry off his wounded and was obliged to burn part of his baggage. Twelve siege-guns (24 pounders) were captured. Send this to Prague, Leipsig and Frankfurt."

Happy is the hero who can be his own rewrite man, and even persuade posterity to believe him.

In fact, on that very evening of July 28 (1813) Soult had decided he must retire, and had made rather a hash of it. He tried a night march over mountain paths in the fog, and as soon as light came Wellington attacked, capturing 1,700 prisoners from Maucune's division alone, and badly damaging several others. Soult's retreat became a rout, and for an hour or two Wellington seriously thought of making an immediate invasion of France, and would undoubtedly have done so but for the Plaswitz armistice. He refrained, and on August 3 he was back at Lesaca, writing placidly to Bathurst:

"We have had some desperate fighting in these mountains, and I have never known the troops behave so well."

Soult admitted nearly 13,000 casualties, and if he admitted that number they must have been serious indeed. The attempt to reverse the verdict of Vittoria had failed utterly; Pamplona was still closely blockaded; the siege-guns taken temporarily away from San Sebastian were brought back; and Soult noted with alarm the weakening morale of his troops. At Echelar on August 2 (for instance) Barnes's brigade of the Seventh Division had made a charge against overwhelming numbers, and should have been beaten off with ease. The charge succeeded; and this triumph, which would have been quite impossible in earlier days, was but one of many indications of the Allied supremacy over Soult's more and more disheartened army of Spain.

It is an interesting comment on the sort of person who was running this war in England to discover that Bathurst, the Minister of War, remained entirely ignorant of the fact that the battle of the Pyrenees was the longest and the biggest battle Wellington and his men had yet won. Bathurst merely wrote: "I congratulate you on your distinguished success," and then complained that Wellington's dispatch had not given the number of prisoners captured, although when Wellington wrote there had not been time even to begin counting them. There were in fact about seven thousand.

There was a pause; and then at the end of August fighting flared up again. Soult pressed forward near the sea in a last desperate attempt to relieve San Sebastian, whose cannon fire he heard dying away as Graham's men stormed into the town; and Wellington drove him back at San Marcial in the only battle he fought with Spanish troops alone. It is said that the Spanish general sent back for the help of the British brigades drawn up as his reserve; and that Wellington refused, seeing that the attack on the Spanish lines was faltering, and anxious for the Spaniards to have the sole credit for the victory. For him the day must have been a queer one, since he was half-way between the mountain battle and the assault on the shore fortress. San Marcial was a considerable affair, since Soult lost four thousand men, and the Commander was able to give the Spaniards high praise for their conduct:

"They were beat back . . . in the most gallant style by the Spanish troops, whose conduct was equal to that of any troops I have ever seen engaged."

It was another story at San Sebastian. The town indeed was captured, with Major Snodgrass and his Portuguese behaving "handsomely", but the casualties were well over two thousand, and the apparently inevitable scenes of arson, murder, pillage, drunkenness, and rape followed the fall of the town. Several officers were murdered by their own men in vain efforts to restore discipline and order, and all the goodwill gained at San Marcial was lost in a very natural Spanish resentment at these outrages, of which the anti-British party in Spain took the fullest advantage. The Peer was suffering from an extra bad attack of lumbago on that August 31; and his spirits were not improved by the loss at San Sebastian of Sir Richard Fletcher, the engineer who had carried out the ideas for the Lines of Torres Vedras.

During the sack of San Sebastian, General Rey and about one thousand survivors of the garrison took refuge in the castle, which surrendered on September 8, after the town had been gutted by intoxicated madmen. If we have to allot blame for these horrible disorders to anything but the nature of men, we might surely blame

General Rey and the principal inhabitants of the town for not ordering the destruction of all liquor before the assault, which they knew was coming. They had by this time plenty of experience of what happened at the storming of towns, whether the attacking troops were French, British, Spanish, or Portuguese; and they knew all the vilest excesses came from drunkenness. At San Sebastian the Portuguese regiments were as bad as the British; and it seems a little hard to blame Wellington for brutalities which he could not stop but which General Rey could have prevented by smashing every barrel and bottle in the town.

Pamplona held out much longer than San Sebastian; for Wellington was determined not to sacrifice men in a direct assault on that almost impregnable fortress. It did not in fact surrender until the last day of October 1813; and on October 7 Wellington made a sudden surprise attack on the lower reaches of the Bidassoa, which carried his army on to what Imperial propaganda called the "sacred" soil of France. Sacred or not, the British army were there; and their Commander had certain ideas as to how they were to behave. He revived in Orders the stale fiction of war with the government and not with the nation of the enemy; pointed out (more cogently) that French disasters in the Peninsula were largely due to their cruelty to civilians; and drew the moral that good behaviour in conquered France would pay. But he did not push his invasion, even though the rumours of Leipzig had come in and the Russians were clamouring as usual for a second front. Wellington was not too eager to invade a country "where everybody is a soldier" and "where the population is armed and organized", with a force largely composed of Spaniards and Portuguese burning to revenge in kind the murders, arsons, rapes, and robberies so long practised on their own countries. He knew that the French were openly saying they would make no resistance if the English came alone, but that they knew perfectly well what the Spaniards and Portuguese intended and would rise *en masse* against them.

For some weeks Soult had been building a feeble parody of the Lines of Torres Vedras, which showed how completely the French generals misunderstood the peculiar complex of circumstances which made the fortification of the Lisbon peninsula so effective. Wellington decided to take these field-works, and a day or two before the battle of the Nivelle in which they were stormed, he demonstrated to his staff how the apparently formidable works could be carried:

"They dare not concentrate a sufficient body to resist the attacks I shall make upon them," Wellington said. "I can pour a greater force on certain points than they can concentrate to resist me."

In any event, this is exactly what happened on the day of the attack (November 10, 1813) when one position after another fell to overwhelming attacks, so that at nightfall Soult had to order the abandonment of his "impregnable" right wing, where the four French divisions spiked their guns and got away only just in time to avoid complete encirclement. The fighting of a single day made the intense engineering work of many weeks totally useless, and Wellington's headquarters sprang forward from Lesaca up in the Pyrenees to St. Pé on the river Nivelle. There was a curious little episode that evening, concerning a French colonel who had been captured by the Rifle Brigade. The staff began asking him questions before dinner, to which they got only grunts and surly monosyllables in reply. Wellington whispered to them to leave the colonel alone until after the soothing operation of dinner and a few glasses of Madeira. Pledging his captive guest with great courtesy, Wellington apologized for entertaining a distinguished guest in a mere barn, adding:

" 'But you, Monsieur le Colonel, who have served all over the world, have probably been used to such things, and indeed your Emperor himself must of late have had some hard nights' lodging. . . . By the bye, where *were* Imperial Headquarters when you last heard of him?'

" 'Monseigneur, there are no Imperial Headquarters.' "

Wellington and his staff exchanged glances. They had heard vague rumours of the battle of the nations at Leipzig, but this was the first authentic sign of a great new disaster to the Empire. Though small in comparison, that day on the Nivelle had not exactly been a help to the Emperor, Soult having lost fifty-nine guns and four to five thousand men. Even Napoleon's reserves could not stand this continued drain of man-power; and the conscripts drafted to fill the gaps were now mere cannon fodder in comparison with the brave and skilful veterans who were lost.

Such being the case, why did Wellington not push on into France at once? "It has not ceased raining since the 10th," he wrote to Henry Wellesley on November 19, "and I have put the troops into cantonments." Every ford on the numerous rivers flowing from the Pyrenees became impassable, roads and fields were quagmires, ankle-deep, knee-deep in sticky mud. So drenching was the rain that Wellington left his leaky barn for the house of the parish priest of St. Pé, with whom and other inhabitants he spent the days talking French politics. For close on ten years no responsible Englishman had been in touch with any Frenchmen but *émigrés* and prisoners, and Napoleon's censorship and

G*

propaganda were so effective that (for example) many French people had never heard of the battle of Trafalgar, and the inhabitants of southern France were astounded at being invaded—their latest news was of driving the frightened Leopard into the sea. On the other hand, with Napoleon's defeat growing ever closer, it was very important for the British Government and its General to find out what sort of peace would be acceptable to the French people. Already royalist *émigrés* and minor Bourbons were pestering Wellington, and assuring him that Bordeaux and the whole Midi were eager to rise for Louis XVIII. The real fact, which not even Wellington saw fully, was that the French people were so completely sick of the war that they were willing to accept any solution which gave them peace and security.

Such ends were hardly furthered by a Portuguese soldier who murdered a whole French family because French soldiers had murdered his family. And when the Spaniards began robbing, murdering, and burning in a big way, Wellington settled the matter drastically by sending the whole Spanish army back to Spain in disgrace. The remedy was a desperate one, for as he wrote ruefully to Lord Bathurst:

"If I could now bring forward 20,000 good Spaniards, paid and fed, I should have Bayonne. If I could bring forward 40,000, I do not know where I should stop. Now I have both the 20,000 and the 40,000 at my command, upon this frontier, but I cannot venture to bring forward any for want of means of paying and supporting them. Without pay and food, they must plunder; and if they plunder, they will ruin us all."

There was a great shortage of hard cash at this period, and the British Government was unable for a time to send out the usual amounts of silver and gold. On one occasion during this shortage the Peer had to borrow money from his staff officers to pay for a special messenger. A little later, he became a coiner, collected some of the criminals of his army and turned English and Spanish coins into French five-franc pieces. Great care was taken to see that they conformed to Napoleon's standards of weight and alloy, and a secret mark was put on the coins so that in the future the French mint could withdraw them.

It was during this wet and penniless winter that the Emperor in his distresses suddenly remembered King Ferdinand of Spain, and tried to negotiate a separate peace with him in exchange for his freedom: an event which would have left the Anglo-Portuguese army in a nasty hole. Wellington gloomily thought these intrigues might succeed, especially "if Boney had less pride and more common sense". Nothing, he suspected, was more astonishing than the lack of common sense in

the world, for "if the Spaniards had had more common sense they
would never have undertaken the war", and now that they had nearly
won it they were not unlikely to throw away all they had fought for.
However, though Ferdinand signed a treaty (which he had no intention
whatever of keeping) the Cortes and Regency refused to ratify, which
the Peer said was "behaving very handsomely"—and breathed again.
The real dupe of the proceedings this time was the Emperor, who was
so anxious to believe that the Treaty of Valençay would accomplish
what he expected that he withdrew troops from Soult and Suchet
before it ever came up for ratification. It was harsh yet poetic justice
that the master trickster of the Spaniards should in his own turn and
need be tricked by them.

The only military action during these winter months was a double
attack by Soult on each wing of Wellington's army in turn, an action
which did some damage but failed completely in its object of crushing
either wing separately. Wellington had guessed what was coming
(since his position was cut in two by the river Nive) and had repeatedly
warned his two wing commanders, Hope and Hill. There are many
personal stories of Wellington during the five days of this desperate
fighting. One of the most authentic concerns a battalion of Hope's
army who were hard-pressed and beginning to waver when Wellington
rode up:

" 'You must keep your ground, my lads,' cried he, 'There is nothing behind
you. Charge! Charge!' Instantly a shout was raised. Many fugitives, who had
lost their own corps, threw themselves into line upon our flank. We poured in
but one volley, and then rushed on with the bayonet. The enemy would not
stand it; their ranks were broken, and they fled in utter confusion."

It is an interesting point of difference between Wellington and his
subordinate commanders that while Wellington was saving his men,
in this very same battle and almost at the same time Sir John Hope had
to be saved by his troops. Sir John was one of those generals who wear
their hats crooked, write flamboyant communiqués, and behave as if it
were the duty of a commanding officer to act like a sniper or a sniper's
target. He was always getting into trouble and costing valuable lives
for his rescue; and not very long after this was wounded and captured
by the French. A more heartening episode of this battle of the Nive
was that three German battalions deserted from the French by night,
and were promptly sent off to join the armies on the other front.
Indirectly this was a greater blow than it seemed, for both Soult and
Suchet in Catalonia became so suspicious that they disarmed all
German and Spanish troops in their armies.

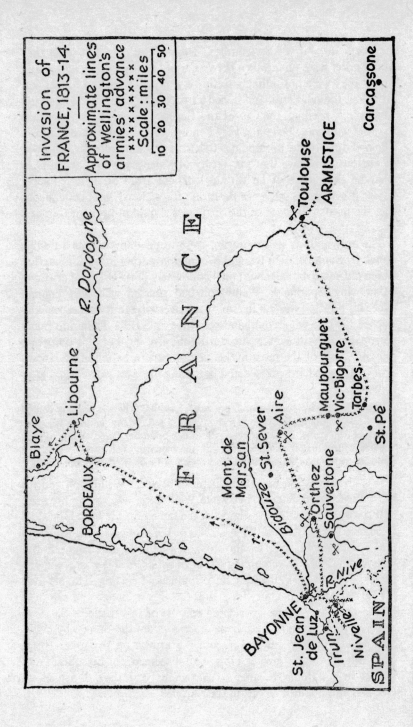

Invasion of
FRANCE, 1813-14.
Approximate lines
of Wellington's
armies' advance
×××××××
Scale: miles
10 20 30 40 50

R. Dordogne

FRANCE

Libourne

Blaye

BORDEAUX

Mont de Marsan

Bidouze

St. Sever

Aire

Maubourguet

Vic-Bigorre

Tarbes

St. Pé

Toulouse

ARMISTICE

Carcassone

Orthez

Sauveltone

R. Nive

BAYONNE

St. Jean de Luz

Irun

Nivelle

SPAIN

Once more the Basque country was drenched in rain, and as Wellington's veterans shivered in their huts and ruins, the Emperor in the north took advantage of the mistrusts and disagreements of the Allied sovereign, to launch his last and perhaps his most brilliant campaign, while Lord Castlereagh in a post-chaise toiled interminably over German roads to catch up with the kings and try to make them see reason. Castlereagh arrived just in time to prevent a fatal quarrel between the Emperors of Russia and Austria. Meanwhile, royalty which had been conspicuously absent from Wellington's headquarters during six years of hard knocks (the Prince of Orange excepted) suddenly turned up as Victory began to smile. The French royal Duc d'Angoulême arrived with an aristocratic attendant, but they were not much of a success:

"Lord Wellington was in his manner droll towards them. As they went out, we drew up on each side, and Lord Wellington put them first; they bowed and scraped right and left so oddly, and so actively, that he followed with a face much nearer a grin than a smile."

Yet Wellington could discover no particular enthusiasm for the old royal family, and none at all for the alternatives of a regency for the King of Rome, the rule of one of the Marshals, or a republic—which gave everyone the jitters with memories of Robespierre. Then what the devil did they want? he asked testily. A cynic muttered that Buddha would make a very good king of France, and another hinted that Gascony had been very prosperous under the Angevine kings of England. As for the peasants, they were enjoying a brief period of "taxless anarchy" and praying that this unexampled prosperity might last—the mad English over-paid in cash for everything.

Napoleon was forced to draw on Soult for another 14,000 men, and that was really the end of what had once been the army of Spain, as it was the last effort also before the Emperor's fall. Wellington's operations settled into a pursuit of Soult, plus the blockade of Bayonne and the friendly occupation of Bordeaux. On February 12, 1814, the army moved forward once more, and when the Second Division hesitated at Garris, a familiar figure in grey rode swiftly up behind them with the sharp order to "take that hill at once". Soult's army fell back, and a day or two later lost the line of the river Bidouze and then the line of the river Saison; and there Wellington halted while he himself rode back thirty miles in the hope of shepherding Sir John Hope's men over the perilous passage of the Adour towards Bayonne. But a savage gale was blowing, and he returned once more to his

manœuvring against Soult, who now abandoned the Gave d'Oloron
and fell back upon Orthez and the Gave de Pau. There, rather to
Wellington's surprise, Soult decided to make a stand; and there
Wellington attacked him, failing at first against Soult's concentration
to his right, but finally driving the French army back in headlong
retreat after bitter fighting, taking 6 guns and 1,300 prisoners, and
disabling four of Soult's generals. Wellington and Alava were both
slightly wounded by half-spent bullets which hit them in the buttocks.
A week later Wellington was still limping. Hastily Soult fell back on
St. Sever, so hastily that he had no time to destroy his magazines, all of
which, including the great central depot at Mont de Marsan, were
captured.

The end was very close now, and Soult must have known it, as each
morning brought him the ever-growing lists of deserters, and the
northern Allies pressed on to Paris. The English troops soon learned
to recognize these deserters in the villages by their close-cropped heads
and the new civilian clothes given them by sympathetic villagers. On
March 1 (1814) Wellington occupied Soult's former headquarters at
St. Sever, and Hill attacked the Marshal in his positions on the Aire
forcing him to fall back wearily in the direction of Toulouse, while
snow fell and Wellington rode through the storm wrapped in a white
cloak and fighting a heavy cold. Bordeaux rather startlingly put up the
white cockade and declared for King Louis, and Wellington gathered
up his troops for the last blow while the Allies marched on Paris.

There was a sharp brush at Vic-Bigorre on March 19; on the
twentieth an engagement at Tarbes, and Soult only just extricated
himself in time from a great encircling movement. On March 24,
Soult brought his army into Toulouse, 8,000 of them without boots,
while 5,000 new deserters and stragglers were scattered over the
countryside. Nevertheless, in the battle of April 10 for Toulouse, the
French stood up to the attack with surprising courage, and (owing to
Picton's disobeying his orders) actually inflicted more casualties than
they suffered: 4,568 to 3,236. But this last flash of resistance was as
useless as the bloody sortie from Bayonne a day or two later; after
dark on April 11 Soult marched off what was left of his army in the
direction of Carcassonne, leaving behind many guns, 1,600 wounded,
and "large quantities of stores".

Before 6 a.m. on April 12, messengers arrived at Wellington's
headquarters begging him to enter the city at once, and declaring
for Louis XVIII. At about eleven, the deputy-mayor, council,
band, and city guard, and a large crowd awaited Wellington at one

of the gates, ready to hand over the keys and to proclaim the loyalty to Louis XVIII they had so long and so skilfully concealed. By accident Wellington slipped into the town by another gate, and passed through streets already clinking busily with hammers and chisels as they smashed the Emperor's busts and chipped off the N's and B's. The mayor and his train made a rush for the town hall where "Wellington showed himself at the window, amidst the shouts and waving handkerchiefs and hats of everyone". His lordship then announced a ball that evening at the Prefecture, and sent Marshal Beresford in hot pursuit of Soult with three divisions and the cavalry.

At 5 p.m. there was a rapid clatter of hoofs, and Colonel Ponsonby galloped up to headquarters with electrifying news sent from Bordeaux by Dalhousie—the Emperor had abdicated at Fontainebleau on April 6! There was a dinner that night with several of the chief citizens of Toulouse—Picton, Freire, Alava, Alten (of the King's German Legion), about forty in all—when in came Colonel Cooke and the Marquis de Saint-Simon with official dispatches and private letters from Paris. The first envelope Wellington opened contained a wildly excited note from Lord Burghersh, beginning: "Glory to God and to yourself, the great man has fallen!" Wellington called for champagne, and with his usual deliberate calm proposed the health of Louis XVIII, "which was very cordially received with three times three". If his lordship expected the matter to rest there, he was deceived. General Alava suddenly jumped to his feet and "with great warmth" gave "the health of Lord Wellington, *Liberador d'Espagna!*" Instantly there was pandemonium, every man on his feet and "a general exclamation from all these foreigners":

> "*El Liberador d'Espagna!*"
> "*Liberador de Portugal!*"
> "*Libérateur de la France!*"
> "*Libérateur de l'Europe!*"

The formality of "three times three" was lost in a frantic cheering which lasted for ten minutes. Lord Wellington looked surprised and "confused", and to stop the apparently endless demonstration got up to speak. Excited witnesses afterwards vowed that for a moment that usually cold clear eye was dimmed with emotion, but if so it was only for an instant. As he looked searchingly down on those red shouting faces, common sense insisted that his guests were drunk—"Lord Wellington bowed, and immediately called for coffee".

CHAPTER XVIII

The Captured Eagle Escapes

THE bugles sounded reveille, and the British Army of the Peninsula awoke to a hangover and the slowly dawning realization that the war was successfully ended—which for many of them meant going to fight another and most unpopular war in North America. Probably the coolest head among them was still that of their Commander, who was abstemious in his wine-drinking, averse to being carried away by fits of popular hysteria, and not to be moved from calmly realistic views of human beings. A less scrupulous or less restrained man might have chosen to overlook the fact that his Liberator-of-Europe audience were drunk, or might even have been drunk himself. As Wellington sustained that test of his vanity with tranquil good sense, so he passed unscathed through the ordeal that same evening at the Toulouse theatre, where an excited French crowd cheered him for wearing the white cockade of the Bourbons, and in a frenzy of loyalty sang the old royalist song, "*O Richard, O mon roi . . .*" having suddenly discovered that for twenty years they had accidentally been on the wrong side. Even Lord Burghersh's gush already quoted: "Glory to God and to yourself, the great man has fallen!" passed without comment to the Wellington correspondence book. With the King's government to be carried on, orders to be carried out, and some sort of arrangements to be made for reducing (if possible) the general confusion in Europe, life was too short for any foolery. There was still, as this great world-policeman perceived, constabulary duty to be done.

Taking first things first, there was Soult to be watched. Alarmed over the probable loss of his valuable plunder and insufficiently convinced by the reassurances of the provisional French Government, the stern old warrior refused to accept the armistice. He did indeed receive Colonel Cooke, the British commissioner, with that unpleasant courtesy which rival warriors reserve for each other in such circumstances, but he frightened the French commissioner, the Marquis de Saint-Simon, out of his wits by pointing sternly to the fleur-de-lis in that gentleman's buttonhole and telling him "in low menacing tones" that he "deserved hanging". The little Marquis fled to the more amiable and less self-enriched Marshal Suchet, who received him more kindly; and Colonel Cooke reported to his chief. Wellington contented himself by "observing" the enemy, whose motives and bluff were perfectly clear to him. Soult did not mean to fight for anything more important than his own bank balance; and meanwhile the Hôtel de France, Toulouse, sheltered the most amiable of Spanish ladies as well as British General Headquarters. The capitulation of Marshal Soult was not long delayed, and very soon *S.M. L'Empereur* was on the way to Elba under an armed guard amid the hostile demonstrations of his former loyal subjects.

All this was entirely satisfactory from the point of view of the Tory Government in England, but there was a fly in their ointment, a cloud on their horizon, a lurking suspicion in their triumph, which seem never to have been even vaguely guessed at by the innocent cause of their distrust. For a brief while and until they knew him better the Government seems to have been worried by the military phœnix it had accidentally brought into being through no fault of its own. With all that jealousy of their own power so characteristic of a narrow oligarchy they glumly reflected that it was no good smashing a foreign dictator if they had bred up a military dictator of their own. The Tories boasted frequently of the support they had given Wellington, but the Government knew perfectly well that, since Salamanca at least, Wellington had supported them and that he knew it as well as they did. The pride, the pomp, and petulance which Richard Wellesley had brought back from India seemed an evil omen—they had learned with dismay that Arthur Wellesley had the devil's own will and that the stoutest generals and most undisciplined peers quailed and wilted under his mere frown. The Tory Government also knew that Wellington was by far the most popular man in England, as much revered as Nelson after Trafalgar, with the added indecency of being alive to profit by it. Why couldn't the fellow have got himself decently and heroically slain in the assault on Toulouse?

Precedent—for in every emergency a cabinet consults precedent—was of no avail, for the sufficient reason that no English general since Marlborough had embarrassed his Government with such victories, and Marlborough had been rendered harmless by his Government before his war was over. But what the Tories could do to preserve the sacred spirit of liberty they did. The Peninsular Army was shipped off directly to America out of the control of its late Commander with indecent haste; for like that Commander, many of them had been continuously on active service without furlough for five years. A nice rest under the fire of American sharp-shooters was clearly well earned. Negotiations with the possible traitor were entrusted to Castlereagh, who was soon able to report joyously that the Field-Marshal showed no particular anxiety to return home, and then that he had fallen at once into the booby-trap of accepting the post of ambassador in Paris, thus combining the minimum of home influence with the maximum of foreign unpopularity. As Napoleon remarked in his famous interview with Lord John Russell on Elba, the appointment was "tactless", for nobody, especially a Frenchman, "likes to be constantly reminded that he has been defeated". The Emperor, who for once fell into the common error of judging other people by himself, seems to have shared the Tory Government's suspicion, for he astonished Lord John by assuming that England would at once embark on a series of wars of aggression. And when the diminutive but bright little Whig asked why, the Emperor murmured something about Wellington not being content to remain where he was after such military successes—for the Bonaparte propaganda against the Duke as a soldier only began at Saint Helena.

To do them justice the Tory Government quickly recovered from whatever suspicions they might have had, for, in accepting the doubtful honour of Ambassador to France, Wellington had written with his invariable plain sober honesty: "I must serve the public in some manner or other; and as, under existing circumstances, I could not well do so at home, I must do so abroad." To make doubtly sure, Castlereagh summoned him from Toulouse to Paris for "consultations" (about what?) and then sent him off on a fool's errand to Madrid with the addition of a ducal coronet, characteristically announced by the recipient to his ambassador brother Henry some three weeks later as follows: "P.S. I believe I forgot to tell you I was made a Duke." In Paris, Wellington met the Tsar and the other royalties, whom he greatly surprised by turning up at military parades dressed in the frock-coat and top hat of an ordinary English gentleman. He was introduced to Metternich and Blücher; and as he lay asleep in his post-chaise while horses were being changed somewhere on the Toulouse–Paris road, Soult, travelling the same route in the opposite direction, ventured a peep at his old adversary, remarking afterwards that it was the only time he "had caught Lord Wellington napping".

The new Duke of Wellington, in Spain Duque de Ciudad Rodrigo, began his diplomatic career with an assignment which was doomed to failure from the outset. Six years of grim suffering and heroic resistance on the part of the Spanish people had resulted in the

LORD JOHN RUSSELL

From the painting by G. F. Watts
[*The National Portrait Gallery*]

restoration of Ferdinand VII, despotism, and bigotry, a consummation which that singular people accepted with almost unanimous enthusiasm. They cheered themselves hoarse when Ferdinand repudiated the constitution he had been made to swear to on the frontier by the liberals; with joy they welcomed the revival of the Inquisition, and went frantic with happiness as they obliterated the word "Liberty" wherever it happened to be written up publicly in Madrid. The British Government, Tory though it might be, was shocked, and felt with some justice that this was not altogether what it had spent so much money to obtain. Not very hopefully they dispatched the Duque de Ciudad Rodrigo to protest, and though Wellington admitted that Ferdinand was "by no means such an idiot" as people thought, he added that nothing was to be done towards persuading the Spanish King to adopt a more liberal form of government. After all, why should the King grant liberty when the majority of his own subjects didn't want it? So Ferdinand dodged the subject, and contented himself with receiving the Duke as a Grandee of Spain of the First Class. The Spanish Guards shuffled their feet in a peculiar way when Wellington entered the royal antechamber, and he was told to keep his hat on in the royal presence. When the time came to enter the throne room, the other Grandees allowed the Duque de Ciudad Rodrigo to go in first (he was a foreigner and didn't understand their ways and some had even heard that he had been slightly connected with the great Spanish victories at Salamanca and Vittoria) and then all the other Grandees rushed at the door and pushed and shoved and elbowed in a free-for-all scrimmage, for all were equally grand Grandees and so none could yield precedence to another, thereby beautifully combining the advantages of aristocracy and democracy in one stately ceremony.

So, with nothing more achieved than saving the lives of some Spanish Liberals, his grace's travelling carriage was turned northward, and for the last time jolted over the war-worn roads of Spain and France. At Bordeaux he halted to write a farewell Order of the Day to his army, and then continued on his way to Calais, where he took ship for Dover and so returned home after an absence of more than five years. It was now midsummer and the war had ended in April, but if the Government had hoped that this lapse of time would deaden the feelings of the people towards "that long-nosed bugger that licks the French", they were greatly mistaken. As the Duke's ship slowly entered Dover harbour, those on board suddenly became aware that every square foot of ground was occupied by an intensely excited

and huzzaing crowd, through whose solid phalanxes a devoted body-
guard at last hewed a way for the Duke to reach the Ship Inn. There he
endeared himself further to the hearts of his countrymen by ordering
tea and buttered toast, a homely combination which is almost unobtainable outside the British Isles.

Now, if there was anything in the aristocratic thesis that the
emotions and reactions of the fickle crowd are groundless and worthless, it stands to reason that their plaudits ought to be ignored as much
as their catcalls. The usual practice of the high and mighty had been
to accept the plaudits as a well-earned tribute to their virtues, and to
ignore the catcalls as mere vulgar vileness, probably paid for by the
Opposition. Not so the Duke. That one-track honest mind believed
that if you chose to ignore the hisses, you must in common justice
ignore the cheers. So for sixty odd miles of dusty turnpike road a
spare, hook-nosed gentleman sat bolt upright looking desperately to
his front, while for mile after mile after mile the horses clattered past a
solid double lane of his humbler but most enthusiastic fellow-subjects,
who made his sixty miles from the coast to London one long roaring
cheer. True, there was plenty of beer in it, and there was plenty of
mere flag-wagging nationalism, but there was also plenty of equally
sincere praying may-God-bless-him as well; for most of these simple-
minded people believed that after God and Horatio Nelson, this hook-
nosed Arthur Wellesley had saved them from great humiliation and
great danger. So they cheered him loudly and honestly and—pity 'tis,
'tis true—in his honest code of aristocratic aloofness he had to look
aristocratically and coldly to his front.

Either by accident or design, Prinny and the visiting royalties from
the Continent had been sent that week to Portsmouth for a naval
review, so that no public reception could be arranged for the return
of the successful Commander of the united armies of England, Spain,
and Portugal. Indeed the official attitude seemed to be that they had
heard a vague rumour of a Mr. Arthur Wellesley, who had landed or
was about to land at Dover. The large and populous town of London
refused to accept this official view, and turned out in unprecedented
numbers to welcome the man who was in his own country a sort of
military classic—everybody had heard of him and nobody had seen
him. According to one authority "the people took the horses from his
carriage", dragged it through the streets, and then "carried him in
their arms" to the arms of his Duchess, in Hamilton Place. Although
this authority is Gleig, an officer who turned clergyman and became a
personal friend of the Duke, he seems to be wrong—other authorities

maintain that the Field-Marshal evaded the crowd and was smuggled privately into his home by the servants' entrance.

It would be hypocrisy to suggest that the reunion with Kitty was a source of much rapture. The ashes of their romance had long since grown cold. But it would also be an error to suppose that her martial Lothario failed either in respect or a certain grim fondness for the mother of his children. As for the children, whom he loved with a passion he strove desperately to hide beneath his aristocratic coldness, they presented the disconcerting phenomenon of babies changed by five years' absence into energetic small boys in the brawling stage.

From his home the Duke went at once to see his mother, pushing his way alone through the excited crowds, who never suspected that the little hook-nosed gentleman in a blue coat and a topper was the hero they were longing to lynch with love. Much had happened since Lady Mornington had declared Arthur "food for powder", and it is to be hoped that mother and son had by now both forgotten that unlucky prophecy. Richard the favourite, in spite of his enlarged views, excellent taste and elegant Latin verses, had been thrown into the shade. Like Letizia Bonaparte, Lady Mornington had unconsciously darkened more and more into the character and the very appearance of a Roman matron as her son's military career progressed in glory. Portraits of Lady Mornington in her old age show a most formidable old lady, looking as if she were telling all her sons to come home with their shields or on them. Unluckily, we have not the slightest knowledge of what she and her son said to each other on this interesting occasion. We do know that Arthur once more set out on foot to pay his respects to Richard, bumped into him in a crowd which recognized them and began cheering and dangerously pressing round in admiring affection, from which they fortunately escaped to the home of their married sister.

The next six weeks were a round of glory and gratification such as is reserved only for the successful destroyers of human life on a large scale. The honours varied from being feasted by the Prince Regent (who understood this kind of thing) to receiving the degree of Doctor of Laws (*honoris causa*) from the University of Oxford. The House of Lords witnessed a ceremony which has never happened before nor since in the centuries of its existence—namely, the reading of patents as Baron, Viscount, Earl, Marquess, and Duke for one person, so that entering the building officially still a commoner, he took his seat as a Duke, and there received the thanks of that House for his services to his country. Later, in the Commons, the Chancellor of the Exchequer (having read a message from the Regent) moved that an income of £10,000 a year be voted the Duke, with permission at any time to commute it for £300,000 to purchase an estate. Mr. Whitbread and Mr. Ponsonby of the Opposition now outdid themselves, for having spent the whole of the Peninsular War period in denouncing the Allied Commander as incompetent and a liar, they now tried to embarrass the Government by complaining of its meanness to the national hero, and forced through an amendment granting an addition £100,000—a wonderful snub to Government and delightful for the taxpayers they represented. When the Duke ceremoniously attended the Commons to express his gratitude, the Speaker used words which were unfortunately pompous and yet did contain the gist of the matter:

"It is not, however, the grandeur of military success which has alone fixed our admiration, or commanded our applause; it has been that generous and lofty spirit which inspired your troops with unbounded confidence, and taught them to know that the day of battle was always a day of victory; that moral courage and enduring fortitude, which, in perilous times, when gloom and doubt had beset ordinary minds, stood nevertheless unshaken; and that ascendancy of character, which, uniting the energies of jealous and rival nations, enabled you to wield at will the fate and fortunes of mighty empires."

Then the tumult and cheering, the speeches and the honours, the feastings and the ladies, dropped away, and the King's retained servant once more boarded a ship on His Majesty's service. But the respite from campaigning, the success and the world's word had done Wellington good, had relaxed the austerity a little and sent a frosty gleam into his bleak loneliness. Watching his young men dancing gaily he had remarked wistfully that there had been too little of that kind of thing in his own life, and that he intended henceforth to surround himself with young people. As he came out of the opera with his platonic adorer, Lady Shelley, on his arm, people spontaneously made way for him. He was so pleased that he bade the lady observe how fine it is "to be a great man"—a piece of naïveté which would be ridiculous in a man less frank and unaffected. It *is* pleasant to be treated everywhere as the greatest man in your country and to know that you have deserved the tribute without claiming it, so why not make the admission frankly? Moreover, the brief visit to England enabled him to catch up with some new developments of public opinion:

"I was not aware till I had been some time here of the degree of frenzy existing here about the slave trade. People in general appear to think that it would suit the policy of the nation to go to war to put an end to that *abominable* traffic;

and many wish that we should take the field on this new crusade. All agree that no favour can be shown to a slave-trading country. . . ." [Letter to Sir H. Wellesley, London, July 29, 1814.]

Agitation against the slave-trade had begun as far back as the seventeenth century among a few idealists in England and New England; Parliament had forbidden the trade to Englishmen in 1807; and in 1814 the feeling against slave-trading had reached an intensity in England comparable with that of the abolitionist movement in the Northern States a few decades later. Even a Tory Government could not resist such pressure, and, to do them justice, they seem to have been sincere in their efforts to suppress the trade, which was then (1814) entirely in the hands of foreign powers. Abolition of the slave-trade (emancipation of all slaves in British colonial territory was delayed for some years) occupied a good deal of the Duke's attention in his early days as a European diplomat. In his patient methodical way, the Duke read all the anti-slavery literature fired at him by such philanthropists as Wilberforce, Clarkson, and Zachary Macaulay, and espoused their views to which he did his best to convert such cynics as Talleyrand and the other diplomatic representatives of Europe.

Before proceeding to Paris, and thence later in the year to the Congress of Vienna, as an emissary of peace, the Duke was sent by his Government to the Low Countries to advise on its fortification and defence against possible French invasion. This indeed lends point to Napoleon's remark about the tactlessness of sending a victorious general as ambassador to his late enemy! With the best intentions in the world, a man who has destroyed a nation's army can hardly set about fortifying a frontier against its future armies, and then smilingly bow himself in as an emissary of goodwill. From our point of view the only interesting item in the Duke's long (and no doubt efficient) report on the defence of Belgium is the inclusion among good defensive positions of "the entrance of the forest of Soignies"—a battle-ground which the French call Mont St. Jean and the rest of the world Waterloo.

From August 1814 until late in January 1815 Wellington played his part as ambassador, living in a splendid Parisian mansion which had belonged to Bonaparte's sister, Pauline Borghese. After years of rough billets and "cold meat", the luxuries of Paris must have seemed an odd change for the better, even though the Duchess came to live with him. This did not prevent his seeing Mlle. Grassini whenever he wanted; and for the first time in his life he had the fun of Christmas with his children. Meanwhile the official business of interviews, levees, receptions, notes, and correspondence went on with the usual meticulous attention to duty. Sometimes the sardonic "commander-of-the-forces" touch comes into his official correspondence with the Foreign Office, as when he comments on an oculist who was impatient to learn French methods of eye treatment without knowing a word of French, or gravely reports on a scholar from Cambridge who wanted all the editions of Demosthenes in the Paris public libraries sent to his hotel because he didn't feel well enough to go to the libraries himself. Again, when the French Government complained of the conduct of an Englishman who had got himself arrested in France, the Duke replied that the "man appears to be what in England is known as a vagabond", and recommended that he be expelled. His observation of those currents of feeling which so largely determine the behaviour of nations was still keen:

> "I believe the truth to be that the people of this country [i.e. France] are so completely ruined by the revolution and they are now suffering so severely from the want of the plunder of the world, that they cannot go on without it; and they cannot endure the prospect of a peaceable government." [Letter to Lord Bathurst, December 17, 1814. Quoted by Gleig.]

Meanwhile the crowned heads of Europe had been knocking together for some time in Vienna in the fascinating but hopeless tasks of redrawing frontiers to please everybody and devising that "perpetual peace" which has figured in the preambles of so many treaties. The Prince de Ligne's over-quoted gibe that the Congress "*ne marche pas, il danse*" was not even original, since a very similar joke had circulated thirty years before about the protracted trial of Warren Hastings, and the jest failed to take into account either the complexities of the situation or the necessity for exhausted delegates to recuperate in feminine company. After the usual jockeying for position (should there be a Big Four or a Big Five or even a Middle-Sized Eight?) there was the gratifying shock of discovering the existence of secret treaties, and the ferocious squabbling of the Powers over boundaries and annexations. Russia wanted Poland, Prussia wanted Saxony; and by way of simplifying matters France, Austria, and England made yet another secret treaty to fight Prussia and Russia under certain contingencies. The Emperor of Russia introduced a discordant note into the Congress by the tactless suggestion that henceforth the foreign policy of the Powers ought to be based not upon Machiavelli but upon the Sermon on the Mount. He proposed a "Holy Alliance" of Christian kings to maintain these principles, which Castlereagh managed to evade signing on constitutional grounds, while secretly emitting the opinion that the Tsar's plans were "a piece of sublime mysticism and nonsense". Metternich thought them a consummate piece of hypocrisy to hide Russian ambitions.

So protracted were the negotiations that Castlereagh was forced to return to England to face the House of Commons and defend himself, his policy, and his colleagues. The rest of the Cabinet had now come to know Wellington at closer quarters, and perhaps had discovered that, though a soldier, he was perhaps rather more intelligent than they were and certainly quite as honest. They agreed to let him represent his country at the Congress of Vienna, and with his invariable courage and integrity he there upheld the cause of Liberalism. Let no one start and protest—in those days and in that company at Vienna English Constitutional Tories like Castlereagh and Wellington were considered almost Jacobins. After the terrific struggle "to liberate the world from the tyranny of Napoleon", it must have been disconcerting even to a Tory Cabinet to find what in fact they had set free. Thus, in Spain the utmost efforts of the Duque de Ciudad Rodrigo failed to effect more than the saving of a few Liberals from the scaffold; and Ferdinand absolutely refused to go even so slight a way on the path of representative government as to set up Wellington's project of a Spanish House of Lords. In Italy, the Pope's government abolished street lighting as being too revolutionary and democratic, and in Turin, the King of Savoy, Victor Emmanuel, for the same reason grubbed up the French botanical garden and forbade his subjects to use the road built by Napoleon over the Alps. New school histories were being issued in France which omitted all mention of the Revolution, and taught that great victories were "won for King Louis XVII and King Louis XVIII by their famous General Buonaparte". In the midst of all this obscurantism the Tsar Alexander shines an archangel of sweetness and light, and the Duke glows a distant but steady beacon of common sense.

Suddenly these unpleasant dovecots were fluttered by heart-shaking tidings—The Eagle had escaped from Elba. Perhaps the imperial bird did not "fly from steeple to steeple" with all the majesty and amid all the demonstrations of popular joy claimed by the Bonapartist legend, but the Emperor's rapid promenade from Antibes to Paris was certainly an impressive demonstration of what can be effected by a dominating personality and judicious bribery. The Emperor's plans were greatly aided by the fact that his road was echeloned with French regiments on their way to attack Murat, King of Naples. Ney provided a pleasing example of soldierly honour—after solemnly pledging his word to Louis XVIII that he would be faithful unto death and capture Napoleon (with the entirely unnecessary addition that the Corsican should be brought captive to Paris in an iron cage) Marshal Ney, Prince de Moskowa, went over to his old commander the moment he saw him, and the two gentlemen roared with laughter over the jest at dinner. As to public opinion it is neatly enough expressed and satirized by the (probably apocryphal) items of news which are supposed to have appeared in the Paris newspapers at different dates, as follows:

(1) The Corsican ogre has landed at Antibes.

(2) General Bonaparte has reached Lyons.

(3) Last night His Majesty the Emperor entered his palace of the Tuileries.

It is said that when the news was told the Tsar, he went into fits of laughter at the thought of all the energy and time wasted in their futile political intrigues. Indeed, if political mankind were capable of learning a lesson, this was a very instructive one. But the Congress was far from sharing the view that the Emperor's escape and return were a laughing matter. We have all read in history books how the delegates of eight countries to the Vienna Congress solemnly declares Napoleon "*hors la loi*", and if we happen to see the document in question we shall find that he was proclaimed "*hors les relations civiles et sociales*", which perhaps comes to much the same thing, especially since he was handed over to "*la vindicte* publique*". Meanwhile Louis XVIII issued an ancient feudal writ ordering his officers to "*courir sus*" the usurper; and then immediately fled to Ghent. The Congress agreed with alacrity to receive subsidies from England and appointed the Duke to command the Allied armies in the Low Countries; they also agreed to furnish armies themselves, but except for Prussia and some of the smaller German states these were very slow in arriving—Austria was involved in its war for Naples and the Russians had a very long way to march.

The news of the Emperor's last gamble for power reached Vienna on March 7, 1815; before dawn on April 5 Wellington was in Brussels, and took command of the miscellaneous military forces there assembling.

---

* *Vindicte* meant justice, not vengeance.

CHAPTER XIX

Waterloo

THEY gave him a raw, miscellaneous, and numerically inferior army to oppose the greatest general and the best soldiers of the age. In one of those sudden rare outbursts of temper, which were the only sign Wellington ever gave of frayed nerves and maddening responsibilities, he described this army as "infamous"; but that was before they fought the campaign. It was certainly a curious rag, tag and bobtail the Duke managed to collect in Belgium during that spring of 1815, while Europe waited breathlessly for the moment when the Great Adventurer would strike. The betting was heavily against Wellington and the Prussians, the only allies yet in the field on the western front, for the Austrians had their troubles in Italy with Murat. The Duke's army consisted of Dutch and Belgians, levies from the Hanseatic towns, Brunswickers, Hanoverians, English, Scotch, and Irish line regiments of recruits mixed up with a few Peninsular veterans, the Guards, and the Household cavalry. But the main strength of the British army, the Peninsular veterans, "my old Spanish infantry", were scattered over the world, at Mobile and Pensacola, in Canada, in Ireland, on the high seas. Meanwhile, the British Government neglected to call out the militia (which would have freed regular troops for service overseas) and the Horse Guards as of old was penurious with trained battalions and lavish with incompetent generals. "Before you send any more General Officers let me see more troops," the Duke pleaded; but still the generals arrived and the battalions lingered. Even guns were doled out in penny numbers, and there were not even enough drivers for the wagon train.

Who should be living in Brussels in those days but the Parliamentary Mr. Creevey, the gentleman who had made such reputation as a military critic in the House by denouncing the Duke as a charlatan and a liar. To his surprise Creevey found the Duke good-humoured, not seeming "to resent or recollect these former bickerings". Early in June they met by accident in the public park and a remarkable conversation ensued:

"Will you let me ask you, Duke, what you think you will make of it?"

"By God!" said the Duke, stopping short, "I think Blücher and myself can do the thing."

"Do you calculate upon any desertion in Bonaparte's army?"

"Not upon a man, from the colonel to the private in a regiment, both inclusive. We may pick up a Marshal or two perhaps, but not worth a damn."

"Do you reckon upon any support from the French King's troops at Alost?"

"Oh, don't mention such fellows! No, I think Blücher and I can do the business." He then pointed to a British private who was looking at the statues in the park. "There! It all depends upon that article whether we do the business or not. Give me enough of it, and I'm sure."

The search for "that article" was hectic and often disappointing. As the finest available substitute, the Duke pleaded for 14,000 of his old Portuguese trusties—brigaded with the redcoats they could be depended on to give Boney a surprise. But the Government of Portugal declined, and so lost the opportunity of being accidentally covered with glory. The absence of all electric forms of communication and all sea-locomotion but wind and sail added extreme uncertainty to the quantity and quality of troops drifting back from America—bits of regiments turned up at odd times, or by a stroke of luck a convoy would come in with two or three battalions complete. Sir Thomas Picton arrived, eccentrically garbed as usual, and after an exchange of discourtesies with his old chief went off to command the advance-guard. Leaving no stone unturned that might lose a battle the Horse Guards sent out Lord Anglesea (then Lord Uxbridge*) to command the cavalry and to try to act as second-in-command. I say "try", because on the one occasion when he screwed up courage to make an attempt at playing that part he was immediately crushed by the Duke's solemn irony. On the eve of Waterloo, Uxbridge ventured to ask for the Duke's plans and was met with another question:

"Who will attack the first to-morrow—I or Buonaparte?"
"Buonaparte."
"Well, Buonaparte has not given me any idea of his projects; and as my plans will depend upon his, how can you expect me to tell him what mine are?"

Before Uxbridge could protest against the obvious unfairness of this put-off, the Duke rose, placed a hand on the shoulder of his brother peer, and added with sardonic irony:

* The spirited action of Lord Uxbridge in attending the solemn funeral of his amputated leg after Waterloo pleads greatly in his favour.

"There is one thing certain, Uxbridge; that is, that whatever happens you and I will do our duty."

So the crowded days ticked busily away from early April until mid-June. There had been a "Boney's-coming" panic in Brussels at the end of March, but this had vanished as soon as the Duke appeared from Vienna, only to recur again whenever the outposts or an over-anxious spy sent in false information of a French advance. The more serious tourists got to be quite ashamed of running away and then coming sheepishly back again. When the real attack did come and the Prussians were driven back from Charleroi, a conscientious Hanoverian general who had promptly forwarded all the false reports held up the true one for investigation, so that the news was many hours late in reaching the Duke. Hence the stories that "Wellington was surprised" at Waterloo, stories which give Anglophobe historians much comfort, although one would think that if the Duke really were surprised it is all the more to his credit that he got out of the scrape so handsomely. Not until four o'clock in the afternoon of June 15, 1815, did Wellington receive news that the French were attacking the Prussians in force, and it was long after dark before he received information sufficiently accurate to determine his point of concentration. He then ordered his divisions to march on Nivelles-Quatre Bras at dawn next morning. Undoubtedly he was late, but that is not the same thing as being "surprised".

"Tell me, Duke," said a lady suddenly at dinner many years later. "Is it true that you were surprised at Waterloo?"

"By God, not as surprised as I am now, mum."

Apocryphal stories cluster as thickly round the legend of the campaign as false rumours about its reality. Certainly "there was a sound of revelry by night" at the Duchess of Richmond's ball, for Wellington thought it would reassure the panic-stricken and intimidate the ill-affected of Brussels if he and his generals and staff attended the dancing while the regiments were mustering and tramping to their rendezvous. Was it true that a message was brought to Wellington that evening as he sat in a room apart from the dancers, and that after reading it he sat intensely concentrated and then issued a series of orders, while one by one his officers slipped away? Perhaps. Was it true that he then sent for a map of the district, pointed to Quatre Bras, saying: "I shall meet him here, and if that fails, *here*," drawing his thumb-nail along the ridge of Waterloo? The story was vouched for by a Scottish Duke; but then the Prince Regent himself was convinced that he had led the cavalry charge at

Salamanca. What is beyond dispute is that there were "sudden partings, such as press the life from out young hearts . . ."

Almost as much ink as blood has been shed over the Waterloo campaign and the great battle. Many French accounts are fantastic in their inventions, excepting of course the professional military studies which are excellent. The sunken road into which Victor Hugo hurled the French cavalry never existed, and the French cavalry in fact arrived intact and were "walking about" the British squares for a couple of hours—the story of the cavalry falling into the sunken road seems to be Hugo's vague reminiscence of the disaster which befell the (British) Twenty-First Light Dragoons at Talavera. From Talavera also comes Chateaubriand's picturesque account of the troops of the two armies drinking from a little stream in a lull of the battle—there was certainly no stream across the Waterloo battle-field and no such prolonged lull. Chateaubriand goes on to say that the English were "entirely beholden to the Scots and Irish for their victory", and then adds exultantly and without noticing the contradiction that "every noble family in *England* had to mourn its dead". Michelet surpasses them all. He had read somewhere that the *Écossais Gris* (The Scots Greys) played a dramatic part in the battle, and that they were reckoned a very fine regiment. Now *gris* in French can mean "drunk" as well as "grey", and in Michelet's veracious account of Waterloo the charge of the Scottish cavalry regiment becomes: "Wellington made one of his finest regiments drunk and sacrificed them to the last man!"

On the English side the reader of the numerous personal narratives of the battle gradually learns with growing interest that this great contest seems to have been won by the special contribution of each narrator; while the one man who might safely have been absent and had little to do with the victory was the Duke of Wellington. This fact must have been noted in the last century, since it produced a popular satirical recitation: "How Bill Adams Won the Battle of Waterloo". If "Bill Adams" was a collective symbol for "Thomas Atkins" there would be a great deal of truth in the claim, for it was the dogged courage and fire-power of the infantry squares which decided the issue. But the various claims of the various officers may be dismissed at once. Lord Uxbridge told the Duke of York who told Greville that it was Uxbridge not Wellington who won the battle. He certainly obeyed gallantly Wellington's order to the heavy dragoons to charge at Waterloo, lost some hussars while commanding the rear-guard after Quatre Bras, and very nearly lost Mercer's battery of Horse Artillery by an injudicious order. On the very battle-field Sir Hussey Vivien infuriated the peppery Tomkinson (of the dragoons) by claiming to have "saved the battle" on his own initiative through a charge which occurred by order of Wellington himself, and after the French army was in full retreat. Shaw Kennedy claims that his disposition of the Third Division saved the day, and even a humble battery commander describes the mountains of dead of the Old Guard left by the miraculously effective firing of his guns. . . . There are legions of such tales.

Need it be added that the Duke did *not* say, "Up Guards, and at 'em"? And if General Cambronne said, "The Guard dies but does not surrender", he was the wrong man to say it, for on the night of Waterloo he was to be found waiting hat in hand and a prisoner at Wellington's headquarters.

There were two contemporary rumour factories hard at work behind the lines of the contending armies. One was French head-quarters, for the Emperor had long before consecrated his talents and those of able literary subordinates to the creation of that propaganda which is not embarrassed by truth or facts. On the other side was the whole city of Brussels, aided and abetted by the Court of His Most Christian Majesty at Ghent. Between them they contrived to keep the world in a terrific uproar of misinformation and alarmist turmoil. The best imaginative recreation of those three hectic days in Brussels is Thackeray's in *Vanity Fair*. More recently the publication of the Creevey papers has given us an actual contemporary account of the hopes and fears and mistakes of people in Brussels.

On the morning of June 16 at 8 o'clock the Duke and his staff rode out of Brussels, and Mr. Creevey saw them go. He did not see, of course, the interior of Lady Dalrymple Hamilton's bedroom where the maid had just then drawn the curtains and exclaimed: "O my lady, get up quick! There he goes, God bless him, and he won't come back till he's King of France!" In the afternoon between four and five, Mr. Creevey became aware of the sound of cannon in the distance, which later became "distinct and regular". That night he met his friend Captain Hamilton who had just ridden back from the battle of Quatre Bras where he had seen the Duke of Brunswick killed—Hamilton was full of admiration for the conduct of the Allied troops.

On the seventeenth, Mr. Creevey "felt easy" when he saw "the streets filled with British troops". This Parliamentary critic of the Peninsular War failed to realize that these "troops" were merely the baggage train. ("All the baggage . . . to proceed immediately from

thence to Hal and Bruxelles". Wellington to Hill, June 17, 1815.)
Later in the day, Captain Hamilton somewhat alarmed the Whig
M.P. by the news of Blücher's defeat at Ligny and the retreat of both
the Prussian and British armies.

On June 18 (Waterloo Day) Mr. Creevey was much relieved when
he saw the "troops" (who he still hadn't realized formed only the
baggage train) moving up towards the army. About three in the
afternoon he walked out to the western suburbs and found the whole
Sunday population drinking at cafés and listening to the long rumble
of artillery fire. At four, Mr. Creevey received the palpitating news
that the French were in Brussels! Rushing into the street he was just
in time to see the last of the Cumberland Hussars (a volunteer regiment
of Hanoverian gentlemen) who had bolted from the battle-field and
clattered hell for leather through Brussels on their way to Antwerp
screaming that the French were at their heels. Mr. Creevey was
naturally much alarmed and depressed; but then was greatly cheered
shortly afterwards to see a body of about fifteen hundred French
prisoners escorted by Life Guardsmen who were displaying two
captured eagles. Half an hour later a burst of shouting announced
more prisoners. Then Mr. Creevey ran into another Member of
Parliament, who had been watching the battle from afar, but was
weighed down with pessimism, and horrified Mr. Creevey by opinion
that "everything looked as bad as possible". Mr. Creevey at once set
out agitatedly to see his friend the Marquis Juarenais. On the way he
met a wounded British guardsman who said, "The French are getting
on in such a manner I don't see what's to stop them". At the Marquis's
house was a young English officer, wounded and fainting, who said the
French must reach Brussels that night. Returning home in dismay,
Mr. Creevey then heard the unpleasant news that his friend General
Barnes (Wellington's Adjutant-General) had been wounded.

Between ten and eleven that night, long after the sound of the
cannon had died away, Captain Hamilton came in wounded and said
that the wounded General Barnes was also on his way back. Both the
General and his aide-de-camp thought the battle lost, and urged Mr.
Creevey and his family to fly. But Mrs. Creevey was too ill to be
moved, and all Mr. Creevey could do was to order "the young ladies"
(his stepdaughters) to lie down without undressing. Mr. Creevey not
unnaturally slept very badly, but at 4 a.m. was a little comforted to
find that no French had arrived and to see more British "troops"
(another baggage train) moving in the right direction. He dressed, and
at six in the morning went round to the Marquis again, where he

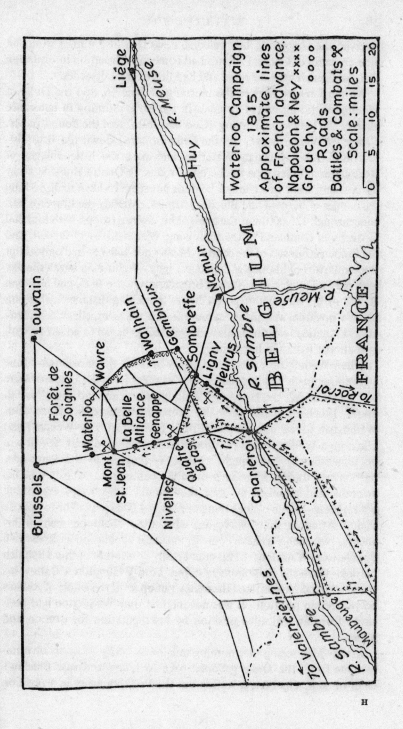

Waterloo Campaign
1815
Approximate lines
of French advance.
Napoleon & Ney ××××
Grouchy oooo
Roads ———
Battles & Combats ✗
Scale: miles
0 5 10 15 20

H

received the staggering but welcome news that at 3 a.m. a wounded aide-de-camp of General Alten's had come in with certain information that the French were defeated and had fled in great disorder. . . .

We must return now to the morning of June 16, and the Duke of Wellington riding out of Brussels in the early morning in ignorance alike of the lady's maid crying "God bless him" and the doubts in Mr. Creevey's Whiggish eye. As the Duke cantered down the Brussels–Charleroi road, through Waterloo and past the little villages of Rosomme and Genappe to the cross-roads at Quatre Bras, he knew his concentration was late but he does not seem to have realized fully the danger of his own and Blücher's armies. Already the Emperor had concentrated 125,000 men, the finest of his veteran troops, with Marshal Grouchy in command of the right wing, Marshal Ney of the left, and the Emperor himself of the centre. Meanwhile Blücher had only about three-quarters of his men gathered at Ligny. Wellington began the day with only a Dutch and a Nassau brigade at Quatre Bras, and less than 30,000 of his men within a few hours' marching distance. The Emperor's position was most favourable, his plans excellent, his army almost fanatically enthusiastic—and yet things began to go wrong with him almost from the beginning.

When Wellington arrived at Quatre Bras on the morning of June 16 nothing much had happened. Ney's orders from the Emperor were to "brush aside" the troops of Wellington's army and then "to fall upon" Blücher's flank while the Emperor attacked his front. But Wellington's local commander (Prince Bernard of Saxe-Weimar) had taken up a Wellingtonian position on a reverse slope, and Ney (it will be remembered) had fought against Wellington in the Peninsula, particularly during Masséna's unhappy campaigns. If Ney and his veterans had attacked at once they would have swept everything before them—at ten o'clock there were only 4,000 men in line to oppose them. After carefully surveying what little could be seen of his enemy, Ney seems to have come to the same conclusion as Reille two days later at Waterloo: "This could easily be another of those Spanish battles—when the right moment comes Lord Wellington will show his troops." And Ney ordered the attack put off until the whole of Reille's corps were in position. It was not the first time Wellington had been saved from an awkward position by his reputation for caution and guile.

Meanwhile, seeing that nothing much was going on in his own immediate front, the Duke galloped over to Ligny and saw Blücher's chief of staff, Gneisenau, setting out the Prussian army in a position where every man was visible to the enemy and a target for the admirable French artillery. In his bluff way the Duke expressed his surprise at this order of battle, adding that if he put his own men out in full view like that he should expect to see them "damnably mauled". Gneisenau fatuously answered that "Prussians like to see their enemies when they fight", which was not the point of the criticism. The Duke shrugged, promised to bring up his men to assist if not attacked too heavily, and rode back to Quatre Bras. Ney attacked Wellington's line just before the Duke returned (about 2 p.m.) and the Emperor attacked the Prussians between two and three. The tragedy of the day from the French point of view is that the general reserve under D'Erlon spent the whole day marching and countermarching under orders and counter-orders, when its presence on either battlefield would have been decisive. The fault was nobody's but Napoleon's, who most unaccountably made a similar error two days later with Grouchy's corps.

Quatre Bras was a series of desperate encounters in which at each serious crisis some of Wellington's reinforcements came up in the nick of time, while Ney (as we have seen) never got his reserves. The first French attack was just on the point of succeeding when the Duke turned up, and Sir Thomas Picton arrived with the Fifth Division (British). Then Ney was reinforced by Kellermann's cavalry, but Wellington received Alten's British division. Finally the division of Guards turned up after a long forced march, but with enough punch left to drive the French back to where they had begun the battle, which thus ended as a draw with losses of over four thousand to each side. The fighting had been fierce. The Allies had lost the Duke of Brunswick, and Wellington himself at one moment only escaped the French cavalry by jumping his English hunter over a line of Scottish Highlanders. At the end of the day the French were back precisely where they had started the battle, and Ney had been unable to attack Blücher's flank as the Emperor had ordered. On the other hand, Ney had prevented the Duke from going to help Blücher, who was forced to retire from Ligny after losing 20,000 men to the Emperor's 11,000. In a great cavalry charge, Blücher himself was unhorsed, ridden over, and very nearly captured.

Napoleon, then, had not done badly, but not so well as he thought he had. His bulletin claims a "complete victory" over "the united Prussian and English armies", which is untrue. One would not insult the Emperor's intelligence by assuming that he believed his own bulletins, but his subsequent orders show that he over-estimated the damage to Blücher as much as he appeared to under-estimate Welling-ton as a general, since he followed up neither army on the morning of June 17, but wasted the precious hours in gossiping and useless reviews. He was so certain that the Prussians were finished and flying to Liége that when in the afternoon he sent Grouchy with 30,000 men after them, much time was wasted on the Namur road while the Prussians were in fact rallying on Wavre where reinforcements awaited them. Meanwhile the Duke had begun to withdraw his infantry at 10 a.m.; and when the Emperor sent his cavalry in pursuit about 3 p.m., it was too late, especially as there was a terrific thunder-storm with torrents of rain, such as preceded the Duke's Peninsula victories. The troops of both armies had miserable wet bivouacs that night; and the French were without rations, while many of their regiments did not come up until after midnight. Wellington had sent to Blücher, offering to fight if assured of the support of one Prussian army corps. Blücher wrote promising two (Bülow and Pirch) and more if possible; i.e. any troops not needed to contain Grouchy, of whose position and numbers the Prussians were now fully aware.

Wellington was up early on that morning of Sunday, June 18, 1815. By 3 a.m. he had written four letters, one of them a long one in French to the Duc de Berri at Ghent, arranging for the escape of Louis XVIII to Antwerp if things went wrong, but "*j'espère, et plus, j'ai toute raison de croire, que tout ira bien*". To the British ambassador in Brussels he wrote "Pray keep the English quiet if you can. Let them all prepare to move, but neither be in a hurry or a fright, as all will yet turn out well". He wrote to the Governor of Antwerp to declare a state of siege, to break the dikes, and notwithstanding the state of siege to allow free entry to the King of France and to all "families, either English or of any other nation". Finally he sent Lady Frances Webster a note warning her to be ready to leave Brussels at a moment's notice. As soon as it was light, the Duke mounted his thoroughbred "Copenhagen" and rode out to supervise the drawing up of his army, which on that memorable day was made up as follows:

British	23,991
King's German Legion	5,824
Hanoverians	11,247
Brunswickers	5,935
Nassauers	2,880
Dutch-Belgians	17,784
Total	67,661

Wellington had 156 guns, manned by 5,645 men. Against this miscellaneous collection Napoleon could bring 74,000 veteran troops, all Frenchmen, armed with 246 guns. A day's march to his right, Wellington had another 14,000 men intended to guard against a flanking movement which would have forced him to retreat and to uncover Brussels. The Duke is much criticized by military experts for wasting these men in parrying a movement the Emperor never intended; yet, oddly enough, when Reille was asked his opinion by Napoleon on the battle morning, he advised exactly the move to Wellington's right flank which the Duke always maintained Napoleon should have made and which he dreaded.

That morning the Emperor had no intention whatever of making any cautious manœuvre. If Wellington made a stand, Napoleon meant to smash his army to fragments by terrific frontal attacks, although he must have known that no frontal attack had ever succeeded against the Duke's armies. The Emperor was confident, over-confident, as he sat down to breakfast at eight, hours after his adversary was out on horseback placing his men: "It is too late for Wellington to retreat, he would be completely destroyed. He has thrown the dice, and they favour us." At that moment the first outposts of Prussian cavalry already were to be seen beyond Planchenois, and the corps of Bülow and Pirch had been toiling since dawn through the narrow muddy lanes. Oddly enough there were several generals among Napoleon's staff who had faced Wellington before—Soult, Ney, Reille, D'Erlon, Foy. . . . The Emperor would not listen to their protests and warnings. To Soult he was insulting:

"Because you have been beaten by Wellington, you consider him a great general. And I tell you that Wellington is a bad general, that the English are bad soldiers, and the whole thing will be a walk-over. . . . We shall sleep in Brussels to-night."

No such memorable and eloquent sentences came that morning from the Duke, prosaic and practical as ever. As rain-storms swept over the ground he put on a cloak remarking: "I never get wet if I can help it." A staff officer of the Third Division asked how his grace wished the division drawn up, and was told "in the usual way". He was in no hurry to begin the battle, although "if I had had my old Spanish infantry I should have attacked Buonaparte at once"; every minute of the morning the Emperor wasted brought the muddy Prussian columns that much nearer. Apparently the Duke was still worried about his right, for the farm of Hougoumont on the right was better fortified and garrisoned than the other farm of La Haye Sainte which was the key to his centre—he could not even then believe that the "greatest captain in history" would send close columns against the musketry of the British line exactly as Junot had done at Vimiero, and with exactly the same result.

The battle of Waterloo has been one of the most described of battles, yet there is no agreement on even so trifling a matter as the exact hour when the battle began. Even the rival commanders are at variance, for the Duke's official dispatch says that it began "about ten o'clock" with "a furious attack on our post at Hougoumont", while Napoleon says his troops were not in position until ten-thirty when "a profound silence reigned over the battlefield". Perhaps the most effective way to understand the main action is to take Shaw Kennedy's advice and divide it into five acts, like a great classical tragedy.

Act I lasted from about 11.30 a.m. to about 1.30 p.m. The French artillery opened a "very heavy cannonade" and three divisions under Jerome Bonaparte attacked the farm of Hougoumont. Some of the Nassau garrison gave way, and as Wellington sent in the Guards to restore the position he pointed to the Nassauers and remarked sarcastically (in French) to the Austrian General Vincent: "And these are the gentlemen with whom we are supposed to win battles!" Attacks, costly to the French in man-power, continued on Hougoumont all through the day, but the hard-pressed Guards never lost the post. During the two hours of this subsidiary operation (which was of course a failure) Ney was busy preparing an attack on the centre with D'Erlon's corps of thirty-two battalions arranged in four vast clumsy columns—the Emperor's idea being that the mere sight of such masses would terrify the British infantry as it had so often terrified continental infantry.

Act II lasted from about 1.30 to 3.30 p.m. The Emperor was just about to give the word to launch this imposing attack when Destiny tapped him on the shoulder—a staff officer suddenly noticed and pointed out heavy masses of troops advancing on the right flank about six miles away. Who could they be? Not Grouchy, for a report had lately come in from him showing that he was moving on Wavre and that he still thought the main Prussian army had retired on Liége. At that moment a German hussar prisoner was brought in, and admitted that the whole of Bülow's corps was marching to Wellington's aid. These were unpleasant tidings, but the hopeful Emperor believed he could still beat Wellington, and the order was given to Ney to break the Allied centre. This attack turned out a bad business for the French,

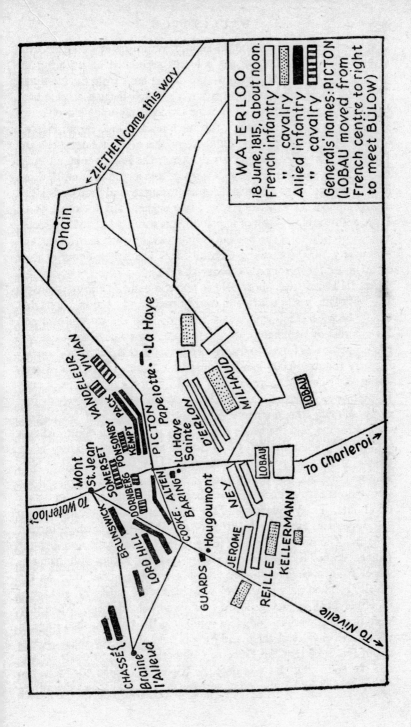

WATERLOO
18 June, 1815, about noon.
French infantry
" cavalry
Allied infantry
" cavalry
Generals' names: PICTON
(LOBAU moved from
French centre to right
to meet BÜLOW)

ZIETHEN came this way

Ohain

La Haye
VANDELEUR
VIVIAN
PACK
PONSONBY
Papelotte
KEMPT
PICTON
D'ERLON
MILHAUD
LOBAU

Mont
St. Jean
SOMERSET
La Haye
Sainte
DORNBERG
ALTEN
BARING
LOBAU
NEY
To Charleroi →

To Waterloo

BRUNSWICK
COOKE
Hougoumont
JEROME
REILLE
LORD HILL
GUARDS
KELLERMANN

CHASSÉ
Braine
l'Alleud

TO NIVELLE →

in spite of their numbers and the support of furious covering fire from seventy-four guns. One of the columns succeeded in capturing the gardens of La Haye Sainte, but were driven back from the buildings. The other three columns drove Bylandt's Dutch-Belgian brigade back in confusion, but behind them came immediately upon Picton's two British brigades, with whom a furious musketry duel raged, Picton's line defeating five times their number. At this moment Somerset's and Ponsonby's brigades of heavy cavalry smote the French columns in the flank, Picton yelled to his men "Charge!" and a second later fell dead. The French columns broke in disorder, losing several thousands killed and wounded, 3,000 prisoners, and two eagles. The enclosure of La Haye Sainte and the farm of Papelotte, temporarily lost to the French, were promptly retaken; but the British cavalry pursued too far and lost nearly 1,000 (including General Sir William Ponsonby) of their 2,500 under French cavalry counter-attacks.

Act III lasted from about 3.30 to about 6 p.m. The Prussians were late, very late, partly because of muddy roads and a fire in Wavre, but chiefly because Gneisenau intentionally delayed the troops, owing to his mistrust of Wellington. But they were now coming up at last and the Emperor was forced to detach two brigades of cavalry and Lobau's infantry (about 10,000 men) to guard his flank. It must have been about this time that there was that brief lull in the fighting mentioned by many eye-witnesses when the heavy smoke of battle slowly drifted away showing the remnants of Picton's redcoats still holding an unbroken line, and the whole Allied army gave them a cheer. Almost immediately what was left of D'Erlon's and Reille's infantry made unsuccessful attacks on Hougoumont and La Haye Sainte. Then Ney, who had command of all forward operations, ordered the first of the tremendous cavalry charges which began at four and lasted for nearly two hours. Forty squadrons of the Emperor's finest cavalry rode up the slopes and attacked the artillery and the infantry, which formed squares. The British guns kept firing to the last moment, and then the gunners rushed for shelter to the nearest square, taking with them one wheel from each gun so that it could not be carried off. As the cavalry reached the squares they were blasted by musketry, and taken on either flank as they galloped round and behind them. When they were thus thrown into complete confusion, the Duke dashed some of his reserve cavalry at them and hurled them down the slope. It was about this time that the Duke of Cumberland's Hanoverian hussars fled the field. But this was only the beginning. Time after time the fifteen British and Hanoverian squares were charged, and dreadfully thinned by artillery-fire and snipers. Ney called on two more cavalry divisions and then the heavy cavalry of the Imperial Guard; Wellington used up all his reserve infantry and all his cavalry except Vivian's and Vandeleur's light brigades. Yet after two hours of this, the greatest cavalry action of the Napoleonic wars, the decimated squares still stood intact with all the guns beside them. Only one square, of Hanoverians, was lost owing to a mistaken order to open out, given by the Prince of Orange. In all, there were four great charges of the French cavalry, of which the third containing seventy-seven squadrons, mostly fresh men, was the most formidable. Yet by six o'clock they had accomplished nothing decisive, and were themselves destroyed as a fighting unit.

Act IV lasted from about 6 to 7.30 p.m. Where were the Prussians? Wellington had joined battle on the understanding that they would be up at noon, and it was now six. No wonder he looked anxiously at his watch. But just about this time a staff officer reported to him that Ziethen's corps was coming up on the left, and the Duke himself then noticed the smoke of Bülow's attack on distant Planchenois which had in fact been going on for some time. Already the Emperor had been compelled to send four regiments of his Guard to reinforce Lobau. At this hour (6 p.m.) Blücher had managed to bring up 29,000 men and 64 guns. Seeing the failure of the French cavalry, Napoleon now ordered Ney to attack again with infantry. The fresh divisions of Bachelu and Foy were hurled against the weary squares, which instantly formed line and swept the new attackers away with their deadly musketry. But at six-thirty the French scored their first real success, a most dangerous one to the Duke's whole centre—the survivors of Major Baring's German Legion defending La Haye Sainte ran out of ammunition, and were bayoneted to the last man.

This was the real crisis of the battle. The La Haye Sainte position was the key to Wellington's centre and within sixty yards of his main line; all the troops in that area were exhausted by the incessant fighting; and Blücher's attacks so far had done nothing to relieve the intense pressure. But what was left of the French infantry was also too exhausted to press on, and Ney sent to the Emperor for more infantry —"More infantry!" exclaimed the Emperor. "Where am I to get it? Do you expect me to manufacture infantry?" The Duke received the somewhat appalling news that La Haye Sainte had gone, as he stood behind Maitland's brigade of Guards to the right of the Nivelles road, and heard it with his accustomed calm. By the time Ney was able to renew the attack, the Duke had acted. He knew that Ziethen was now

H*

in touch with his extreme left, and therefore ordered his remaining cavalry from the left to the centre, Kielmansegge's Hanoverians were brought in from the right, and the Duke himself led up the Bruns-wickers and some Nassau troops, as Ney about seven-thirty advanced to the attack with the last reserves of the Guard and what was left of the French infantry.

Act V lasted from about seven-thirty until dark. Everything the French had left was thrown into this last attack against the Anglo-Allied line, except for two battalions of the Guard sent to hold Planchenois and another two (some say three) battalions held as a defence to the Emperor's person. The Emperor had now for some time left his chair in front of La Belle Alliance from which he had directed his troops, and advanced bit by bit along the road, gesticulat-ing, talking feverishly, and taking snuff at every moment. The Guard, as they passed, saluted him with loud shouts of "*Vive l'Em-pereur!*" Meanwhile Wellington had ridden back behind Maitland's brigade of Guards, which he now saw would be the centre of an attack which was being made all along the line. Marcognet's division attacked Best's brigade, Alix attacked Lambert and Kempt, Donzelot's division attacked Alten. The Old Guard came on in echelons, and the first column met Halkett's brigade and withered away under its shattering musketry fire, and the grape-shot of the artillery. The second column approached the Guards who were lying down to shelter from the French artillery. The Duke called to them: "Stand up, Guards!" and then to their General: "Now, Maitland, now's your chance!" The Guards gave them a devastating volley at close range and then charged, firing as they advanced, driving the column of the Old Guard down the hill in confusion. At the same moment Colonel Colborne swung the Fifty-Second out of line and took the third French column in flank, smashing it and rolling it back on the fourth column (the reserve of two battalions) and also on to the remains of Reille's men falling back in disorder from Hougoumont. A cry went up: "*La Garde recule!*"— Adams's and Halkett's brigades rushed forward, Ziethen broke through on the extreme left of the British line, Bülow again took Planchenois and the Prussian cannon-balls began falling on the Charleroi road, Wellington threw in his last cavalry brigades and galloped along his whole line shouting to the brigades to charge, and waving his plumed hat in the direction of the French. The retirement became a rout. The French troops near Planchenois were the last to give way, and the three reserve battalions of the Guard retained their formation and discipline, defying capture when the rest of the army were in Stendhal's words "like a lot of sheep running away". The haggard and now speechless Emperor was hurried into his carriage, which he was forced to abandon in the choked bottleneck of Genappe and take to a horse to escape the Prussian cavalry. It was a strange reversal of fate for the General who at three that afternoon had sent out to Paris and the world the official announcement of a "complete victory".

Night had fallen on the battle-field, on the fugitives and their pursuers, when Blücher and Wellington met at La Belle Alliance (according to Blücher) but (according to the Duke) not far from Genappe. They shook hands with warm feelings—each had kept his word loyally, a practice which might well be revived in international affairs. Through an interpreter the two Commanders agreed that the Prussian cavalry should continue the pursuit, while the exhausted Anglo-Allied army bivouacked on the field of battle. Then the weary Duke rode slowly back to his quarters in Waterloo, across a battle-field where 45,000 dead and wounded men lay in an area of three square miles. The human cost of that decisive day had indeed been heavy. The French losses have never been accurately known because the whole army dispersed in flight and many of the men went straight to their homes, but unwounded French prisoners were not far short of 7,000 and the killed and wounded between 30,000 and 40,000. No less than 150 French guns were abandoned on the battle-field, and Blücher's men picked up sixty more during the night. The Prussians reported casualties of 6,999. Wellington's killed and wounded numbered 16,186, of whom 11,678 were English and Hanoverians. The loss in British officers, especially of high rank, was heavy—620 killed and wounded, including every member of the Duke's personal staff.

It is said that as Wellington rode back along the muddy *pavé* that night he was recognized in the bright moonlight, and faintly cheered by his wounded men lying on the ground—which, if it really happened, must indeed have been a ghostly and ghastly experience. As usual after a battle, however victorious, the Duke was in a mood of deep depression, partly of course from fatigue and over-exertion, but chiefly because he could not bear the casualties. He dismounted stiffly after nearly eighteen hours in the saddle; and "Copenhagen", still lively, lashed out and just missed killing him. That night "he ate little and ate in silence", looking up quickly whenever the door opened, in the vain hope that it might be one of his missing officers returned in safety. As he went to bed, he lifted his hands and said solemnly: "The hand of God has been over me this day."

He did not sleep long, for in the small hours they woke him to say farewell to one of his staff, Colonel Gordon, who was lying in the house, and who was dead when the Duke reached him. Then Hume, the Surgeon-General, came in with the preliminary casualty list, and as he read the seemingly interminable list of officers' names the Surgeon-General saw with awed amazement that tears were running down the Duke's face. During the battle he had maintained a composure which some thought callous, for when Uxbridge was wounded at his side and exclaimed: "I've got it at last!" the Duke merely remarked: "Have you, by God?" And when Picton's death was reported he said nothing for a time, and then only "I'm sorry Picton's gone".

The distress of hearing the casualty list made further sleep impossible, though Wellington must have been wearied out by the three days and nights of incessant work and anxiety. At any rate, he washed and shaved, and then began his unemotional and unboastful Waterloo dispatch, perhaps the most temperate account of a great victory ever written by a conqueror. He must have broken off this writing at dawn to ride into Brussels "to arrange some matters" (presumably cars and billets for the huge numbers of wounded, and some stop-gap staff officers) and there finished his dispatch and wrote a number of other letters. He must have been early in Brussels, since there exists a note to Lady Frances Webster timed "$\frac{1}{2}$ past 8 in the morning", saying, after the announcement of the victory:

"My loss is immense. Lord Uxbridge, Lord Fitzroy Somerset, General Cooke, General Barnes, and Colonel Berkeley are wounded: Colonel de Lancey, Canning, Gordon, General Picton killed. The finger of Providence was upon me, and I escaped unhurt."

Just about eleven on this morning of Monday, June 19, Mr. Creevey came in to congratulate the Duke on his victory:

"It has been a damned serious business," said the Duke with the greatest gravity, "Blücher and I have lost 30,000 men. It has been a damned nice thing —the nearest run thing you ever saw in your life. Blücher lost 14,000 on Friday night, and got so damnably licked I could not find him on Saturday morning; so I was obliged to fall back to keep up my communications with him."

The Guards, he went on, had done amazingly well in holding Hougoumont against repeated attacks, and "he praised all our troops, uttering repeated expressions of astonishment at our men's courage".

Mr. Creevey asked if the French had fought better than the Duke had seen them fight before, and the Duke said No, they always fought the same since he first saw them at Vimiero. And after a pause he added: "By God! I don't think it would have been done if I had not been there." Finally Creevey asked if he thought the French would be able to take the field again, and got this reply:

"No, certainly not. Every corps of France, but one, was in the battle, and the whole army went off in such rout and confusion I think it impossible for them to give battle again before the Allies reach Paris."

Before leaving Brussels that day the Duke dined with Frances, Lady Shelley, and her husband, where he walked up and down the room exclaiming: "Those Guards—those Guards, what fine fellows!" At dinner "the tears rolled down his cheeks and he could not recover his spirits at all". "Next to a battle lost," he told Lady Shelley, "the greatest misery is a battle gained."

Over in England and especially in London those June days had passed slowly under a pall of anxiety and depression. The stock market was down to its lowest in years, members of the Government looked gloomy, society was dispirited except for that gallant band of Opposition supporters who always disliked the Government more than the enemy. The most alarming rumours flowed in from the Continent and circulated with that astonishing superiority of speed which falsehood seems always to have over truth. None passed on these rumours with deeper satisfaction than the Opposition supporters just mentioned. Later in the afternoon of June 22 some of them stood talking eagerly in the large bow-windows of a fashionable club. A young Whig peer was listened to eagerly; he "knew for a fact" that the Prussians were wiped out, that the Anglo-Allied army was destroyed, Wellington himself killed, and the Emperor in Brussels—"the Government must fall when this news is known . . ."

At that moment someone who was staring out the window touched his arm and said quietly: "Look there!" Everybody turned, and what they saw was a chaise and four horses driving briskly down the street, followed at a run by a cheering mob. From the windows there stuck three French Imperial eagles.

The Tower guns began to fire a salute of 101 guns, and the church bells were rung.

CHAPTER XX

The Eagle Recaptured

CONTACT between the French and Prussian outposts was made on June 15, 1815; on June 18 Wellington stood at bay at Waterloo; and on July 7 the troops of Wellington and Blücher entered Paris. The Emperor had abdicated once more, and was a hunted fugitive desperately scheming to escape to America through the naval blockade. It so happened that at Waterloo the Emperor met the only two Generals who were not afraid of his reputation; and though there may have been some occult point in the Emperor's battle-field witticism that "these English are too stupid to know that they are beaten" he lived to learn that they were not too stupid to know when they had won. The remark of course was in line with the Emperor's usual propaganda, which now in July 1815 rebounded against him like the most unpleasant of unwanted boomerangs. Most people in Europe had been expecting an easy triumph for the French army, so that its shattering defeat was as astonishing as it was welcome to a world sick of war. An interesting example of this state of opinion and of the power of Napoleonic propaganda was related many years afterwards by Daniel Webster, who told an acquaintance in London that the United States envoy, John Quincy Adams, accustomed to Bonaparte's boastful bulletins, could not believe at first that the Duke's modestly worded dispatch announced a real victory, and for some days Mr. Adams firmly believed the Allied armies had been defeated. Even the Duke seems not altogether to have realized at first the completeness and magnitude of his victory, for on June 23 (1815) he wrote:

"I may be wrong, but my opinion is, that we have given Napoleon his death blow; from all I hear his army is totally destroyed, the men are deserting in parties, even the Generals are withdrawing from him. . . ."

The sudden reflux of opinion and feeling carried the Duke and his reputation on the crest of the wave, making him temporarily the most influential person in Europe. Even the French concurred for a few weeks, since the discipline and moderation of the British army contrasted so sharply with that of the Prussian, and Wellington's moderation with Blücher's brutal desire for vengeance. Public opinion may be wrong in its hero-worshipping, particularly since the growth of newspaper heroism, but in this case it was not altogether wrong: Waterloo was Wellington's battle. Of course the Prussians are entitled to all praise for their share; they are an essential part of the calculations; if they had not been willing to co-operate there would have been no battle, Wellington would have retired and waited for reinforcements. The Prussians did come up, but about six hours late, so that with his makeshift army Wellington had been compelled to face all day the repeated attacks of the finest soldiers in Europe animated by patriotism, devotion to the Emperor, and the fear of disbandment and half-pay if they lost the battle. The Emperor's tactics that day resulted in an unusually short battle line considering the number of men involved; and this exactly suited Wellington, who had long been accustomed to oversee as many details of a battle as possible and always to be present in person at critical points and moments. When the Nassauers began to abandon Hougoumont, the Duke was there to send in the Guards with a bluff: "In with you, my lads, and don't let me see you again." He had a more ceremonious "Now, gentlemen, for the honour of the Household Cavalry" when he threw the Life Guards against the French squadrons. He could even find a moment to notice the smart movement of a battery of horse-artillery he had ordered up, and to speak a word of commendation. According to Shaw Kennedy it was the Duke who rallied the Brunswickers at the crisis after La Haye Sainte fell, and the Duke who took command of the Fifty-Second after Colborne's unauthorized movement and directed their advance just before he gave the order for the whole line to attack.

The contrast between the two Commanders is not uninteresting. The Emperor still retained his marvellous intellect; his plans and projects were more grandiose than ever; and he had not lost his faculty for striking expressions. But the intellect was no longer served by the body; the planner was no longer a man of action; and he used his verbal dexterity to wound his last best friends. Obese and talkative, Napoleon sat consuming snuff on a chair in front of La Belle Alliance, when he should have been up with Ney to take advantage of the break-through at La Haye Sainte. When he left the battle-field it was in a luxurious travelling coach, fitted out with gold and an ostentatious library. Wellington, spare, austere, taciturn, was intensely active for more than twenty hours, most of the time in the saddle. How little he regarded his personal safety is showed by the fact that every one of his staff was a casualty, and that he and others believed his own escape to be almost miraculous, a special favour of God. He was entirely concentrated on the immediate task before him, and behold! the uninspired Anglo-Irishman beat the great master of modern warfare. Heine has bitterly lamented that his demigod Napoleon should have fallen to one so ordinary as Wellington, seeing in the tragedy a symbol of that fate which condemns all that is beautiful, gifted, and superior to fall before the commonplace—so that even God cannot be worshipped until He has been murdered. Not aspiring to these tragic heights, we may perhaps guess at a lesson for power and greatness in these contrasts.

Already in the first days of the march on Paris the Duke provided another contrast, this time with his friend and ally, Prince Blücher, who clearly had never made war against Mysore and the Mahrattas in the midst of an immense population whose hostility could be fatal, but whose tolerance (if not friendship) could be brought by justice, good faith, moderation, hard cash, and respect for castes. Prussia had been savagely treated by Napoleon, had suffered deeply, and had much to avenge, while, as Mr. Guedalla points out, Wellington represented a country which had not been invaded. The Duke's commonplace idea of the purpose of waging war was to bring about a victorious (and, if possible, lasting) peace as soon as possible. He therefore refused to treat with the French Provisional Government in Paris, with which Blücher agreed; and, considering the French King an ally, Wellington invited Louis XVIII to take possession of the towns and fortresses as they fell into English hands. With this Blücher strongly disagreed, as he would have liked to prolong a state of anarchy in France. Relations with his *"lieber Kamerad"* became distinctly strained when they reached Paris, and the Duke strongly objected to a Prussian levy of a hundred million francs on the town, while he posted a sentry on the Pont de Jena to prevent the Prussians from blowing it up. In justice it must be said that the bridge was preserved, not by the British sentry, but by the incompetence of the Prussian engineers who failed to blow up either the bridge or the representative of their dear ally. Luckily the Allied sovereigns began arriving in Paris before the "dear Allies" got to blows, and Blücher retired to St. Cloud where he could gratify his stout old German heart by turning a French palace into a German barracks.

The army was still advancing on Paris when the flood of congratulatory letters began to rush in upon its Commander. One of the earliest, certainly the most florid and probably the most sincere came from Prinny, who had sense enough to admire his soldier without envy or suspicion. Roused to enthusiasm by three French eagles and a good deal of claret His Royal Highness wrote:

"My dear Wellington,

I lose not a moment in communicating to you the fulness of my joy and admiration at the unparalleled triumph of your last and greatest achievement. Greatest, my dear Lord, not only in military glory, but in political importance; and not only in this proof of what all believed, that even the consummate genius of the Corsican could not withstand the superior genius of our own hero, but in the now nearly realised expectation, resulting from this victory, that England, under the auspices of her transcendent General, is again destined to rescue the world from tyranny and oppression. . . ."

From which it appears that the Regent was not only the fountain-head of Mr. Turveydrop's manners, but the model for Mr. Micawber's prose style. There was indeed nothing but magniloquent flattery left for the Regent to bestow on his "hero", and even Parliament could only give him thanks and more money (£200,000) for the upkeep of Strathfield Saye. It was therefore ungrateful of the Duke to remark later to Mr. Creevey apropos the Prince Regent: "He looks and talks so like old Falstaff that, dammee, I'm ashamed to enter a room with him."

Meanwhile what had happened to the Emperor? After his abdication he had vanished, and there was good reason to suppose that some of Louis XVIII's Cabinet (though not indeed the King himself) were communicating with the fugitive and trying to arrange his escape in the hope that he might make himself a nuisance to the New World, and especially to the English who had just restored the said Cabinet to power. Castlereagh and Wilson Croker (Secretary to the Admiralty) were now in Paris, and agreed with the Duke that Fouché, Talleyrand, and Jaucourt were communicating with Napoleon by means of the semaphore, which of course was much quicker than the swiftest messenger. The three Irishmen decided to try what could be done with a little guile, for there was a strong feeling that Bonaparte ought not to be allowed to escape. Together they concocted a careful letter to the naval commander of the British blockading squadron telling him to go on shore and get the Emperor (if he was still on land), but

" . . . if the ship in which Buonaparte may be, should, by an obstinate re-sistance, drive you to extremities, Lord Castlereagh feels that you ought not, for the sake of saving her *or any one on board her*, to take any line of conduct which should increase in any degree your own risk." [Italics are the author's.]

In other words, go and get Boney alive or dead, but get him. Of course the Secretary of State for Foreign Affairs and the Secretary of the Admiralty (who is not a Sea Lord) had no right to give orders to a naval officer, but Castlereagh only made it a strong request, and

Croker put the letter into naval officialese. They relied on the relevant captain or admiral grasping the situation and acting accordingly; and then showed the letter to the three French Ministers who naturally were not acquainted with the niceties of British authority and its devolution, and were quite unaware that the letter was a bluff. As loyal Ministers of Louis XVIII they could not object to the dispatch of the letter, but oddly enough a few hours later the Emperor wrote his celebrated Themistocles letter to the Prince Regent and surrendered to Captain Maitland on the *Bellerophon*. In view of the Emperor's later feigned indignation and protests that he had been "betrayed" and that he had received promises and agreed on terms with Captain Maitland, it may be as well to quote that officer's letter to Croker:

H.M.S. Bellerophon Basque Roads, 14th July, 1815

"Sir,

    "For the information of my Lords Commissioners of the Admiralty I have to acquaint you that the Count Las Cases and General Allemand this day came on board H.M. ship under my command with a proposal for me to receive on board Napoleon Bonaparte, for the purpose of throwing himself on the generosity of His Royal Highness the Prince Regent.

    "Conceiving myself authorised by their Lordships' secret order, I have acceded to the proposal, and he is to embark on board ship to-morrow morning. *That no misunderstanding might arise, I have explicitly and clearly explained to the Count Las Cases that I have no authority whatever for granting terms of any sort, but that all I can do is to convey him and his suite to England, to be received in such manner as His Royal Highness may deem expedient.*" [Captain Maitland to J. W. Croker. Italics are author's.]

It seems clear that the French Ministers must instantly have sent to Napoleon by semaphore signal the gist of the Castlereagh-Croker letter, and that this so much frightened the Emperor that he determined to surrender at once. Captain Maitland's letter makes it equally clear that the stories of the Emperor's being "betrayed" and taken to England on false pretences are pure invention. Indeed, the complaints of the Emperor and the Bonapartist party on this point seem ungrateful, for Blücher had given orders that the (now ex-) Emperor was to be shot on sight as a brigand.

Evidently that July 13 (1815) was the day which Wellington and Castlereagh had decided on for a show-down with the somewhat shifty French Ministers, for after the business of the letter about Napoleon had been disposed of, the Duke turned to Fouché and reminded him that although the Governor of the Vincennes fort had hoisted a white flag he had not yet surrendered the fortress, although Fouché had promised it for that morning. Fouché shrugged his shoulders, looked "penitent", said the Governor was obstinate and wouldn't obey orders, and ended, "What can I do?"

"It's not my business to tell you what you ought to do," said the Duke reddening, "But I'll tell you what I'm going to do. If the fort is not surrendered by ten to-morrow morning, I shall take it by assault. Do you understand?"

Fouché tried to get a little more delay, but the Duke was adamant— "if the place isn't surrendered by ten, it will be captured by twelve." He turned to Croker who was sitting at a writing-table and said:

"Croker, you never saw a fight; be with me at 9 o'clock to-morrow morning; I shall give you some breakfast and mount you on a good horse, and take you to see the show—a show which I shall be very sorry to exhibit, but which such an outrage on good faith and honour forces upon me."

Next morning Croker turned up for breakfast and found that everything had been duly prepared for the assault. However, he was disappointed of his show, for the place was immediately surrendered.

This firmness in handling anything which looked like subterfuge or dishonest dealing is in sharp contrast with the Duke's policy of conciliation and goodwill to France, which he was able to impose on his own Government and on the rest of the Powers by the extraordinary prestige he had acquired by his victory. It is worth noticing that this policy was not the result of feebleness nor of what would now be called "political idealism", but of the Duke's invariable common sense and plain dealing. He saw, perhaps more clearly than anyone else, that a policy which is a half-hearted compromise between revenge and appeasement is fatal because it enrages without seriously weakening the vanquished. If the Powers really intended to make France harmless as a military power, "let them take from that country its population and resources as well as a few fortresses". If they were not willing to take drastic action, then the sensible course was to make a reality out of the fiction that they were only at war with Bonaparte as the allies of Louis XVIII, and to make that King's government as strong and popular as they could. There is perhaps nothing unusual in a professional soldier proving to be less bloodthirsty and vindictive on grounds of pure morality than civilians and "statesmen", but it is surely to the Duke's credit that he used his victory and his prestige so sensibly. Add to this that a little later he, and he alone, after months of hard work succeeded in hammering out a solution of the reparations problem, ruthlessly scaling down the demands of the "dear Allies" and consulting many prominent bankers to be sure that France could pay without undue strain what he ordered. Again there was nothing remarkable in the excogitation of a war reparations scheme which was unanimously accepted; but that a man should find a war reparations scheme which actually *worked* is almost awe-inspiring. Perhaps young Arthur Wellesley had not been so far wrong when he told a sceptical mother that he thought his abilities were financial. Europe owed to this dual functioning of common sense the longest peace it has known for centuries, and that is surely a greater claim to glory than all the Duke's victories from Assaye to Waterloo.

As long as there was danger that the Teutonic Powers would insist on the dismemberment of France, Wellington was the most popular man in that country; and naturally that popularity waned rapidly as soon as there was nothing more to be gained from him. Something of the kind was inevitable, owing to the political factions into which France had been shattered by the Revolution and its results. No more curious example of the political incoherence of that great country, and the extent to which political expediency was carried, could well be invented than the sober fact that His Most Christian Majesty was compelled (or thought he was compelled) to include among his Ministers, Fouché the Jacobin regicide and Talleyrand the unfrocked priest, both of whom had been in the service of Bonaparte for years. But the most dangerous factions were the "ultras", the bigoted Church and State men more royalist than the King; and the Bonapartists. The former hated Wellington because he counselled moderation in French home affairs and supported a constitutional as against an absolute monarchy; and the latter hated him because he had defeated the Emperor, ruined their military careers, and thwarted all hope of a regency for the son of Napoleon and Marie Louise. In attacking Wellington, the Bonapartists were also attacking the monarchy he had restored; and, acting literally on Voltaire's ironical advice about calumny, they lost no opportunity of discrediting the man who had saved their country from humiliation and dismemberment.

It is said that at one of Louis XVIII's levees, the French Marshals present ostentatiously turned their backs on the Duke when he entered. The King began a diplomatic apology to rub the insult in, but was interrupted by the hearty remark: "Not the first time I've seen the backs of the French Marshals, sire!" This (probably apocryphal) story is true enough in spirit, showing the lengths to which Bonapartist hostility was prepared to go, and the cheerful contempt with which the Duke received it. Anti-Wellington activities of the Bonapartists reached a climax in February 1818 when a determined attempt to assassinate the Duke, as his carriage was turning into the Embassy in Paris, very nearly succeeded. The author of this attempt was an ex-soldier named Cantillon, to whom the grateful Napoleon bequeathed a considerable legacy, from funds which the Emperor knew to be imaginary—which is perhaps the poetically just way to reward an assassin who fails. The Duke thought otherwise, and shook his head over Napoleon, "a sad fellow", who ought to have known better than to encourage inefficient criminals with fraudulent legacies.

This attempted assassination occurred towards the end of the occupation of France by the armies of Russia, Austria, Prussia, the Low Countries, England, and the minor German states—all of them, by the way, under Wellington's command. It would be impractical as well as tedious to enumerate the many episodes which were used to discredit the Duke with Frenchmen; but two are inevitable, if only because Byron has given more than a century of vitality to his own versions of them, which are really not justified by the facts. The first and more important concerns the shooting of Ney for treason by the monarchical French Government. Now, although Louis XVIII had to condone a perfectly enormous amount of treachery and to work with men who had deserted him at a moment's notice for the Emperor, he could not without a complete loss of national discipline openly pardon Ney. Even so, the French Government, while excluding Ney from the general amnesty, had permitted him to live incognito in a remote part of the country until, unluckily, an over-zealous local official saw fit to arrest him and send him to Paris, where of course he was court-martialled and condemned. Great efforts were made to induce the Duke to intervene with the King on Ney's behalf, and it was claimed that Ney ought to benefit by Article 12 of the Convention of Paris (which the Duke had signed) covering the safety of persons and property in the surrendered city. But this was a palpable quibble, and nothing in the Convention abrogated the right of the French King to take proceedings against any of his subjects considered guilty of high treason. The Duke was certain that such cases as Ney's were not intended to be covered by the Convention, and in addition he was equally clear that he could not and must not interfere with "the workings of the French King's Government in domestic affairs". If he did, the cry would at once go up that the French Government was a "mere puppet" of the English. There are some heart-rending letters from Ney's wife, which must have been difficult to resist, but the Duke held firm, and Ney was shot—outside the Closerie des Lilas. Where-upon the Bonapartists circulated the story that the Duke could have

saved him if he had wished, and had refused to intervene only because
he was jealous of Ney's military glory! Byron took up the cry in
"Don Juan", Canto 9:

> "Glory like yours should any dare gainsay,
>   Humanity would rise and thunder 'Nay!' "

with the footnote: "Query—*Ney?*—PRINTER'S DEVIL". The passage
is amusing and good invective; especially when a soldier's complaint
of the food shortage *after Talavera in* 1809 is used to bolster an
insinuation that the Duke starved his sentries *in* 1816! But, as a boxer,
Byron knew that in the politics of those days there were no Queens-
berry rules.

The other episode which was used as propaganda against the Duke's
popularity with the French people was the return to their several
owners of the works of art "collected" by the armies of the Emperor
and the Republic. Some such act of reparation was anticipated early,
for under date July 14, 1815, Croker records a visit to Denon, the
amiable and intelligent Director of Fine Arts at the Louvre. Croker
found Denon in a state of high agitation, wailing that the French art
collections would be (in Croker's words) "plundered of their plunder"
by (Denon's words) that "animal indécrottable", Prince Blücher. The
weak side of the case for the Allies was not that there was any doubt
about the pictures and statues having been looted, but that in 1814 they
had condoned the offence by not insisting on their being returned.
Except that they were angry with the French for the Hundred Days
there was no more reason why the works of art should be restored in
1815 than in 1814. But once the Allied council had made the decision,
the Duke was not the man to shrink from enforcing it. Indeed he
approved of it on principle, holding that the constant spectacle of such
trophies was a standing invitation to the French people to invest in
more such profitable military adventures. And as Louis XVIII, for
reasons of his own, perpetually put off the restorations he had agreed
to, the Duke sent his redcoats to collect the works of art and to see
them dispatched to their proper owners. Whereupon, judging him by
the standards of their own Marshals, the Bonapartists let it be known
far and wide that the Duke was taking these valuable objects for
himself. That such stories could be circulated and believed indicates
the standards of public morality which had prevailed in France since
the Revolution.

Hypocrisy is the tribute vice pays to virtue, and calumny is the
measure of a living man's superiority over his contemporaries. The

Duke in his time received a superabundance of these testimonies, but they do not appear to have worried him in the least. When a Mr. Denys officiously handed on the rumours to the effect that the Duke was pillaging the Louvre, this characteristically sensible reply was returned:

"The Duke is very much obliged to Mr. Denys for his advice regarding the false reports in circulation on the subject of the specimens of the arts in the Museum. The Duke has long learnt to despise this description of report, which he never considers sufficiently deserving of his attention to contradict. These reports originate with those who know they are false; and as soon as contradicted, others would be circulated of the same description. The Duke, therefore, considers it best to leave the public to discover the truth as they best can."

It would be interesting but seems impossible to know just how far this lofty disdain for detractors was innate and how far it had been cultivated or even assumed out of deference to aristocratic standards. Sadly enough, men are more sensitive to one libeller than to a hundred panegyrists, especially when they have grown accustomed to praise. In later life the Duke refused to read histories of his wars because "I might be tempted to reply" and "I will have nothing to do with writing a book". Nevertheless in 1816 he *did* write a memorandum in reply to Ney's wife, and many years later he *did* write a long and interesting comment on Clausewitz's criticism of the Waterloo campaign. In this respect it might be noted that the account of the Russian campaign in 1812 in Walter Scott's *Life of Napoleon Bonaparte* is based on a memoir supplied by the Duke. Since the (far from complete) printed collections of the Wellington correspondence occupy about thirty-five large volumes, he did pretty well altogether for one who disdained authorship.*

Similarly, while he may have disdained rewards as much as he disdained calumny, he did pretty well. During the period just after Waterloo "it snewéd in his hous" of royal and military orders, Eagles Red, White, and Black, Lions Gold and Ordinary, Elephants, Crosses, Grand Crosses, and Saints. The Duke must have possessed the greatest collection of official babules in Europe, as he certainly acquired the largest bundle of Field-Marshal's batons—those of England, Portugal, Spain, Russia, Austria, Prussia, the Netherlands, and France. During the period of the Allied occupation of France, 1815–1818, he was in supreme command of all the armies, which at one period amounted to the (then unprecedented) number of 900,000. Since he was drawing Marshal's pay from five countries, perhaps he

* See Appendix.

deserves credit for disinterestedness in labouring to reduce the time of the occupation, as he lost his pay with the ending of his command.

The indisputable fact that never once in his long career did he use his power or persuasion to advance his money interests,* was one reason why his friends in Parliament had so little difficulty in persuading the House of Commons to vote him such large sums of money. Although he received £600,000 and the estate of Strathfield Saye,. his pay as a Field-Marshal, £50,000 as his share of the Peninsula prize-money, a similar or larger amount as his share of the Waterloo campaign prize-money, and an annuity of 20,000 florins from the Low Countries which went with his title of Prince of Waterloo. He was also given estates in Portugal, Spain, and Belgium, but is said to have been consistently defrauded of the revenues by dishonest stewards.

The rewards to the army were as follows. For the Peninsular War, prize-money of £800,000 divided according to rank. It must be remembered that those under the rank of ensign had means of picking up money forbidden to officers. Thus, the rank and file must have collected at least a million sterling from Joseph's treasure chests at Vittoria—there are well-authenticated cases of men who picked up $1,000 or more in gold that day. Moreover, pillage of slain enemy soldiers and officers nearly always yielded results, since even then the French were a thirfty, saving race. Rifleman Harris, who had no share in the Vittoria spoils, brought home two hundred gold guineas as his earnings as a sharp-shooter. For the Waterloo campaign close on one million sterling was given as prize-money, with two years' immediate seniority for all present at the battle of Waterloo. (The effect of the latter privilege was to bring them in one day two years nearer to their seniority pay.) Finally, well over another half-million was raised by public subscription for pensions to widows, orphans, and wounded, in addition to the usual not very generous grants from Government. It is true that from our point of view a disproportionately large share of this money went to the officers, but it is also true that Wellington's rank and file were far better treated in the matter of money reward than their continental allies and enemies, even though they were "the scum of the earth".

Are we to count the social lionizing of the Duke among compensations or among bores? On the whole, he seems to have enjoyed it, particularly that part of his social duties which consisted of being kissed by enthusiastic and pretty ladies of high birth and politics. In

---

* At Seringapatam and after Salamanca he complained officially of insufficient pay.

the latter half of 1815 it seemed as if everyone in Great Britain who could raise the fare went to Paris to gaze on their hero and to make the acquaintance of the world's intellectual capital, which few of them had seen for a quarter of a century. Croker has noted the curious and picturesque detail of the Life Guards doing police duty on the boulevards, and Walter Scott surprised the Duke by refusing technical information for his projected life of Napoleon, eliciting later the pungent reflection from the Duke that "I didn't know he only meant to write a novel". In fact, the Duke seems to have anticipated Mr. Henry Ford's views on history, since he constantly discouraged contemporary historians and refused to believe that the truth could be written. Meanwhile, the cosmopolitan smart set dined and danced in Paris; and the hungry veterans of the *Grande Armée* had leisure to muse on military glory and its rewards.

The field of Waterloo now became an obligatory station on the grand tour of Europe, much to the profit of the Belgian peasantry who collected and perhaps manufactured battle relics, and drew on a traditionally fertile imagination for authentic anecdotes of the contest. In the early days the battle-ground was singularly like those of our own times, allowing for the change in weapons. Croker, who saw it a few weeks after June 18, found the highway for miles "strewed with soldier's hats and caps, broken arms, bones of horses and other reliques of an army", while on the actual field he noticed the immense litter of "cartridges and waddings of the cannon, letters which had been torn out of the pockets of the killed and wounded", "torn remains of hats, caps and helmets", "the house and offices" of Hougoumont "burnt and battered with shot, the trees around it cut to pieces . . . the fields around it broken up with graves". But in a very short space of time all these uncomely memorials of strife had disappeared, and the tourist could indulge his emotions uncontaminated by brutal facts:

> "And Ardennes waves above them her green leaves,
> Dewy with nature's tear-drops, as they pass,
> Grieving, if aught inanimate e'er grieves
> Over the unreturning brave. . . ."

CHAPTER XXI

Peace

IN LATER days the Duke said that the greatest moment in his military life was when he led his troops from Spain across the Nivelle to invade France. We can easily see why, since this was done in spite of the utmost resistance of an enemy long supposed to be "invincible", and achieved six months before any other of the Allies set foot on French soil. For others his greatest military moment fell between seven-thirty and eight on the evening of June 18, 1815, when he galloped along his battle lines waving his cocked hat to launch the regiments in pursuit of the broken French army. It was more than the end of Napoleon's dream of universal dictatorship, it was the end of France as a successful aggressive power. Certainly that moment at Waterloo was the dramatic climax of Wellington's life, and the thirty-seven years or so he had yet to live were in the nature of an anti-climax. It is as a soldier that he won his fame, and the last hour at Waterloo was the culmination and the abrupt end of his active life as a soldier. He never again commanded an army in the field.

Yet successful peace-making is much harder than successful war-making, and if mankind were not incorrigible idiots they would cease to admire the "heroes" who triumph at the expense of their blood and wealth and turn their gratitude to the more obscure but more worthy people who labour for peace. If Wellington has a claim to be considered a great man as he certainly may claim to be a picturesque and thoroughly sincere "character", it is because he was a successful soldier who disliked war, a conqueror who never acquired Napoleon's cynical disregard for human life, and because he earnestly worked for peace. Whatever his mistakes as a politician in his own country, an authority so good as Bagehot thought that the Duke's influence in the House of Lords probably averted a revolution in the troublous days of 1830–1832. Whatever his mistakes as the arbiter of Europe in 1815–1818, it can be said definitely that firstly he made not the slightest attempt to exploit the situation for his own aggrandizement and indeed faced great obloquy in doing what he thought was right, and secondly that he used his great influence in those critical years on the side of moderation and appeasement.

The Prussian scheme for the subjugation and division of France was a natural result of Prussian conceit and love of revenge; but there would have been a real logic in it if the French nation remained uncured of its aggressive militarism. Wellington thought it was cured, because of his talks with Frenchmen of all classes (including the *curé de Pé*) in the south of France in 1813–1814, and because he believed the Hundred Days was a last desperate fling of the French army which the nation had to endure but did not support. Would the whole armed resistance have crumbled with such startling rapidity, the Duke argued, if it had really been supported by the nation? Unluckily, the Duke's solution of France's problems by a constitutional monarchy with representative government through an upper and a lower house was a failure. One of the grimmest legacies of the French Revolution was that division into irreconcilable factions, which has prevented France from achieving a permanent form of government strong enough to defend the country from its enemies without, and flexible enough to avoid revolution within. It is astonishing how these dissensions have been prolonged from generation to generation. There is a story of the small daughter of a Republican family who asked: "Mamma, are *all* Democrats wicked?" and was told: "My dear, they are born bad and get worse with age." What we laugh at as a joke of exaggeration was not far from being a real and widespread state of mind in the France of 1815 onwards. Where political parties represent irreconcilable factions Parliamentary government becomes impossible—eventually there must be a revolution or a civil war. By 1818 almost the only things on which all Frenchmen were agreed were hatred of Wellington and the impatient desire to get rid of the Allied armies of occupation under his command.

There exists an interesting letter of the Duke's written to the English diplomat, J. C. Villiers, in 1818, which shows that already he saw that his efforts to give France a stable government had failed and unerringly laid the blame where it belonged—on "Monsieur", the King's brother, then Comte d'Artois, later Charles X, who was thrown out of France in the Revolution of 1830. Here is what the Duke wrote of the coming elections in France:

"I entertain no doubt how this contest will end. The descendants of Louis XV will not reign in France; and I must say, and always will say, that it is the fault of Monsieur and his adherents.

"I have been in France since the year 1814, and if I have not been an actor in all the scenes which have taken place, I have been too much interested in them not to have paid attention to them; and I have been placed in a situation to have a knowledge of everything that was passing; and, notwithstanding my respect for Monsieur, I cannot but be of the opinion which I have just now communicated to you. . . .

"I wish Monsieur would read the histories of our Restoration and subsequent Revolution, or that he would recollect what passed under his own view, probably at his own instigation, in the Revolution.

"The conduct of the Royalists in joining with the Jacobins against the Moderate party certainly led to the King's death.

" . . . The Sovereigns of Europe will meet in the autumn of this year, to consider of the state of France and the Federal system for Europe to adopt in reference to that state. We are bound to the dynasty of Monsieur in no way, excepting by a consequence to be drawn from our engagement to restore the fortresses; and this may be depended upon, that if he and his party (for it is nonsense to suppose that he is not the head of a party) go on as they have done, the Powers of Europe will unite in a system to avert from themselves revolutionary changes, leaving France to herself, and Monsieur to find his own way through them. I know, and Monsieur will then see clearly, that he has not a chance of reigning; and he will then repent, but too late, the false direction which he has given to his party during the reign of his brother." [Letter to J. C. Villiers, January 11, 1818.]

A little over twelve years later, in August 1830, the writer of that letter was Prime Minister of Great Britain, and he received the following communication which shows how accurately he had foreseen the future of Charles X:

"I have just returned from on board the *Great Britain*, American vessel, in which the late royal family of France are embarked. They anchored at Spithead about two o'clock this afternoon.

"The King and Dauphin look well, but evidently are much dispirited and dejected. I delivered to the latter your Grace's message, which he communicated to the King, who informed me that he had written to the King of England and to your Grace, requesting permission to be permitted to remain in England until he hears from the Emperor of Austria, in whose dominions he has asked an asylum." . . . [Letter from Sir C. Campbell, Portsmouth, August 16, 1830.]

Thus ended in failure the Duke's well-meant attempt to play the part of Warwick the King-Maker in France, and the constitutional monarchy of Louis Philippe which followed only lasted eighteen years. In history "ifs" are always sheer waste of time, but it now seems clear that the only chance for the restored Bourbons in 1814–1815 would have been to adopt a régime as comparatively liberal as that of Louis Philippe, with the possibility of a peaceful evolution towards more democratic forms of government. In 1830 it was already too late. The Comte d'Artois (Charles X) has much to answer for—he and his party turned the French Revolution into violence in 1789 and made the reconciliation of parties impossible in the period after the restoration of 1815. One of the most disquieting lessons of history is the repeated examples of the irreparable damage which can be done by a few obstinate fools and bigots. Before blaming the Duke too heavily for his failure (along with the other Allied statesmen and kings) we might remember that the alternatives to Louis XVIII were: (1) the Emperor Napoleon, who had just given a striking example of peaceful good faith; (2) a regency for his son, which would have opened the way for every conceivable intrigue and disorder; (3) one of the Marshals as king, which would have been an invitation to all the others to conspire; (4) a republic which was then impossible, for "Republic" still connoted "Robespierre and the Terror" and sent a shiver down the spine of every honest man in the country.

It would be quite wrong, of course, to say that the Duke was wholly or even chiefly responsible for the treaties and various decisions of the post-war conferences and congresses. He *was* responsible for urging Louis XVIII to return to France within a few days of Waterloo when the fortress of Cambrai was handed over to the French King by the British troops, and he *was* responsible for the decision to treat France with moderation instead of severity. So that while he would not have been entitled to all the praise if these measures had completely succeeded (i.e. in giving Europe a permanent peace and France a stable government), neither can he be wholly blamed for their eventual failure.

On the other hand, Wellington does deserve praise for his settlement of the reparations to be paid by France to the various European Powers to compensate the losses of private citizens—or rather a fraction of the losses—inflicted by the armies of the Republic and the Empire. It is curious to note how, in the reaction against the apotheosis of the Duke in his old age, even an impartial historian seems to deny this claim to achievement, when he says:

"Before the end of the session of 1818, by the intervention of the Tsar through Pozzo di Borgo and with the final consent of Wellington it became possible to regulate the responsibilities of France towards her foreign creditors and the Powers."

The sentence is loosely worded, but I think would suggest to any reader unfamiliar with the subject that the Tsar and Pozzo di Borgo settled the matter, and that Wellington (who seems to be suggested as some vague obstacle to settlement) finally consented to it. Nothing can be further from the truth, which is that, after more than two years of fruitless wrangling over the question, the Tsar "finally" in the autumn of 1817 suggested that Wellington be appointed arbitrator, which was agreed to; and that after months of intensely hard work the Duke produced a settlement acceptable to all parties in April 1818. As I wrote I have before me the relevant letters of the Tsar and his representative, Pozzo di Borgo. The Tsar writes to Wellington from Moscow (in French) under date (presumably Old Style) October 30, 1817, and among other things says:

" . . . you have more than once contributed to the conciliation of the most important interests by your wisdom and moderation . . . if I had a wish to utter, it would be that the unanimous consent of my Allies and of the other interested parties might be given to the handing over to you of the principal control of the negotiations which ought to be opened in Paris on the question of these 'créances particulières' and on the fairest way of deciding it by a common agreement." [Translated.]

The language is fustian, but it is clear that the Tsar wanted the Duke to take over and settle the reparations problem. Pozzo di Borgo's letter (Paris, November 21–December 3, 1817) is more specific:

"His Majesty the Emperor has added a proposal which he considers necessary to the result desiderated by the common interest, namely, that you, My Lord, should be entrusted with the principal control of this great problem, and that you should be placed at the head of the Conference effectively, so that among all these conflicting claims there may be found a compromise to form the basis of the wished for agreement. . . ."

Wellington replied to this letter on December 4, 1817, and again I translate:

"If however the Powers of Europe, on the proposal of H.M. the Emperor see fit to entrust me with the principal control of the negotiations, I shall not only not refuse but shall be grateful for the confidence reposed in me by the Powers and for the honour done me. . . ."

It is plain from these letters and the many documents included in the Wellington *Dispatches* that the Tsar proposed that the Duke should be entrusted with the unpleasant job of reparations arbitrator, that the Tsar included a memorandum of generalities, leaving to the Duke the real tussle of getting money out of France and distributing it among hungry European governments without being torn to pieces. The claims amounted to something approaching a milliard of gold francs, a colossal sum for that epoch. Here is a table of claims, which is incomplete for it does not include Spain, Portugal, England, or Russia:

Austria	200,000,000	gold francs
Prussia	120,000,000	,,
Bavaria	73,000,000	,,
Holland	65,000,000	,,
Sardinia	70,000,000	,,
Hamburg	70,000,000	,,
Bremen and Lübeck	4,500,000	,,
Denmark	42,000,000	,,
Saxony	20,000,000	,,
Tuscany	4,000,000	,,
States of the Church	30,000,000	,,
Hanover	25,000,000	,,
Saxony and Prussia	15,000,000	,,
Switzerland	12,000,000	,,
Small Powers	25,000,000	,,
Total	775,500,000	,,

It is a notorious fact that little creditors and small landlords are the most exacting, and representatives of small powers the most querulous and verbose in cases where there is money to be claimed; which explains why the Duke shied like a frightened horse away from the Tsar's further proposal of a "general conference of delegates" of all the interested Powers. (Spain weighed in after the above list was drawn up with a modest little bill for 263,331,912 francs and 85 centimes.) The prospects of a settlement in such a pandemonium seemed to the Duke extremely dim. He thought there would be more chance if he did things himself, and after four months of intensely hard work he actually persuaded everybody concerned to agree to the following settlement:

Anhalt Dessau	373,507	gold francs
Anhalt Bernbourg	350,000	,,
Austria	25,000,000	,,
Baden	650,000	,,
Bavaria	10,000,000	,,
Bremen	1,000,000	,,
Denmark	7,000,000	,,
States of the Church	5,000,000	,,
Spain	17,000,000	,,
Frankfurt	700,000	,,
Electoral Hesse	507,099	,,
Grand Duchy of Hesse, etc.	8,000,000	,,
Hanover	10,000,000	,,
Hamburg	20,000,000	,,
Ionian Islands, etc.	3,000,000	,,
Lübeck	2,000,000	,,
Mecklenburg Schwerin	500,000	,,

Duchy of Nassau	127,000	gold francs
Duchy of Parma	1,000,000	,,
Prussia	52,003,289	,,
Low Countries	33,000,000	,,
Portugal	818,736	,,
Saxony	4,500,000	,,
Sardinia	25,000,000	,,
Saxe Meiningen	20,694	,,
Switzerland	5,000,000	,,
Tuscany	4,500,000	,,
Wurtemberg	400,000	,,
Saxony and Prussia	2,200,000	,,
Electoral Hesse, etc.	14,000	,,
Hesse Darmstadt, Bavaria	200,000	,,
Hesse Darmstadt, Prussia and Bavaria	800,000	,,
Total	240,664,325	,,

At this distance of time it is hard to say whether these figures represent a just settlement or whether they were imposed by the Duke's cold blue eyes and the knowledge that he had 150,000 soldiers under his command in France. Certainly in view of all that the country suffered so courageously in the common cause, Portugal seems to have been shabbily treated. At this distance of time it is impossible to get at the rights and wrongs of the individual states, but the miracle is that, first, such a sum of money could have been wrung from a reluctant France; second, that agreement on its disposal could have been reached among so many hungry little governments; and third—wonder of wonders—that the money was actually paid in full. And, final miracle, the creditors did not have to lend five times the amount in order to get paid.

It is well to remember that while this complicated work was going on, the Duke was constantly being asked his opinion officially on a multitude of public concerns, and that he kept up an intense correspondence with the Government of his own country and representatives of many others. In addition he was responsible for the behaviour and good condition of a large miscellaneous army billeted in a hostile country, over which he reigned from his headquarters in Cambrai. Infinite were the forms of mischief in which the members of the army felt impelled to indulge, from generals who would go hunting on the private property of indignant French princes, to subalterns who insisted on committing riots in public places where they had no business to be, to privates who would try to take back to England at the public expense young women to whom they were not even married. All these and a thousand other military details were passed on to the

Commander of the Forces, and dealt with according to regulations supplied by the wisdom of the Duke of York and his forgotten predecessors.

By way of recreation there were libel actions to be brought (unsuccessfully) against the editors of Belgian newspapers, and the immense hubbub which followed Cantillon's attempt on the Duke's life; there were the drawing-rooms and feasts of polite society in Paris and London, and the inspection of Belgian fortresses; and there were military reviews and manœuvres for the entertainment of princes and potentates. The reviews were perhaps the least troublesome of all these diversions, though no doubt the private interviews with ladies whose names have been carefully shrouded from a profane posterity were the most agreeable. In 1815 the Duke displayed his army outside Paris for the benefit of the foreign potentates, and amazed them by throwing his divisions swiftly into the positions they had occupied in the battle of Salamanca, and then just as the kings and laymen were wondering what on earth these complicated manœuvres meant, aides-de-camp galloped from the Duke's side to the divisional commanders, and lo! the whole army broke off its operations and formed immediately in review order. The Prussians could scarcely believe that it was all done without rehearsal, without markers or ground tape.

Apropos a farewell review of the Allied armies in the late summer of 1818 the generalities of history are suddenly made lively and particular by a visit of Mr. Creevey, observant, indiscreet and garrulous as ever, to the Duke at Cambria. Frankness being a comomn quality of the great Tory and the little Whig, they got on famously; and particularly in the matter of the Royal Dukes. Mr. Creevey remarked that the Government (the Duke's friends) had "cut a contemptible figure" owing to their "repeated defeats" in the Commons in trying to get more money for the Dukes of Clarence, Kent, and Cumberland on their respective marriages. "By God!" said the Duke, "they're the damndest millstones about the necks of any Government that can be imagined. They have insulted—personally insulted—two thirds of the gentlemen of England, and how can it be wondered at that they take their revenge upon them when they get them in the House of Commons? It is their only opportunity, and I think, by God! they are quite right to use it."

It was in that interview or one very close in time that the Duke made his courtier-like comparison of the Prince Regent to Falstaff; and not to be single in literary comparisons he found another for Queen Victoria's father, the Duke of Kent:

I

"God dammee! d'ye know what his sisters call him? By God! they call him Joseph Surface."

Mr. Creevey was one of those friends of the people who like comfort and the flesh-pots, and are by no means averse from luxury when it is paid for by others. Imagine his dismay when, during a series of military reviews to which he had been invited by the Duke, he found the inn he had been told was the rendezvous for dinner "the most wretched concern I ever beheld," so "small and wretched" that Mr. Creevey thought it must be a mistake until the Duke came out "of a wretched little parlour", and shouted that dinner was ready. Horror upon horror! Dinner was "brought in by two dirty maids" and "consisted of four dishes, two partridges . . . a fowl . . . fricassee of chicken . . . and something equally substantial". Mr. Creevey could not believe his ears when he learned that the Duke had left Paris at 5 a.m. and had driven 130 miles that day, with nothing for his party to eat but a cold fowl. Finally, "although the fare was so scanty, the champagne the commonest of stuff, and the house so bad, it seemed to make no impression on the Duke. He seemed quite as well pleased and as well satisfied as if he had been in a palace".

At the military review Mr. Creevey characteristically—for was he not a political friend of the people—saw only the two Dukes, the Royal and the Promoted, and his seeing eye delighted in the contrast between them. The Duke of Kent looked "atrocious" in the "jacket and cap of his Regiment" and "but for his blue ribbon and star he might have passed for an orderly sergeant". "Look on this picture and on that!" What a contrast was the other Duke, the world's Duke, a Duke taken to Mr. Creevey's heart and forgiven his connections with the Tories—"the Duke of Wellington's appearance was, as it always is on such occasions, *quite perfect*. I have never seen any one to be compared with him".

They met again later for dinner in Valenciennes where the new Duchess of Kent was accompanied by a lady-in-waiting, unsympathetically described as "an ugly old German female companion", who had to be taken down to dinner by someone. Mr. Creevey caught sight of Wellington moving anxiously among his staff officers and other male guests before dinner, inquiring irritably: "Who the devil is to take out the maid of honour?" None could imagine, though all wished to avoid the misfortune; and then suddenly the Duke remembered that after all they were an army of occupation in a conquered land, and turned to a staff major eagerly: "Dammee, Fremantle, find out the Maire, and let *him* do it!"

Reparations were to be paid, the Allied armies withdrawn, and there was to be another conference, this time at Aix-la-Chapelle—all of which it was hoped would give France tranquillity and political stability. But what hope of political honesty could there be when almost every political leader and representative except the fanatics of the extreme Right and extreme Left was a turncoat; and how could the French people, or the Government for that matter, be brought to respect a constitution not yet agreed on, when for a quarter of a century there had been a hail of constitutions, most of them dead before they were even proclaimed? The long despotism of the French kings seemed to have doomed France to political incompetence, and the Revolution with its legacies of violence, suspicion, and intrigue, seemed to leave no political alternative save futility or violence. Revolution and counter-revolution followed one another even when the great Revolution was supposedly ended; for 1815 was followed by 1830 and that by 1848 and that by 1851, and Napoleon III went out in the revolution of 1870, and the communists of 1871 went down before the Prussian bayonets, as did the Third Republic in 1940. Naturally, the Duke foresaw none of this beyond the possibility of the 1830 revolution (which nevertheless surprised him when it came); and in 1818 all he saw was that the French people were growing restive, and all he wanted was to get his soldiers out before they got involved in a new war with the civilian population. Hopes of a perpetual peace, of goodwill among the nations, of a European order had already faded. And yet someone at Aix had the idea of an international police force, or something on those lines, for among the innumerable papers and plans of the Conference one's eye suddenly is attracted by: "Project of the Formation of an European Army." It was to consist of Belgian, Dutch, French, Austrian, Russian, Prussian, and other troops to be stationed in northern France and the Low Countries, under the command of the Duke of Wellington, *"un chef qui a si bien su s'appro-prier la confiance générale"*. The plan seems to have attracted no attention; and remains a yellowing scrap of paper in the Wellington archives.

At Brussels in October (1818) the Duke and Mr. Creevey met and talked again with their usual frankness. Creevey asked if Sir Hudson Lowe were not acting as "a harsh gaoler of Buonaparte at Saint Helena?" "By God! I don't know," replied the Duke, "Buonaparte is so damned intractable a fellow there is no knowing how to deal with him. To be sure, as to the means employed to keep him there, never was anything so damned absurd. I know the island of Saint Helena

well . . ." And he went on to outline a scheme which would have
given the captive Emperor the liberty of most of the island without the
risk of escape. "As for Lowe," the Duke went on, "he is a damned
fool." He was a damned fool because he tried to induce the Duke to
equip his army "on the Prussian model". ". . . I was obliged to tell
him I had commanded a much larger army in the field than any
Prussian general, and that I was not to learn from their service how to
equip an army."

Later Mr. Creevey turned the conversation on to politics, and
received a curious statement from one who for years was destined to
be the oracle and dominant influence in the House of Lords: "Nobody
cares a damn about the House of Lords; the House of Commons is
everything in England, and the House of Lords nothing." There was a
rumour going round that the Duke had been offered the post of Master-
General of the Ordnance, which carried with it a seat in the Cabinet.
Mr. Creevey asked if the rumour were true, and got an evasive answer;
but already the shrewd little man sensed a change in the Duke's
manner, a dropping of the soldier's breezy frankness and irreverence,
the taking on of a quasi-official sedateness Mr. Creevey found irritating and deplorable. He didn't like the notion of the Duke joining a
Tory Government—had the Duke forgotten that he was "the retained
servant of the monarchy" and not a colleague of Liverpool, Aberdeen,
Castlereagh, Eldon, and the forgotten nonentities of the Tory Cabinet?
Mr. Creevey could not forgive this decadence; and while the Duke's
toadies rejoiced, his friends in many parts of the world were troubled.
Alava, the Spanish soldier, friend and companion of many a march
and uncomfortable billet and victorious fight, who for years lived as
the Duke's guest at Apsley House—Alava put what many were
thinking into a few words: "He should have remained the soldier of
Europe."

Yet, summing him up, Mr. Creevey has left a remarkable tribute to
the Duke, coming as it does from a Whig who had so violently hated
him and his family, who had opposed the Peninsular War in Parliament, and whose judgments on his contemporaries are usually the
reverse of flattering:

"It is a very curious thing to have seen so much of this said Duke as I have
done at different times, considering the impostors that most men in power are
—the insufferable pretentions one meets with in every jack-in-office—the uniform frankness and simplicity of Wellington in all the conversations I have
heard him engaged in, coupled with the unparalleled situation he holds in the
world for an English subject, make him to me the most interesting object I
have ever seen in my life."

CHAPTER XXII

Rich and Poor: The Two Nations

MR. BENJAMIN DISRAELI, the satirical novelist, never forgave and seldom forgot any one who had placed obstacles in the way of that rising young politician, Mr. Benjamin Disraeli. This was particularly the case with those older members of his own party to whom he was accustomed to refer as "the pseudo-Tories". Just how it was that young Mr. Disraeli and his friends had rediscovered the true-blue brand of Toryism, which had been for so long mislaid, is one of those profound mysteries only to be explained by those initiated into the high secrets of Parliamentary politics. On the other hand, there can be no secret about the reasons why, in the 1820's, 1830's, and 1840's, the ageing Duke mistrusted Mr. Disraeli. In the first place he took his information from Croker (the gentleman who had insulted Keats), who seems to have been an uncommonly bad judge of talents when unsupported by great wealth and a title; and Croker gave a bad report, fully repaid by Dizzy's virulent caricature of him as Rigby in *Coningsby*. But Dizzy himself was enough to put the old Duke off—those flamboyant garments with loud rings and a cane, the Byronic pose, the glossy dyed ringlets clustering about the impressive profile, that flow of exuberant eloquence, the flashes of brilliant wit, the fashionable novels, the genius for political invective which crushed no less a person than Sir Robert Peel, all these would inevitably disquiet the old leader of the Tories in the Lords. Add to this that Dizzy was a kind of proto-Fascist, a Radical turned Tory because he saw no chance of office in a Whig Cabinet where every post was booked for a member of a great family, and it is easy to understand both the Duke's mistrust and the resentment of his destined successor to the leadership of the Tory party.

Thus, no one can be surprised that Dizzy's novels are unfavourable to the Duke, although there is something to be said for the main trend of the novelist's argument: That the honesty and directness of purpose of a soldier totally unfit him for a political career. The Duke, Mr. Disraeli thought, "watches events rather than seeks to produce them", whatever that may mean. But Dizzy could not write or speak on any topic without hitting out at last one striking phrase, even if it was one so idiotic as "being on the side of the angels" in a discussion of Darwinism. There he was floundering in the morass of his ignorance; but, when judging politicians, Dizzy knew what he was talking about, and he said of the Duke that "*he knew nothing about England*". This *boutade* contains a profound truth, for when the Duke returned permanently to England in 1819, at the age of fifty, few indeed of his adult years had been spent in that country. In his case, we could reverse Kipling's line and ask, What do they know of England who only the Empire know? The limits to the experience and knowledge of an overseas soldier and administrator are so considerable that the entrance of such men into home politics is always looked on with suspicion and dislike. Let them take their money and titles, and go fox-hunting or write their memoirs. Wellington, it is true, could claim that he had sat in Parliament for a time, before he became famous, but what he didn't know, when he returned home as a Cabinet Minister with an influence far exceeding his nominal position, was nothing less than the English people and the industrial revolution. Against these two powers the Duke fought blindly and disastrously for his reputation, so that the worshipped hero of 1814–1815 was by 1830–1832 the most unpopular man in England, in positive danger of his life from angry crowds—an interesting example of a man brilliantly successful in a war where (unknown to himself) he was backed by the will of his own people, the spirit of the times, and the good wishes of mankind, turning to failure when that support was withdrawn because he failed to recognize the signs and trends of the newer age, a fresh generation, another world.

The pity of it is that as a human being the Duke was fundamentally quite capable of understanding both the advantages of the industrial system and of justice to the workers. He himself was a model landlord, year after year re-investing the rents of his estate to improve the buildings and agricultural output, though he admitted that few other landlords could afford to do this. Incidentally, it may be said that the Duke's support of the Corn Laws, which pressed so heavily on the workers, was due to the fact that alleged agricultural experts had sold him the idea that improved methods would so increase production that the protective tariff would not keep up the price of home-grown wheat—which might possibly have been true but for the great increase of population. In commercial transactions indeed the Duke's standards were not such as can be approved of in a society blessed with the enlightenment of private enterprise. The Strathfield Saye steward came to him one day, and announced with much pride that he had bought a new farm for the Duke at considerably less than it was worth. The Duke asked how much the difference amounted to and, when told, sternly ordered the steward to go at once to the former owner and pay him the extra money. Practices so contrary to good business ethics naturally made the Duke unpopular in business circles.

This sort of chivalry in the "last of the Barons" is perhaps less surprising than his genuine interest in new inventions and their application, together with his turn of mind for little inventions on his own. And in this respect he was in amusing contrast to the enlightened radicals.

"March 16, 1825. Sefton and I have come to the conclusion that our Ferguson is *insane*. He quite foamed at the mouth with rage in our Railway Committee in support of this infernal nuisance—the locomotive Monster, carrying *eighty tons* of goods, and navigated by a tail of smoke and sulphur, coming thro' every man's grounds between Manchester and Liverpool. . . .

"June 1st, 1825. Well—this devil of a railway is strangled at last."

Such was Mr. Creevey's contribution to the march of time; but such was not the Duke's view. Indeed it was when he had gone (as Prime Minister) to give his countenance to the opening of this very railway that he witnessed the distressing death of his much disliked colleague Mr. Huskisson, who was run over by Mr. Stephenson's "locomotive". And if this patronage of new railways be considered merely one of the thousand-and-one public demonstrations to which members of a Government are doomed without necessarily approving either the occasion or its object, there is plenty of evidence that the Duke was born to sympathize with the age of gadgets, which was getting well under way even in the 1820's. He was a reader of newspaper advertisements, and could never be prevented from buying any new invention which happened to catch his eye. Thus he was one of the first to buy a new patent safety razor (they existed over a century ago), and though he would not "endorse the product" (conduct unbefitting an officer and a gentleman) he could not or did not attempt to stop the proud or shrewd manufacturer from framing the Wellington cheque and hanging it up in the front office. The Duke must have been one of the first if not the first man in England to abandon open fires for central heating. In 1834 Lord Mahon at Strathfield Saye was shown the "new apparatus for warming the house by tubes of hot water", which cost £219—pretty cheap considering the size of the house. When his niece and her children were coming to stay with him in winter and the anxious mother asked for "a warm room", with what pride of ownership the Duke wrote back (by return of post, of course) that he "could not give you a cold room"—even the bath-rooms, it appears, were heated.

Moreover, the Duke was something of an inventor himself, particularly in the matter of warm, comfortable clothes, in designing which he ignored both current styles and æsthetic principles. The Wellington boots, for instance, were not pretty but they were practical —or at least he thought they were, which sufficed; and such was the prestige of the inventor that every Eton schoolboy owned a pair, though forbidden to wear them at the school. Capes, overalls, and even "boas" are credited to his inventive mind, and a guest at Strathfield Saye testifies that for a whole week-end the ladies (especially) had to see and test a special finger-bandage which the Duke had just invented, and of which he appeared to be much prouder than of Assaye and Waterloo. He drank iced water in a country where that useful fluid is too often still served lukewarm. He was all for speed; and drove very fast horses along narrow winding lanes, with a speed and negligence which greatly alarmed unwarned fellow-travellers, especially since the Duke talked the whole time and never paid any attention to fogs. He invented a special glass window, with holes for the reins, which he closed in cold or wet weather. "Luckily," remarks one of the victims, "the horses were tractable."

Here then was a man who was free from the prejudice against new inventions which marked such a pioneer of political freedom and enlightenment as Mr. Creevey. The Duke was in sympathy with the epoch of machines—the application of science to industry—which in 1818 was already decades old in the pioneer country of industrialism, England. (It is as well perhaps to recall that coal was being extensively used for smelting iron and for working the textile machinery in England long before the end of the eighteenth century. By 1835 England was producing 60 per cent of the world's manufactured cotton goods, and the annual output of iron was around 1,300,000 tons—an unprecedented figure for the time.)

That his personal servants were devoted to the Duke proves nothing, for such people are often devoted to perfectly worthless persons, who happen to possess the art of arousing that love of serving a "great" man which seems innate in subaltern spirits everywhere. Even the fact that the Apsley House coachman threw "two shillingsworth of brandy and water hot" in the face of a pub acquaintance who maligned the Duke shows little but an excess of servile zeal. But the evidence goes to prove that the Duke was both a decent landlord and a humane general, at a time when neither animal was particularly common.

How then does it happen that the Duke as a politician became, at any rate in the mythology of excited Radicals, the very symbol of reaction; that his political career might be summed up as "attacks which failed" and "retreats which were carried out only just in time to avoid disaster"; that, in short, the Duke's political career was on the whole as feeble as his military career had been masterly?

There are a number of snap answers to these rhetorical questions which any reader who has done me the honour of coming thus far is as able to make as I am. To answer them fully and conscientiously would require a long and minute synopsis of English history and an analysis (or psycho-analysis) of the English character (which is actually neither incomprehensible nor a monument of pure cussedness), but merely undisturbed by anomalies and impervious to criticism. It is just possible that the Duke might have done better if he had been permitted to be a dictator, instead of being one head in the "republic of a Cabinet"; and it does seem a little unfair to blame the Master-General of the Ordnance for failing to solve or even perhaps to understand social and economic and political problems which baffled everybody else. If time and fate had permitted, would England have been better governed by a Cabinet consisting of Adam Smith, Malthus, Ricardo, Godwin, Coleridge, Lord Byron, Lord Shaftesbury, and young Mr. Shelley? Considering what a mess is made of government by one generation after another of practical men, it seems a pity that some such fantastic combination of rulers as this was never tried.

The situation to which the new Cabinet Minister posted home was far from reassuring, and few could have blamed him if he had refused office and had retired (he was now fifty) to fox-hunting, the invention of gadgets, attending concerts of Ancient Music, and going about with pretty women. For one thing, the triumphs of Toulouse and Waterloo were already stale by 1819, and no crowds gathered to cheer the hero. To do him even the barest justice, it must be admitted that he cared little enough one way or other. What he had to worry about was the situation of the country he was to help to govern. The long war had involved enormous expenditures and subsidies to Allies, and Castlereagh had very wisely refused to take any indemnities; England was burdened with a public debt higher than any nation had ever before contracted, the House of Commons was restive over taxation, and the distress of the people was so acute that "crime and violence" were rapidly reaching a revolutionary pitch. So acute was the danger in those first post-war years that even the insurgent though virtually unenfranchised middle class joined with the dominant aristocratic oligarchy to resist the anger and despair of the maddened working class.

Since the quarrel and duel between Canning and Castlereagh, the Tory Cabinet had been dominated by Castlereagh and the Lord Chancellor Eldon—that skilful lawyer who handed down the decision that Shelley was unfit to associate with his own children. Absorbed by the war and the complex diplomatic negotiations following it, Castlereagh left the home front almost entirely to Eldon, who discovered that the cry of the oppressed, the widow, and the fatherless was high treason and Jacobinism. Reforms at least half a century overdue were obstinately refused; and bread riots were suppressed by force. In 1817 the window of the Prince Regent's coach was smashed, whereupon the Government suspended the Habeas Corpus Act and passed a series of repressive measures. The hoped-for and much heralded trade prosperity which was to have followed the war did not occur, all countries being exhausted and more or less ruined by war and civil war. The simplest facts appear to have been hidden from this Cabinet, who do not seem (for instance) to have understood why "sedition" calmed down for a while after the abundant harvest of 1817 and flared up again when the crops failed in 1819.

It is easy enough to see why such a Government confronted by such a situation welcomed effusively the support of the man who *had been* the most popular man in the country, and who certainly both possessed and deserved a reputation for integrity and success. If we may judge by the Wellington letters, he seems to have had nothing to do with internal affairs during that critical year of 1819, and seems rather to have been used to relieve Castlereagh of part of the burden of foreign affairs. Yet even if the Duke had been entrusted with the conduct of home affairs, there is not the slightest reason to suppose he would have been any more intelligent, humane, or far-sighted than his colleagues. He had been "conditioned", as we should say to-day, by his birth and upbringing, by his profession and career and interests, to complete identification with the aristocratic party and a firm (if naïve) faith that they and they alone made the strength, safety, happiness, and glory of the realm. He could scarcely have mistrusted the people more if he had been one of the people's friends, those Whig peers who "*jogged* along" on £40,000 a year, and jeered at Tories and *jacquerie* alike over 10 p.m. rere-suppers of oysters and hot pheasants, wheeled round on trollies by obsequious flunkeys. His share of home government was limited to sending arms from the Ordnance department to local military commanders who asked for them for the sinister purposes of "keeping order", and to advice on the best way to use the veterans of Salamanca and Waterloo in shooting down their hungry fellow-citizens.

By way of feeding the hungry, the Government with an empty exchequer voted one million pounds to build new churches in a country which already had far too many old ones.

"Fifty thousand agitators" came together in Manchester on August 16, 1819, and marched with huge banners inscribed "Liberty or Death", "Equal Representation or Death". By order of the magistrates the yeomanry charged the large but peaceable procession; one citizen was killed and at least forty injured, although the so-called "mob" were wholly within their constitutional rights. By way of helping to assuage bitter feelings, the Tory Government forced the Prince Regent to send a letter congratulating the magistrates on what was immediately nicknamed "the Battle of Peterloo", before there had been any inquiry into the occurrence and before the magistrates had been legally exonerated for the use of force against the people. In other countries and in other times it might seem absurd to make so much fuss about a riot, but Englishmen as a rule will not permit their fellow-countrymen to be knocked about by policemen or soldiers in the interests of rich men's pockets. Even the rich men object to it. Thus a peer of the realm exhaled his discontent against his brother peer, Castlereagh:

> ". . . The vulgarest tool that Tyranny could want,
> With just enough of talent, and no more,
> To lengthen fetters by another fix'd,
> And offer poison long already mix'd.
>
> An orator of such set trash of phrase
> Ineffably—legitimately vile,
> That even its grossest flatterers dare not praise. . . .
>
> A bungler even in its disgusting trade,
> And botching, patching, leaving still behind
> Something of which its masters are afraid,
> States to be curb'd, and thoughts to be confined,
> Conspiracy or Congress to be made—
> Cobbling at manacles for all mankind. . . ."

The heir to a baronetcy and an estate of one million dollars expressed himself in this address to his poorer countrymen on the event at Manchester:

What is Freedom?—ye can tell
That which slavery is, too well—
For its very name has grown
To an echo of your own.

'Tis to work and have such pay
As just keeps life from day to day
In your limbs, as in a cell
For the tyrant's use to dwell. . . .

'Tis to see your children weak
With their mothers pine and peak,
When the winter winds are bleak,—
They are dying whilst I speak.

'Tis to hunger for such diet
As the rich man in his riot
Casts to the fat dogs that lie
Surfeiting beneath his eye;

'Tis to let the Ghost of Gold
Take from Toil a thousandfold
More than e'er its substance could
In the tyrannies of old. . . .

And at length when ye complain
With a murmur weak and vain
'Tis to see the Tyrant's crew
Ride over your wives and you—
Blood is on the grass like dew."

"My dear Byng,

"The accounts which I saw yesterday of the proceedings of the Radicals in different parts of England tend to prove that we are not far removed from a general and simultaneous rising in different parts and at different places. It is probable they will first *meet* in this manner and try their ground, and see how the troops are disposed of, and then proceed to business, which will be neither more nor less than the Radical plunder of the rich towns and houses which will fall in their way. . . .

WELLINGTON."

How reconcile the views of the Peer and the Poets? It is impossible. "The lists are set from of old, and the warfare endureth for ever".

Those idealistic moralists, the Greek dramatists, had a conception of Justice—of Right—which differs from that of the Hebrew prophets. Nobody ever knew a prophet who was not right all the time; but Æschylus said, No, a man or a party or a cause, or a nation might start with Right and Justice and then act in such a way that Right and Justice abandoned them and went over to the other side. Right and Justice are not static, Æschylus thought, but something elusive and shifting, a balance of good and evil, inclining now one way and now another. Adopting this hypothesis, we might argue that the English Tories had a narrow or even a wide margin of Right in opposing the dictatorship of Napoleon, and in their not very strenuous efforts to support milder forms of government in Europe; but that Right fled from them in horror when they became nothing more than the ugly watch-dogs of rich men's wealth and privileges, the obstinate guardians of long-established abuses. Unfortunately for "our hero", he was one of them, convinced in his own mind that he was defending "hearth, home, altar, throne" and all the rest of the unnecessary virtues. Such is the limitation of horse sense. Of course, these people who rioted and shouted and carried banners and threw stones were ugly and dirty and ragged and uneducated and none too honest about other people's property. With a bitterly unconscious irony they had invented the proverb which said you might as well be hung for a sheep as a lamb, because husbands and fathers were hanged for stealing a lamb to feed starving women and children; and if they had stolen a sheep, well, the food might have lasted a day or two longer and the man's death be that much more worth while. Common sense is valuable; but it doesn't cover everything as charity is said to do. In those days there was a need of faith, almost a mystic faith, to believe that these ignorant violent people could in their children become decent civilized people if only they were freed and decently treated. But you had to take the risk of freeing them. Arthur Wellesley, Duke of Wellington, had too much common sense to believe in freeing them, too great a feeling of responsibility to the Throne (Prinny and his brandy bottle) to take the risk.

On the other hand, it cannot be denied that there was something in the Duke's notion of "Radical plunder", even though it may have been founded on prejudice and memories of the behaviour of his own soldiers. There are human beings in every class, pickpockets in every crowd, and it would be remarkable indeed if a political demonstration of the dispossessed was made up wholly of honest men and pure enthusiasts. In his admirable book, *The Pre-Raphaelite Tragedy*, Mr. William Gaunt has summed up with appalling accuracy the different "revolutionary" types encountered by William Morris more than half a century later:

"There was the smooth, glib educated agitator, out for political advancement; the comic ignoramus to whom Socialism was an excuse for slipping out to a game of billiards and a pint of beer; the sinister refugee from the Continent whose aim was chaos and pillage; the fiery artisan with sufficient intelligence to feel inferior—and the muddle-headed labourer whose real ambition was to become a respectable member of the middle-class."*

The excellent though depressing merit of that passage lies in the fact that with alterations, not in kind but in degree (such as "champagne" for "beer"), it might stand as the description of almost any revolutionary political party that ever existed. Gazing from the eminence of his position on Luddites, rick-burners, machine-smashers, and the unemployed generally, the Duke made no subtle distinctions—they were all of the "sinister refugee from the Continent type" and were only prevented from subverting all that was worth having by "the grace of God and our miraculous institutions". As he explained it all (in French) to Alava, the Duke seemed to glow with honest patriotic pride:

"You will have seen with pleasure how well we have arranged matters here. In Europe you would like to have our Constitution; but what you don't want is our solidity, our conservation of property—the basis and strength of our Constitution. Note that we maintain this conservation on a level with our liberties, and that this guarantee makes us enemies of all the so-called Liberal class in France, the Low Countries and Germany. Why? Because they only want to plunder, they talk of Liberty with the sole object of pocketing other peoples' goods, and they can't endure a country where liberty is established and founded on order and on the security of property." [Letter to Alava, London, February 21, 1820. Translated.]

Unluckily the Duke nowhere explains just why it was a "miraculous institution" to throw yeomanry squadrons against an unarmed mob, while "whiffs of grapeshot" in France were mere plunder. Really, at this distance of time a very nice discrimination is required to distinguish between the royalist and clerical White Terror of Europe and the law-and-order programme of the Tory English Government. Moreover, the Duke and his political friends held views about "Liberty" which would have been strenuously denounced and opposed by many if not most of their countrymen from the days of King John and the Great Charter onwards. The Duke seems to have overlooked the fact that his "Constitution" included a Habeas Corpus Act (1679) and a Bill of Rights (1689). Suspension of Habeas Corpus is *always* an attack on the liberties of the people, whether the suspender be James II or Castlereagh, Abraham Lincoln or Winston Churchill. It is true that the Duke of Wellington was not a member of

* Quoted by permission of the American publishers, Messrs. Harcourt, Brace & Co., Inc.

the Cabinet which suspended Habeas Corpus (without even the excuse of war) in 1817, and that when the suspension period ended in 1818 the Act was never again suspended in England until it got into a new war for freedom. But he was a member of the Cabinet which introduced the infamous "Six Acts"; which, among other things, virtually made Habeas Corpus a dead letter. By Act of Parliament magistrates could confiscate arms and stop the publication of "seditious and blasphemous libels", such as the writings of Shelley and Leigh Hunt, the latter of whom was imprisoned. A Stamp Act made newspapers so expensive that only the upper classes could afford them, and other Acts forbade all assemblies except those called by the magistrates. Thus free assembly, free speech, and free expression of thought in print were abolished in the name of the Duke's "miraculous institutions". Even the Whig peers couldn't stand this, and warned the Government that one result of their Acts would be "secret cabals and conspiracies".

Even in political debate a true word is sometimes spoken by chance, and it was not long before Lord Holland's warning was justified by events. Only two days after the Duke's "miraculous institutions" letter to Alava (February 23, 1820) the Government received warning of the Cato Street Conspiracy, a sort of minor Gunpowder Plot; for Thistlewood and his friends proposed to murder the whole Cabinet as they sat at dinner with Lord Harrowby in Grosvenor Square. Ministerial heads were to be stuck on pikes, the Bank of England and Newgate prison were to be freed of their respective treasures, and the republic proclaimed at the Mansion House. The plot seems to have been revealed by one George Edwards, and must have provided rather startling news for the Cabinet. Unanimously they voted down a blithe proposal of the Duke's (doubtless supported by plenty of "by Gods" and "dammees") that they should go on with the dinner, each Minister taking a brace of pistols to shoot it out with the conspirators. Not unnaturally, the rest of the Cabinet preferred to have the enemy arrested by Bow Street runners. Thistlewood and his misguided friends were hanged.

"It came out upon the examination," said the Duke long afterwards to Gleig, "that I was to be taken care of by Mr. Ings. Mr. Ings, it seems, had watched me often, but never caught me alone, till one afternoon in the beginning of February (1820) he saw me leave the Ordnance Office. He crossed the street and walked after me, intending, when I got into the Green Park, to stab me from behind. But before reaching St. James's Palace, a gentleman with only one arm met me, and turning round, walked with me through the park to Apsley

House. Mr. Ings was afraid, in the circumstances, to go on with his job, and I escaped. And all this I quite believe, for I recollect meeting Lord Fitzroy Somerset [*who lost his arm at Waterloo*] that day; and just as we resumed our walk, I saw a suspicious-looking person pass us and go up St. James's Street."

An odd experience for "the Liberator of Europe".

CHAPTER XXIII

Politics

GEORGE III died on January 29, 1820, after the longest reign in English history except that of Queen Victoria. Since the old man had been blind and mad for many years while Prinny for all practical purposes had been King, one would suppose that the event would have caused no more than a token crisis and that official grief which is allotted to official personages. But no; for reasons which are lost in obscurity the death of this aged and pathetic lunatic was the occasion for a first-class political crisis, including (as we have just seen) an ambitious attempt to change the Government by murdering it. Possibly, even probably, the real reason for the "crisis" was the fixed resolve, not merely of the Whigs, but of the greater part of the nation, not to be bullied any further. It shows what a national will can do through a legislative body, even when that legislature is so little representative of the people as the pre-Reform Parliaments of George IV. Here was a "strong" Government, controlling both Houses, backed by the King, supported by almost unprecedented new laws of a repressive kind and the immense influence of the Duke of Wellington, yet forced by public opinion to abandon measures it wanted to pass, and to pass others it didn't want. And the very first of its defeats occurred over a measure started by the King himself concerning a matter painfully connected with His Majesty's domestic comfort.

At least since the days of Thackeray it has been almost obligatory to abuse Prinny as a drunk, a glutton, a bigamist, a dissipater of the nation's money, and altogether a thoroughly bad bargain for John Bull. Even among contemporaries the *nimmukwallah* Duke had to confess he was ashamed of his master; and the irreverent Mr. Creevey noted that His Majesty had given up wearing stays—"Prinny has let out his belly with the awful result that it has fallen about his knees"; and the only posthumous friend Prinny ever had in the world is Mr. Shane Leslie, whose witty monograph is warmly recommended. As a matter of fact the people do not seem to have disliked George IV, who after all gave a lot of support to cricket and horse-racing. At all events the philanthropical Lord Shaftesbury noted in his diary with surprise and chagrin that nobody seriously attempted George IV's life, whereas already no less than "four attempts have been made on this mild and virtuous young woman", by which he meant Queen Victoria. There is something to be said for Mr. Leslie's defence, and I incline to believe that Prinny's bad posthumous press has been due to three crimes: (1) He welched on the Whigs in 1812 and they never forgave him; (2) he offended the middle class by opposing Parliamentary Reform; and (3) he definitely angered the middle class by his love of the arts and by spending public money on them. The English cut off King Charles I's head for making a collection of pictures and projecting a palace by Inigo Jones; so one may well imagine the fury when a degenerate successor to pudding-witted George I cultivated music, admired painting and architecture, and studied literature. Not even the ugliness of the Brighton pavilion was accepted as an excuse. It was clear that the King had a great deal of taste and the fact that most of it was bad did not excuse him.

Whose fault was it that Prinny was a bigamist? Not his. He married Mrs. Fitzherbert in the sight of God and a parson, and there was nothing to prevent the couple jogging comfortably through the various stages of a happy marriage except George III's eccentric Royal Marriage Act and his insistence that the Prince must marry some "dreadful German woman", and produce a royal heir. Much righteous indignation has been expended against Prinny for approaching the altar of second matrimony so staggeringly under the influence of brandy that he had to be physically supported by his royal brothers. No wonder he was drunk, poor devil, having been compelled to abandon the woman he liked and to marry another he hated at first sight. And no wonder they parted almost immediately after the birth of their daughter, Charlotte. For years the Princess Caroline lived abroad in more or less disreputable company. According to the Duke, she must have been a volatile and lively creature, for on one occasion she remarked to him significantly (and in French) that "the men in this country are devilishly afraid of a rope"—referring, so the Duke believed, to the fact that death was the penalty inflicted on any man having carnal knowledge of the Heir Apparent's wife. By the death of George III, Caroline became Queen Consort of England, and maddened her husband by announcing that she would return to England to take her part in the coronation and her place in the State and society—wherein she was aided and encouraged by the Whigs, delighted to have a chance of paying Prinny for his refusal to back them in 1812.

The King decided on a divorce, which in those days meant a special trial in the House of Lords, and dragging the whole scandal before a coarse and ribald public, amid the ceaseless catcalls of libellous publications and hideously vulgar caricatures. The Duke opposed these legal proceedings. How, he asked, could the King take action against his wife for adultery when he himself had been notoriously unfaithful to her? The sensible thing to do would be to send out at once some good-looking young man (he instanced Frederick Lamb) to win over the various dependents who controlled the Queen's decisions, and thus keep her abroad permanently by appealing to their enlightened self-interest:

"You are going to lose your golden eggs—you are going to kill your goose! Once in England, and you will not be able to live with her on your present footing, and retain your present allowances."

This judicious advice was neglected, and the Queen came to England, prompted by Brougham's advice in all her actions. There were hootings and scandal when she tried to force her way into the Abbey at the coronation, but somehow she was turned back (they had no right to do it); and so was not present at the gorgeous coronation banquet where the Duke and Lord Anglesea clad in medieval dress rode into Westminster Hall and the Champion was mounted on a circus horse which had been carefully trained to walk backwards so the rider need not turn his back on the King as he retired—but unluckily the circus horse was so well trained that it insisted on entering backwards, and thus bore the champion backside foremost into the presence of his Sovereign.

The Queen's trial was conducted with the solemn pomp and exterior decorum appropriated to legal farces. Office-hungry Whigs whooped up the affair in hopes of defeating the Government, though there were some men who felt that checkmating and humiliating the King over his divorce might not be the best preparation for an offer to serve as His Majesty's confidential servants. The Duke stood by his master, though privately indicating his distaste for the public scrubbing of all this royal linen, dropping his jaw in a rare but characteristic grimace of disgust as he remarked that the King could hardly be degraded lower than he had already degraded himself. Brougham, the future Whig Lord Chancellor (satirized by T. L. Peacock as "the learned friend"), outdid himself in frenzies of forensic eloquence; the Government's majority dropped to nine; and finally the Cabinet decided it must abandon the King and his divorce suit. Retaining his imperturbable common sense, the Duke did not allow this disaster to distress him—Francis Ellesmere saw him at Almack's with Lady

Harrowby on his arm at this time, and was "struck with the good-humoured and joyous expression of his smile, but more with the unusual length and size of his watch-chain and appendages". He even retained enough of his boisterous sense of humour to tease Mr. Creevey, by pretending that the Government was going to produce "two naval officers" who would prove the Queen an adultress. Since Mr. Creevey had been longing for a lucrative sinecure since long before Trafalgar, this ominous "news" gave him a feverishly sleepless night; and apparently he never realized that "the Beau" had been pulling his leg. Perhaps the highest level of national decorum was reached when a band of enthusiastic supporters of "the injured Queen" mobbed the Duke and threatened him with violence if he didn't say "God save the Queen". It was a military maxim of the Duke's never to fight against hopeless odds. "Well, gentlemen, since you will have it so, God save the Queen—*and may all your wives be like her.*"

The proceedings against the Queen were finally dropped and the Government was saved from defeat, leaving Prinny brooding angrily in various palaces and Mr. Creevey with a quivering lip as he thought of the snug little office that might have been his—there was nothing for His Majesty to do but grin and bear it, while Mr. Creevey composed another of his orations against holders of sinecures. The Duke went off to stay with Lady Shelley, who was relieved to find that he seemed never to have heard of "my young kinsman, Percy Bysshe Shelley" and the things he wrote. (The Duke is Laoctonos in "Swellfoot the Tyrant.") Like Napoleon, the Duke was a very poor shot—the excellent ones were heroes like Louis XVIII and Charles X who never wasted any time directing armies. But it must be admitted that at Lady Shelley's shooting party the Duke abused his position as a military genius. He frightened little Fanny Shelley into hysterics, and wounded (1) a dog, (2) a keeper, (3) an old woman:

"I'm wounded, my lady," she wailed, but Frances, Lady Shelley, was not lady of the manor for nothing.

"My good woman," was her monumental and incredible rebuke, "this ought to be the proudest moment of your life! You have had the distinction of being wounded by the GREAT DUKE OF WELLINGTON!"

The Duke—how excellent is common sense—ignored this tribute, apologized to the old lady, and handed over the gold coin that happened to be in his pocket.

The year 1820 passed into 1821, and the Government was fast reaching a peak of unpopularity, in spite of the fact that it had been forced to reduce expenditure and taxation and that (small thanks to it) there was some improvement in trade. Revolution and Red Radicalism turned a little good-humoured, and when George IV went to the theatre nobody shot at him (he was not "mild and virtuous") but cockney voices from the gallery yelled: "Where's your wife, Georgie?"

When the cockney turns good-humoured the dynasty is safe, even though the stalls indignantly sang in answer to the ribald voice "God Save the King" and "Rule Britannia", though what Prinny had done to help Britannia rule the waves would have puzzled even Mrs. Fitzherbert to say. That year, 1821, was coronation year in London; and May 5 in Saint Helena was the day when the Emperor lay dead, bequeathing the world the poison of his legend, to France an unending tradition of political faction, and to the would-be assassin of Wellington ten thousand francs. It is said (but on uncertain authority) that when the Emperor was buried in the lonely glen with military honours, the British regimental flags that dipped to his coffin were inscribed: "TALAVERA", "PYRENEES". If this is not true, it ought to be; for in 1815 the Emperor's last letter as a free man announced what was actually his surrender to "the most powerful, the most constant and the most generous of my enemies".

The Emperor was dead; but Europe, even if not actually at war, was far from being tranquil. In Spain, Ferdinand who had insisted upon ruling as *Rey neto* (i.e. absolute king) had exasperated *los Liberales* to another of the innumerable series of *pronunciamientos* which have afflicted the Spanish people and found himself virtually a captive with a written Constitution to obey as long as it could be enforced. In France, M. de Chateaubriand had abandoned literary rhetoric for politics, and as Foreign Minister was rattling the Gallic sabretache and threatening "intervention" in Spain in the name of the Bourbon family pact. The British were strongly in favour of an opposite policy baptized "non-intervention", which led M. de Talleyrand to make an (unaccepted) contribution to the dictionary of the French Academy: "Non-intervention, a mystical and diplomatic word having much the same meaning as 'intervention'." The usual remedy of a conference was not lacking. Castlereagh refused to have England represented at the Congress of Troppau, for its object was to devise means for keeping the continental peoples subject to the oppressions of absolute monarchy. And if this be considered merely another case of the pot calling the kettle black, it might be urged that the pot had been cleaned up before, and was about to be cleaned up again, with considerable energy.

Meanwhile the Tory Government continued its losing struggle

against public opinion, the ever-increasing demand for reforms, and the rapidly growing economic power of the middle-class industrialists. It was a strange world, this, of self-righteous reformers who worried so intensely about French and Portuguese support of the negro slave-trade, and never noticed that the children of their own countrymen were being dragged from the workhouses to the deathly slavery of Lancashire cotton factories:

> "For oh," say the children, "we are weary
>   And we cannot run or leap;
> If we cared for any meadows, it were merely
>   To drop down in them and sleep.
> Our knees tremble sorely in the stooping,
>   We fall upon our faces, trying to go;
> And, underneath our heavy eyelids drooping
>   The reddest flower would look as pale as snow.
> For, all day, we drag our burden tiring
>   Through the coal-dark, underground;
> Or, all day, we drive the wheels of iron
>   In the factories, round and round.
>
> "For all day the wheels are droning, turning;
>   Their wind comes in our faces,
> Till our hearts turn, our heads with pulses burning,
>   And the walls turn in their places:
> Turns the sky in the high window, blank and reeling,
>   Turns the long light that droops adown the wall,
> Turn the black flies that crawl along the ceiling:
>   All are turning, all the day, and we with all.
> And all day, the iron wheels are droning,
>   And sometimes we could pray,
> 'O ye wheels' (breaking out in a mad moaning)
>   'Stop! be silent for to-day!' "

There is no available evidence that His Grace the Duke of Wellington was aware of these horrors, though he did bestow a well-deserved sneer on the anti-slave-traders who derived "large incomes from the enslavement of their fellow-countrymen". But in these years the Duke's attention (as was, after all, natural) was directed to the field of foreign affairs where he had played so splendid a part. Greece—Mexico—Spain—Italy—Turkey—Russia—obviously there would have to be another Congress. . . . Meantime the Duke erupted in a stupendous and majestic display of Minutes and Memoranda: Upon the proposed transfer of works and buildings in the Canadas to the Ordnance; On the reduction in the Ordnance; On the revision of various points of Ordnance equipment; On the supply of forage to the

horses of the Ordnance; On the state of affairs between the Russians
and the Turks; On the Treasury Minute respecting the transfer of the
barrack and store Departments; Arrangements for the Carriages of
Persons going to the Irish Ball; Examination of the present expense of
the Diplomacy of the Country; On the system of Defence adopted by
the Prussians; On the necessity of defending the mode in which the
duties of the barrack Department are to be carried on . . . Barracks
at Trinidad . . . Public Buildings at Foreign stations . . . Abolishing inspectors . . . Cape of Good Hope . . . The Store in Tooley
Street . . . Preventive service in Ireland. . . .

It is scarcely surprising that Castlereagh decided to get rid of this
omniscient and energetic colleague by sending him to the Congress of
Verona; and it is the less surprising since that unhappy statesman must
have felt with acute anguish that his mind was lapsing into madness.
The Foreign Secretary believed he was threatened by blackmailers—
but How? Why? by Whom? There is no evidence that these blackmailers were anything but a delusion, although there is always the
possibility that evidence has been withheld and destroyed. Yet the
black shadow certainly descended on Castlereagh with great swiftness.
The Duke's Memorandum on the Last Days of Lord Londonderry
shows this clearly.

On August 3, 1822, Wellington and Castlereagh met at dinner and
the Duke thought Castlereagh "in particularly good spirits"; but, on
August 6 and 7, the Duke thought him "very low, out of spirits, and
unwell". On the ninth (the morning of the day the Duke was to start
for the Continent) he had an interview with his colleague, which
convinced him that his old friend was going mad. After listening to
Castlereagh's delusions, the Duke said with his usual simplicity and
directness:

"From what you have said, I am bound to warn you that you cannot be in
your right mind."

Covering his face with his hands and weeping Castlereagh admitted
the dreadful truth. The Duke offered to abandon his mission and to
stay with him, but Castlereagh refused; and Wellington went home to
write urgent letters of warning to Arbuthnot and Dr. Bankhead. The
doctor obviously suspected some form of suicidal mania, for he
deprived Castlereagh of weapons and razors, and even arranged to
stay in the house and to watch over the patient alternately with his
wife. Unluckily, as often happens, the cunning of the madman
outwitted those trying to protect him from himself. Castlereagh found

razors which had been overlooked in a travelling case, went to his dressing-room and then sent a message for the doctor, who came rushing in to find his patient apparently staring at the ceiling. To his horror, the raised face uttered a few words and then fell back still further as the body toppled into Dr. Bankhead's arms, showing the throat completely severed.

Suicides among politicians then were as frequent as they are among poets now. It is thought that the politicians ate and drank too much. Accustomed as the world was to seeing its political leaders do themselves justice, the death of Castlereagh in this tragical manner caused an outburst of grief among his friends and of hysterical rejoicing among his enemies. The epigrams written by Lord Byron on this occasion reflect little credit on either his lordship's talents or his good taste:

> "Oh, Castlereagh! thou art a patriot now;
>   Cato died for his country, so didst thou:
> He perish'd rather than see Rome enslaved,
>   Thou cutt'st thy throat that Britain may be saved!"

There can be no doubt that Castlereagh in his time had been the best-hated man in England, which is perhaps a genuine tribute to his ability and character. If he oppressed his fellow-citizens, he did much to secure peace among foreigners; along with Wellington and the Tsar Alexander he deserves credit for the "moderate" settlement in 1815 which gave Europe nearly half a century of comparative peace in which to prepare for a new and bloodier set of contests. But animosity against Castlereagh was not silenced even at his grave-side. It is said that the mob cheered and booed derisively as his coffin was carried into the Abbey, and it is certain that Lord Byron celebrated the burial with this refined quatrain:

> "Posterity will ne'er survey
>   A nobler grave than this;
> Here lie the bones of Castlereagh:
>   Stop, traveller, and . . ."

Yet even Castlereagh had friends to mourn him, and among them was Wellington who owed him even more than he owed to his brother Richard and to William Pitt.

This abrupt and tragical end to Castlereagh came near to being as tragical for the political party he had so long supported by his energy and talents. There was only one possible successor—the dead man's rival, George Canning, the greatest orator in England, but an

isolationist whose foreign policy was the exact opposite of the colla-
borationist Castlereagh. Canning had resigned from the Government
rather than support the prosecution of the Queen, and the susceptible
Prinny had taken this as an insult to his feelings as a gentleman. It
fell to the Duke to put it bluntly:

"You're not a gentleman, Sir."
"Not a gentleman! ! !" exclaimed poor Prinny, falling back into his chair
in the extremity of agitation.
"No, sir, you are King of England, and have to carry out his duties."

Ben trovato, perhaps, but the Duke certainly had every excuse for
giving the rebuke, though it may not have been on this occasion.
Indeed, during the worrisome days when His Majesty had to be
persuaded into accepting the impugner of his honour as his Secretary
of State for Foreign Affairs, the Duke was confined to Apsley House
with an illness which might have killed him. Thinking he might as
well profit by the delay in his setting out for Vienna and Verona, the
Duke (ever anxious to try something new) allowed a quack specialist
to try to cure him of a growing deafness, which this Mr. Stephenson
proceeded to attempt by the method of syringing the ear with "a
strong solution of caustic". The result may be best described in
Wellington's own words:

"I don't think that I ever suffered so much in my life. It was not pain; it was
something far worse. The sense of hearing became so acute, that I wished myself
stone deaf. The noise of a carriage passing along the street was like the loudest
thunder, and everybody that spoke seemed to be shrieking at the very top of
his voice."

It is not surprising that when his own physician saw him next day, he
found the Beau in a most un-Beau-like condition: " . . . Sitting at a
table, unshaved and unwashed, with bloodshot eyes and a flushed
cheek . . . when he rose he staggered like a drunken man." Mr.
Stephenson had come close to a medical murder of the saviour of his
country; and Dr. Hume thought that another hour of the intense
inflammation would have affected the Duke's brain. It is characteristic
that, when later the unhappy Mr. Stephenson came to apologize, the
Duke cut him short:

"Don't say a word about it; you acted for the best; it has been unfortunate,
no doubt for both of us, but you are not at all to blame."

He even went so far as to agree not to say a word about the fact that
the wretched man had permanently destroyed the hearing of one ear,

but refused to allow the man to go on attending him, which favour Mr. Stephenson begged for, to save his practice. "No, I can't do that, for that would be a lie." And so, after a delay of some weeks, the Duke set out for the Congress of Verona by way of Paris, completely deaf in one ear—which is perhaps not wholly a drawback to a diplomat—and bearing a complex set of instructions from Canning, beginning with "The Turkish question, internal and external" and ending with "the Slave trade, the Austrian debt and the late Russian ukase". But in spite of these drawbacks, the Duke started on these new continental wanderings in almost a holiday spirit. He was not now accompanied, as he had been in 1821, by Prinny, who had insisted on being personally conducted over the Fields of Waterloo by "Arthur". The Duke afterwards reported:

"His Majesty took it very coolly. He never asked me a single question, nor said one word, until I showed him where Lord Anglesea's leg was buried, and then he burst into tears."

A day in June may be rarer than a day in any other month except February, but can there be anything duller than an international conference or congress of long ago, which settled difficulties which soon came unsettled again and failed to deal with problems which evaporated of their own accord a century past? His Grace the Duke of Wellington represented his country at the Congress of Verona with dignity and efficiency, but at this distance of time only the frivolity of the poet survives in the satirical "Age of Bronze" which made its mocking bow to the Congress and the leaders of Europe:

> "Who now assemble at the holy call?
> The blest Alliance, which says three are all!
> An earthly trinity! which wears the shape
> Of heaven's, as man is mimick'd by the ape.
> A pious unity! in purpose one—
> To melt three fools to a Napoleon . . .
>
> Resplendent sight! Behold the coxcomb Czar,
> The autocrat of waltzes and of war!
> As eager for a plaudit as a realm,
> And just as fit for flirting as the helm;
> A Calmuck beauty with a Cossack wit,
> And generous spirit, when 'tis not frost-bit;
> Now half dissolving to a liberal thaw,
> But harden'd back whene'er the morning's raw;
> With no objection to true liberty,
> Except that it would make the nations free . . ."

But as we all know the home folks best, the noble poet reserved his choicest lines for his own country:

"Shall noble Albion pass without a phrase
From a bold Briton in her wonted praise?
'Arts—arms—and George—and glory—and the isles—
And happy Britain—wealth—and Freedom's smiles—
White cliffs, that held invasion far aloof—
Contented subjects, all alike tax-proof—
Proud Wellington, with eagle beak so curl'd,
That nose, the hook where he suspends the world!
And Waterloo—and trade—and—(hush not yet
A syllable of imposts or of debt)—

And ne'er (enough) lamented Castlereagh,
Whose penknife slit a goose-quill t'other day—
And "pilots who have weather'd every storm"—
(But, no, not even for rhyme's sake, name Reform)' . . .

Alas, the country! how shall tongue or pen
Bewail her now *un*country gentlemen?
The last to bid the cry of warfare cease,
The first to make a malady of peace. . . .

The *landed interest*—(you may understand
The phrase much better leaving out the *land*)—
The land self-interest groans from shore to shore,
For fear that plenty should attain the poor. . . .

See these inglorious Cincinnati swarm,
Farmers of war, dictators of the farm;
Their ploughshare was the sword in hireling hands,
Their fields manured by gore of other lands;
Safe in their barns, these Sabine tillers sent
Their brethren out to battle—why? for rent!
Year after year they voted cent per cent,
Blood, sweat, and tear-wrung millions—why? for rent!
They roar'd, they dined, they drank, they swore they meant
To die for England—why then live?—for rent!"

The poet has dragged us from the heights of an international congress to local affairs which have neither interest nor parallel in more enlightened ages. The Congress met to preserve the peace of Europe, and dissolved, having agreed that France must be allowed to attack Spain in the interests of peace, order, and religion. Since this was one of the events the Duke had been sent to Verona to prevent, it can hardly be said that his mission was a complete success. There was really only one step which would have prevented France (backed by the rest of the autocratic powers) from again invading Spain—the threat of a declaration of war by Great Britain. And there were at least two excellent reasons for not making such a threat: one, because it might easily have led to another European war; two, because such a war would have been so unpopular that the Government trying to wage it would certainly have been thrown out. Herein the Congress of Verona was important, for it marked the point when the Government of England ceased to believe in the efficacy of joint action by the Powers, and retired into an isolation which was none the less a retrogression because Canning chose to give it the epithet of "splendid". Seven years of "co-operation" between the Powers had revealed difficulties which had not been foreseen by those who had seen in the Holy Alliance the machinery for a new epoch of perpetual peace. Autocratic governments interpreted "the peace of Europe" as the perpetuation of the kind of government they approved; having complete control over their subjects, they could send them to war to restore autocracy wherever it was menaced, while a country with even imperfect representative government could only resist if backed by public opinion. It would have been hopeless for Liverpool, Canning, and Wellington (even if they had wanted) to appeal, only a few years after the end of a world war, for a new war on behalf of Spanish *Liberales* whom many Englishmen distrusted, however much they hated the oppression of Ferdinand VII. Perhaps Canning was right to withdraw, and to be content with keeping the Russians back in Alaska and with the recognition of the independence of the new Spanish republics in South America.

When we are tempted to think of the Duke of Wellington in those days as a buttress of reaction, we ought in fairness to compare the representative Parliamentary system (however defective and in need of reform) for which he stood with the royal dictatorships of the Continent. During four days at Verona the despots tried to wheedle, threaten, or entrap him into some "formula" which would commit England to the support of the autocratic *status quo* throughout Europe; and during four days he said "No". Nor did he make any mistake in gauging the situation with regard to Spain and France and their curious underground intrigues. From Paris he had written (probably not without a touch of his usual irony) that for some reason the French clergy seemed to think that a war with Spain would be to their advantage. Oddly enough, the Spanish clergy seemed to think that being invaded by the French would be to *their* advantage.

Publicly the Duke talked of the "grave difficulties" of campaigning in Spain and of the terrific "resistance of Spanish guerrillas"; but in private he expressed the view that the Spaniards would only put up a token resistance and that a French invasion would be a walk-over. When the war came, this proved to be the case.

Out of the dim vistas of these forgotten world politics comes one curious little human incident—during the Congress of Verona the Duke often played at cards with Marie Louise, ex-empress of France and widow of Napoleon, and the gold coins they played for were "napoleons". This anecdote would seem a pure invention but for the fact that the Duke himself confirmed it. He had met her first in Vienna in the year 1815, he said:

"It is a very curious thing . . . she afterwards said to someone: 'The Duke of Wellington little knows the service he has done me by winning the battle of Waterloo!' The fact is, she was then with child by Neipperg—whom she afterwards married; and if Napoleon had prevailed she would have had to return to him in that state."

He was back in London in time for Christmas, and in the usual family festivities had a day or two of leisure to observe that his sons were growing up in the disconcertingly rapid manner of all children. The Duke's fondness for small children, particularly in his old age, has been dwelt on with more than necessary rapture and emphasis by his literary henchmen, who produced this pleasing trait as a trump card in defence of the "iron" Duke as a human being. They had to make the most of it, for there is nothing to show that he ever played cricket or liked any dogs but foxhounds. As a father the Duke appears to have been rather impeccable than either delightful or friendly. In the eighteenth century it was not customary for noblemen to have very much to do with their children; the custom was to hire a clergyman or "an Oxford man extreamely read in Greek" to undertake the more humdrum paternal duties. The Duke was unlikely to abandon any conservative custom, and as early as 1817 selected for this purpose (rather surprisingly) the vicar of Brighton, the Rev. H. M. Wagnert, who held the post seven years. This reverend gentleman was summoned to General Headquarters in France, and told that "my boys are to serve the King" and must therefore be brought up "as Christian gentlemen, in all singleness and simplicity, every consideration being postponed to that of duty". At Eton the boys were not allowed to buy anything for which they hadn't the cash, and when they went to Oxford in 1824 the heir was allowed £800 and the younger son £500 a year, and "I expect they will not run in debt". This was generous, though not extravagant. At a rather earlier date the Duke submitted the boys' Greek and Latin verses to the taste and judgment of their Uncle Richard, the ex-Viceroy, who of course commended them, adding these characteristic remarks on a classical education and the limits to which it should be applied to young nobles:

"I consider these efforts as the true foundation of distinction in the progress of life. Not that I should wish to see your sons distinguished as writers of Latin verse in future times, but these exercises at school are essential to the accurate knowledge of the great fountains of ancient genius, science, and taste, as well as of the ancient examples of virtue, honour, and glory. The habit of composition in the ancient languages is most useful, if not absolutely necessary, to those who desire completely to understand those languages; at all events, it is useful to employ young persons in acquiring such accomplishments. . . ." [Letter from Lord Wellesley, May 2, 1821.]

But why is it useful? Alas, the great man did not tell his brother, so that Arthur could only sigh over the lack of these "accomplishments" in himself, and hope that his sons would turn out more successfully than their father. Meanwhile the Duke wrote regularly to Mr. Wagner, laying particular stress on mathematics.

On the home political front the years 1822–1827, from the death of Castlereagh to the end of Liverpool as Prime Minister, witnessed a sudden change which was marked by at least a beginning of long-overdue reforms. If it can be said truly that Castlereagh inherited the repressive side of his great master, William Pitt, it is equally true to say that Canning carried on the earlier Pitt policy of progressive reform which had been lost in the whirlpools of the French Revolution. Canning's energy was immediately demonstrated in various legal, commercial, and financial changes; and he introduced into the Government an alleged "financial genius", Huskisson, who in deference to the King's susceptibilities was only allowed to sit on the Board of Trade though he was actually doing the work of Chancellor of the Exchequer. The Whig opposition, which throughout the war and early post-war period had been factious, querulous, and even downright treacherous to their country, suddenly became the most co-operative of Parliamentarians. Indeed, with one important exception—Parliamentary Reform—Canning's policy and views were closer to the old Whigs than to the old Tories; and the Duke had been responsible for bringing him back to power! At this distance of time we are apt to overlook the rebelliousness of the English people during the first half of the nineteenth century, forget that again and again the country was on the very verge of revolution, "only averted by some happy stroke of fortune". It is a fact that in 1832 arms were secreted in many cottages for the rebellion which would have occurred if the Reform Bill had not passed:

"A Whig nobleman," wrote G. W. E. Russell in 1897, "of great experience and calm judgment, told me that if Princess Victoria had died before William IV, and thereby Ernest Duke of Cumberland had succeeded to the Throne, no earthly power could have averted a revolution. 'I have no hesitation in saying,' I heard Mr. Gladstone say, 'that if the repeal of the Corn Laws had been defeated, or even retarded, we should have had a revolution.' Charles Kingsley and his fellow-workers for Social Reform expected a revolution in 1848."

This latent revolutionary situation was not a product or plagiarism of the French Revolution (as Croker and others so loudly proclaimed) but a genuine home-grown article, a continuation of the same process and lines of thought which had produced the Great Rebellion against Charles I in the 1640's, the Revolution against James II in 1688, and the American Revolution against George III in 1776. Everybody knows that this happened, but it seems to be forgotten when the Duke's behaviour as politician has to be explained. We have seen how his temperament, his extraordinary career, and his associates inevitably made him a Tory (though a special kind of Tory, with a lofty ideal of his duties to the Throne oddly contrasting with his personal contempt for George IV and William IV); but it was the fact that (in one case) Ireland and (in others) England were perfectly ready to rise in rebellion which caused the Duke to retreat from the great Tory positions —opposition to the repeal of the Corn Laws and to Catholic Emancipation. The most he could do was to fight Parliamentary delaying actions from the House of Lords, which he did with some skill; but Dizzy's contention that he knew nothing about England certainly seems borne out by his action in 1830–1832 when he misjudged the temper of his fellow-citizens and very nearly precipitated a revolution. Canning was then dead, but if he had been alive would he have done any better? More clearly than the Duke or than any one else at that time Canning saw that Parliamentary Reform must lead eventually to democracy and universal suffrage. Like a true Whig, Canning mistrusted the people, and would have viewed the Durham-Grey-Russell Reform Act with as much dismay as the Duke and his friends. What would he have done, what *could* he have done that the Duke failed to do? The best would have been to give way sooner and with a better grace. And if Canning's claim to be considered the "great statesman", which it is denied that the Duke ever was, is founded on his foreign policy, we may ask how those who have experienced our nationalist wars can applaud his principle: "Every nation for itself, and God for us all". If that was "Liberalism" may we be spared from it—better a hundred times the fumbling attempts of Castlereagh and the Duke at some kind of European order. Was it statesmanship in Canning to support order at home and anarchy abroad?

Whatever the Duke's attitude towards Canning's policy in home and trade affairs, he can claim no merit except that of acquiescing (if he did acquiesce) in the secrecy of Cabinet meetings. But the two men soon began to differ, and to get on each other's nerves over foreign affairs. The Duke had lived so long abroad that it was easier for him to get on affably with foreign gentlemen than with home-grown riff-raff; and he certainly disliked Canning's England *ueber alles* pronouncements— later carried to the extremity of impudence by Canning's pupil, Palmerston, in his "*civis Romanus sum*" oration. Soon the buzz went round that the Duke and Canning were no longer seeing eye to eye, or at any rate were seeing each other with jaundiced eyes. Prinny naturally was delighted—he had always disliked "that fellow" Canning, and had only consented to take him into so important a place in the Cabinet because "Arthur" had insisted. Now Arthur was finding out that Mr. Canning was no gentleman. So Prinny invited Arthur to come on a fishing trip with him and the lady of the seraglio, Lady Conyngham, at Virginia Water—a small but picturesque pond which Prinny had succeeded in enclosing for his own entertainment. It must have been a great moment for Prinny when he could say "I told you so" to the impeccable Arthur, who would obstinately refuse to admit that His Royal Highness (now Majesty) had charged at the head of the Household Cavalry at Salamanca. Surely Arthur would now at least admit how much credit was due to Prinny for sending reinforcements out just before Salamanca!

"You remember, Arthur, how I forced the Cabinet to send you twelve thousand men for Salamanca?"

"Sir, I was in Spain."

Prinny could only console himself by hoping that Canning and Arthur would soon quarrel; and they did—in the autumn of 1824. Already they were wiring rather acid notes to each other in July, and in October they began to misunderstand each other vehemently about a possible diplomatic visit of Canning to Paris. The Duke, writing from the Royal Lodge, mentioned having heard about it "in the Equerrys' room here yesterday". Mr. Canning could not "account for the reports of the 'Equerrys' room'" . . . "if His Majesty has

changed his opinion, he will, no doubt, lay his commands upon me".
The Duke retorted that "it is quite obvious to me that you have not
considered my letter in the sense in which I wrote it". Mr. Canning
replied with a tart letter whose "only object is to set you right as to the
supposed object of my supposed journey". (Prinny was now enjoying
the correspondence immensely.) His Grace replied that "it is quite
impossible that the object of Lord Westmorland's visit to the Lodge at
Windsor can have been what you imagine". Mr. Canning snapped
back; the Duke started to write a conciliatory letter, but his third
paragraph begins: "You will find it very difficult to convince the
world," whereupon Mr. Canning saw "no occasion to give you the
trouble of coming up to town", and then wrote a letter to the Prime
Minister showing that he suspected Prinny and Arthur of dirty work
behind his back:

"I have the highest respect for the Duke of Wellington, and I do not presume
to limit the confidences of the King. But when one finds that all that passes
between the King and oneself is repeated as a matter of course to a third person,
and that third person one who thinks himself at liberty to repeat it to others,
at the same time that he conceals the fact of his knowing it from one's self, it
is high time to look about one, and to beware of what Burke calls 'traps and
mines'." [Letter to Lord Liverpool, October 17, 1824.]

Canning enjoyed a high reputation as a man of letters, though
"one" would not think so from his second sentence in that extract.
As to the grounds of the disagreement, the quotations given should
show that they were little more than the normal unfriendly relations of
political colleagues. (Where did politicians acquire the tradition of
professing the "greatest respect" for rivals whom they detest and
obviously wouldn't dream of respecting?) The significant thing about
this quarrel is that its cause was so obscure and trivial. It was a clash
of divergent temperaments, two men "getting on each other's nerves",
rather than any important difference of principle. They continued to
work together but with a good deal of mutual suspicion and ill will,
which on the Duke's part extended to all the "Canningites", Huskisson, Palmerston, and the rest. Yet on the home front 1824 was a good
year for the Government; the removal of some trade restrictions and
the partial recovery of the world from the war resulted in a large
increase of trade and national income. They were even too successful.
The profit motive got out of hand, not for the first or last time; in 1825
there was wild speculation despite repeated warnings from Canning
and Huskisson, with the usual results—a sudden slump followed by a

panic and bank crashes which nearly brought down the Bank of England. The Ministers were frantically abused for misfortunes which were due to the greed and selfishness of speculators; and those who for some reason are known as "wise men" blamed the disaster on a variety of more or less irrelevant causes. The panic began on Christmas Day, 1825, Santa Claus refusing to deliver the goods to redeem the paper promises:

"For my part," said the Duke reminiscing, "I was in the Cabinet in 1826, and I well remember that had it not been for most extraordinary exertions— above all on the part of old Rothschild—the Bank must have stopped payment."

The Duke, it appears, was then a bimetallist and wanted the Bank to hold a reserve of silver as well as of gold, but the orthodox economists would not hear of it.

Meanwhile the Tsar Alexander had died at Taganrog on Christmas Eve (1825) and was succeeded by Nicholas I. The connection of this event with the independence of Greece and of the Duke of Wellington with both may seem remote, but was not so in fact. All remember the superb advertisement given to the Greeks by Lord Byron's death at Missolonghi in 1824, but all may not remember that in 1825 the Greeks were everywhere defeated and being massacred by Turkish and Egyptian armies. By one of those singular anomalies, so common in power politics, the cause of the Greeks was warmly upheld by the serf-owning Russian autocracy while the Parliamentary majority of (more or less) free England was adverse or at best unenthusiastic. The reasons? Well, if the Russians could get themselves into a popular war with the Turks on behalf of the enslaved and oppressed Greeks, then Russia would, if successful, weaken an old enemy, might get the Dardanelles, Constantinople, and an outlet to the Mediterranean. Strange to relate, the British Government did not want their Russian friends in the Mediterranean; but on the other hand almost everyone in England except the Government was enthusiastically pro-Greek. It was an awkward situation. Alexander had been prepared to negotiate and to arrange a compromise solution, but what would Nicholas do? Canning had an idea—why not send the Duke on a special embassy to St. Petersburg, ostensibly to offer congratulations on the new reign, actually to negotiate? "I hope," Canning noted, "to save Greece through the agency of the Russian name upon the fears of Turkey without a war." He suggested the matter to Prinny, which resulted in a marvellous royal letter (Most secret and confidential, *and for yourself alone*) from Prinny to the Duke, ending up:

"Advice I do not pretend to offer, but, as to *my* wishes, they are to be summed up in very few words indeed; and not to repeat all I do so sincerely feel personally towards you, I must say, that your absence for any length of time, or rather, *the want of your presence*, would be *quite intolerable to me*, besides, the risk, which your health would run, perhaps even your life, which is too *frightful a consideration*, either for the private man that *loves you*, or the public man that cares for his country, or for the interests of all Europe, to entertain or tolerate for a single instant." [The King to Field-Marshal the Duke of Wellington. Royal Lodge, December 27, 1825.]

Nicholas succeeded to the throne through the abdication of the Grand Duke Constantine, an event foreseen by the Duke and referred to by him in the letter to Canning which accepted the mission:

"I should not be surprised if Constantine were to abdicate. This act will show that he agrees with others in thinking that assassination is the legitimate charter of the Russian people." [Letter to Canning, January 1, 1826.]

The difference between the characters of Canning and Wellington as well as the "differences" (in the other sense of the word) which marked their hostility are rather well brought out by a remark of each at this time. "The Duke of Wellington" said Canning superciliously "would not have done for any purpose of mine a twelvemonth ago", implying both his own superiority and his ability to use the Duke as a tool whenever he wished. In replying to George IV's letter, the Duke wrote: "I am at all times ready and willing to serve your Majesty in any station in which it may appear to your Majesty and your servants that I can be at all useful to your service." It is the old principle of service to the State expressed with proud if formal humility; whereas Canning sounds merely like an ambitious man pushing his own schemes and career.

There was some reason for Prinny's elaborate verbiage in presenting the idea of such a mission, for in those pre-railway days a journey across central Europe by sledge in midwinter was a hardship if not a danger to a man approaching sixty who, in spite of his austere manner of living, had been liable to occasional fits of dizziness or fainting since the fatal operation on his ear. But such considerations did not worry the Duke, whose attention was chiefly turned to the problem of defeating the vermin of Eastern European inns and posting houses, to which end he devised a sleeping-bag of silk—a substance he thought would be difficult for the enemy to penetrate—of a light colour which would at once show the number and dispositions of the enemy troops. As to the subject of his mission, he was not hopeful. If the Russians wanted to fight the Turks he didn't quite see how they were to be stopped, and what he was worried about was not the freeing of the Greeks but the averting of another European war. It seems that those who criticize the Wellington of these years and his foreign policy at all times overlook the fact that preventing another major war was the dominant thought—one might almost say, the obsession—of his mind. He really had been sickened by the carnage and misery of the war years and, like many soldiers after the war of 1914–1918, was determined "it shan't happen again". And, as long as he lived, it didn't. He had a great dislike for blood-thirsty civilians who indulge in bellicose and intransigent sentiments which other men have to make good with their lives. As late as the last year of William IV, when the Duke was ceasing to be a leading figure in politics, he is to be found writing to deplore "the propensity of the government and of their majority in the House of Commons to go to war with Russia". Twenty years later that "propensity" led to the Crimean War.

By the middle of February (1826) he was in Berlin, conferring with the King of Prussia and firing off rapid notes to Canning, from some of which it appears that he had already abandoned his views on bimetallism and inclined to the belief that the "value" of silver would decline continuously. There he received a communication from his brother Henry Wellesley (ambassador to Vienna) containing the flattering intimation that Metternich "is quite prepared to enlist himself under your banners, and to leave the interests of Europe in your hands, satisfied that they cannot be placed in better". He was at Riga on February 26, and in St. Petersburg on March 2 (1826), where he remained until April 6. His mission succeeded in the sense that there was no war; but how far was this due to the Duke and his influence? He seems to have been nonplussed by the complicated court intrigues of the Russian palace, and to have been received by the new Emperor rather as a venerated survivor of another epoch than as a leading figure of the day. In the matter of ceremony he received all those attentions which seem to be so pleasant to elderly (or as they now prefer to be called, "elder") statesmen. On arrival he was asked whether he wished to be treated in accordance with his rank as a Russian Field-Marshal (then the highest in the Russian Empire) or merely as Prinny's envoy—of course, choosing the latter and receiving the honours of the former, in harmony with the quaint workings of what is sometimes referred to as the diplomatic mind. On leaving, the Duke was overwhelmed with gifts, from autographed portraits of notables to magnificent sets of sable furs and malachite vases of exemplary uselessness from the imperial manufactory. The record of his daily industry in St. Petersburg may be read in the not very thrilling dispatches he wrote; and even on the journey home he was not idle, drawing up a judicious and (on the whole) not inhumane memorandum on the subject of military punishments. He was back in London April 27 (1826); and the Russian trophies were added to the many others adorning or concealing the walls of Apsley House. The 1815 trophies were already acquiring the melancholy interest of associations with the departed, for Blücher the co-victor of Waterloo had long since gone to his account, haunted by the strange fantasy that he was pregnant of an elephant by a French soldier. Could outraged France have asked more in the way of *revanche?*

A little stiffly, for age would begin to assert itself despite the tennis-court at Strathfield Saye and the hunting field, the Duke took up his London round of Parliamentary, palace, and social duties. Yet age in politicians, as the citizens of most countries find to their cost, never cools ambition and is very seldom thought a bar to political promotion. In the Duke's case it must be admitted that he bore his late fifties amazingly well, showing the passage of time only in greying hair, in an occasional peevish damning of red dispatch boxes, and in an ever-growing dislike for Canning and his friends and their goings-on. The Duke particularly objected to Canning's habit (afterwards so fully developed by his pupil, Palmerston) of taking important action as Foreign Secretary without consulting his colleagues. There were domestic troubles in Spain and Portugal, threats of trouble between Spain and Portugal—a matter of direct concern since ancient treaties bound England to the defence of Portugal—and the Greek troubles seemed no nearer settlement than before the Duke's mission to St. Petersburg. Some even were found to whisper that "Wellington had been hoodwinked" by that affable but Byzantine court. Then suddenly Canning withdrew the British minister from Madrid and, much to the Duke's disquiet, sent troops to Lisbon. "Mr. Canning", primly remarked a hanger-on of the Duke, "was not in all respects a favourite with the Duke, who admired his talents, but distrusted his political honesty".

Among the numerous Wellington papers for the year 1826 the most staggering is a long letter to Mr. Robinson (Chancellor of the Exchequer) on the Poor Law. This amazing document should be quoted in full, but even the last paragraph is deserving of meditation:

"I confess I doubt the success of a pauper emigration to the Cape of Good Hope, or to the convict colonies in Australasia. We must not expect that all these pauper colonists will succeed as agriculturists; some must continue labourers. There is no demand at the Cape for more than a certain number of the latter, on account of the existence of slavery in that colony; and there can be no demand for labourers in Australasia, where there are still so many convicts unemployed." [London, October 20, 1826.]

Less repulsive to a modern reader and in the genuine Wellington style are the instructions issued to the small expeditionary force sent to Portugal. There the Duke knew what he was talking about, and from a practical military point of view every sentence is of gold. Nothing could more strikingly justify the instinctive rightness of judgment of the English people in their dislike for entrusting their government to a soldier, no matter how successful in the field and how honourable in his intentions and conduct. The proper place for the Duke, as he himself admitted, was as Commander-in-Chief of the Army; and in the autumn of 1826 it became evident that the Duke of York was at last to be cashiered by "the fell Sergeant" Death. (Prinny's lament, "Alas! my poor brother!" happened to be the slogan a century later on an English advertisement of the beef extract, Bovril, where a bull is lamenting over his bottled brother—none the less appropriate for that.) What chiefly bothered the Duke was the funeral pomp ordered for his predecessor—"It cannot be military, because we have not enough men in England to bury a Field-Marshal!" And perhaps that remark illustrates the obverse of the remark about soldiers as civilian rulers— namely, the unwisdom of entrusting the military defence of a country entirely to juntas of landowners, capitalists, and friends of the people.

But the Duke of York was dead, he who as Commander-in-Chief had done his damnedest to secure the defeat of as many British armies as possible, who had nearly wrecked and always handicapped the career of the one efficient and intelligent General in the service, and who had done all he could to vilify that General and his achievement when the wars were over. Visitors to London may have been puzzled to explain the existence of a large and ugly pillar crowned with an indistinguishable figure at the far end of the piazza overlooking the Mall at the terminus of Lower Regent Street. That is the monument to the Duke of York, "Who had ten thousand men; He led them up to the top of the hill. And led them down again". It is not possible to omit quoting the Duke's reply to a certain Mr. Glenny who asked his support for this unnecessary boosting of the Duke of York to a level with Nelson:

"There is nothing that would gratify the Duke in a greater degree than to promote any plan which has for its object to mark the public grief for the loss of the late Duke of York, or the public respect for his Royal Highness's memory. But as plans are sometimes formed upon occasions like the present which have not exactly those objects in view, and the Duke has not had the good fortune of seeing the prospectus to which Mr. Glenny refers, or of knowing who are the members of the committee with whom the Duke is desired to associate, he hopes he may be permitted to request to be furnished with such information before he gives his answer."

This is followed by one of the innumerable Memoranda to the Cabinet which haunt the pages of the Duke's correspondence like extremely heavy ghosts. Yet the first paragraph of this one is sober, striking, and memorable:

"The Duke of York is supposed to have owed £200,000 at the period of his death, for the payment of which no provision is made."

At any rate, the Duke had not lost his gift of irony as he grew older, nor his capacity for pungent criticism, as witness the following letter:

"Woburn Abbey, 13th January, 1827

"My Dear Mr. Canning,

"I return you Count Palmella's proposed alterations of the convention, with a Memorandum upon them. I have had many transactions with this gentleman, and he certainly is the most difficult to deal with I have ever met. He must have been educated by a Portuguese Jew attorney."

It was a bitter blow for the Horse Guards clique to have their prime enemy appointed their master, and, by way of showing their displeasure, Torrens (the Military Secretary) was made to draw up a long and pompous General Order in which the new Commander-in-Chief lamented and praised his predecessors in a strain of fulsome adulation, and by implication promised to carry on the old system and to protect its beneficiaries. Imagine the fury when by return of post they received a peremptory refusal to publish their Order and a command to publish this Order:

"In obedience to His Majesty's most gracious command, Field-Marshal the Duke of Wellington assumes the command of the army, and earnestly requests the assistance and support of the general and other officers of the army to maintain its discipline, good order, and high character." [January 25, 1827.]

It is perhaps hardly worth noting that forty years had elapsed since the new Commander-in-Chief entered the army as "a penniless ensign". The British army, someone has said, was then ruled by a clique within a caste. The Duke belonged to the caste but not to the clique, and there is no difficulty in imagining the consternation and fury of the survivors of the old clique at this change of dynasty, and their rage at the snub they received when at the very outset they tried to impose themselves on him by sending him *their* General Order for him to sign.

"I dare say that this order will not be approved" wrote the Duke to Torrens as he refused to sign the Horse Guards Order and sent his own, adding significantly: "But nothing that I shall do for some time will be approved, and I must follow the unbiassed dictates of my own understanding." An opportunity for using that "understanding" was provided almost immediately by an inventive gentleman who strongly urged that the British cavalry be equipped with lossos. Certainly the idea of the Life Guards charging with brandished lariats is exhilarating, but it seems the Duke's "unbiassed dictates" were against the plan.

But this flower of forty years' growth was of remarkably short duration. On February 17 the Prime Minister was smitten by apoplexy and thereby "deprived of his understanding". Coarse-minded, ribald Whigs might ask sarcastically what difference that made to a Tory Prime Minister, but his afflicted monarch and colleague thought otherwise. The Ministry had to be reconstituted; Canning and not Peel collected the succession, whereupon all the "old Tories" (including Eldon and the Duke) sent in their resignations. A letter from Canning (April 11, 1827) which was seen and apparently approved by Prinny gave the Duke great offence, as may be seen from his resigning as Commander-in-Chief (which is not a political office) as well as from the Cabinet. In a Memorandum the Duke expressed his feelings in these strenuous words:

"I could not exercise that command with advantage to his Majesty, the government, and the public, or with honour to myself, unless I was respected, and treated with that fair confidence by his Majesty and his minister which I think I deserve; and nobody will consider that I was treated with confidence, respect, or even common civility, by Mr. Canning in his last letter." [Memorandum on quitting the Cabinet, April 13, 1827.]

Lord Anglesea (the Uxbridge of Waterloo) was appointed Master-General of the Ordnance; Prinny himself took over as Commander-in-Chief (Palmerston did the work); and the town produced a derisive caricature of the Duke as "Achilles sulking in his tent". That not too intelligent critic failed to note that this was the first time the Duke had been out of a job since his return from India in 1805.

"Curious times these, Duke," said Mr. Creevey, meeting him as he came out of Arbuthnot's house. The Duke agreed, and was actually beheld walking arm-in-arm with a Radical—a false omen, for it was now beginning to be thought among the really crusted Tories that only the Duke could "save the country from disaster". It certainly was a fact that Canning only remained in power through the support of the Whigs.

CHAPTER XXIV

Prime Minister

"CURIOUS times" indeed, when liberal and enlightened England cheered the freeing of the Greeks by the action of an Anglo-Franco-Russian fleet which (contrary to orders) smashed the Turkish fleet at Navarino, but when none of the said liberal and enlightened appeared to notice that every day more and more men, women, and children were being poured into unventilated, unregulated factories whose only but sacred purpose was Mr. Gradgrind's longing to make as much as he could from overworking and underpaying his "hands". One voice raised in protest was that of the Tory Laureate, Southey, crushed by the liberal and enlightened Mr. Macaulay who proved statistically that the workers now had more cotton stockings than ever before and that poor-rates were declining in manufacturing districts, but said nothing about death-rates or about the non-statistical human misery rates which appalled Southey. "Curious times", too, when the owners of these dingily grey slaves were more and more insisting on a political power to match their economic power, when they muttered questions as to why Roman Catholics should not sit in Parliament (much they cared), when they asked grumblingly why the Corn Laws should keep up the price of wheat to benefit landowners since free trade in wheat would enable them (the manufacturers) to cut starvation wages lower still. And not only they but men everywhere began to ask why on earth Parliament should be elected on the population basis of the fourteenth century, so that Cornwall had only one less member than all Scotland, ruined ghost towns like Old Sarum returned two members when great industrial cities had none at all, and when (according to Croker) 203 seats were entirely controlled by Tory peers and 73 Whig peers. Among the Tories Lord Lonsdale controlled nine seats, the Marquess of Hertford 8, Duke of Rutland 6, Duke of Newcastle 5; and so on and so on through most of the peerage. It might be noted as a matter of curiosity that the Duke of Wellington controlled no seats at all.

Not much of this worried Mr. Canning. So far as he knew he had no relatives working in factories; he lived on his wife's income; he had no prejudices about Corn Laws and Catholics; but he wanted no Parlia-

mentary Reform which would destroy the power of the aristocracy
which had fostered him and made his career. He saw nothing funny in
the remark of an opponent: "Mr. Canning is a very eloquent man, but
even he cannot pretend that a decaying tree stump is the people".
That is just what Mr. Canning did want to pretend. Unluckily for
him, he had caught a cold at the funeral of the Duke of York, and
never managed to throw it off. Like another of the Duke of Wellington's enemies, he lasted exactly a hundred days, dying on August 8,
1827.

Would the King "send for" the Duke? was the question everybody
was asking as soon as it was known that Canning was about to die.
For after this fit of political Achilles' sulks nobody could maintain that
the Duke was a no-party man solely desirous of "carrying on the
King's Government", however much he might continue to believe he
was. To a cynical world he had become the likeliest candidate for the
leadership of the Tory party. But the King did not "send for" the
Duke; Prinny was still angry with Arthur for foisting Canning on him
and then quarrelling with Canning, with the result that his affectionate
Sovereign was left wide open to the horrors of Mr. Canning's
eloquence and liberalism. The King sent for Lord Goderich (né Mr.
Robinson), and told him to form a Government; which to the best of
his meagre abilities he did, on August 13, 1827. Four days later the
Duke was writing:

"I have received your Majesty's most gracious commands conveying to me
the offer of the command of your Majesty's army, which I accept. . . ."

So once more he was Commander-in-Chief *de jure* as well as *de
facto*; but not for long. Mr. Robinson was no fire-ball as a politician;
moreover he was hysterical and lachrymose, which got on Prinny's
nerves. There was another political "crisis" at the end of December
1827, and after trying various other people the King sent for the Duke,
who found his gracious Sovereign lying in bed clothed in disreputably
tarnished silken night-clothes and an old turban. "Arthur," said the
familiar voice, "the Ministry is defunct!" The Duke was loyal but
cautious: "I told his Majesty that I was so situated professionally that
I could not say that I would form a government of which I should be
the head without consulting others." Croker saw him in the thick
of it a few days later at Apsley House "beset and plagued with
importunities" and feeling, he said, "like a dog with a canister
tied to its tail". He pointed to a heap of green bags and red boxes,
exclaiming:

"There is the business of the country, which I have not had time to look at
—all my time being employed by assuaging what gentlemen call their feelings.
In short, the folly and unreasonableness of people are inconceivable."

No doubt this expressed the Duke's sentiments at large, but might
it not also have been a hint to Mr. Croker that he was wasting valuable
time? Eventually, in spite of the gentlemen and their feelings, the new
Ministry was formed; and men watched curiously to see how the great
soldier would conduct himself in the perils and ambushes of Parliamentary warfare. Early impressions, as usually happens, were not
unfavourable:

"The Beau," Mr. Creevey noted, "is rising most rapidly in the market as a
practical man of business. All the deputations come away charmed with him.
But woe to them that are too late. He is punctual to a second himself, and waits
for no man." [March 20, 1828.]

Troubles began early, as was inevitable. The Opposition uproar
about the danger to the country and breach of the Constitution caused
by the Commander-in-Chief being First Lord of the Treasury, was
evaded by handing the army temporarily over to the faithful Hill, of
Peninsula fame. Prinny's Protestant conscience and sentiments, which
he fancifully asserted "for years and years have never varied", were apt
to flare up when he saw the Archbishop or the Duke of Cumberland,
or wanted to worry Arthur. In May (1828) the Duke got rid of the
excellent Huskisson and the other Canningites, and turned himself into
a thoroughly Tory Government. The manœuvre by which Huskisson
and his friends were got rid of was not quite on the highest level of
public morality—the Duke chose to misread a letter which gave him
the chance to ask for Huskisson's resignation as a definite declaration
that his colleague had resigned. Good politics, perhaps, but not
worthy of the Duke. On the other hand, there is no foundation for
Dizzy's sneer that the Duke replaced the Canningites with "second-
rate generals". He did put the best Peninsula generals into the
military posts which every Government filled with generals, and he put
a soldier instead of a civilian at the head of the War Office. But every
other important post (except his own) was filled by a civilian, and if the
generals were "second-rate", they were the best England had and a
vast improvement on their predecessors and successors. More comic
than worrying was a singular contest over authority with the Duke of
Clarence (afterwards William IV) who had persuaded Prinny to give
him the wholly decorative post of Lord High Admiral of England, and
then infuriated the ancient sea-dogs at the Admiralty by hoisting his
flag and giving orders as if he were a real sailor.

Apropos Clarence, it might be observed that in addition to the large annual sums paid the King, a country still struggling under an immense war debt was paying annually £250,000 in pensions to members of the royal family, some of whom were entirely German.

Nine months of office had taught the Duke something when he wrote this letter:

Stratfield Saye, 29th October, 1828

"My dear Sir,

"I have received your letter of the 28th inst, and return the enclosure. You must have been very much surprised when you received it; more particularly as you are not aware of the advantage which I possess in the proffered assistance of nearly every gentleman in England, who has nothing to do but to amuse himself, and is tired of his usual amusements, and of reading the newspapers.

"There is not a subject of public interest upon which I do not receive hundreds of letters, numerous almost in proportion to the difficulty and importance attached to each. Corn, currency, poor-laws, payment of the national debt, adjustment of the Roman Catholic question, are the favourite topics; and to read this correspondence it might be believed that there would be nothing so easy as to arrange all our difficulties. Political arrangements and objects of minor importance are not beneath their notice; and I have come to the conclusion that the English are the most officious people that I have yet met with.

"I must say for this gentleman that he has not the same excuse for his officiousness that others might have. It appears that he has something to do. To be sure he does not like his employment. . . ."

The Duke would have been staggered and incredulous if informed by the tutelary observator of England that what he mistook for sarcasm was only a sober description of how great countries were to be governed in a not very distant future.

It was under date February 3, 1829, that Mr. Creevey noted excitedly: "Everyone was up with the news of the day—that Wellington had decided to let the Catholics into Parliament"; but this revolutionary measure had in fact been secretly under Cabinet consideration for some time, and they had come to the conclusion that the step was necessary to prevent a rebellion in Ireland, and as the last logical stage in the progressive freeing of Roman Catholics from legal disabilities. To speak of this change as "revolutionary" now looks absurd; but it must be remembered that the Reformation in England had been carried through and from time to time perpetuated by Acts of Parliament which specifically constituted England a Protestant country. The King only reigned as a Protestant, the Bishops sat in the Lords as Protestants, and it was held by lawyers that even the writs summoning Members of Parliament were only issued to them as Protestants. Thus, what now seems an act of merely elementary and long-delayed justice was in fact equivalent to an amendment to the Constitution in the United States, and one not unlike permitting avowed American monarchists to sit in Congress. The awkward thing was that the Duke was head of a party which was pledged to resist any such alteration in the laws, and the mere hint of their intentions in the King's Speech infuriated many of the Government's supporters. Prinny himself was against it, though, amusingly enough, as early as 1797 he had twice memorialized William Pitt urging the necessity and justice of the measure. When, on January 28, 1829, the Duke mentioned his new plans for Catholics, Prinny exclaimed in anguish: "Damn it, do you intend to let them into Parliament?"

The Duke did, and thereby delighted his political opponents as much as he offended his supporters:

"Well, the Whig croaking must end now," Mr. Creevey noted. "The Beau is certainly immortalised by his views and measures as detailed by Peel last night. I certainly, for one, think it an unjust thing to alter the election franchise from 40s. to £10; but considering the perfection of every other part and the difficulty there must have been in bringing Prinney up to this mark, I should, were I in Parliament, swallow the franchise thing without hesitation."

Mr. Creevey might have noticed that this seems to have been the only Bill ever before an English Parliament since the Tudors which restricted rather than extended the franchise; but he was tighter than he knew about the difficulty with Prinny. Prinny's brother, the Duke of Cumberland, was a rabid Protestant and a bitter enemy of the Duke, and used his great influence to obstruct and delay, while Prinny himself had a wonderful time expounding his views and defending his Protestant conscience over the brandy bottle. On one occasion he discoursed for five and a half hours without allowing the Duke to get in one word—he not infrequently was thus eloquent, so that the Duke had to write all the answers by letter next day. Prinny even threatened to abdicate, but ended up by kissing the Duke, who reported that the interview with His Majesty had been "very painful". A few days later there was again talk of abdication, and after another long and exhausting interview Peel and Wellington retired convinced that the King meant to dismiss them. At the last moment Prinny sent a note accepting the situation.

Rows with Prinny were by no means the full extent of the Duke's Catholic Emancipation troubles. There were the Bishops, particularly the Irish Protestant Bishops (there was still an Established Protestant Church of Ireland), and numerous influential Tory peers and members. One of these arguments led to consequences of a scandalous and notorious nature. Lord Winchilsea published a letter (in the *Standard*, March 16, 1829) announcing the withdrawal of his support from the non-sectarian University of London. The Duke, it appears, had been in favour of including some kind of religious instruction, on which Lord Winchilsea thought fit to write:

". . . I considered that the noble Duke at the head of his Majesty's government had been induced on this occasion to assume a new character, and to step forward himself as the public advocate of religion and morality.

"Late political events have convinced me that the whole transaction was intended as a blind to the Protestant and High Church party, that the noble Duke, who had for some time previous to that period determined upon 'breaking in upon the constitution of 1688', might the more effectually, under the cloak of some outward show of zeal for the Protestant religion, carry on his insidious designs, for the infringement of our liberties, and the introduction of Popery into every department of the State."

Lord Winchilsea was a very silly man, but this letter forced the Duke to take a dramatic step he had never taken in his long career as a soldier. After vainly attempting to reason his adversary into withdrawing the charges and printing an apology, the Duke sent one of his tough letters which ended:

"I now call upon your Lordship to give me that satisfaction for your conduct which a gentleman has a right to require, and which a gentleman never refuses to give."

The seconds were Lord Falmouth and Sir Henry Hardinge; the weapons, pistols; the time 8 a.m. on March 21, 1829; and the place "about half a mile on the other side of the river" over Battersea Bridge. Hume, the Duke's doctor, had been routed out early by Sir Henry for an affair of honour between gentlemen, and was "overwhelmed with amazement" and "greatly agitated" when the Duke suddenly rode up to him, saying in a laughing manner: "Well, I dare say you little expected it was I who wanted you to be here." And undoubtedly it was an odd experience for a respectable doctor to be brought along to see the ruler of his country break its laws. The Duke was in a hurry—a few curiosity-mongers were already gathering:

"Now then, Hardinge, look sharp and step out the ground. Damn it! don't stick him up so near the ditch. If I hit him, he will tumble in."

Sir Henry had lost an arm at Waterloo, so Dr. Hume loaded the pistols, the Duke fired and missed (his shooting improved but slowly), and Lord Winchilsea solemnly and magnanimously fired in the air; after which his second announced that he was ready to sign and to publish "an apology in the most extensive or in every sense of the word". When that was finally agreed to, Lord Falmouth began excusing himself for his share of the proceedings, but the Duke interrupted him: "Good morning, my Lord Winchilsea; good morning, my Lord Falmouth"; touched "the brim of his hat with two fingers", mounted his horse and with his second "rode quickly off the field". As may be surmised, the news that the Prime Minister had fought a duel caused an enormous public sensation. Prinny was delighted, and opined that "gentlemen must not stand upon their privileges", adding that he should have done the same thing himself in the Duke's place. On the other hand, Jeremy Bentham wrote a long and scolding letter beginning "Ill-advised Man!" and denouncing in no unmeasured terms the "plague" of duelling and the wickedness of the Duke. "Compliments. The Duke has received his letter," was the reply.

In the midst of all this excitement the Bill passed its third reading in the Commons by 320 votes to 123; and though the Lords raged against it, they let it pass. Was it, as some said, the first stage in the separation of Ireland from the Empire and the handing over to hostile, or at best indifferent, keeping naval bases vital to the defence of England? Croker said bitterly: "What was denied to reason and policy is surrendered to intimidation," which might stand as the motto of his political party and of his country. As for Mr. Creevey, he positively condescended to praise the Duke to his face:

"Well, upon my soul, Duke, you are the first of mankind to have accomplished this Irish job as you have done, and I congratulate you upon it most sincerely. You must have had tough work to get through."

Theoretically and to a very large extent practically (be it said to his credit) the Duke ignored blame and praise alike. As a ruler he believed it was not his business to court popularity but to do what he considered right and just. Gross calumny and libel might be justly resented with a pistol at twenty paces in the case of a gentleman, with a lawsuit in the case of newspaper publishers, and contemptuous silence in the case of "the mob". And yet—"I hate meddling with the Press. The perpetual interference with the Press was one of the rocks on which my predecessors struck". It is a little hard for us to realize that this Wellington Government, which to us looks so reactionary, was being violently attacked for its supposed betrayal of Church and State.

The Winchilsea episode is a case in point, but that was only one of many. One of the greatest difficulties the Duke had to contend with was the forty years' long delay in accomplishing necessary changes. He saw this perfectly well. As early as October 1828 he writes in exasperation: "The difficulties of the times have been accumulating for nearly forty years; and I must find a way out of them!!!" More than a year later, after a particularly trying encounter with Prinny, he broke forth with a most unaccustomed vehemence:

"If I had known in January 1828 one tithe of what I do now, and what I discovered in one month after I was in office, I should never have been the King's Minister, and should have avoided loads of misery! However, I trust that God Almighty will soon determine that I have been sufficiently punished for my sins, and will relieve me from the unhappy lot which has befallen me! I believe there was never a man suffered so much; and for so little purpose!" [Letter to Sir W. Knighton, November 10, 1829.]

This was one of the sudden outbursts of ill humour by which the Duke got rid of his "nerves"; as when he had denounced the troops in the Peninsula as the "scum of the earth", or in the Waterloo campaign when he wrote that everything was going on as badly as possible—although actually he was rapidly moving on Paris. Yet after the passage of the Catholic relief act there was a temporary lessening of revolutionary heavings, and even for those comparatively quiet days little went on or seemed to threaten. There was the "Eastern Question", which was in time to become such a bore; there were the usual troubles in Greece, Spain, Portugal; and the usual home front worries. At last, it seems, some realization of the consequences of the industrial revolution was beginning to reach even the Government; and for the first time the Duke's papers (1829–1830) contained reports on labour and wages. Under almost the identical date when one correspondent wrote that "pauperism, which forty or fifty years since was scarcely felt, except as to the impotent poor, is now a general system" and another spoke of cotton operatives' wages in Cumberland of four shillings a week, Mr. Creevey recorded with an admiring groan that Lord Dudley was in "a state of lingering existence under the frightful pressure of £120,000 a year". From which it would appear that under "our miraculous institutions" an obscure peer was held to be as valuable as twelve thousand artisans.

Perhaps the most curious episode in this calm period between the dying away of the Catholic storm and the full fury of the Reform hurricane, was the case of Mr. Comyn which illustrates at once the instant resentment of these aristocrats at any attempt by their beloved

SIR ROBERT PEEL

From the portrait by John Linnell
[*The National Portrait Gallery*]

Sovereign to act without their consent and also that genuine respect for the Law (even when it affected one of their own order), which must be counted to them as virtue.

Mr. Comyn was an Irish gentleman who had been tried and convicted of arson, then a capital offence. Friends intervened, and misrepresented the case to Prinny, who without consulting the Government wrote to the Lord-Lieutenant of Ireland (Duke of Northumberland) saying: " . . . I am desirous of exercising the best prerogative of the Crown—that of mercy—in saving his life, leaving to your Grace the commutation of punishment you may think fit". Immediately a volcano blew up in Prinny's face. Northumberland wrote to the Duke: "How could we punish the humble Whiteboy, if an offender of this kind be suffered to escape?" Peel fumed: " . . . the same post which brings me a letter from the Lord Lieutenant, proving this Comyn to have committed the triple offence of perjury, forgery and arson, and informing me that he has resolved that the law shall take its course, brings me one from Windsor, apprizing me that the King has actually signified his commands for the remission of the capital sentence. This is quite intolerable . . ." (Peel to Wellington, April 13, 1830.) The Duke was "much concerned" when he heard this, and announced ominously, "I am going to Windsor this morning".

It looked as if Prinny was in for one of those majestically respectful wiggings the Duke knew so well how to administer, but on reaching Windsor he found ample confirmation of rumours which had reached him that the King was ill and—"I did not talk to him about business of any kind". At sixty-seven even Prinny's excellent constitution was wrecked by a régime of huge meals, strong liquors, and no exercise. He had heart disease, dropsy, and gout, yet even in this his last illness continued to eat heartily—"his appetite is *too* good", the Duke reported. Then began the usual routine of daily health bulletins to the press, daily communications with the Heir Apparent (Clarence), and the usual whisperings and murmurings of political changes. The first bulletin was issued on April 15 (1830). Early on the morning of June 26 the King woke and, feeling faint, asked for sal volatile and water, which he found he was unable to drink. He sent immediately for his doctor, and pressed the hand of Sir Wathen Waller, exclaiming: "My boy, this is death!" And it was.

"Arthur" was one of the executors, and discovered that the King had for years carried a miniature of Mrs. Fitzherbert hung round his neck under his clothes. Later, going through the pockets of innumerable

suits of royal clothes, the Duke grimly collected a large pile of forgotten love letters, fans, and other trinkets expressing feminine
interest in His Majesty as a man. The new King, with his immense
family of illegitimate children and his colourless lawful Queen,
promised no such interest. The difficulty was that the Duke of
Clarence had for so long been a snubbed nonentity that this sudden
elevation to the throne over-excited him; and those nearest to him
were the least certain that he was altogether sane. He damned the pen
he had to use at his first Privy Council, excitedly rebuked the officers
who (rather excusably after 115 years of Georges) said "George"
instead of "William" when the oaths were administered, and to the
Duke's horror and manifest discomposure got up to make a speech.
Luckily this turned out to be "merely a little natural and pretty
funeral oration over Prinney", when the Duke had expected some
serious indiscretion. Equally unfounded were the Duke's more serious
apprehensions that the King would remember the snubs administered
to the Duke of Clarence and insist on putting Lord Grey into the
Ministry. In later years the Duke likened his relations with William
before and after his accession to those attributed by Shakespeare to
the Chief Justice and Henry V. Later in his reign this merry old
monarch celebrated New Year's Eve by dancing a country dance with a
"nautical, quizzical, clumsy, monstrous old Admiral", Lord Amelius
Beauclerk. The heights to which William IV's after-dinner speaking
could reach had long been suspected, but were only fully revealed
when he invited himself to dinner at Apsley House along with that
model couple, the King and Queen of Württemberg. Rising somewhat
unsteadily His Majesty broke forth into a panegyric on conjugal
fidelity, which convulsed the guests, since he was a bigamist, and his
host, the Duke, notorious for affairs with women. The King then
ordered the band to play "See the Conquering Hero Comes", and
delivered another panegyric on Marlborough and Wellington and how
they had beaten the French. Catching sight at that moment of the
French ambassador, His Majesty then went to extraordinary pains to
prove that in fighting Napoleon the British army had really been
winning victories for his friend and ally, the King of France. The
French ambassador kept bowing his acknowledgments of these
compliments whenever he caught the name of the King of France, for
with that exquisite tact of which only Foreign Offices are capable, the
French envoy did not understand a word of English. The eloquent
Billy wound up this extraordinary performance with fulsome expressions of confidence in the Duke's government. Those present

could not decide whether they were more delighted by the King's eloquence or by the various expressions on the Duke's face.

Meanwhile a series of events were in progress which were destined to drive the Duke from office, to make him for a time the most unpopular man in England, and to change the ancient Constitution. Oddly enough, this sequence began in Algeria where, under pretext of punishing the Bey for undoubted acts of piracy, the French had begun a set of military operations meant to give them possession of the country. The Duke was all in favour of hitting pirates hard, but not at all pleased by the idea of France expanding in the southern Mediterranean. His views were conveyed to the French Ministry, but since Charles X and Polignac knew that peace was the Duke's most cherished possession, they felt sure he would not go to war to protect Algeria, and so went right ahead with their plans. It was so certain that the Duke would not go to war unless compelled, that the general election of July 1830 (necessitated by the demise of the Crown) was fought on slavery and economy, and then on means rather than principles, for all agreed that economy was needed, and few opposed the abolition of slavery throughout the Empire. (Slavery was not in fact abolished until August 1833; and cost the British taxpayers twenty millions sterling in compensation to the slave-owners.) It is a very curious fact that the Whigs of the Macaulay type who were most urgent and (be it admitted) sincere for abolition of black slavery were precisely the people who in the name of *laissez-faire* most strenuously opposed any mitigation of the lot of white slaves in their own factories and in their own land.

The French aggression in Algeria was promptly punished. Polignac and Charles chose the very moment when their main strength, the army, was away in Africa to issue a series of decrees altering the electoral laws and abolishing the freedom of the press—in fact, attempting to restore the *ancien régime*. Paris rose and manned the barricades:

"The last account is of the 29th at night. There had been a terrible massacre in the streets; but it appears that the troops had had the worst of it. The drapeau tricolour was flying upon the Tuileries, and upon the Column in the Place Vendôme. La Fayette had taken command of the Garde Nationale. . . . Some of the troops of the line had gone over, according to the accounts of yesterday; but surrendered according to the accounts of this day. . . . The Guards were still fighting in the Rue St. Honoré." [Wellington to Peel, July 31, 1830.]

So little had Charles X understood the situation that when he was told "all is over", he thought the words meant that the attempted revolution had failed, not that it had succeeded and that nothing remained to him but ignominious flight. The Duke's 1818 prophecy about the Bourbons had come true; but he took no pride in that piece of foresight. On the contrary, he was depressed by this destruction of his handiwork. There were "bitter pills to swallow". Europe looked from Paris to London a little anxiously—would the conqueror of Waterloo accept this excellent pretext for another European war and more military triumphs? Metternich was quite ready, but after carefully re-reading the peace treaties the Duke came to the conclusion that he had no right to interfere and that the "ordonnances" of Charles X had put the French King hopelessly in the wrong. Nothing for it then but to swallow the bitter pills, and accept the new government:

> "If we don't quarrel with them they must set these matters to rights, or quarrel among themselves, or quarrel with us. Any one of these would be better for us, and for the world, than that we should at this moment quarrel with them."
> [Wellington to Lord Aberdeen, August 12, 1830.]

It is very strange that the Duke so misjudged events and feelings at home as apparently to believe that this sudden successful upsurge in France would have little or no influence in England. The elections had left him weaker in the Commons, and though Huskisson was killed in September in the railway accident, the Duke was no more friendly to the surviving Canningites, especially as Lord Grey was to be included in the Cabinet as the price of their support. Yet as late as October 10, 1830, the Duke was writing tranquilly to the Lord-Lieutenant of Ireland that "the harvest has I believe been good everywhere", "the people are satisfied", "the price of wool has risen" and "manufacturers and trade were never in a better state". To be sure, there was a "good deal of uneasiness" about the Continent, and "men's minds were unsettled" about such trifles as "Parliamentary Reform, Slavery, Tithes, Taxes &c". It is astounding that a sensible man could be so blind to what was brewing, for under the guidance of Macaulay's persuasive black-is-black-and-white-is-white eloquence, public opinion and the Whig opposition had suddenly seized upon the subject of Parliamentary Reform with astonishing eagerness. Like a flag or a good catchword, "Parliamentary Reform" became a symbol of things far beyond its obvious and practical meaning—it became the battle-cry of freedom for the distressed, the hopeful, the embittered, and the adventurous.

Parliament met on October 26 (1830) in a state of excitement contrasting sharply with the comparative apathy of the election.

The Duke and his supporters entirely misjudged the strength of this feeling and the extravagant hopes aroused by the various schemes of Parliamentary Reform. Many opponents of Reform were perfectly aware in their hearts that they only opposed it because it was contrary to their interests; and others, more honest if less intelligent, could only plead that though the existing system was indefensible in theory it "worked well enough in practice". One of the few persons who honestly believed the existing system was both theoretically and practically right and ought not to be changed was the Prime Minister, the Duke of Wellington. He can hardly be accused of inconsistency—in his maiden speech before the Irish House of Commons forty years earlier he had defended Catholic Emancipation and announced his opposition to Parliamentary Reform. The whole point, of course, was that Catholic gentlemen might sit in Parliament without the slightest threat to the power of the aristocracy, but a redistribution of seats to represent the people, even to the extent they had been represented from the Plantagenets to the Stuarts, would inevitably destroy the power of the nineteenth-century aristocrats. Why, it is often asked, did the Duke—so reasonable, so horse-sensical—refuse any and all of the very moderate Reform measures first put forward by Grey and Russell? It was a matter of principle. He saw that if he admitted there was a case for handing a few seats, even one seat, over to the new industrial cities, if he agreed to any alteration, he thereby admitted the principle that the existing system could be improved and should be altered along lines of greater popular representation. This, he held (and incidentally quite rightly) would inevitably lead in time to complete adult suffrage; which in turn he thought would overthrow the aristocracy, destroy the "unique balance" of the Constitution, and lead to the decline and fall of the British Empire.

That is why the Tories in the Commons threw out Russell's very moderate proposals in the autumn session of 1830; an action which caused intense public irritation. But the mine which blew up his administration, his party, and his class was in fact fired by the Duke himself. Answering an attack by Grey in the Lords, the Duke produced an extempore speech which roused the enormous Reform party throughout the country to frenzy. He said that he had never read or heard of any measure of Parliamentary Reform which would improve the existing system; that he was "fully convinced" the existing Legislature "answers all the good purposes of legislation" and was better than that in any other country; that "the system of representation" possessed "the full and entire confidence of the country"; that if he had to form a Legislature for any country, he would try to form one exactly like that existing in England although "the nature of man is incapable of reaching such excellence at once"! And he wound up with this memorable defiance:

"Under these circumstances, I am not prepared to bring forward any measure of the description alluded to by the noble Lord. And I am not only not prepared to bring forward any measure of this nature, but I will at once declare that, as far as I am concerned, as long as I hold any station in the government of the country, I shall always feel it my duty to resist such measures when proposed by others."

In the utterly injudicious and indeed unnecessary defiance of this statement appears the difference between a great leader of armies and a great Parliamentary leader. The Duke had read his Cæsar too closely and the history of his own country too carelessly if he thought a patrician could successfully defy the people who had overthrown the papal power in England, defied Elizabeth, executed Charles, thrown out James, and struggled against George III even to applauding the defeat of their own soldiers by the American patriots. In a matter of weeks, almost days, the whole country was in an uproar; there were nightly "seditious meetings" in the Rotunda at Blackfriars; and the Duke had to issue operation orders for the defence of Apsley House, dated November 9, 1830, and beginning:

"In all probability the windows on the park front of Apsley House will be broken between sunset and the hour at which the park gates are shut. . . ."

Servants with loaded muskets were to be stationed at every window and even in the Duchess's bath-room, but they were not to fire unless the gates were broken down or the crowd came over the railings.

The supreme humiliation came on the occasion of the annual Lord Mayor's banquet at the Guildhall, when the Cabinet was forced to admit that it was unsafe for the King to drive through the streets of his own capital, and therefore had to advise him not to attend. This was worse than scandalous, it was ridiculous. Richard Wellesley spoke of the decision contemptuously as "the boldest act of cowardice I have ever known"; and long afterwards the Duke admitted that the decision had cost him "more anxious consideration" than any other "crisis in my military or political life". He maintained that there had been a conspiracy "to cut the traces of the King's carriage at Ludgate Hill and seize his person as a hostage until the Reform Bill should be carried".

Such a situation could not be prolonged. On November 15 (1830) the Tories were defeated in the Commons on another issue—the Civil List; and next day the Government resigned. The Duke had talked himself out of power with a single speech; yet he still thought he could defeat Reform and flattered himself that resignation on another and minor issue was a masterly manœuvre which "prevented the discussion of Parliamentary Reform".

CHAPTER XXV

The Reform Bill

THE battle of the early Reform Bills—there were no less than three—lasted from November 1830 until June 1832, and was a notable example of political warfare at its most bitter and most intense; "a revolution by due course of law" as the Duke rightly said. It was also the Duke's last real political fight, and the most mortifying defeat a proud man could suffer. He began the battle by misunderstanding the situation and underestimating the power and passion of national feeling; he fought against the measure with injudicious obstinacy, and then, when it was too late, tried to form a Ministry to pass a modified Bill, only to be deserted by most of his old friends and party; finally, he permitted the Bill to pass just in time to avert civil war, though not sporadic acts of violence. It was doubtless owing to the rigid limits of mere common sense that he ever got into this the worst scrap of his career; but then it was common sense that eventually got him out of it, and again common sense which led him to recognize tacitly, if not openly, that he was not the man to be Prime Minister. Whatever his subsequent influence and position as an "elder statesman", his action in 1834 showed that he knew the battle of Reform had been the Waterloo in reverse of his political career.

On November 6, 1830, only ten days before his cabinet resigned, the Duke wrote a letter to Maurice Fitzgerald* in Ireland. Unfortunately Fitzgerald's letter to him seems to have been lost, but it is clear that he had written to warn his chief of the gathering storm and the danger to the Government in the poular sentiment over Parliamentary Reform. Clearly Fitzgerald had an uneasy feeling that something ought to be done about it, and for his pains received this frosty answer:

"I have not leisure to discuss Parliamentary Reform either in writing or in conversation. I confess that I doubt that it will be carried in Parliament.

"If it should be carried it must occasion a total change in the whole system of that society called the British Empire; and I don't see how I could be a party to such changes, entertaining the opinions that I do. . . ." [November 6, 1830.]

* He was the Knight of Kerry.

So far the letter is sheer miscalculation and party prejudice, but now mixed in with it comes that note of "straightforward simplicity" which so much attracted others besides Mr. Creevey:

"To tell you the truth I must add that I feel no strength excepting in my character for plain manly dealing. I could not pretend that I wished sincerely well to the measures, which I should not become merely a party but the principal in recommending."

There is something disarmingly pleasant in this frank admission, which is none the less effective for the awkward second sentence; the man is thinking of what he means and not at all of how he is saying it.

Here certainly is a first miscalculation, pardonable perhaps in one so far removed from common sources of opinion, but which should have been corrected by defeat in the House of Commons. Not at all. Here are some recollections of a conversation with the Duke, held between the dissolution in November 1830 and the re-convening of Parliament in February 1831, as set down by the Tory soldier-parson, Gleig:

"I don't see how these men are to carry on the government," the Duke said, "so as to maintain order at home or peace abroad. It's very well for Lord Grey to talk about standing out for reform, retrenchment, and non-intervention. Reform, as he calls it, he may or may not get; retrenchment I'll defy him to carry farther than we have done, unless he sacrifice the great institutions of the country; and as to non-intervention—with all the sympathies of his party enlisted on the side of democracy, that is in his case impossible. Mark my words; you'll see the Belgian insurrection taken up, and a French army in the Netherlands before many months are over; and then, if Austria, Russia and Prussia move, what is to save Europe from a renewal of scenes which no man who has once taken part in them would ever desire to witness again?"

The line of argument by which a change in British Parliamentary representation was to lead to a European war is not conspicuously strong, but interesting as showing how avoidance of war was still a ruling motive with the Duke, and also as showing that he still completely failed to understand the home political situation. Meanwhile, Lord Grey refused to take office without the King's consent to a Reform measure; and when Parliament met he appointed a committee to examine and report on that subject. The two most eminent members of this committee were Lord John Russell, a future Prime Minister; and Lord Durham, who was later responsible for a complete change in English colonial policy, laying the foundation for the present system of self-governing dominions.

This committee made some extraordinary discoveries. There was no uniform system of election, but at least four main groups: (1) nomination boroughs, the owners of which had the absolute right to appoint anyone they liked as members, and to sell this right for what it would fetch; (2) rotten boroughs, where the few privileged electors regularly sold their votes for a considerable fee, of which they proudly boasted; (3) boroughs with sufficient voters to make bribery difficult; and (4) boroughs with such a democratic electorate that it included "potwallopers", i.e. any one who could prove he cooked his food within the borough limits. The committee discovered such interesting facts as that one member represented a district which had long ago been engulfed by the sea; another spoke on behalf of a beautiful green field; and yet another had been unanimously elected by a picturesque ruined wall. Meanwhile large towns had no representatives at all, and had to be content with that strange substitute ingeniously labelled by Tory apologists, "virtual representation"—by which presumably was meant that since somebody sat in Parliament, all those who had no vote were "virtually" represented by someone they hadn't elected, could not petition, and could not reject!

All this information and the proposed new bill were kept very secret by the government of Lord Grey; and the Duke clearly had no hint of what was coming, while still strangely in the dark about the intentions and feelings of most of his countrymen. He had indeed begun to frighten himself—or at least was attempting to frighten his more naïve supporters—with that perennial bogy man of all generations of reactionaries, a conspiracy of "agitators" subsidized by foreigners:

> "I entertain no doubt that there exists a formidable conspiracy. But as yet I don't believe that we have got a trace of it. . . .
>
> "I am inclined to think that the operations of the conspirators in this country are conducted by Englishmen. But that the original focus is at Paris.
>
> "We have in this country unfortunately a very numerous class of men, well educated, who have no means of subsistence, and who have no employment. These are the gentlemen who go about in gigs.
>
> "You will ask how are these men subsisted? How are the gigs &c., paid for? I answer that I know that the *Société Propagande* at Paris had at its command very large means from subscriptions all over Europe. . . ."

If "the men who go about in gigs" were intended for Cobbett and his "Rural Rides", it was an extremely bad shot. A couple of black eyes would most likely have been the only return to any propagandizing Frenchman who had tried to buy Cobbett's pen.

On March 1, 1831, Lord John Russell introduced the first Reform Bill in one of the great speeches of his career. The House listened, at first with mild interest, then with amazement, then with delight on one side and noisy fury on the other—this was no mere tinkering, but a comprehensive change in the Constitution, abolishing scores of seats and re-allotting them to the new industrial towns. Even the Bill's most ardent well-wishers scarcely believed it could pass, and as Russell read the lists of seats to be forfeited and re-allotted he was constantly interrupted by Tory jeers and insults. Those "sober wise men" who unfortunately are always with us described the Bill as "Utopian". The debate lasted three weeks. On March 14 (1831) the Duke wrote that "notwithstanding the cry in the newspapers, the well-judging people in the country, as well as in London, are against the measure". His advice was that the Tories should divide against the second reading, which they duly did on March 21, with this interesting result: for the Bill, 302, against it, 301; majority, 1. The Tories were filled with incredulous horror and dismay and rage. Macaulay, who sat in that Parliament and indeed made a brilliant speech on this very Bill, has described the looks of his political enemies at this dramatic moment, in a great purple passage—Herries looking like Judas, Twiss with "the face of the damned", and Robert Peel with fallen jaw. In an age like our own, when man has been so prodigal of vast butcheries, appalling destructions, unlimited confusions, we may well envy the destiny of men who could derive so much excitement, emotion, and virtuous dismay from such innocent occurrences.

The drama of the Reform Bill was, however, very far from exhausted by this exciting division. In April the Government was defeated on a minor issue, and cleverly took advantage of the position to persuade the King to dissolve Parliament; which of course meant a general election. In spite of the huge number of boroughs controlled by wealthy Tories, Grey and his friends knew that public excitement would give them a majority, and the Tories knew it also. Therefore, although the decision to dissolve had been kept secret, the Tories were actually moving an address against dissolution in the upper House when the roar of ceremonial guns announced that the King was coming down to dissolve Parliament. Bedlam broke out in both Houses, and the Speaker and the Lord Chancellor were unable to control their members. Every man was on his feet shouting and gesticulating, angry Tory peers shaking their fists under the noses of Whig Dukes, while, in the Commons, Peel was raving, Burdett stamping and throwing his arms about, and Hardinge bawling that the next guns to fire "will be shotted and take off your heads!" The Whigs had dished the Tories again; and they knew it.

That night huge mobs swarmed along London's streets, smashing the windows of any house which had not put out illuminations for Reform. One of the biggest crowds swept down Piccadilly and swirled round Apsley House, which stood aloof in darkness and silence. There was a terrific yell, and then showers of stones in an instant smashed every window of the house and fell into the rooms, damaging furniture and even some of the pictures captured from Joseph at Vittoria. Still the mansion remained dark and silent. Curiously enough, the only great personage who had been absent from Parliament that day was the former Prime Minister, the one great man in London who did not know what had happened was the Duke of Wellington. As the stones crashed into his house he was sitting alone by the body of his dead wife.

It is true that their romance, such as it was, had long been a burned-out ash, that she had exasperated him with her gush, her hero-worship, her financial incompetence, her myopia, her timid inability to play the part of Duchess of Wellington; true that he had long since gone his own way about the world and that that world knew he had been consistently unfaithful to her. But men are odd in their ways—after all, she was his wife and the mother of his children, and, as she lay there dying, he knew he was going to miss her. Perhaps it came into his mind that he had been wrong when he said so bitterly that many women had been attracted to him by his fame and the excitement of his life, but that none had ever loved him. Hadn't his wife loved him? At any rate she died happy and reconciled, for a little before her death she had discovered that her wonderful Duke still wore on his arm concealed by his sleeve a "circlet" she had fastened there many years before at their betrothal.

Meanwhile the battle of the Reform Bill continued in the leisurely fashion of those days, the election taking place in June 1831 and giving the Whigs a majority of about one hundred. This victory furnished the Tory opposition to Reform with the best argument they had yet found—if the present system can so clearly decide against us, they asked, where is the necessity for Reform? By way of answer, the Whigs introduced another Bill, and the Duke reflected pessimistically over the late dissolution:

"It appears to me that we are in a bad way. I don't believe that the King of England has taken a step so fatal to his monarchy since the day that Charles I passed the Act to deprive himself of the power of proroguing or dissolving the Long Parliament, as William IV did on the 22nd of April last.

". . . The dismay of all reasonable men upon what is going on is beyond description. It is impossible that there should not be reaction. . . ." [Letter to Duke of Buckingham, May 21, 1831.]

In the summer the second Bill passed the Commons by a large majority; but the Lords threw it out by a majority of 41. Then came "the reaction", but not exactly of the kind the Duke had anticipated. There were riots all over England. In Bristol somebody knocked down the Tory candidate, and the exhilarated mob then set fire to the town hall and the city jail. The Duke refused to see these actions as anything but sporadic and the work of imaginary agitators; yet he was taking up a new attitude—perhaps there ought to be a little bit of Reform, not enough to harm the great aristocratic oligarchy, but enough to confuse and hold off the enemy:

"It is doubtless true that many still continue to consider reform necessary, and I confess that I don't see how we can escape reform in some shape or other if the King should live. In this view of the case, and supposing that the moderate class can get the upper hand, the rejection of the bill will have a good effect; it gives us time, at all events."

Parliament was prorogued until December; and the mob again smashed the Duke's windows. Early in November he planned to go to Walmer Castle; and received news from Gleig that there was a plot among some alleged desperadoes of Deal to assassinate him on a lonely part of the turnpike. Here the Duke was in his element. He immediately replied:

"It is my duty to go to Walmer and to Dover, and I am not to be prevented from doing so either by threats of insult or injury. . . . I shall therefore set off to-morrow morning; and I hope to arrive early in the day. I suspect that those who will attack me on the road will come rather the worst out of the contest, if there should be one."

And to the Deputy-Governor of Dover Castle:

"In respect to insults to me, those who wish to insult me are perfectly welcome. I defend myself if they attempt injury. . . . I shall certainly attend at Dover on Wednesday and Thursday. The magistrates of the town have the power, and they know best how to protect the Lord Warden from insult and injury."

Among the guests at Walmer Castle at this time were Croker, Stanhope, and Gleig, so that we suddenly get several glimpses of the Duke's ordinary life and doings. He attended (for instance) the christening of Gleig's child, inspected a regiment of yeomanry collected by his old enemy Lord Winchilsea, went to Dover to carry out his duty as Lord Warden, and got up at six every morning to write letters to the political allies who pestered him for and with advice by every post:

"You see how they come about me," he said irritably to Gleig. "They were never satisfied till they got rid of me as a minister; and now they want me to put my neck in the halter for them."

He even wrote letters (and memoranda for the Ministry, since he was still *nimmukwallah* and must therefore help even the bitterest political enemies in whatever concerned the King's service) with his guests laughing and chattering about him in the same room. He also talked a good deal, not apparently very much about the present and the distasteful topic of Reform, but about the great days of the war—with Alava who had shared the ardours and endurances of the campaigns, with Gleig who had been in the Pyrenees as a very youthful subaltern, with Croker who thought he knew everything and seemed to question the Duke on his battles with a view to catching him in error, and especially with Lord Stanhope, a young man agog to hear tales of the brave days of old from the hero of them. One contemporary event they did discuss with some attention was cholera, which had crossed Europe from the Near East and had finally broken out in London:

"The only thing I am afraid of is fear," said the Duke. "I told Lord Grey at Windsor that I was quite sure if three or four hundred *Notables* were to leave London for fear of it, they would be followed by three or four hundred thousand, and that then this country would be plunged into greater confusion than had been known for hundreds of years."

The battle of the (now third) Reform Bill began again in December 1831 with a crescendo of national frenzy which now seems inexplicable and, to put it mildly, unintelligent. Matthew Arnold has pungently criticized his countrymen for their faith in the efficacy—the almost sacrosanct omnipotence—of political machinery. The excitement about the Reform Bill may have been in Arnold's mind when he made that criticism. Certainly, the most extravagant hopes were circulating in 1831–1832 about the new epoch which was to follow the passage of "the Bill". Croker found a sort of hunger-march of working men begging their way to London "to carry the Bill, which would put down machinery and enable poor men to earn a living". Others, who ought to have known better, were certain that if only "the Bill" were passed, there would be a new age of peace and prosperity, the ancient

"Saxon constitution" (whatever that may have been) would be restored, the national debt would be instantly paid off, and there would henceforth be neither political parties nor political corruption. A continuation of the steady decline in political corruption is all that followed the Bill, though it might be argued that even this was not the direct result of the Bill but of other and older national changes which went unrecorded by Act of Parliament.*

What exactly was the change made by this third and much fought-over Reform Bill which, after six months of vicissitudes, finally became law in June 1832? In the first place, it disfranchised no less than 143 seats in the House of Commons, taking 30 from the rotten boroughs, 111 from the nomination boroughs, and one each from the constituencies of Weymouth and Melcombe Regis. Twenty-two large towns, Birmingham, Leeds, Manchester, *et cetera*, received 44 of these seats; 21 were allotted to the same number of fair-sized towns which hitherto had been compelled to put up with "virtual representation" (i.e. no representation at all); and the remaining seats were given to the counties. There was also an extension on franchise, giving the vote to 40-shilling leaseholders and copyholders as well as freeholders and (in the counties) to tenants paying £50 a year rent. If Croker was right in his estimate of about 240 seats controlled by the peers, there still remained about one hundred boroughs not covered by this Bill, which was supposed to be so revolutionary. Possibly the extension of franchise made bribery even in those seats too expensive and difficult, though it may merely have given rise to that perfect type of voter who "took a guinea from each side and then voted according to his conscience".

Once more the Bill passed the Commons on its second reading, and actually squeezed through the Lords with a majority of 9; but it was certain in the spring of 1832 that the Lords would again throw it out in committee. What was to be done? There was one last desperate remedy, namely, to create enough new peers (in this case about sixty) to pass the Bill; but the opposition to this measure was so considerable that Lord Grey and many of his colleagues hesitated. The long strain of the political battle was telling on several of them—Lord Brougham, for instance, was taken ill, and it was reported that Lord Althorp was so worried he was afraid he might commit suicide! However, when the Lords at last threw out the Bill early in May, the Grey Ministry offered the King a choice of making the new peers or accepting their

* See Bagehot's *The English Constitution* for handsome tributes to the Duke and Peel in ridding politics of corruption. Bagehot was a Liberal.

resignations. He chose the latter, and sent for the Duke to form a Government, with the idea that the Tories under his leadership might pass some sort of a Reform Bill and write into it "the principle of conservatism". As the Duke wrote to Gleig:

> "Is it true that we cannot do any good by mending the bill? The metropolitan representation is ruin. We may, possibly we shall, get rid of that. The democracy has, by the bill, a positive gain of sixty-four members. We may reduce those members very considerably. We may improve Schedules A and B. We may improve the £10 franchise. All this would be important if the measure is to be carried into execution." [Duke to Gleig, May 2, 1832.]

Now it was possible for the Duke to turn this political back somersault and to propose the introduction of a "conservative" Reform Bill after he had declared emphatically that no Reform was needed and that he would oppose all Reform—it was possible because he still claimed that he was solely the King's servant and therefore outside any political party and hard-and-fast political allegiance. This was the argument by which he had persuaded the Tories to pass the relief Bill for Roman Catholics; but this time it didn't work. Apart from two Generals, Murray and Hardinge, and a couple of nonentities, every one in the Tory party from Peel to Croker absolutely refused to have anything to do with such unparliamentary behaviour. They couldn't understand the Duke and he couldn't understand them. He judged the situation more as a General than as a politician—if the army was in a tight spot, between Talavera and the Portuguese frontier for example, you retreated promptly and saved every man and gun you could. Why not retreat from superior Whig forces in Parliament, and save as many seats as possible, keep the franchise from being too widely extended? This sort of common sense was wholly outside the views and ethics of the political men, who for lack perhaps of other virtues were compelled to make a virtue of consistency. As one of them was to write:

> "The future historian of the country will be perplexed to ascertain what was the distinct object which the Duke of Wellington proposed to himself in the political manœuvres of May 1832. It was known that the passing of the Reform Bill was a condition absolute with the King*; it was unquestionable, that the first general election under the new law must ignominiously expel the Anti-Reform Ministry from power; who would then resume their seats on the Opposition benches in both Houses with the loss not only of their boroughs, but of that reputation for political consistency, which might have been some compensation for the parliamentary influence of which they had been deprived.

* This is false, the King wanted "a" not "the" Reform Bill.

It is difficult to recognise in this premature effort of the Anti-Reform leader to thrust himself again into the conduct of public affairs, any indication of the prescient judgment which might have been expected from such a quarter. It savoured rather of restlessness than of energy; and, while it proved in its progress not only an ignorance on his part of the public mind, but of the feelings of his own party, it terminated under circumstances which were humiliating to the Crown, and painfully significant of the future position of the House of Lords in the new constitutional scheme." [Coningsby, by the Rt. Hon. Benjamin Disraeli.]

The attempt to make a strategic political retreat failed miserably; indeed it ended in a surrender, with the Duke having to confess to the King that he could not form a Government, and in his giving his promise to keep enough peers away from the House for the Bill to pass without further creations. This may have been "humiliating" for the Duke, but how can it have been so for the King?—since all he wanted to avoid was the necessity for making fifty or sixty new peers, and avoiding this unpleasant act was the net result to the King of the Duke's "manœuvres". The Duke put his own situation in a nutshell when he wrote to another Tory peer: "It is quite hopeless to obtain any unanimous opinion from our friends upon Parliamentary Reform". Since they wouldn't collaborate with him in putting through a modified Bill, they got the whole Bill and nothing but the Bill; which received the royal assent on June 7 (1832). The opposition benches in the House of Lords were empty. The Bill had passed; and the hero of the Peninsular War and of Waterloo was the most unpopular man in England.

He soon had an opportunity of learning this fact beyond any possible mistake through an episode which he never forgot nor forgave, any more than the smashing of his windows while his wife lay dead in the house. The universal excitement over "the Bill" did not die away immediately but was translated into uproarious rejoicing among the "lower orders", and even school children were seen parading with placards: "The Reform Bill has passed". The bitter resentment and anger generated by opposition to the Bill was still fiercely burning eleven days after its passage—June 18, 1832, seventeenth anniversary of Waterloo. On the evening of each Waterloo Day the Duke's custom was to give a great dinner at Apsley House to some of the officers who had been present, but otherwise he did not treat the day as a holiday. On this particular anniversary he had official business at the Tower of London, to be followed by an interview with the Solicitor to the Treasury in Lincoln's Inn, where he had appointed a meeting with Lord Eliot and Lord Granville Somerset.

L

The Duke set out with his unvarying punctuality, riding a horse and accompanied by a mounted groom. He dispatched his business at the Tower, and had just started back when he was recognized and almost instantly surrounded by an angry and rancorous mob. Attracted by the hoots and threats, members of the City police attempted a rescue but were swept aside; one man even seized the Duke's bridle, but was forced away by the groom. The Duke refused to put his horse to a gallop, and continued on his way at a walk, looking steadily to his front and paying not the slightest attention to the screaming and murderous throng. Luckily for him, passers-by came to the aid of the reinforced police; and a man driving a phaeton (or tilbury) kept close behind, so that the crowd could not press too heavily on the Duke.

With this singular escort for a Field-Marshal, he arrived at Lincoln's Inn, transacted his business, and then started home, guarded by Lincoln's Inn lawyers. A zealous solicitor seized a "bawling butcher" with one hand and knocked him down with the other, to the intense gratification of the assembled citizens. A *cortège* was then formed, with (the future) Lord St. Leonards walking in front of the Duke's horse, a peer at each stirrup, and the groom behind. Policemen came in to swell the little force, but St. Leonards forbade them to draw their truncheons and sent a body of them on ahead to occupy a place where street repairs were in progress and therefore plenty of stones available for mob ammunition. In this manner they proceeded as far as St. James's Palace, and "there being only a few stragglers left, the Duke and his companions shook hands" with their rescuers and trotted off to Apsley House. The only sign given by the Duke on this five-mile ordeal that he was not a "cast-metal man" (as Carlyle melodramatically called him) was when he touched his hat to a man named Martin Tupper who was loudly shouting: "Waterloo! Waterloo!"

The next day at the Ascot race-meeting a man called Collins threw a stone at King Billy with such accurate aim or good luck that he hit that startled monarch on the head. This was particularly hard upon William since he had been in favour of Reform all along, and had gone through a great deal of trouble and annoyance to get the Bill passed.

Such episodes confirmed the Duke in a settled pessimism of belief that all was over with England except the burial.

"The government of England is destroyed. A Parliament will be returned by means of which no set of men whatever will be able to conduct the administration of affairs and to protect the lives and properties of the King's subjects."

He thought that "if the Political Unions are not put down they must govern the country", as the Jacobin Club had governed France during the first Revolution. On the other hand he was able to report:

"I think that I have got the better of the mobs in London by walking about the town very quietly, notwithstanding their insults and outrages." [Letter to Bishop of Oxford, August 1832.]

But he agreed that he had better not visit Canterbury for the present, since the ill-affected of that cathedral town had just turned out in force to hoot and stone His Grace the Archbishop, Primate of all England. Still, the Duke had not lost his sardonic humour. During the period just before the election of the first Reformed Parliament, Croker sent the Duke a wordy four-page letter detailing at great length all the weighty and cogent reasons why he, the said Croker, would never again condescend to stand as a candidate for Parliament. In reply he received this masterly snub:

"London, Aug. 14th, 1832
"My dear Croker,
"I have received your letter. I am very sorry that you do not intend again to be elected to serve in Parliament. I cannot conceive for what reason.
"Ever yours most sincerely,
"Wellington"

The long-range result of the Reform Act and its successors was to transform England from an oligarchy of aristocrats into a democracy administered by aristocrats; and though the tendency of the late nineteenth and the twentieth centuries was more and more to thrust out the aristocracy from executive and administrative control, the nation even now instinctively turns to the descendants of its old leaders in times of crisis. The Duke in 1832 thought the process of change to democracy would be much quicker than it proved to be; and was correspondingly depressed. But he was not a defeatist like Croker, and he was utterly free from Croker's self-centred vanity and self-importance which made him affect to disdain a seat in a democratically elected Parliament and to imply that his absence would be felt as a snub. This sort of thing seemed to the Duke ridiculous— hence his snub to the omniscient Croker. Certainly the Duke disliked the situation. "The bill is now the law of the land", he said, "and has effected the greatest revolution that ever occurred without bloodshed in any country." But there was no sense in taking up a position of perpetual boycott, as Croker proposed and practised. "As good citizens and loyal subjects," the Duke continued, "we must conform ourselves" and "in the meanwhile it is our duty . . . to render the fall of our great institutions so gradual that it shall do as little damage as possible".

When the first Reform Parliament met in 1833 the Duke went down to have a look at the monsters, and added a new slang phrase to the language by reporting that he had never seen so many "shocking bad hats" in his life. Here he was undoubtedly prejudiced, for in fact the first Reform Parliament contained a greater number of distinguished men than its predecessors. The hats may have been shabbier, but the heads inside them were better. But if the Revolution which brought them into power had been "bloodless", people began to realize that this moderation was partly due to the Duke and his common sense. He had fought a good political fight, but if he had chosen to make the fight a last-ditch affair, as his warmer followers wished, there could easily have been a new civil war. Fair play at least demanded that this should be recognized, and now that the Duke seemed to be taking leave of party politics and devoting himself to the restraint of the Tory majority in the Lords, people began to forget the unsuccessful Prime Minister and to remember once more the victorious General of Salamanca, Vittoria, Toulouse, and Waterloo. Mobs ceased to follow him, the hooting died away, and, as in the great days just after the war, men took off their hats as the Duke went by, and a little ashamed, a little apologetically, muttered something about God bless him. Even in the hunting field he discovered that, as he put it, he was "getting up in the market", men making way for him, opening gates, and so on. They "seemed anxious to be kind", he thought. But the most curious step upwards from the depths of unpopularity on the way to national apotheosis came, as was fitting, from the home of lost causes, the city of dreaming spires, Oxford, which appointed a flattered but embarrassed Duke its Chancellor. He pointed out that he "knew less Latin and Greek than a boy in the remove at Eton", which was putting it mildly; but then Oxford was not electing him Chancellor because of his scholarship. Nor could the Oxonians have been greatly influenced by the first volumes of his dispatches,* interesting as they are, which Colonel Gurwood was beginning to publish.

Yet there was at least one eminent person who demonstrated his opposition to the move. Archbishop Whately stormed into the office of the Lord-Lieutenant of Ireland (who happened to be the Duke's elder brother, Richard) and greatly startled that dignified gentleman by requesting to be made a cornet of dragoons. Asked why, the reverend prelate replied with much scorn that he had as good a right to

* See Appendix.

command cavalrymen as the Lord-Lieutenant's brother had to be Chancellor of Oxford University. Nevertheless, in June (1834) the Duke went up to Oxford to be installed, accompanied by some of his friends, including Croker who complained that the Duke was "a sad hand at popularity hunting". What seems to have made the greatest impression on the Duke was the truculent energy of the undergraduates:

"I perfectly understand now," the Duke reported later, "how revolutions are got up in such places as the École Militaire in Paris, and in Warsaw."
"Boisterous, were they?"
"Boisterous! You never saw anything like it in your life. Let those boys loose in the state in which I saw them, and give them a political object to carry, and they would revolutionise any nation under the sun."

This was naturally very enjoyable, or at least as enjoyable as excessive animal spirits in other people can be; but the drawback to the whole entertainment was that the Duke had to begin the proceedings at the Sheldonian by making a speech in Latin.

"How did you manage, Duke?" he was asked.
"Well, any speech is difficult, but a Latin one was impossible; so in this dilemma I applied to my physician, as most likely, from his prescriptions,* to know Latin, and he made me a speech, which answered very well. I believe it was a very good speech, but I did not know much of the matter."

All that has been recorded of this Latin speech is that in reading it the Duke gave wrong quantities to "Jacŏbus" and "Carŏlus", having perhaps over-rehearsed these nice points. But that did not matter in the least so far as the enthusiasm of his audience went. On his entering the Sheldonian there was a "burst of applause" which lasted for ten minutes, the "shouts of the men" and "even the voices of the women" making a tremendous din amid the waving of handkerchiefs. Later in the proceedings (after everyone had recovered from the shock of Jacŏbus and Carŏlus) an undergraduate named Arnold (not Matthew who was then only twelve) read a poem, which was listened to with that semi-silent boredom an audience always devotes to the recital of poetry and sermons. Suddenly the poet declaimed these lines:

"Till on that plain, where last the Eagle soared,
War's mightier master wielded Britain's sword,
And the wild soul the world could scarce subdue,
Bowed to thy genius, Chief of Waterloo."

* Most unfair of the Duke. Sir Henry Halford was a fine scholar, with a wide reputation as a Latin poet.

Electrified by these none too perfect lines, or perhaps merely enchanted by the opportunity to break the tedium of sitting still, the whole audience started to their feet and began cheering:

"At the word [Waterloo] began a scene of enthusiasm such as I never saw; some people seemed to me to go out of their senses—literally to go mad. The whole assembly started up, and the ladies and the grave semi-circle of doctors became as much excited as the boys in the gallery and the men in the pit. Such peals of shouts I never heard; such waving of hats, handkerchiefs, and caps, I never saw; such extravagant clapping and stamping, so that at last the air became clouded with dust. During all this the Duke sat like a statue; at last he took some notice, took off his cap lightly, and pointed to the reciter to go on; but this only increased the enthusiasm, and at last it ended only from the mere exhaustion of animal powers."

It was in fact a "tremendous ovation", and none the less flattering for being wholly spontaneous. Perhaps we should not inquire too closely into the motives of the demonstrators; for since Oxford was the very omphalos of High Church Toryism the demonstration might have been directed less to praise of their fallen champion than to defiance of the wicked Whigs, who even at that moment were busily engaged in such nefarious practices as the abolition of black slavery and attempts to regulate white slavery by a first timid Factory Act. Even Oxford, however, cheered the Duke as the victor at Waterloo and not as the last-ditch opposer of Parliamentary Reform; though in the Oxford of 1834 that would certainly not have been held to his discredit.

The autumn of 1834 had in store an even greater compliment, and marked a greater progress towards that universal, almost sentimental, approbation the Duke was beginning to deserve so richly through advancing age and harmlessness. The first Reform Parliament was not doing so well politically as might have been imagined from its immense majority. That very majority was a drawback, since a party so large had no fear of the Opposition and therefore was the less likely to restrain expressions of the internal dissensions inevitable in any political party, but especially in a large new one. Already Lord Grey had resigned as Prime Minister in a Cabinet re-shuffle, and his place had been taken by Lord Melbourne—an aristocrat of airy and irresponsible habits whose terror as a revolutionary force is not apparent at this distance of time. Lord Althorp, pillar of the Whigs in the Commons, was suddenly removed to the Lords by the death of his father; and at the same time Billy the King was much offended by a speaking tour of Scotland undertaken by Lord Chancellor Brougham, a man of tumultuous but tactless energy, of whom it was said that "if he were a horse, nobody would buy him". Brougham's loud speaking about himself, the King, and the Ministry greatly offended William, who said the Chancellor was a mountebank an "itinerant mountebank"; and dismissed the Ministry on the first available pretext. The dismissed Lord Melbourne carried with him a letter from the King for the Duke of Wellington.

Nobody had expected this piece of petulant self-assertion from Billy the King; for the act though constitutionally legal was not even reasonable. Peel, whose hobby was the paintings of the old masters, had gone off on the grand tour of Italy; and the Duke was just starting on his favourite intellectual pursuit of fox-hunting when the King's letter reached him at 6 a.m. "Here's a go for you," Mr. Creevey noted, "the Whigs turned out and Wellington sent for!" His Grace did not approve of His Majesty's hasty action, and even ventured to drop a hint to that effect. Moreover, he respectfully but positively refused to act as Prime Minister. The difficulties of any Government, he said, would be in the Commons, and therefore "I earnestly recommended to His Majesty to choose a Minister in the House of Commons". In other words, "send for Peel". But there existed no telegraph system and no European railway system in 1834; so a King's Messenger was dispatched to find the absent one, and as he bumped laboriously over frozen roads in a post-chaise, the Duke entered on what he afterwards called his "Dictatorship". In sober fact he went to the Home Office, and was duly sworn in as First Lord of the Treasury, Secretary for Foreign Affairs, War and the Colonies. Mr. Creevey thundered against the rule of "this soldier", and a good-humoured opposition caricaturist produced this version of the Cabinet:

First Lord of the Treasury	Duke of Wellington
Home Secretary	Duke of Vittoria
Foreign Secretary	Prince of Waterloo
War and Colonies	Duke of Ciudad Rodrigo
Lord Privy Seal	Count Vimiera
First Lord of the Admiralty	Baron Douro
Chancellor of the Exchequer	Arthur Wellesley
Lord High Chancellor	Viscount Wellington

But on the whole the nation was half amused, half touched by this curious situation, and by the obvious unselfishness and public spirit of the Duke's attitude in standing aside for Peel and offering to serve under him. Nor was this temporary one-man Government inefficient.

Fixing his headquarters at the Home Office but "occasionally roving over the rest", he not only dealt with the whole business of the country but even contrived to clear up arrears left by the outgoing Ministers; an easygoing set, one would imagine, since the premier, Melbourne, was too indolent even to inform his colleagues that they were going out and left them to discover this pleasing fact in the morning newspapers. Meanwhile, a strange deep peace fell upon the country, and elderly ladies who had been incessantly terrified by horrid prophecies of Whig atrocities once more breathed and slept tranquilly, praying ardently for divine support of the great and good Duke and petitioning that his solid reign might last.

It was not to be. Within three weeks Sir Robert turned up from Italy, convinced that the King had made a blunder and that no good could come of the manœuvre. Nevertheless he consented to take office, and put the Duke in the Foreign Office, which he gravely scandalized by introducing habits of strict punctuality and orderly dispatch of business. A dazed French ambassador reported that "thirty minutes with him suffice to transact what can never be accomplished in as many hours with our wavering ministers of France". But the Tories were in a minority in the House of Commons and they lost the general election. Somebody asked the Duke if anxiety about this did not keep him awake at night, and received the memorable reply: "No. I don't like lying awake; it does no good. I make a point never to lie awake." Peel put up a gallant but hopeless struggle in the Commons, where the Whigs were able to defeat him whenever they chose; and they chose pretty frequently. William tried very hard to persuade Peel to remain in office, threatening abdication if he went; but it was obviously ridiculous if not unconstitutional for a Government to attempt to carry on with a perpetual minority in the House of Commons. In April 1835, Peel resigned, and with him went of course the Duke, whose days as Cabinet Minister seemed over. He took up the part of the Nestor of the Lords, soothing fretful land-owners into accepting the inevitable and passing the not very tremendous reforms introduced by Melbourne, whose favourite remark to reformers was: "Why can't you leave it alone?" and who once scandalized his Cabinet by remarking: "It doesn't much matter what we say, so long as we all say the same thing."

The Duke was well out of it. Like Oxford, the nation at large began to remember what he had done on the battle-field and to forget his not altogether happy career as a politician. Even Cambridge received him with enthusiasm, and now as he went about in the last year or two of William's reign the cheers of twenty years before greeted him everywhere.

"I think," the Duke said to Greville, "I think the country is on its legs again."

As for Sir Robert Peel—his patient endurance of a long series of snubs from a hostile House had for some reason convinced what are known as "sober men" of his political genius. In place of the obsolete Duke, Sir Robert quietly bloomed as the new leader of a supposedly regenerated Tory party which hopefully thought to conceal its past by calling itself Conservative. "Sir Robert Peel," says Bagehot, had "the powers of a first-rate man and the creed of a second-rate man. From a certain peculiarity of intellect and fortune, he was never in advance of his time. Of almost all the great measures with which his name is associated, he attained great eminence as an opponent before he attained even greater eminence as their advocate."

CHAPTER XXVI

Last Years

" . . . *we wax old,*
All we wax old and wither like a leaf."

IT was June 18, 1837, the twenty-second anniversary of Waterloo;
and William IV lay dying. The Archbishop of Canterbury had been
praying at his bedside; and the King, remembering what day it was,
hoped wistfully that he might at least live through the anniversary of
the day so glorious to England. The echoes of the Waterloo can-
nonades lived on, it seemed, with peculiar vividness in the hearts and
memories of the Duke's countrymen—partly no doubt from national
vanity but partly because they had ended the long affliction of a more
than twenty years' war. Even the King on his death-bed remembered
it. Then the dying man's thoughts turned to his successor, and he said
it would be a good thing for the sailors to have a beautiful young
Queen to fight for. Unfortunately the Duke had never been able to
return King William's esteem, as is showed by a letter written in the
spring of 1834, which contains the following acid judgment:

" . . . the British public know very little of what our Army is, and of the
difficulty of commanding to their satisfaction one of theirs. Many of them
think it is very like a fleet. *One of these is our most gracious Sovereign.*" [Italics
are author's. Letter to Ellesmere, May 11, 1834.]

Such might almost have stood as the epitaph on poor King William
who had meant well, but as to intelligence—"That's quite another
thing, that's quite another thing!" But what of his eighteen-year-old
successor, who had been roused from her bed in the summer dawn to
learn from the Archbishop and the kneeling Chamberlain that she was
no longer merely Princess Alexandrina Victoria, but Queen of
England? Not many had ever seen her, and few indeed knew anything
of her, for she had been bred with simple strictness and in almost
complete seclusion. Mr. Creevey had once caught a glimpse of her at
the opera when she was twelve, and thought she looked "a very nice
little girl indeed". Introduced to her reigning uncle, Prinny, she had
been greeted with a gruff: "Give me your little paw!" and when
asked by the same Illustrious Personage the name of her favourite

322

tune, had replied with displeasingly fulsome tact: "God Save the King". Apart from such trifling shreds of social gossip, the new Queen was unknown except to her mother and half-sister, her uncle Leopold of Belgium, her governess Lehzen, and a handful of attendants. There was considerable curiosity to find out what she was, not only among that vast public which in the whole of its life catches only a few distant glimpses of the sovereign, but also and especially among those whose rank and position, ambition and duty, would bring them frequently into her presence.

The story has been often told of the sudden enthusiasm created by the little Queen's first appearance before her Council, her extraordinary grace and dignity in spite of round red cheeks and rounder blue eyes, her composure as she read her message in a clear musical voice, so that even "the savage Croker" was tamed, and the Duke swore he could not have asked more of her if she had been his own daughter. And the impression was strengthened when the Council came to do homage. The contrast between this fresh young girl and the tottering remnants of the cohort of her apoplectic uncles was indeed striking, and scarcely a man among all the notables present but rejoiced that the long reign of these "ridiculous and disreputable old men" was over. These cynical grey-haired men seemed to think they had acquired a Walter Scott heroine as their nominal ruler; and engravings of the period show the Queen as a sylph-like creature of unrealistic prettiness managing a large horse like another Diana Vernon. Mr. Creevey contrived to see her with less poetic eyes:

"A more homely little being you never beheld, when she is at her ease, and she is evidently dying to be always more so. She laughs in real earnest, opening her mouth as wide as it can go, showing not very pretty gums. She eats quite as heartily as she laughs. I think I may say she gobbles. She blushes and laughs every instant in so natural a way as to disarm anybody. Her voice is perfect."

However much the Duke might approve of her, a young Queen exactly fifty years his junior could not fail to remind him that age was coming on. At dinner one day he started a new topic for him by speaking of the different ideas people had of what constituted "age", mentioning some schoolboys who had been to dine with him and how they had talked of somebody as "an old man", which said old man the Duke discovered to be exactly twenty. One Saturday in November 1838 he had a fall in the hunting field. With their usual accuracy the newspapers reported that the accident had happened on Sunday, and read him an impertinent lecture on the wickedness and punishment of

Sabbath-breaking. Increasing deafness more and more cut him off from the pleasures of talk and of music, though he still attended the concerts of Ancient Music and brought musicians down to Walmer to entertain his guests. As a woman's heart sinks when for the first time some well-intentioned blunderer remarks how young she looks or, if a stranger, fatuously pretends to mistake her daughter for her sister; so the Duke's intimates felt a pang as he began to boast that he could hunt and shoot and walk as well as twenty years before. He began for the first time to be querulous about the enormous correspondence he invited and prolonged by his own punctilious care in answering, and about the now established custom of consulting him officially on all topics of public interest or worry, especially worry. To this period of his life belongs a curious habit of referring to himself in conversation and letters in the third person, making an implied distinction between that public figure the Duke of Wellington whose burdens were becoming intolerable, and Arthur Wellesley who would have liked to live a simple, frugal life as a country gentleman. There were times when his self-discipline and rigid self-control gave way, when he groaned that he got less rest than "a costermonger's donkey" or broke out angrily:

"Nobody else will do it. The Duke of Wellington *must*."

It seemed as if nothing of the slightest public interest could be undertaken without pestering the Duke of Wellington. Gleig quotes a letter to an unnamed correspondent (perhaps himself) who had worried him about—of all things—Scottish universities:

"London, 12th June, 1836
"The question of Scottish universities has not escaped my attention. Care is taken that nothing should. . . ."

Stanhope a couple of years later saw fit to plague his hero with the "Prospectus of a College of Agriculture for the Sons of Farmers and Yeomen in Kent". Why the devil he had to plague the old man with such officious nonsense it is impossible to tell, but he certainly got an epistolary Roland for his Oliver prospectus:

"My dear Lord Mahon,
"I am the Duke of Wellington and an officer of the army. But there is not an affair of any kind in which I am not required to be a party. And each of these cases is attended by consequences. I am now required to be a party to the establishment of a college in Kent to teach agriculture.

"If there is one thing in the world of which I know positively nothing, it is agriculture; then I observe that I have not an acre of property in Kent; and I know, that as a matter of course, I shall be called upon to establish similar institutions in Oxfordshire, Wiltshire, Somersetshire, Berkshire, Hants, and Surrey.

"What can I answer, my dear Lord? The theory of agriculture is one thing the practical application of the theory in what is called farming wholly different. Treat the theory as you please, you cannot make the good farmer in the Isle of Thanet, or in the neighbourhood of Deal and Walmer, a good farmer even in the Weald of Kent. The practice of farming in both must depend upon experience, teach as you may.

"The scheme reminds me of a lady at Paris who had an opera dancer to teach her daughter how to walk in a garden! . . ." [Letter from Strathfield Saye, December 13, 1838.]

Yes, he was getting older and deafer and shorter-tempered, but that letter shows that he was not losing his wits or his wit. It is a fact that there are still people who think farming and soldiering can be taught on a blackboard or by an opera dancer.

There was another symptom of age which was known only to a very few intimates, but gave them plenty of concern. The Duke had been noted for his cool temper and for his cold justice to all inferiors, but now he would suddenly imagine some fault of service and fly into a temper with his menservants. For instance, he would mislay the book he was reading and then accuse a footman of having taken it away. The man's respectful denials would only serve to put the Duke in a rage, when he would storm up and down the room denouncing everything and everybody. Sooner or later he would discover that he had made a mistake, that he himself had moved the book and then forgotten all about it. This was what worried his friends; but what worried the Duke was the problem in ethics involved. The Duke of Wellington—the national myth—could not apologize to a servant, but then Arthur Wellesley could not leave an injustice unatoned for. He solved it thus:

" . . . he would ring the bell again, and on the servant showing himself, he would ask some ordinary question. The answer being given, he would reply in a tone of marked kindness, 'Thank you, I am much obliged to you'. The valet perfectly understood that this was as much as if he had said, 'I've done you wrong, pray forgive me'. "

That the servants fully understood the Duke and were devoted to him in spite of his occasional outbursts of old man's temper is sufficiently proved by their distress and eager service when he suffered one of his rather frequent illnesses and by the extreme care they gave

him. Stanhope has left an account of one of these illnesses, which
seem to have been a mild form of paralysis complicated by the Duke's
Spartan habit of "bullying" a cold or an attack of constipation by
starving himself. November 18, 1839, the Duke and Stanhope were
out with the hounds. The Duke spoke indignantly of the bad treatment by Government of a British officer in China, and discussed
certain differences between English and German university methods—
he thought German students had insufficient moral discipline and that
it was mistake to pay the professors according to the number of
pupils they could attract. It was a very cold wet day, and the Duke
(who cared no more for hunting conventions than any others) put on a
fur collar and held up an umbrella—which must indeed have been a
curious spectacle if he was wearing hunting pink and a topper. As he
did this he remarked sardonically to Stanhope.

"I think it was Charles II who said that in our climate one may go out every
day of the year—and so one may, if one will only consent to be wet through
—or blown to pieces—or starved to death!"

On the way home from the hunt, the Duke discoursed on bimetallism to a Mr. Latham of Dover, and then left his friends at the
entrance to Walmer Castle. At twenty past six that evening Stanhope
was suddenly called upon by the Duke's footman, William, "looking
as white as a sheet" and saying "he believed his Grace was not very
well"—a rather extreme understatement, since Stanhope on rushing
to the Castle found the Duke just lifted "from the floor to his camp-
bed and apparently insensible; his face like monumental marble in
colour and in fixedness, his eyes closed, his jaw dropped, and his
breath loud and gasping". Slowly the Duke recovered speech and
memory, and then the use of his limbs. Almost his first words were an
order that the dinner he was giving to some garrison officers that night
should not be cancelled. It was several days before he was able to go
about normally again; and then he immediately left for London.
According to Stanhope, the Duke had been treating himself for some
months to a very rigid dieting, without wine, and had eaten practically
nothing for nearly two days! This hardly seems a very intelligent
treatment for a man of seventy about to ride to hounds on a cold wet
winter day.

It is worth noting as an example of the Duke's loneliness in his old
age that nobody was with him at the Castle, and that, if Stanhope had
not happened to be staying near, the sick man would have been left to
the care of his servants and the local doctor.

The oddest and most disquieting symptom of advancing age has yet to be mentioned, and that is the strange case of Miss Jenkins. So painfully ridiculous is the story that when the *Letters to Miss J.* were made public many people refused to believe in their authenticity. But who that has the least acquaintance with the Duke and his style of letter-writing could doubt the authenticity of such a letter as this?

"The Duke of Wellington presents His Compliments to Miss J. She is quite mistaken. He has no Lock of Hair of Hers. He never had one."

Miss Jenkins was a young woman of some physical attractions, but with more zeal than intelligence, who from too much reading of the Bible and evangelical tracts conceived it her duty to save the Duke of Wellington from everlasting damnation by making him into a religious prig. To that end she wrote him a letter of spiritual exhortation, and unfortunately that administrative mania for answering every fool's letter made the Duke reply by return of post. The lady promptly called at Apsley House to leave a Bible and a note, which this time the Duke did not answer. In August of that year (1834) an event occurred which was thus recorded by Mr. Creevey: "Only think of the Beau's flirt, Mrs. Arbuthnot, being dead!" The Duke was more lonely than ever, and after a delay of four months he suddenly wrote again to Miss Jenkins (under the impression that she was Mrs. Jenkins) asking for an interview.

They did not in fact meet until November, when he called on her; and although she afterwards admitted that he had "a beautiful silver head" she abused the occasion by reading to him the third chapter of St. John—the story of Nicodemus. She had just reached the words: "Marvel not that I said unto thee, Ye must be born again . . ." when the Duke suddenly clapsed her rhetorically outstretched hand, exclaiming:

"Oh, how I love you! How I love you!"

For the time being that was all, it appears, and the Duke was then suddenly absorbed by the cares of his temporary dictatorship. Still, he found time to drop Miss J. a note and even called on her, for she had been smart enough to leave his letter unanswered. He said he was going to see the King, and she said she wished it was the King of Kings, and then the Duke said:

"This must be for life! This must be for life!"

Miss Jenkins, who was evidently chaste modesty personified, thought he was asking her to be the new Duchess of Wellington, a misunderstanding which annoyed the Duke very much; and when after a longish silence she wrote to say their love must be purely spiritual, he dashed all her hopes by curtly agreeing. Nevertheless, meetings and correspondence continued at intervals on these somewhat quarrelsome lines. The Duke said he wanted his letters returned or burned, yet he still went on writing more letters in a rather repellingly formal style:

"I don't consider with you that it is necessary to enter into a disputation with every wandering Blasphemer. Much must depend upon the circumstances."

By 1836 he was quite convinced that they could never come to terms —his terms; but the lady continued for years to pursue the will-o'-the-wisp hope of becoming Duchess of Wellington, and worried him with her letters and presents. In 1840 she tried to get into the house to nurse him! The Duke was unalarmed, but frigidly repellent, and told her "he will write no more". Four years later she tried again, and he was foolish enough to see her and to present her with his profile in wax on one of his visiting-cards Then she tried to get money out of him, and received this devastating salvo:

"I will give her any reasonable assistance. . . . But I announce again; that I will never write upon any other subject."

Nevertheless she continued to write him letters until his dying day, and he sometimes replied. Disappointed by the Duke's death of all hopes of a coronet, Miss Jenkins sailed for New York, but without destroying the Duke's letters. She who was afraid to kiss was not afraid to tell.

Meanwhile, the Duke's life as a public man continued. In spite of his paternal feelings towards the new Queen, the two did not hit it off very well at first. Indeed, all the Queen's warmer feelings were concentrated on that gay young man of fifty-eight, her Prime Minister. Lord Melbourne's marriage had been unlucky; his wife was that tempestuous Caroline Lamb whose affair with Lord Byron had been so widely advertised by her, and on both of which—the lady and the affair—the noble poet had bestowed this amiable epitaph:

"Remember thee! Aye, doubt it not.
    Thy husband too shall think of thee:
By neither shalt thou be forgot,
    Thou *false* to him, thou *fiend* to me!"

Twice since then, Lord Melbourne had been cited as co-respondent in
divorce cases, but then on each occasion he had been exonerated by the
jury. Yet no informed breath of scandal touched his relation with
Victoria; though she was certainly half in love with him, he never
passed beyond "the respect of a statesman and a courtier, the tender
solicitude of a parent". Still, the Prime Minister spent his mornings
working with the Queen, his afternoons riding with her, then dined
with her and played chess until he nodded for her to go to bed. The
change in him was amazing. He ceased to be unpunctual, never said
"dammee", and gave up lounging on sofas with his heels higher than
his head. The British mob, incapable of platonic subtleties, whistled
catcalls after the Queen as the cockneys yelled: "Mrs. Melbourne!"

Then almost a tragedy happened. The Government majority fell to
five over some complications arising out of the freeing of the slaves in
Jamaica; and the Whigs decided to resign. Melbourne told the Queen
to send for Wellington, and the Duke told her to send for Sir Robert
Peel, for though "I have always been and always shall be in front of the
battle", still "There is nobody who dislikes so much as I do and who
knows so little of party management—I hate it". He would serve
under Peel or anyone else, as "the retained servant of the monarchy",
but he'd be damned (not of course to the Queen's ears) if he would any
more concern himself with "what gentlemen call their feelings". So,
reluctantly and in tears, the Queen sent for Peel. Now the Tory Peel
was in one respect exactly like the Liberal Gladstone of later days—he
remembered the Queen was a public institution in whose presence he
must always stand, but he forgot that she was also a woman; whereas
the Whig Melbourne and the Conservative Disraeli remembered that
interesting fact before everything. "Everyone likes flattery," said
Disraeli, "and when you come to Royalty you should lay it on with a
trowel." Sir Robert Peel was too honest to lay on flattery even with a
feather, and when he proposed to change the Queen's Whig ladies for
Tories, she first had tearful hysterics and then committed an unconstitutional crime:

"Now, ma'am, about the Ladies. . . ."
"I cannot give up *any* of my ladies."
"What, ma'am! Does your Majesty mean to retain them *all?*"
"*All.*"
"The Mistress of the Robes *and* the Ladies of the Bedchamber?"
"*All*," the Queen repeated with that definitive ring in her voice the world
was to know more about later.

Sir Robert retired, after threatening her with the Constitution;

whereupon she had a good cry, and wrote to dear Lord Melbourne. Meanwhile the costermonger's donkey had been pressed to settle the crisis, and His Grace the Duke of Wellington was announced to the Queen. "Well, ma'am," he began hopefully, "I am very sorry to find there is a difficulty." "Oh!" said the Queen with feminine logic, "*he* began it, not me." The Duke failed to move Her Majesty's determination as completely as he had failed to melt Miss Jenkins's morality. Apprised of all this, the Whig Cabinet swore enthusiastically that they were ready to live and die for such a woman, and unselfishly returned to power. The Queen fancied that "Peel and Wellington looked very much put out" at the ball that evening. She did not know that the Duke had just written a letter to say that Peel had resigned before even taking office, adding with heart-felt sincerity: "Thank God!" But if the Duke was thankful not to be back in political office, he had not lost all his old fire. His ancient enemy, Marshal Soult, had been sent over to represent Louis Philippe at the Queen's coronation, and the two old soldiers appeared in public amid loud cheers. At a banquet to Soult some officious person whispered to the Duke that he ought to propose a toast to the French army. "No, by God," said the Duke suddenly flaring up, "we'll beat 'em, but dammee, we won't drink to 'em." And he didn't.

The reason the Duke left Walmer for London so soon after his illness in November 1839 was to be present at a Privy Council meeting when the Queen announced her intention of marrying Albert of Saxe-Cobourg. (The Duke lost a bet over this.) Earlier in that year he had been brought in to try to make peace between Victoria and her mother, the Duchess of Kent. He succeeded in getting rid of the Duchess's lover, Sir John Conroy, whom the Queen detested; and persuaded Victoria to write affectionately to her mother. The unwearying Duke had to traipse off to the old woman to assure her that her daughter's letter was genuine; whereupon the following strange dialogue is said to have occurred:

"What am I to do if Lord Melbourne comes up to me?"

"Do, ma'am? Why, receive him with civility."

"But what am I to do if Victoria asks me to shake hands with Lehzen?"

"Do, ma'am? Why take her in your arms and kiss her."

"*What!*"

"No, ma'am, no. I don't mean you are to take *Lehzen* in your arms and kiss *her*, but the Queen."

Unfortunately all this valuable diplomacy was wasted, and the factions of the royal family continued to hate each other as usual; and then the Queen proposed to Albert and was accepted, and all life became wonderful. Unfortunately her feelings as a prospective bride and as a sovereign were outraged by the unmanly and unmannerly behaviour of the Tories, who first of all decided that Albert was not worth 50,000 good golden pounds a year and cut him down to £30,000; and then refused either to make him King Consort or even to give him precedence next the Queen—which seems a not unreasonable request from a wife. But the Tories and especially the Duke felt very deeply about the whole topic; indeed the Duke said "with great animation" that "if privilege were thus to be set above law" he should at once emigrate to North America where he was given to understand the law "does at least make itself supreme and paramount". The Queen revenged herself by saying she would invite no Tories to her wedding, and when told that it was absolutely impossible to omit the Duke of Wellington, she said angrily: "What! That old rebel! I won't have him." All the same, he got his invitation; and the foundations of the great Victoria and Albert monument to domestic virtue were laid on February 10, 1840. But it is impossible to leave the year 1839, the Duke's seventieth, without calling attention to his admirable letter to the Rev. Mr. Cruttwell, a well-known currency crank of the day:

"London, 4th July, 1839

"The Duke of Wellington presents his compliments to Mr. Cruttwell, and has received his letter.

"The Duke begs Mr. Cruttwell to publish upon the currency if he pleases, and to speak upon the subject to whom he pleases.

"The Duke desires to have nothing to say to it; and he entreats Mr. Cruttwell not to give himself the trouble of writing to him again."

A few days after the Queen's wedding (1840) the Duke was again taken ill in London, and Croker reported to the King of Hanover (his unpleasant but congenial friend the former Duke of Cumberland) that "I cannot conceal from your Majesty my apprehension that the D.'s public life is over". In March Stanhope thought he looked very ill and late in April—"He is now extremely thin, stoops a good deal on one side, his countenance careworn and pale . . . even in the forenoon he is apt to fall asleep for a few minutes . . . he sways very unsteadily in his saddle . . ." but "his great mind is certainly as great as ever". But was it? One evening the Bishop of London was astounded at receiving a polite but formal letter from the Duke saying that whenever his lordship chose to visit Strathfield Saye he should be shown the Duke's "Waterloo breeches", although the Duke must say he couldn't for the life of him imagine why his lordship should want to see them.

Amazed and scandalized by this ridiculous and indecent communication the Bishop hastened to Lambeth, and with much shaking of good grey heads he and the Archbishop charitably supposed the Duke was losing his mind. Eventually the mystery was cleared up—at Strathfield Saye some young trees planted in 1815 were known as the "Waterloo beeches" and a botanist named R. C. Loudon wished to see them; his handwriting was crabbed; and the busy Duke misread "breeches" for "beeches" and the signature as that of the Bishop of London. All was well that ended well, but intimates were left wondering a little uneasily what might happen next.

What happened proved Mr. Croker to be wrong as usual in his know-all predictions—the Tories came in again in 1841, Peel was Prime Minister, and the Duke in spite of his deafness had a seat in the Cabinet without portfolio. Cabinet meetings are notoriously secret, but it was rumoured that so far as the Duke was concerned the other members " . . . said it loud, they said it clear, They went and shouted in his ear . . ." quite literally, since each in turn got up and stood beside the Duke as he gave his opinion, which must have been a little trying to every one. However, in spite of Mr. Croker and other pessimists, there was the Duke back in the Cabinet, and there he remained for nearly five years, adding the command of the army to his other duties on the death of Hill (of Peninsular fame) in 1842.

Although the Duke had held the post of Commander-in-Chief for a few months in 1826–1827, and Hill had been generally looked on as a kind of deputy to his old chief, still the fact remains that Wellington did not take over the post permanently until he was seventy-three, whereas the Duke of York held it from the time he was thirty-five until his death except for the brief period when the Mrs. Clarke scandal forced a temporary resignation. It is to be feared that the appointment came too late in life, for soldiers of seventy-three are not very open to new ideas and methods, and the Duke was always more pleased to hear that a regiment was keeping up the good old-fashioned ways than to discover any outbreak of intelligence. His influence mingled strangely with that of the Duke of York and Prinny in forming the traditions of the British regular army. Brass-button-polishing, the "Christ!-who's-your-tailor?" attitude, the promotion of incompetent scions of the military clique, clearly derived from York and Prinny; but on the other hand the whooping horse laugh of brigadiers, the two-fingered salute of corps commanders, the religion of fox-hunting, the tendency for officers to be gentlemen and to look on other ranks as His Majesty's lackeys in uniform, come from the Duke. So lasting was this influence that the British Expeditionary Force of 1914 was a slightly modernized version of the six divisions of the Peninsular Army, and relied for its fire-power largely on the musketry with which the Duke had accomplished such military miracles.

Naturally the Duke set his own peculiar standards at the Horse Guards, now that he was there for good. He was not in favour, for instance, of too narrowly professional a training for officers, pointing out that a British officer may have "to serve . . . as governor of a colony or . . . as a magistrate", and therefore must "know something of the Constitution and the laws". He introduced, or rather permitted the introduction of, a new musket, which he would not have called "a rifle" because:

" . . . we must not allow them to fancy they are all riflemen, or they will become conceited, and be wanting next to be dressed in green, or some other *jack-a-dandy* uniform."

He amused himself on inspections by giving pompous field-officers drill problems they could not solve, and then, taking command, showed how the master hand could still control troops. A subaltern on guard who sent him a written message with a gross spelling mistake roused his ire (how the devil had such a fellow got into the army?), recalling an earlier dictum that "it is difficult to employ usefully noblemen's sons who can barely read and write". Breaches of discipline could still make him very angry, as when he declared that two unnamed generals "By God, require a commander-in-chief for themselves; there is no end to their complaints and remonstrances". And he still maintained his own views of the ability of generals, on which topic he expressed himself with complete frankness. Asked to name three generals from whom one might be selected to avenge a defeat in India, the Duke scribbled:

    (1) Sir Charles Napier
    (2) Sir Charles Napier
    (3) Sir Charles Napier

A somewhat less authentic story concerns an early project to put an end to the Indian frontier troubles with Burma by occupying Rangoon. The Cabinet asked the Duke who should be given the command, and he replied instantly:

"Lord Combermere."
"But we have always understood that your Grace thought Lord Combermere a fool?"
"So he is a fool, and a damned fool, but he can take Rangoon."

On the other hand, he evidently did not think that it was any part of the duties of the Commander-in-Chief to educate his fellow-citizens in military history. Somebody wrote him from Belfast to ask whether Napoleon was or was not guilty of murdering his prisoners at Jaffa; and if so was there any military law or circumstance to justify such a proceeding? In reply the "Mr. H." who made the query received this chilling snub:

"F. M. The Duke of Wellington presents his compliments to Mr. H.; he has also received Mr. H.'s letter, and begs leave to inform him, that he is not the historian of the wars of the French Republic in Egypt and Syria."

Also in his capacity as Commander-in-Chief, but influenced perhaps by the uncertain and often gloomy judgment of extreme age, the Duke developed a great fear of foreign invasion, and went so far as to pray in a letter (printed without his consent) that "the Almighty may protect me from being a witness of the tragedy". There was nobody (he says in another letter of later date) "more convinced than I am of the necessity for peace, and indeed good understanding", but he did not think that possible unless he could "see the country in a reasonable state of defence", as it was "before the French revolutionary war". He thought (rather shrewdly) that the development of steam navigation made a surprise night attack on the unfortified English coast easier than in sailing days; and with the army less numerous and effective in 1840 than in 1790 he certainly had some reason to be alarmed. Out of all this came the Volunteer movement in England and a quarrel with the Shelleys, since it was through Lady Frances that the Duke's letter had got into print. No matter what the motives, publication of this sort without the consent of the writer seemed to the Duke an unpardonable breach of good faith and friendship, as bad as taking notes of conversation. He did not know that his intimate friend Lord Stanhope had been doing this for years, but when he discovered that the deceased Gurwood had done so he was furious:

"The Duke does not believe that there is an instance in history of a similar act. It is anti-social; it puts an end to all the charms of society, to all familiar and private communication of thought between man and man. . . ."

Had he forgotten that his friend Croker had edited Boswell's *Life of Johnson*?

He was dead against allowing British settlers in India, and thought the Whig Government had made a great mistake in permitting Europeans to travel in India without special licence:

"The principle of our occupation of India has been the protection of property in land in the hands of the natives; and with a view to the attainment of this object, the positive prohibition of colonisation by Europeans, and that of the purchase of land by Europeans out of the boundaries of the original settlements. . . ."

Obviously, as the Duke himself pointed out, his proper place as a soldier was at the head of the army, as the Lord Chancellor was in his proper place as head of the legal profession. But valuable as his work as an organizing soldier was in the 1840's, it is a question whether the use he made of his prestige in the Lords was not more important, especially in avoiding revolution over Reform in 1830–1832 and the repeal of the Corn Laws in 1846. It is curious indeed that the Duke, after opposing both measures, should finally have persuaded his brother peers to let both pass; for the first limited the political power of the landed aristocracy and the second dealt a heavy blow at their wealth. But the fact is that the Duke knew perfectly well that a country can only be governed by one of two powers, the people or the sword, and on the whole much as he disliked the people he disliked the sword more. That is why he would oppose popular measures with which he disagreed, but never beyond the point where rioting might become revolution. Disraeli (who knew better) has sadly misrepresented the Duke's motives, accusing him of love of office and political inconsistency, when he was really engaged in preserving the "Throne" of which he considered himself the servant and "guiding the Lords to their true position", i.e., from "latent directors" to "temporary rejectors and palpable alterers".

"Rotten potatoes", as the Duke expressed it, "have put Peel in his damned fright", which resulted in the repeal of the Corn Laws. It was an awkward question, incapable of an entirely just solution in an island where the population was beginning to exceed the number which could be fed from the native soil, and where the workers were paid too little to be able to keep the landowners and farmers. There had to be free trade in food, especially when the potato crop failed, although this meant low agricultural wages, poorer profits for farmers, smaller rentals for owners of farm lands. In Ireland more than 20,000 people died of starvation, although close on three million quarters of corn (maize) were given away, while public works projects were financed to take care of 285,000 Irish in 1846 and 734,000 in 1847. And the repeal of the Corn Laws (wheat) was useless to people who had no money to buy bread.

The pros and cons of free trade or a tariff, the good or bad results of repealing the Corn Laws are less relevant to this narrative than the part played in national politics by the Duke and the change in the British Constitution which he guided. This is so well expressed in his famous letter of February 19, 1846, to Lord Derby (then Lord Stanley), leader of the Conservatives after Peel's violent death, that it must be given in the Duke's own words:

"For many years, indeed from the year 1830, when I retired from office, I have endeavoured to manage the House of Lords upon the principle on which I conceive that the institution exists in the Constitution of the country, that of Conservatism. I have invariably objected to all violent and extreme measures, which is not exactly the mode of acquiring influence in a political party in England, particularly one in opposition to Government. I have invariably supported Government in Parliament upon important occasions, and have always exercised my personal influence to prevent the mischief of anything like a difference or division between the two Houses—of which there are some remarkable instances, to which I will advert here, as they will tend to show you the nature of my management, and possibly, in some degree account for the extraordinary power which I have for so many years exercised, without any apparent claim to it.

"Upon finding the difficulties in which the late King William was involved by a promise made to create peers, the number, I believe, indefinite, I determined myself, and I prevailed upon others, the number very large, to be absent from the House in the discussion of the last stages of the Reform Bill, after the negotiations had failed for the formation of a new administration.

"This course gave at the time great dissatisfaction to the party; notwithstanding that I believe it saved the existence of the House of Lords at the time, and the constitution of the country.

"Subsequently, throughout the period from 1835 to 1841, I prevailed upon the House of Lords to depart from many principles and systems which they as well as I had adopted and voted, on Irish tithes, Irish corporations, and other measures, much to the annoyance and vexation of many. But I recollect one particular measure, the union of the provinces of Upper and Lower Canada, in the early stages of which I had spoken in opposition to the measure, and had protested against it; and in the last stages of it I prevailed upon the House to agree to, and pass it, in order to avoid the injury to the public interests of a dispute between the Houses upon a question of such importance.

"Then I supported the measures of the government, and protected the servant of the government, Captain Elliot, in China. All of which tended to weaken my influence with some of the party; others, possibly a majority, might have approved of the course which I took.

"It was at the same time well known that, from the commencement at least of Lord Melbourne's Government, I was in constant communication with it, upon all military matters, whether occurring at home or abroad, at all events. But likewise upon many others.

"All this tended, of course, to diminish my influence in the Conservative party, while it tended essentially to the ease and satisfaction of the sovereign, and to the maintenance of good order. At length came the resignation of the government by Sir Robert Peel, in the month of December last, and the queen desiring Lord John Russell to form an administration.

"On the 12th of December, the queen wrote to me the letter of which I enclose a copy, and the copy of my answer of the same date; of which it appears that you have never seen copies, although I communicated them immediately to Sir Robert Peel.

"It was impossible for me to act otherwise than is indicated in my letter to the queen. I am the servant of the crown and people. I have been paid and rewarded, and I consider myself retained; and that I can't do otherwise than serve as required, when I can do so without dishonour, that is to say, as long as I have health and strength to enable me to serve.

"But it is obvious that there is, and must be, an end of all connection and counsel between party and me. . . ."

It will be observed that the Duke particularly prides himself upon having contributed to the "ease and satisfaction of the sovereign", but these words must be understood in a Pickwickian or constitutional sense. The Prince Consort really deserves all the credit for having at long last abolished the waste and parasites of the royal household and for introducing some order, though it was not (unfortunately) until that worthy prince had died of typhoid that the infamous cesspools under Windsor Castle were abolished. But what confronted the astonished young German husband when he had time to look about him was a state of affairs where one department cleaned the outside of the royal windows and another the inside, where "the Lord Steward laid the fires and the Lord Chamberlain lighted them", where the servants were under all kinds of different royal officers, and so negligent that a quasi-idiot, "the boy Jones" managed to spend three days undetected in the royal apartments and showed such pertinacity in returning that Monckton Milnes promptly nicknamed him "In-I-go" Jones. All these things were outside the Duke's department, though the revelations probably did not surprise him—he had spent his military and political life battling such arrangements.

One last duty, one last flash of his energy remained to show the new age what the Duke had been. It was 1848 and the Duke was seventy-nine, an almost fabulous figure, to whom every man in the street raised his hat, and who had scarcely a living friend of his own epoch. Even Richard Wellesley was dead and buried at Eton. Only Arbuthnot and some of the Peninsular officers remained, but the soldiers he rarely saw except on the annual Waterloo festival. And then came the wave of revolution in 1848, with thrones toppling and kings and ministers flying for safety—providing the strange sight of Metternich in a London hotel and the Prussian Crown Prince at Strathfield Saye. England was not immune. The working classes had long since discovered that the Whigs and the middle class had cheated them in 1832, and some of the smouldering discontent was imperfectly organized in the Chartist movement. In April 1848 Fergus O'Connor threatened to collect half a million ferocious under-nourished Chartists on Kennington Common, and to march them on London. Lord John Russell and his Cabinet took serious alarm. What was to be done? Why, send for the Duke, of course!

The scene must have been a remarkable one, especially since a British Government has very rarely in recent centuries had to consider the defence of London. True, the menace of the Chartists turned out to be chiefly a creation of their own fevered imaginations; but the danger seemed real enough to these politicians when they called on the old soldier to save them—a pity that none of those who had thundered against him forty years before in the House could be present, for almost all that generation had passed away. Macaulay, who was present, never forgot the picture of the Council table covered with maps, worried politicians bending over them and then rapidly regaining courage and confidence as the white-headed old soldier calmly explained his plans and gave his orders—no need to show the troops, they must stay out of sight, but be ready at a moment's notice to move there, to hold there, to attack there. The civilians were so quickly over their fright, thanks to him, that they were ready to smile at the sudden light in the old man's eye, the straightening of his bowed back, and the unexpected ring of command in his voice; but as they watched, the same thought came to them all and checked the smiles—they remembered for how many years their own lives and freedom had depended on that resolute judgment. And what did he feel as he looked over the familiar "Morning States" of effectives, and issued his orders to the commanders of the familiar units, the Guards, the Line regiments, the Royal Artillery? Who can tell? In a few hours it was all over, the giant meeting faded away and, instead of a war, presented a petition. The "retained servant of the monarchy" bowed, and retired.

In those last years the Duke grew very weary of official life and of London, and his best days were those at Strathfield Saye and Walmer —especially at Walmer Castle which he particularly liked, perhaps because it had been William Pitt's favourite home, perhaps because he could take his daily constitutional by going round and round the ramparts with old Arbuthnot. "The rooms most plainly furnished" in these two great country-places "were those which he occupied himself. He slept upon a small iron bedstead . . . without posts or curtains or hangings of any kind; and the bedding consisted of a hair mattress, a blanket, and an eider-down quilt. At Walmer, his bedroom served him as a private sitting-room also". He thought Walmer Castle "the most charming marine residence I have ever seen", and was convinced the Queen had nothing to equal it; but then the Duke was apt to overvalue anything or anybody, that aroused his affections—he petted and boasted, for instance, of second-rate or vicious horses in which nobody else could see any good whatsoever.

The routine of life in the country was seldom interrupted and not changed even in the Duke's extreme old age. He was up early, read and wrote until ten when he breakfasted (more like a modern luncheon); and again retired to his own room until two, when he joined his friends. Dinner was at seven, as he took only two meals a day; and in later years he was a teetotaller though he always served wine to his guests. Punctually at nine he would say: "Will anybody have any more wine?" which meant "It's time to stop drinking", and then at once rise to join the women for coffee. There were never cards, but plenty of books and newspapers, and "the conversation rarely flagged". At eleven-thirty the Duke would light his candle and say: "I'm going to bed; whoever leaves the room last will ring for the lights to be put out." His favourite authors, copies of whose works were kept by his bed, were: "Clarendon, Bishop Butler, Adam Smith, Hume, the Archduke Charles, Gibbon, Leslie and the Bible." The Archduke Charles was the Austrian thought by the Duke to be the one general of his time comparable with Napoleon as a strategist. "Leslie" presumably was the seventeenth-century divine; for it could hardly have been the Duke's acquaintance, Leslie the painter, who wrote a life of Constable and a *Handbook for Young Painters*. Cæsar's *Commentaries*, and Jeremy Taylor's *Holy Living and Holy Dying* were always by his bedside wherever he went.

The intellectual life of his own time seems not to have interested him at all, for Croker and his literary friends were small fry. The Duke did meet Scott and once regretted that he had never known Byron, but he seems to have been quite unaware of the poetic and scientific achievements of Englishmen in his time.* This was perhaps inevitable; the great man of action is almost always mentally behind his times—the influence even of Napoleon arrested the growth of the French mind for a generation. At the same time, the Duke was much persecuted by writers, painters, and sculptors. He got rid of the writers by refusing dedications, forbidding his servants to take in any parcels without a written order from himself, by discouraging writings about

* He read and enjoyed *Pickwick Papers*, but who didn't?

his wars and pretending he never read them, and by refusing to take part in controversies. But, as we have seen, he gave Scott help with his *Life of Napoleon*, and among other things wrote a memorandum on the Russian campaign of 1812 and a reply to Clausewitz's book on the Waterloo campaign. Journalists and newspaper editors he despised as libellers and ignorant mischief-makers, refusing to have anything to do with them or to permit them to visit his army.

Like other wealthy people the Duke bought from the Royal Academy pictures and statues he didn't want. Partly through Prinny's influence, partly through the long connexion between the arts and aristocracy, no gentleman could afford wholly to neglect them. The Duke would stroll down to the annual Academy Show to look round, and even suggested to David Wilkie the subject for a picture, *Chelsea Pensioners*, which the painter had the impudence to rate at a thousand guineas. But the Duke regarded these transactions as an imposition and a folly unworthy of serious men. William Allen sold him a Waterloo picture, and on going for his money found the Duke counting bank-notes. "A cheque will do, your Grace." There was no answer as the Duke rustled over the notes, and Allen tried again in a louder voice: "A cheque will do, your Grace." The Duke growled, "D'you think I'm going to let Coutts' people know what a damned fool I've been?"

It was not the money the Duke minded; it was the constant pestering to sit for this painter and that sculptor, until he broke out in furious protests:

"I can positively sit no longer. I do think that having to pass every leisure hour that one has by daylight in sitting for one's picture is too bad. No man ever submitted to such a bore; and I positively will not sit any longer."

Haydon was one of the pesterers, trying to borrow the Duke's clothes when he couldn't get the Duke, and receiving such volleys of verbal musketry as this:

"The Duke knows nothing about the picture Mr. Haydon proposes to paint. At all events, he must decline to lend anybody his clothes, arms and equipments."

Nevertheless Haydon was eventually permitted to stay at Walmer Castle and, though definitely one of the world's worst painters of subject pictures, produced the most straightforward and interesting portrait of the Duke in old age. The Duke's final word on the subject of sitting for his portrait was reserved for a "foreign prince" who could not be denied, and who insisted on a new marble bust; which meant dreary long sittings. The Duke sat fidgeting and grumbling— why couldn't the fellow be content with a copy of one of the existing busts? Then was an electric pause, and the final verdict: "*Damn him!*"

The results of these tortures seldom interested the Duke—he did not even look at Haydon's picture. His niece said it was very fine, and the Duke said: "Is it though? I'm very glad." And stayed where he was. But he did grow angry when they wanted to move a colossal equestrian statue of him from the top of an arch for purely æsthetic reasons. The Duke didn't give a damn about their æsthetic reasons, he considered that moving the statue (especially after all the pest and bore of sitting for it) was a personal slight. The Queen, the Prime Minister, the Cabinet, the Royal Academy, and the *Times* all wanted it moved; but the Duke did not want it moved, and as long as he lived it was not moved. It was really very odd how people obeyed him, even familiar old Arbuthnot, who continued to live with the Duke after his wife's death. "Now, Arbuthnot," the Duke would say when evening came down on their walk along the beach at Walmer, "you've been out long enough. The dew is falling, and you'll catch cold; you must go in." And Arbuthnot would protest, but always obey.

All these portraits, the caricatures, the Duke's goings and comings in London, had changed the situation entirely from what it was when he returned from the Peninsular War in 1814. Up till then, as we have seen, his face was unknown, and the caricaturists had to draw him as a bulldog labelled "Wellington" worrying a poodle named "Buona-parte". But now that majestic eagle nose, that prominent chin and firm mouth were known to everybody, and as the Duke rode (swaying dangerously) along Rotten Row he was every second touching his hat in answer to the raised hats and bows. Those who could pretend to the honour boasted of their likeness to him, and a Mr. Jones of the Royal Academy was very proud of the fact that he was sometimes mistaken for the Duke. "Strange," said the Duke, when they told him, "nobody ever mistakes me for Mr. Jones." But they did mistake him for Mr. Robinson. One day an unnamed gentleman in the Park, "lifted his hat and bowed and smiled", like the hero in Patmore's "Angel in the House", saying to the Duke, "Mr. Robinson, I believe?" But all he got was a gruff: "If you believe that, you'd believe anything."

As the old friends died off, he made very few new ones, and the losses seemed to break down his iron self-control. They noticed that his face was quivering as he stood by the grave of Richard Wellesley, and when he had to speak of Peel's death in the Lords he made no effort to hide the tears running down his face. Part of the Duke's eulogy of Pool surprised some people at the time and will astonish more now, though for different reasons; he praised Peel for his veracity:

> "In the whole course of my communication with him I have never known an instance in which he did not show the strictest preference for truth. I never had, in the whole course of my life, the slightest reason for suspecting that he stated anything which he did not firmly believe to be the fact. I could not sit down without stating what I believe, after a long acquaintance, to have been his most striking characteristic."

It is perhaps worth noting that among the rulers and statesmen who share with Peel the right to that tribute was the man who uttered it. Few men have had more cause than the Duke to learn by repeated experience how rare are truth and that "common" honesty which is not so common as it might be. He was continually pestered to find posts for deserving people, still more for undeserving people, and still more for money for every kind of rogue and cheat. He gave a gold sovereign to every old soldier who claimed to have served under him, and heaven knows how many were frauds. He subscribed to every conceivable charity, particularly orphanages; for, as he quaintly put it, he had been "the involuntary means of making many orphans, and therefore was bound to do what he could to provide for them". The demands on him by private individuals were incessant. Arbuthnot once found him putting bank-notes into various envelopes and asked what he was doing:

> "Doing? Doing what I am obliged to do every day. It would take the wealth of the Indies to meet all the demands that are made upon me."

His valet secretly communicated with the Mendicity Office and thus saved him from a gang of fraudulent writers of begging letters, who posed as officers' widows and daughters or deceived virgins "anxious to regain a place in society". The prosecution of the gang and the resulting publicity merely gave the clue to others equally unscrupulous. In the last month of his life the Duke was still complaining of this perpetual and apparently incurable affliction:

> "It is certainly very curious that every blackguard beggar, male or female, no matter of what country, considers it the right of each to demand money from me; and that every lady or gentleman, whether I am acquainted with them or not, considers that he has a right to demand the service of my power and influence in favour of some relation of the writer, or that, if I have any office,

or advantage, or benefit in my gift or at my disposal, the applicant considers himself exceedingly ill-treated if I do not dispose of the same as he desires. I am certain it is generally understood that I am a good-natured man, who will do anything; and that moreover I have been highly rewarded and am still in the public service, and that everything I have belongs to the public; as certainly would be the case if I were an *emancipated slave*." [Letter to Rev. G. R. Gleig, September 8, 1852.]

Was it any wonder that he turned more and more to the only new friends he made, the little people who called him "Mister Duke" or "Dukey" and even "Mist' Dook", not one of whom had seen a begging letter or yearned for a plum in the India Office, while all were on the sunny side of ten? Not one of them tried to cut off a lock of his hair when he wasn't looking or sold his last letter to the editor of the *Standard* or tattled his last confidence to the leader of the Radicals or tried to touch him for ten guineas or an ensign's commission in the Guards. Their demands were simple:

"How d'ye do, Duke? I want some tea, Duke."
"You shall have it, if you promise not to slop it over me, as you did yesterday."

Small wonder that in his old age his closest friends were his grandchildren and other young ladies and gentlemen of their age. He had shillings hung on blue and red ribbons to put round their necks, blue for the navy, red for the army. Every night there was a battle of Waterloo with pillows, begun by some bold young woman crashing down the Duke's newspaper with a well-aimed missile. Pompous Lord Aberdeen was much disconcerted on paying a call to find the Duke on his hands and knees under the table with his friends; and a defender of public decorum on a steamboat lost all faith in public men when he learned from a little girl that she had recently been fighting the Duke with a pillow. Haydon saw him rushing after a tiny girl on the Walmer ramparts, shouting: "I'll catch ye! Ha, ha, I've got ye!" And the children adored him. When he called on Lady Wilton at Walmer to say good-bye at the end of the season, three small figures at the door tried to prevent his leaving, and lifted up their voices and wept when he had to insist. But the greatest tribute came from the ringleader of a small gang who were robbing his fruit trees when the Duke's butler surprised them and forbade further depredations:

"Never mind, let's go to the Duke; he always allows everything and gives you what you like directly."

Meanwhile the revolutionary storm of 1848 was blowing itself out.

The French Republic which had expelled Louis Philippe was itself strangled by Louis Napoleon, and the nephew of Napoleon I was proclaimed Prince-President, and most evidently meant to make himself Emperor. Excited journalists pointed out that the régime destroyed at Waterloo had been restored, and in obedience to Mr. Tennyson indignant patriots rushed to join the Volunteers to repel a French invasion. The Duke appeared to take it all rather calmly, almost as if he guessed that Napoleon the Little would not succeed where Napoleon the Great had failed. After all, he had lived to see a good many changes in France—Louis XV, Louis XVI, the First Republic, the Directoire, the Consulate, the First Empire, the theoretical Second Empire, the Restoration, the Orleanist Monarchy, the Second Republic, the Prince-Presidency, and now the Third Empire. He might have echoed Prince Hal: "Prithee peace, we shall have more anon." The Duke had other things to think of . . . for instance, the Queen had insisted on his being godfather to her latest child who was called Arthur, Duke of Connaught, and who died a very old man not very long ago.

In February, 1852, John Russell and his Whigs were out again, and Lord Derby formed a short-lived and undistinguished Tory Ministry. Lord Derby came into the upper House and sat beside the Duke, who was all agog to hear the names of the new Cabinet; but as the Duke was very deaf and spoke in the sonorous tones of the deaf, and Lord Derby had to speak loudly to be heard by his aged colleague, the whispered conversation carried all over the House. "There is Mr. Disraeli," shouted Lord Derby. "Who?" roared the Duke, "Who?" "Lord St. Leonards." "Who? Who?" "Sir John Pakington." "Who? Who?" "Mr. Henley." "Who? Who?" "Mr. Walpole." "Who? Who?" Even the dignified Lords broke into peals of laughter, for it was only too clear that their venerable leader and the one-time leader of the Tories had never even heard of most of the new Ministers; and the nickname of "The Who? Who? Ministry" was not the least reason why they didn't last long. It was certainly worthy of the Duke that in the last year of his life he should mortally wound a Government with a syllable.

That year they kept his birthday with uncommon pomp—it was his eighty-third—and the crowds cheered him in the street, upon which he commented characteristically: "Cromwell's reflection occurred to me. They would readily follow and pull me to pieces, if convicted of exerting undue influence. . . ." On June 18, the thirty-seventh anniversary of Waterloo was celebrated by the usual banquet at

THE FIRST OF MAY

After the painting of F. Winterhalter in Windsor Castle

[By gracious permission of His Majesty the King]

THE FINAL PORTRAIT

From Count d'Orsay's portrait of The Duke
[*The National Portrait Gallery*]

Apsley House, and there was only one man present who had not been
in the battle, the Queen's husband. The Duke later spoke in the Lords,
and then went down to Walmer, where he entertained the Duke and
Duchess of Mecklenburg-Strelitz, the Russian ambassador and other
guests. (The ladies, a guest noted, were "consumed with curiosity"
when a special messenger arrived with dispatches for the Russian
ambassador.) When they had departed, the Duke went over to
Folkestone to call on his old friend Croker, who luckily made notes of
the conversation. It was nearly all about the past and even the remote
past. The Duke talked of his sitting in the old Irish Parliament before
he was of age; of how he had settled the reparations problem in 1818
"after four or five months of hard judicial application"; of his horse
"Copenhagen", long since dead and buried at Strathfield Saye; of how
he called his Peninsular regiments "my old Spanish infantry", because
he had read as a boy that the old Spanish infantry were "the best in the
world"; of how his success in Spain had been largely due to the fact
that he was "a conqueror without ambition", "no one suspected me of
any design to become King of Spain or Portugal, like Joseph or Soult
or Junot". He began telling them about a Spanish lady who during
the war had carried messages concealed on her person, but interrupted
himself and changed the subject, because (so Croker surmised)
"there was obviously some little waggish circumstance he could not
mention before my ladies". He denied that he drew his sword at
Waterloo or that he charged as a common trooper; he also denied that
he said: "Up Guards and at 'em!" He chuckled as he told an
anecdote about a Spanish princess he had recently met at Windsor,
who was astonished at hearing him describe the royal palaces of La
Granja and Madrid in a way which showed he must have lived in
them. The Queen had to tell the foreign lady who this singular old
gentleman was.

At the railway station an old soldier came up, and the Duke gave
him the usual sovereign. The man, an impudent and slightly drunk
Irishman, asked to be recommended as a warden of the Tower, but
was told:

"No, no, I can't do that. All I can do now is to reward current service—the
Cape and India; everyone must have his day."

That was on September 4, 1852. On the eighth of the month his
younger son, Charles, with his wife and children came to stay at
Walmer; and on the twelfth the Duke wrote in high glee:

M

"I had a letter this morning from a madman, who announces that he is a messenger from the Lord, and will deliver his message to me to-morrow morning: we shall see."

On the morning of September 14 the Duke did not get up at his usual hour. After waiting for some time his valet re-entered the bedroom:

"It is getting quite late, your grace; it is past seven o'clock."

"Is it?" said the Duke, and then, "Do you know where the apothecary lives?"

"Yes, your grace."

"Then send and let him know that I should like to see him. I don't feel quite well, and I will lie still till he comes."

The doctor arrived and said that nothing was wrong; but shortly after he had gone the Duke had such difficulty in breathing that he was lifted from the camp-bed to an arm-chair. At seven o'clock that evening he was dead.

They took his body up to London and laid the coffin in the Great Hall at Chelsea, where the Queen and two hundred thousand of her subjects moved past it in silence. They constructed a pompous funeral car to carry him past the innumerable silent people to St. Paul's, where twenty thousand men and women were gathered to see his coffin lowered into the crypt. Soldiers from every regiment and branch of the service had marched behind the car; and as the coffin disappeared the herald read the interminable list of the titles and honours of "The Most High Mighty and most Noble Prince, Arthur, Duke of Wellington . . ." The Queen cried over it all, and the Poet Laureate published an Ode; but the hush, the grief, the indrawn breath of that vast multitude, as the coffin passed through the streets to the funeral music of massed bands and the boom of distant guns, were the true mourning. They seemed to think there was no one to take his place.

The Duke of Wellington as Author

Just as Monsieur Jourdain found that he had been talking prose all his life without knowing it, so the Duke discovered that he had been unwittingly an author for something like forty years when Gurwood began publishing his dispatches. This must have been a shock to one who in refusing dedications, etc., was accustomed to complain that he was "much exposed to authors". Gurwood's series of volumes had an important influence on English public opinion and the Duke's reputation, laying a foundation for the near idolatry with which he was regarded in his last years. Until Gurwood's edition of the first set of dispatches began coming out many Whigs and many of the Duke's personal enemies were convinced that he had no gifts as an administrator and that he owed his victories to the actions of subordinates. The Greville *Memoirs* leave very little doubt that the fountain-head of these disparaging and scandalously untrue assertions was the Commander-in-Chief of the British Army, H.R.H. the Duke of York, aided and circularized by H.R.H. the Duke of Cumberland who hated Wellington with a bitter hatred. People who wanted to believe ill of the Duke could scarcely have had better authority than his own (nominal) commanding officer. Under date September 22, 1837, the long-converted but once bitterly hostile Creevey notes: "I have taken to Wellington and his dispatches again, and the more I read of him the fonder I am of him. He really is in every respect a *perfect man*." The Duke's own judgment was honestly enthusiastic, for he said to Lord Mahon apropos the Indian dispatches: "I have been much amused at reading them over—the energy and activity are quite as great then as ever afterwards. I don't think I could write better now, after all my experience."

Many short extracts from letters, dispatches, and correspondence will be found in the body of this book; but it seemed a good idea to include in an appendix some longer pieces of writing which could not have been quoted without holding up the narrative. There now follow:

1. The Waterloo Dispatch.

To Earl Bathurst

Waterloo, 19th June, 1815.

My Lord,

Buonaparte, having collected the 1st, 2nd, 3rd, 4th, and 6th corps of the French army, and the Imperial Guards, and nearly all the cavalry, on the Sambre, and between that river and the Meuse, between the 10th and 14th of the month, advanced on the 15th and attacked the Prussian posts at Thuin and Lobbes, on the Sambre, at day-light in the morning.

I did not hear of these events till in the evening of the 15th; and I immediately ordered the troops to prepare to march, and afterwards to march to their left, as soon as I had intelligence from other quarters to prove that the enemy's movement upon Charleroi was the real attack.

M*

The enemy drove the Prussian posts from the Sambre on that day; and General Ziethen, who commanded the corps which had been at Charleroi, retired upon Fleurus; and Marshal Prince Blücher concentrated the Prussian army upon Sombref, holding the villages in front of his position of St. Amand and Ligny.

The enemy continued his march along the road from Charleroi towards Bruxelles; and, on the same evening, the 15th, attacked a brigade of the army of the Netherlands, under the Prince de Weimar, posted at Frasne, and forced it back to the farm house, on the same road, called Les Quatre Bras.

The Prince of Orange immediately reinforced this brigade with another of the same division, under General Perponcher, and, in the morning early, regained part of the ground which had been lost, so as to have the command of the communication leading from Nivelles and Bruxelles with Marshal Blücher's position.

In the mean time, I had directed the whole army to march upon Les Quatre Bras; and the 5th division, under Lieut. General Sir Thomas Picton, arrived at about half-past two in the day, followed by the corps of troops under the Duke of Brunswick, and afterwards by the contingent of Nassau.

At this time the enemy commenced an attack upon Prince Blücher with his whole force, excepting the 1st and 2nd corps, and a corps of cavalry under General Kellerman, with which he attacked our post at Les Quatre Bras.

The Prussian army maintained their position with their usual gallantry and perseverance against a great disparity of numbers,[1] as the 4th corps of their army, under General Bülow, had not joined; and as I was not able to assist them as I wished, as I was attacked myself, and the troops, the cavalry in particular, which had a long distance to march, had not arrived.

We maintained our position also, and completely defeated and repulsed all the enemy's attempts to get possession of it. The enemy repeatedly attacked us with a large body of infantry and cavalry, supported by a numerous and powerful artillery. He made several charges with the cavalry upon our infantry, but all were repulsed in the steadiest manner.

In this affair, His Royal Highness the Prince of Orange, the Duke of Brunswick, and Lieut. General Sir Thomas Picton,[2] and Major Generals Sir James Kempt and Sir Denis Pack, who were engaged from the commencement of the enemy's attack, highly distinguished themselves, as well as Lieut. General Charles Baron Alten, Major General Sir C. Halkett, Lieut. General Cooke, and Major Generals Maitland and Byng, as they successively arrived. The troops of the 5th division, and those of the Brunswick corps, were long and severely engaged, and conducted themselves with the utmost gallantry. I must particularly mention the 28th, 42nd, 79th, and 92nd regiments, and the battalion of Hanoverians.

Our loss was great, as your Lordship will perceive by the enclosed return; and I have particularly to regret His Serene Highness the Duke of Brunswick, who fell fighting gallantly at the head of his troops.[3]

Although Marshal Prince Blücher had maintained his position at Sombref, he still found himself much weakened by the severity of the contest in which he had been engaged, and, as the 4th corps had not arrived, he determined to fall back and to concentrate his army upon Wavre; and he marched in the night, after the action was over.

This movement of the Marshal rendered necessary a corresponding one upon my part; and I retired from the farm of Quatre Bras upon Genappe, and thence upon Waterloo,[4] the next morning, the 17th, at ten o'clock.

The enemy made no effort to pursue Marshal Blücher. On the contrary, a patrole which I sent to Sombref in the morning found all quiet; and the enemy's vedettes fell back as the patrole advanced. Neither did he attempt to molest our march to the rear, although made in the middle of the day, excepting by

1 This is a mistake; Napoleon was outnumbered at Ligny.

2 Picton was wounded at Quatre Bras, but did not report the fact, and went into Waterloo with two broken ribs and an infected wound.

3 Cf. Byron: "He rush'd into the field, and, foremost fighting, fell."

4 Wellington is giving his own headquarters.

following, with a large body of cavalry brought from his right, the cavalry under the Earl of Uxbridge.

This gave Lord Uxbridge an opportunity of charging them with the 1st Life Guards,[5] upon their *débouché* from the village of Genappe, upon which occasion his Lordship has declared himself to be well satisfied with that regiment.

The position which I took up in front of Waterloo crossed the high roads from Charleroi and Nivelles, and had its right thrown back to a ravine near Merke Braine, which was occupied, and its left extended to a height above the hamlet Ter La Haye, which was likewise occupied. In front of the right centre, and near the Nivelles road, we occupied the house and gardens of Hougoumont, which covered the return of that flank; and in front of the left centre we occupied the farm of La Haye Sainte. By our left we communicated with Marshal Prince Blücher at Wavre, through Ohain; and the Marshal had promised me that, in case we should be attacked, he would support me with one or more corps, as might be necessary.

The enemy collected his army, with the exception of the 3rd corps, which had been sent to observe Marshal Blücher, on a range of heights in our front, in the course of the night of the 17th and yesterday morning, and at about ten o'clock[6] he commenced a furious attack upon our post at Hougoumont. I had occupied this post with a detachment from General Byng's brigade of Guards,[7] which was in position in its rear; and it was for some time under the command of Lieut. Colonel Macdonell, and afterwards of Colonel Home; and I am happy to add that it was maintained throughout the day with the utmost gallantry by these brave troops, notwithstanding the repeated efforts of large bodies of the enemy to obtain possession of it.

This attack upon the right of our centre was accompanied by a very heavy cannonade upon our whole line, which was destined to support the repeated attacks of cavalry and infantry, occasionally mixed, but sometimes separate, which were made upon it. In one of these the enemy carried the farm house of La Haye Sainte,[8] as the detachment of the light battalion of the German Legion, which occupied it, had expended all its ammunition; and the enemy occupied the only communication there was with them.

The enemy repeatedly charged our infantry with his cavalry, but these attacks were uniformly unsuccessful; and they afforded opportunities to our cavalry to charge, in one of which Lord E. Somerset's brigade, consisting of the Life Guards, the Royal Horse Guards, and 1st dragoon guards, highly distinguished themselves, as did that of Major General Sir William Ponsonby, having taken many prisoners and an eagle.

These attacks were repeated till about seven in the evening, when the enemy made a desperate effort with cavalry and infantry, supported by the fire of artillery, to force our left centre, near the farm of La Haye Sainte, which, after a severe contest, was defeated; and, having observed that the troops retired from this attack in great confusion, and that the march of General Bülow's corps, by Frischermont, upon Planchenois and La Belle Alliance, had begun to take effect, and as I could perceive the fire of his cannon, and as Marshal Prince Blücher had joined in person with a corps of his army to the left of our line by Ohain, I determined to attack the enemy, and immediately advanced the whole line of infantry, supported by the cavalry and artillery. The attack succeeded in every point: the enemy was forced from his positions on the heights, and fled in the utmost confusion, leaving behind them, as far as I could judge, 150 pieces of cannon, with their ammunition, which fell into our hands.

I continued the pursuit till long after dark, and then discontinued it only on account of the fatigue of our troops, who had been engaged during twelve hours,

---

5 Uxbridge's error with Mercer's Battery of R.H.A. and the mess with the hussars are not mentioned. The charge of the Life Guards extricated Uxbridge's hussars from an awkward situation.

6 Too soon; should be "about eleven".

7 The Duke diplomatically omits to say that he sent in the Guards after the Nassauers retired without orders.

8 About 6 p.m. The context makes the event seem to have occurred earlier in the battle.

and because I found myself on the same road with Marchal Blücher, who assured me of his intention to follow the enemy throughout the night. He has sent me word this morning that he had taken 60 pieces of cannon belonging to the Imperial Guard, and several carriages, baggage, &c., belonging to Buonaparte, in Genappe.

I propose to move this morning upon Nivelles, and not to discontinue my operations.

Your Lordship will observe that such a desperate action could not be fought, and such advantage could not be gained, without great loss; and I am sorry to add that ours has been immense. In Lieut. General Sir Thomas Picton His Majesty has sustained the loss of an officer who has frequently distinguished himself in his service; and he fell gloriously leading his division to a charge with bayonets, by which one of the most serious attacks made by the enemy on our position was repulsed. The Earl of Uxbridge, after having successfully got through the arduous day, received a wound by almost the last shot fired, which will, I am afraid, deprive His Majesty for some time of his services.

His Royal Highness the Prince of Orange distinguished himself by his gallantry and conduct, till he received a wound from a musket ball through the shoulder, which obliged him to quit the field.

It gives me the greatest satisfaction to assure your Lordship that the army never, upon any occasion, conducted itself better. The division of Guards, under Lieut. General Cooke, who is severely wounded, Major General Maitland, and Major General Byng, set an example which was followed by all; and there is no officer nor description of troops that did not behave well.

I must, however, particularly mention, for His Royal Highness's approbation, Lieut. General Sir H. Clinton, Major General Adam, Lieut. General Charles Baron Alten (severely wounded), Major General Sir Colin Halkett (severely wounded), Colonel Ompteda, Colonel Mitchell (commanding a brigade of the 4th division), Major Generals Sir James Kempt and Sir D. Pack, Major General Lambert, Major General Lord E. Somerset, Major General Sir W. Ponsonby, Major General Sir C. Grant, and Major General Sir H. Vivian, Major General Sir O. Vandeleur, and Major General Count Dornberg.

I am also particularly indebted to General Lord Hill for his assistance and conduct upon this, as upon all former occasions.

The artillery and engineer departments were conducted much to my satisfaction by Colonel Sir George Wood and Colonel Smyth; and I had every reason to be satisfied with the conduct of the Adjutant General, Major General Barnes, who was wounded, and of the Quarter Master General, Colonel De Lancey, who was killed by a cannon shot in the middle of the action. This officer is a serious loss to His Majesty's service, and to me at this moment.

I was likewise much indebted to the assistance of Lieut. Colonel Lord Fitzroy Somerset, who was severely wounded, and of the officers composing my personal staff, who have suffered severely in this action. Lieut. Colonel the Hon. Sir Alexander Gordon, who has died of his wounds, was a most promising officer, and is a serious loss to His Majesty's service.

General Kruse, of the Nassau service, likewise conducted himself much to my satisfaction; as did General Tripp, commanding the heavy brigade of cavalry, and General Vanhope, commanding a brigade of Infantry in the service of the King of the Netherlands.

General Pozzo di Borgo, General Baron Vincent, General Müffling, and General Alava, were in the field during the action, and rendered me every assistance in their power. Baron Vincent is wounded, but I hope not severely; and General Pozzo di Borgo received a contusion.

I should not do justice to my own feelings, or to Marshal Blücher and the Prussian army, if I did not attribute the successful result of this arduous day to the cordial and timely assistance I received from them. The operation of General Bülow upon the enemy's flank was a most decisive one; and, even if I had not found myself in a situation to make the attack which produced the final result, it would have forced the enemy to retire if his attacks should have failed, and would have prevented him from taking advantage of them if they should unfortunately have succeeded.

The operation of General Bülow upon the Enemy's flank was a most decisive one; and even if I had not found myself in a situation to make the attack which produced the final Results, it would have forced the Enemy to retire if his attack should have failed and would have prevented him from taking advantage of them if they should unfortunately have succeeded.

Wellington

FACSIMILE OF PORTION OF DISPATCH QUOTED ABOVE
From Lord Robert's The Rise of Wellington

Since writing the above, I have received a report that Major General Sir William Ponsonby is killed; and, in announcing this intelligence to your Lordship, I have to add the expression of my grief for the fate of an officer who had already rendered very brilliant and important services, and was an ornament to his profession.

I send with this dispatch three eagles, taken by the troops in this action, which Major Percy will have the honour of laying at the feet of His Royal Highness. I beg leave to recommend him to your Lordship's protection.

I have the honour to be, &c.
Wellington.

2. Letter supplementary to above.

Bruxelles, 19th June, 1815

My Lord,
I have to inform your Lordship, in addition to my dispatch of this morning, that we have already got here 5,000 prisoners, taken in the action of yesterday, and that there are above 2,000 more coming in to-morrow. There will probably be many more.

Amongst the prisoners are the Comte de Lobau, who commanded the 6th corps, and General Cambronne, who commanded a division of the Guards.

I propose to send the whole to England, by Ostend.

I have the honour to be, &c.
Wellington.

3. Private letter to Marshal Lord Beresford on Waterloo.

Gonesse, 2nd July, 1815

My dear Beresford,

I have received your letter of the 9th of June. You should recommend for the Spanish medal for Albuera according to the rules laid down by the King of Spain for the grant of it. I should think it should be given only to those who were there and actually engaged.

I am, as soon as I shall have a little time going to recommend officers for the Order of San Fernando, and will apply to you for a Portuguese list.

You will have heard of our battle of the 18th. Never did I see such a pounding match. Both were what the boxers call gluttons. Napoleon did not manœuvre at all. He just moved forward in the old style, in columns, and was driven off in the old style. The only difference was, that he mixed cavalry with his infantry, and supported both with an enormous quantity of artillery.

I had the infantry for some time in squares, and we had the French cavalry walking about us as if they had been our own. I never saw the British infantry behave so well.

Boney is now off, I believe, to Rochefort, to go to America. The army, about 40,000 or 50,000, are in Paris. Blücher on the left of the Seine, and I with my right in front of St. Denis, and the left upon the Bois de Bondy. They have fortified St. Denis and Montmartre very strongly. The canal de l'Ourcq is filled with water, and they have a parapet and batteries on the bank; so that I do not believe we can attack this line. However, I will see.

Believe me, &c.

Wellington.

We believe Wrede is with the Bavarians at Chalons this day.

4. To Viscount Castlereagh, on the policy of the Allies towards France after the defeat of Napoleon in 1815.

Paris, 11th August, 1815

My dear Lord,

I have perused with attention the memorandum which you have sent me, and have considered well the contents of those written by the Ministers of the other powers.

My opinion is, that the French Revolution and the treaty of Paris have left France in too great strength for the rest of Europe, weakened as all the powers of Europe have been by the wars in which they have been engaged with France, by the destruction of all the fortresses and strongholds in the Low Countries and Germany, principally by the French, and by the ruin of the finances of all the Continental Powers.

Notwithstanding that this opinion is as strongly, if not more strongly, impressed upon my mind than upon that of any of those whose papers have lately come under my consideration, I doubt its being in our power now to make such an alteration in the relations of France with other powers as will be of material benefit.

First; I conceive that our declarations, and our treaties, and the accession, although irregular in form, which we allowed Louis XVIII to make to that of the 25th of March, must prevent us from making any very material inroad upon the state of possession of the treaty of Paris. I do not concur in Prince Hardenberg's reasoning, either that the guarantee in the treaty of the 25th of March was intended to apply only to ourselves, or that the conduct of the French people since the 20th of March ought to deprive them of the benefit of that guarantee. The French people submitted to Buonaparte; but it would be ridiculous to suppose that the Allies would have been in possession of Paris in a fortnight after one battle fought if the French people in general had not been favourably disposed to the cause which the Allies were supposed to favour.

In the north of France they certainly were so disposed, and there is no doubt they were so in the south, and indeed throughout France, excepting in Champagne, Alsace, parts of Burgundy, Lorraine and Dauphiné. The assistance which the King and his party in France gave to the cause was undoubtedly of a passive description; but the result of the operations of the Allies has been very different from what it would have been if the disposition of the inhabitants of the country had led them to oppose the Allies.

In my opinion, therefore, the Allies have no just right to make any material inroad on the treaty of Paris, although that treaty leaves France too strong in relation to other powers; but I think I can show that the real interests of the Allies should lead them to adopt the measures which justice in this instance requires from them.

There is such an appearance of moderation in all that has been written upon this subject, that we might hope there would be no material difference of opinion on the disposal of what should be taken from France, supposing that it should be decided that France is to make a cession; and therefore I do no more than advert to that objection to the demand.

But my objection to the demand of a great cession from France upon this occasion is, that it will defeat the object which the Allies have held out to themselves in the present and the preceding wars.

That which has been their object is to put an end to the French Revolution, to obtain peace for themselves and their people, to have the power of reducing their overgrown military establishments, and the leisure to attend to the internal concerns of their several nations, and to improve the situation of their people. The Allies took up arms against Buonaparte because it was certain that the world could not be at peace as long as he should possess, or should be in a situation to attain, supreme power in France; and care must be taken, in making the arrangements consequent upon our success, that we do not leave the world in the same unfortunate situation respecting France that it would have been in if Buonaparte had continued in possession of his power.

It is impossible to surmise what would be the line of conduct of the King and his Government upon the demand of any considerable cession from France upon the present occasion. It is certain, however, that, whether the cession should be agreed to or not by the King, the situation of the Allies would be very embarrassing.

If the King were to refuse to agree to the cession, and were to throw himself upon his people, there can be no doubt that those divisions would cease which have hitherto occasioned the weakness of France. The Allies might take the fortresses and provinces which might suit them, but there would be no genuine peace for the world, no nation could disarm, no Sovereign could turn his attention from the affairs of this country.

If the King were to agree to make the cession, which, from all that one hears, is an event by no means probable, the Allies must be satisfied and must retire; but I would appeal to the experience of the transactions of last year for a statement of the situation in which we should find ourselves.

Last year, after France had been reduced to her limits of 1792 by the cession of the Low Countries, the left bank of the Rhine, Italy &c., the Allies were obliged to maintain each in the field half of the war establishment stipulated in the treaty of Chaumont, in order to guard their conquests, and what had been ceded to them; and there is nobody acquainted with what passed in France during that period who does not know that the general topic of conversation was the recovery of the left bank of the Rhine as the frontier of France, and that the unpopularity of the Government in the army was to be attributed to their supposed disinclination to war to recover these possessions.

There is no statesman who, with these facts before his eyes, with the knowledge that the justice of the demand of a great cession from France under existing circumstances is at least doubtful, and that the cession would be made against the inclination of the Sovereign and all descriptions of his people, would venture to recommend to his Sovereign to consider himself at peace, and to place his armies upon a peace establishment. We must, on the contrary, if we take this large cession, consider the operations of the war as deferred till France shall find a suitable opportunity of endeavouring to regain what she has lost; and, after having wasted our resources in the maintenance of overgrown military establishments in time of peace, we shall find how little useful the cessions we shall have acquired will be against a national effort to regain them.

In my opinion, then, we ought to continue to keep our great object, the genuine peace and tranquillity of the world, in our view, and shape our arrangement so as to provide for it.

Revolutionary France is more likely to distress the world than France, however strong in her frontier, under a regular Government; and that is the situation in which we ought to endeavour to place her.

With this view I prefer the temporary occupation of some of the strong places, and to maintain for a time a strong force in France, both at the expense of the French Government, and under strict regulation, to the permanent cession of even all the places which in my opinion ought to be occupied for a time. These measures will not only give us, during the period of occupation, all the military security which could be expected from the permanent cession, but, if carried into execution in the spirit in which they are conceived, they are in themselves the bond of peace.

There is no doubt that the troops of the Allies stationed in France will give strength and security to the Government of the King, and that their presence will give the King leisure to form his army in such manner as he may think proper. The expectation also of the arrival of the period at which the several points occupied should be evacuated would tend to the preservation of peace, while the engagement to restore them to the King, or to his legitimate heirs or successors, would have the effect of giving additional stability to his throne.

In answer to the objections of a temporary occupation, contained in Prince Hardenberg's paper, drawn from the state of things in Prussia, I observe that the temporary occupation by the troops of the Allies of part of France will be with views entirely different from those which dictated the temporary occupation of Prussia by the French troops; and if the measure is carried into execution on the principle of supporting the King's Government and of peace, instead of, as in Prussia, with views of immediate plunder and ultimate war, the same results cannot be expected.

I am likewise aware of the objection to the measure, that it will not alone eventually apply a remedy to the state of weakness, in relation to France, in which the powers of Europe have been left by the treaty of Paris; but it will completely for a term of years. This term of years, besides the advantage of introducing into France a system and habits of peace, after twenty-five years of war, will enable the powers of Europe to restore their finances; it will give them time and means to reconstruct the great artificial bulwarks of their several countries, to settle their Governments, and to consolidate their means of defence. France, it is true, will still be powerful, probably more powerful than she ought to be in relation to her neighbours; but if the Allies do not waste their time and their means, the state of security of each and of the whole, in relation to France, will, at the end of the period, be materially improved, and will probably leave but little to desire.

5. Extract from Memorandum on the war in Russia in 1812.

. . . Napoleon, aware of the difficulties of subsistence in that country for a large army, formed squadrons, regiments, and brigades of carts loaded with provisions and other necessaries for his army, which followed its movements through Prussia, in which country it was provisioned on its passage, under the treaty of alliance with the King of Prussia. Droves of cattle were moved through Germany from Italy and France. Yet so little did these arrangements answer the purpose intended, that before the army quitted the Duchy of Warsaw we see complaints of the plunder of the country, and remonstrances from Napoleon to his marshals of the evil consequences (compared to those in Portugal) which must result from the irregularity of the troops, and from the mode in which they took provisions from the enemy.

At Wilna, the first place at which a halt was made within the Russian frontier, and at which an hospital was to be established, we see what the means were which this army of 600,000 men possessed.

This army of 600,000 men could establish hospitals for only 6,000 men at Wilna. These were without provisions, beds, covering, or even straw to lie upon, and even unprovided with medicine. Yet it is a curious fact that the Wurtemberg army had an excellent hospital at Wilna, because the King of Wurtemberg paid the expense of the hospital for his troops. This fact shows to what circumstances all these difficulties were to be attributed. At Vitepsk, where another hospital was formed, we see by the account that hospitals for only 1,400 men could be formed; Russians and French in equal numbers; the Russians having been left for three days without assistance, when they were taken into the French hospitals.

The surgeons were obliged to use their own shirts for dressings, as well as those of the wounded soldiers. It must be observed that these hospitals were for wounded only; the sick shifted for themselves as they could. At Smolensk, on the second night after the establishment of the hospitals in that town, every-thing was wanting to dress the wounds of the wounded soldiers, and paper found in the archives was used instead of lint.

After the battle of Borodino 20,000 French wounded were left in the Abbaye of Kolotskoi. Ségur says, "Les ambulances avaient rejoint, mais tout fut insuffisant;" that is, nearly three months after the frontier had been passed; and Larrey, the chirurgien-en-chef, complains in a publication, that no troops were left with him pour requérir those articles which were necessary from the neighbouring villages. Pour requérir is, in plain terms, envoyer à la maraude —plunder in order to supply the hospitals!!

The causes of the failure of these measures of precaution are worth discussing, as the discussion will convey to the minds of the reader of this paper the real cause of the disasters of the French army in Russia.

The truth is that Napoleon learnt at Paris and Dresden, and the information was confirmed on his arrival at Koenigsberg from Dresden, that the Emperor of Russia had collected his army in the neighbourhood of Wilna. He conceived that he should surprise his enemy in that position and defeat him; or that in his retreat he would have it in his power to fall upon and destroy some detached corps. Forced marches were then to be undertaken, even from the Vistula, and were continued till the army reached the Dwina and the Dnieper. The carts, the carriages, the cattle, and all the supplies brought from France and Italy, were left behind; all the difficulties of the enterprise were forgotten, and nothing thought of but the prospect of finding the enemy en flagrant délit, and of destroy-ing him at one blow.

It is curious to read the statement in Ségur, which is confirmed by all who have written the history of this war, of the loss sustained by the army in the first marches from the Niemen and the Vilia. Not less than ten thousand horses and many men are stated to have been left dead upon the road, and thousands of stragglers from their regiments were wandering about the country. This loss is attributed to the storm of rain which occurred at that period. But those who know what an army is well know that a storm of rain in the summer, whatever its violence and character, does not destroy the horses of an army. That which does destroy them, that which renders those who survive nearly unfit for service throughout the campaign, and incapable of bearing the hardship of the winter, is hard work, forced marches, no corn or dry fodder at the period at which the green corn is on the ground, and is invariably eaten by the horses of the army. It is the period of the year at which of all others a commander who cares for his army will avoid enterprises the execution of which require forced marches or the hard work of the horses.

In like manner, storms of rain do not destroy soldiers of the infantry, exposed to them in a greater degree than other men; but forced marches on roads destroyed by storms of rain, through a country unprovided with shelter, and without provisions, do destroy soldiers, as every one left behind is without resource, is exposed, unsheltered and starving, to the effects of the storm; he cannot follow and overtake his corps, and he must perish. . . .

Called together by the conscription, each battalion of the French army had in its ranks good and bad, of high, low, and middle-class, men of all trades and professions. The French soldiers scarcely required the usual discipline or punish-ment inflicted on soldiers to keep them in order. The good, under the super-intendence and encouragement of the officers, took care of the bad, and kept them in order; and they were upon the whole the best, the most orderly and obedient, and the most easily commanded and best regulated body of troops that ever existed in Europe. They were destroyed by their privations. The French

Revolution first introduced into the world new systems of war, the objects and result of which were to render war a resource instead of a burthen to the belligerents, and to throw the burthen upon the country which unfortunately became the seat of its operations. The system of terror and the misery of the people in France; and the conscription, the execution of which was facilitated by the first; placed at the disposal of the government of the day the whole of the serviceable male population of the country. All that the government had to do or did with them was to organize them into military bodies, arm them, and have them taught the first movements of their arms and of their military exercises. They were then poured into some foreign country to live upon its resources. Their numbers stifled or overcame all local opposition; and whatever might be the loss or misery which the system itself might occasion in the French armies, the first was of men who when dead could not complain; the success stifled the complaints of their survivors.

Napoleon was educated in this system. He succeeded to the power it gave to the government, and carried its action to the greatest possible extent. The system of his tactics was founded upon forced marches. War, being the principal resource of his government, was to be carried out at the smallest possible expense of money to his treasury, but at the greatest possible expenditure of the lives of men, not only by the fire of the enemy, but by privations, fatigue, and sickness. Till this Russian war he had never thought of supplying his armies with the necessaries requisite to enable such great bodies to keep the field. His object was to surprise his enemy by the rapidity of his marches, to fight a great battle, levy contributions, make peace, and return to Paris. But these objects were always attained at the expense of the utmost privations to his troops.

These privations, which must have rendered the soldier unfit for service, and must have destroyed him at once if not relieved by breaches of order and discipline, and by plunder and its consequences, occasioned all these evils, till the army, however well composed originally, and however orderly and well disciplined and formidable as a military body to its enemies, became at last a horde of banditti, all equally bad, and destroying itself by its irregularities. Indeed no other army, excepting the French army, could have subsisted in the manner in which the French army did. No other army known in Europe is sufficiently under command.

His mode is really curious, and worthy of observation. The army started with a certain number of days' provisions upon the men's backs, seldom less than seven days, and sometimes provision, that is to say, bread or biscuit, for fourteen days. Cattle were driven with the army to supply the rations of meat. These articles were procured either from magazines, or from some large town, or from some rich well-populated district in which the troops might have been cantoned. The cavalry could not be loaded with provender for the horses for more than three or four days.

Thus provided, the army started upon its expedition by forced marches. In very few days it was generally discovered that the soldiers, unable to carry their loads upon these forced marches, had either consumed in two or three days that which ought to have lasted seven or ten days, or had thrown it away, or the General commanding, being apprehensive that the provisions which his troops had in possession would not be sufficient to last till he should be able to have another regular issue, commenced to procure supplies by what was called la maraude; that is to say, neither more nor less than plunder.

Authority was then given to send out a certain number of soldiers of each company to obtain provisions at each village or farm-house in the neighbourhood of the road by which the army marched, or of the ground on which it encamped. These soldiers were to force the inhabitants to deliver these provisions without payment or receipt; and it may well be believed that these acts of violence were not confined to forcing the delivery of provisions. Other articles of value were taken at the same time, and by the use of the same coercive measures; and it is not astonishing that officers and soldiers so employed should become habitual plunderers.

The provisions thus brought in were issued among the troops under the command of the officer who had sent these detachments on the maraude. It is obvious that even this system, bad as it was, could not be resorted to with any prospect of success where the country through which the army marched was thinly peopled, or if the army was making extraordinary forced marches, or in the neighbourhood of the enemy; but it must be observed, that even if not resorted to by authority, it was invariably by the private soldiers, and not unfrequently by the officers of the French army, on their own account. They generally required the food because they had consumed or thrown away the enormous loads which had been packed upon them. But even if they did not necessarily require it, biscuit or ammunition-bread, and the meat of an animal but just killed after a forced march, is but bad food in comparison with what can be got from almost any village in the country; and, in addition to the food, the man à la maraude could pick up money and other valuable property.

It must be observed that a French army, after quitting its magazines or a friendly country, never received a ration of provisions not procured à la maraude; and that this army which entered Russia, from the time it quitted the Niemen, in June, 1812, till it returned to Smolensk, in November, 1812, excepting perhaps some of the Guard, never received a ration which was not procured à la maraude.

In all these accounts it is frequently stated that Napoleon complained that his orders were not obeyed, and that magazines of provisions for his army were not formed, upon the retreat, at the places at which he had ordered that they should be formed. This may be true. But it must be observed that these orders were not given as other Generals at the head of armies have given similar orders, pointing out the places where, and the means by which, these provisions were to be collected and stored in magazine; and by supplying the money necessary to pay for their cost. There was but one resource for collecting these magazines, that was, la maraude.

Officers were placed in fortified houses or posts in the towns and villages on the high road from Smolensk to Moscow, with orders to collect magazines to supply the troops in the post, and to assist the reinforcements, recruits and traineurs, coming up to join the army, and eventually the army itself. Was money placed at their disposal to purchase these supplies in a country overrun with Jews, who, if money had been produced, would have procured provisions in exchange for it from any distance? No! The officer in command of such post was to plunder the villages in his neighbourhood, already ruined and exhausted by the passage and operations of two hostile armies, and by the repeated plunder which they had suffered by detachments or single traineurs.

If Napoleon entertained expectations that magazines would have been formed in such situations, it is not astonishing that he should have been disappointed on his retreat; it would have been astonishing if any officer had been able to collect a magazine under such circumstances.

At Smolensk and at Orcha on the Dnieper, on the return of the army, in November, 1812, it appears that magazines of provisions were formed; that is to say, some of the squadrons, regiments, and brigades of carts before mentioned had found their way to, and had discharged their loads into, the magazines at those places; but the army was at that time in such a state of disorganization that those magazines were of little or no utility. The truth is, that nearly the whole army was, from the period of the commencement of the retreat, à la maraude in search of provisions. Nobody would believe that there could be any regular issue of provisions from any magazine; and no officer or soldier would join his corps in hopes of obtaining his portion of such an issue. Besides, the truth is, that the officers of the French commissariat and the gardes magazines, etc., were so little accustomed to make such issues, that they were not expert in the performance of this part of their duty. They performed it but slowly; and men who were starving with hunger and cold were but little disposed to wait to satisfy their appetites till these persons had gone through all the formalities required by their comptabilité, the meaning and use of which they did not understand. It is not astonishing, then, that they should have eaten the horses fit for service, employed in the draught of pieces of cannon upon the glacis of Smolensk, while waiting to receive their rations from the magazines at that town.

The system of the French army, then, was the cause of its irregularities, disorders, and misfortunes; and of its loss.

Some Wellington Source Material

The Manuscript sources are the Apsley House papers, letters and documents in possession of the Wellesley family, and British Museum Additional MSS. On account of the war (1939–1945) I have not been able to consult these papers. It is generally believed that personal and private material in the Apsley House and Wellesley papers may not be published; and this prohibition certainly accords with the views of the first Duke.

The official correspondence and some personal letters of the Duke are contained in three separate collections:

(1) *The Dispatches of Field Marshal the Duke of Wellington . . . from* 1799-1815. Compiled . . . by Lieut.-Colonel Gurwood. 12 volumes.

These volumes contain the cream of the military correspondence, but the index is not good, the notes are scanty, and Gurwood has omitted (most probably by the Duke's orders) the names of every one who is censured or who appears in a bad light or who might be offended. This makes reference difficult, reduces the interest of otherwise fascinating material, and makes some letters and dispatches almost or quite unintelligible.

(2) *Supplementary Despatches, Correspondence, and Memoranda . . . edited by the second Duke of Wellington . . . from* 1794–1818. 14 volumes.

These volumes contain material omitted by Gurwood, and two supplementary volumes (13 and 14) of material which had been overlooked. The second Duke of Wellington was a far more intelligent editor than Gurwood, and he has greatly increased the liveliness of the letters by printing those from other people, as well as many memoranda and documents. This collection covers the period up to the evacuation of the Allied armies from France, and the Duke's permanent return to England in 1818.

(3) *Despatches, Correspondence and Memoranda . . . in continuation of the former Series . . . from* 1818–1832. 8 volumes.

Also edited by the second Duke, and carrying on the correspondence with replies until after the passing of the Reform Bill. Less interesting than the two earlier collections, but of course essential for the biographer and student.

(4) *Letters of the Duke of Wellington to Miss J.* Edited by C. T. Herrick. 1924.

An extraordinary though not very interesting set of letters to Miss A. M. Jenkins, the puritanical young woman who indulged in a long evangelical flirtation with the Duke.

So far as I can discover there is no complete collection of the Duke's letters for the period of 1832–1852, but many of them are scattered about in books of reminiscence and biography, as e.g. Croker's papers and Gleig's Life.

The greatest book ever written or ever likely to be written about Wellington is:

(5) *The Peninsular War*, by Sir C. W. C. Oman. 7 volumes. Speaking as an enthusiast, I am tempted to say that this great work of military history is the most completely satisfactory one-man work by any English historian since Gibbon's *Decline and Fall of the Roman Empire*. It is the masterpiece of the realistic school, as Gibbon's work is the masterpiece of the classical school of historians, and, possessing literary as well as historical merits, it can be read and re-read. Every phase of the struggle, French, Spanish, and Portuguese, as well as British, is made to re-live with amazing vividness and precision. Sir Charles is not very fond of Wellington as a person, but he does full justice to the Duke as General and to the army under his command. The book was written to supplement and correct Napier, but it achieves far more than that—a complete and brilliant record of a great war not too big to be outside the scope of one exceptionally gifted and industrious writer. The bibliography has unluckily never been published. As a valuable pendant to the above:

(6) *Wellington's Army*, by the same author, contains a most valuable survey from the private soldier to the Commander, and a bibliography of about a hundred personal narratives of the Peninsular War. I have not read all of these, but those quoted in this book include:

(7) *Private Journal of F. S. Larpent, Deputy Judge-Advocate-General.*

(8) *Peninsular Journal.* General Sir B. D'Urban.

(9) *Autobiography of General Sir Henry Smith.*

(10) *Adventures of a Soldier.* E. Costello.

(11) *Recollections*, Rifleman Harris.

(12) Grattan's *The Connaught Rangers.*

(13) W. Tomkinson's *Diary of a Cavalry Officer.*

(14) Gleig's *The Subaltern.*

(15) Kincaid of the Rifle Brigade.

(16) Colonel Moyle Sherer.

(17) The anonymous Highlander of the 79th Foot.

(18) Sergeant Lawrence of the 40th Foot.

(19) Captain Blakeney of the 28th Foot.

(20) Captain Mercer's *Journal of the Waterloo Campaign,*

and many others. Some of these (e.g. Gleig, Smith, Harris, Blakeney) have been reprinted in recent times; others equally interesting can only be found in the great public libraries. Among the French narratives the *Private Journal of General Foy* is most interesting and valuable for its revelations of the state of affairs in the French armies in Spain.

(21) Napier's *Peninsular War* can never lose its high position as a magnificent and sustained piece of rhetorical writing, and the descriptions of events where Napier was present have all the value of an eye-witness's report; but the great stylist's prejudices and predilictions make much of his work valueless as history. His Whiggism and quite unfounded hero-worship of Soult must be taken very cautiously. Oman corrects all this.

(22) Robert Southey's *Peninsular War* was killed by Napier's. It is a well-written but rather dull account by a civilian, interesting as the first attempt by an Englishman to do justice to the Spanish and Portuguese share in the war. (Southey knew both languages and had lived in Portugal.) I am indebted to him for the amusing quotations from Opposition speakers in the Commons during the War.

(23) Sir John Fortescue's *History of the British Army*, and *Wellington*.
First-hand records of Wellington's sayings and doings will be found in:
(24) *Stanhope's Conversations with Wellington*. Edited by Philip Guedalla.
(25) *The Creevey Papers*.
(26) J. W. Croker's *Correspondence and Diaries*.
(27) Lord Ellesmere's *Personal Reminiscences of the Duke of Wellington*.
(28) Gleig's *Personal Reminiscences of the Duke of Wellington*.
(29) Sir W. Frazer's *Words on Wellington*.
(30) Greville's *Memoirs*.
(31) *Diary and Letters of Princess Lieven*.
(32) *Diary of Frances, Lady Shelley*.
(33) *Queen Victoria's Letters*.
(34) *Letters of Harriet, Countess Granville*.
(35) *Correspondence of Lady Burghersh with the Duke of Wellington*.
(This contains letters from the Duke.)
(36) *Memoirs of Harriette Wilson*. (Very unreliable.)
(37) Unpublished Journals of the Hon. Mrs. Calvert.
(38) *Life of Lord Granville*, by Lord E. Fitzmaurice.
(39) *Private Correspondence of Lord Granville Leveson Gower*. (Useful.
Contains letters of Lady Bessborough.)
(40) R. B. Haydon's *Autobiography*.
This section might be almost indefinitely extended, since virtually all English
memoirs covering the first half of the nineteenth century contain references to the
Duke. Not all of these are first hand, and it must be remembered that a great
many apocryphal stories and repartees are attributed to the Duke which have
nothing to do with him. One hive of anecdotes which I have used for subsidiary
material is very amusing.
(41) *Collections and Recollections of G. W. E. Russell*.
For Ireland in the eighteenth century I found some background material in:
(42) Lecky's *History of Ireland in the Eighteenth Century*.
(43) Froude's *The English in Ireland*.
(44) A. Young's *Tour in Ireland*.
and for more gossipy and social details:
(45) Mrs. Delany's *Autobiography and Correspondence*.
(46) D. Barrington's *Miscellanies*.
(47) *Maria Edgeworth and Her Circle*, by Constance Hill. (Some details about
Kitty Pakenham.)
For Indian history, social details of society in India, and personal notes on
Wellington, I select:
(48) *History of British India under the Company and the Crown*. P. E. Roberts.
49) *Cambridge History of India*. (Full, learned, and sometimes extremely dull.)
(50) Ramsay Muir's *Making of British India*.
(51) *Memoirs and Correspondence of Richard Marquess Wellesley*. Ed. R. R.
Pearce. 3 volumes.
(52) *Memoirs of William Hickey*. Ed. A. Spencer. 4 volumes.
(53) *Memoirs of George Elers, Captain in the 12th Foot*. Eds. Lord Monson
and G. Leveson Gower.
(54) *Mountstuart Elphinstone*, by J. S. Cotton.
(55) *Memoirs of Sir Philip Francis*. By Joseph Parkes.

(56) *The Francis Letters*. 2 volumes.

(57) *Original Letters from India* (1779–1815), by Mrs. Eliza Fay. Ed. E. M. Forster.

Above all other lives of Wellington the most carefully documented and entertaining is:

(58) Philip Guedalla's *Wellington*.

Other lives to be mentioned are:

(59) Sir H. Maxwell's *Life of Wellington*. (Sir J. Fortescue's *Wellington* is mentioned after his *History of the British Army*.)

(60) *History of the Life of Arthur Duke of Wellington*, by M. Brialmont and the Rev. G. R. Gleig. 3 volumes.

For the Waterloo campaign:

(61) Duke of Wellington's *Memorandum on Waterloo*.

(62) W. Siborne's *Campaign of Waterloo*.

(63) Shaw Kennedy's *Battle of Waterloo*.

For "atmosphere" and details about Waterloo, Thackeray's *Vanity Fair* and *The Creevey Papers* are excellent. Mercer's seems to me the best of the soldier narratives, but there are many others including several Peninsular veterans, among them Harry Smith who immortalized himself by asking "Which way, my lord?" when the Duke ordered his brigade to charge.

Many of the books already mentioned give information on the period 1815–1852. The political novels of Disraeli, especially *Endymion*, *Sybil*, and *Coningsby*, furnish a lot of valuable detail. (Any one who questions my description of Disraeli as a "proto-Fascist" is referred to Chapter XV of *Coningsby*.) For the historical background of the whole period of Wellington's life, volumes 6–11 inclusive of the *Cambridge Modern History* are excellent. Lives of Charles James Fox, William Pitt, Lord Castlereagh, Canning, Sir Robert Peel, the Prince Regent, Queen Victoria, have all furnished material. I should like to call particular attention to:

(64) Shane Leslie's *Life of the Prince Regent*. This witty book makes out a distinct case for Prinny, who has been so vigorously flayed by Thackeray and everybody else anxious to claim respectability.

The *Illustrated London News* for 1852 contains a vast amount of illustrated material on the Duke's life, death, and public funeral.

Among French authors may be noted the Emperor Napoleon, Las Cases, Michelet, Chateaubriand, Stendhal, Victor Hugo.

For the almost endless lists of other books the reader is referred to the bibliographies of the *Cambridge Modern History*, and the bibliographies in Sir Charles Oman's *Wellington's Army* and Philip Guedalla's *Wellington*.

Index

Aberdeen, Lord, 252, 300, 343
Aboukir Bay, battle of (Egypt), 57
Abrantes (Portugal), 136
Achilles (statue of), 4
Acre (Palestine), 57
Adams, General (British), 226
Adams, John Quincy (American Minister in London), 10, 230
Addington, Henry, 1st Viscount Sidmouth, 77, 97
Adour river (France), 197
Æschylus, 260
"Age of Bronze" (Byron), 274
Agraça redoubt (Portugal), 153
Agueda, river (Spain), 169
"*Ah Marmont! Onde vai, Marmont?*", 176
Ahmednuggur (India), 81
Aire river (France), 198
Aix-la-Chapelle (Germany), 251
Alaska, 276
Alava, General Miguel de (Spanish), 198, 199, 252, 262
Alba de Tormes (Spain), 171
Alba de Tormes, battle of (Spain), 142
Albert, Prince Consort, 331, 337
Albuera (Spain), 159
Albuera, battle of (Spain), 160
Albuquerque, Duque d', General (Spanish), 146
Alcantara (Spain), 136, 164
Aldea da Ponte, combat of (Portugal), 161
Alemtejo (Portugal), 160
Alexander I, Tsar of Russia, 57, 104, 109, 197, 202, 209, 210, 245, 246, 247, 272, 282
Algeria, 299
Alix, General (French), 5, 226
Allagoor (India), 62
Allemand, General (French), 234
Allen, William, 340
Allum Shah, nominal Great Mogul, 79
Almack's, 267
Almandoz (Spain), 188
Almaraz (Spain), 137, 141, 167
Almeida (Portugal), 147, 149, 156, 159, 160
Alps, 209

Alten, General (Hanoverian), 199, 218, 219, 226
Althorp, Lord, 311, 318
Amarante (Portugal), 135
American Colonies, 20, 31
Andalusia (Spain), 119, 130, 131, 136, 146, 162
Angel in the House (Patmore), 341
Angers (France), 22–25
Anglesea, William Paget, Marquess of, General (British cavalry leader), 212, 214, 228, 288
Angoulême, Duke of, 197
Anhalt, Bernbourg, 247
Anhalt Dessau, 247
Anson, cavalry General (British), 139
Anstruther, General (British), 123
Antibes (France), 209
Antwerp (Belgium), 220
Appah Sahib (Indian ruler), 71
Apsley House (Wellington's London residence), 2, 4, 252, 256, 263, 273, 285, 290, 298, 302, 308, 313, 314, 327, 345
Aragon (Spain), 137
Aranjuez (Spain), 172
Arapiles, Greater, hill (Spain), 170
Arbuthnots, the, 271, 288, 327, 337, 338, 341–2
Arcot, Nawab of, 55
Areizaga (or Areyzaga), General (Spanish), 142, 146
Aremberg, Prince d', 161
Argaum (India), battle of, 3, 83–86, 87, 91
Armytage, Jack, 22
Arnee (India), 60
Arnold, Matthew, 310
Arnold (Oxford undergraduate), 317
Arroyo dos Molinos, combat of (Spain), 161
Artillery Royal, 108, 338
Artois, Charles Philippe, Count of, *see* Charles XII
Arzobispo (Spain), 141
Aspern and Essling, battle of (Austria), 132
Assaye (India), battle of, 3, 82–84, 85, 87, 91, 107, 236, 256
Asserghur (India), 83